Ruth Chatterton

Actress – Aviator – Author

by Scott O'Brien

Also by Scott O'Brien:

Kay Francis – I Can't Wait to Be Forgotten (2006)

Classic Images Magazine - "Best Books of 2006" Laura Wagner – "O'Brien has a way with words as he beautifully examines Kay's films. He treats her private life with respect, without shying away from some unpleasantries. He skillfully uses Kay's own diary to paint a picture of an independent woman ahead of her time."

Virginia Bruce – Under My Skin (2008)

Daeida Magazine – David Ybarra (editor) – "O'Brien successfully brings Virginia Bruce to life in a way that is believable, intelligent and never pitiable. [He] triumphs in making her more than an actress. *Under My Skin* is by no means a "love letter" to Bruce, but it is a well-researched, tactful, and skilled examination into the tragedy of a talented, beautiful and popular figure in film history, desperate to fall in love and stay in love at any cost. Highly recommended."

Ann Harding – Cinema's Gallant Lady (2010)

San Francisco Gate – Mick LaSalle – "When I was writing **Complicated Women**, I got to know the work of just about every actress who made movies in the early thirties… the actress that I thought was the most gifted and accomplished was Ann Harding. I'm especially impressed that Scott O'Brien has managed to come up with a thick, fact-filled, smart and very readable biography of this *enormous* talent. Harding deserves to be known, and the public deserves to know her."

Ruth Chatterton

Actress – Aviator – Author

A biography by Scott O'Brien

Published in the USA by:
BearManor Media
P O Box 71426
Albany, Georgia 31708
www.bearmanormedia.com

Printed in the United States of America

ISBN 978-1-59393-248-0

Book & cover design and layout by Darlene & Dan Swanson • www.van-garde.com

For my sisters–

Peggy Ann

&

Amy Kate

Contents

1936–Ruth Chatterton's favorite publicity shot from *Dodsworth*
(Ruth's personal collection courtesy of Brenda Holman).

Introduction

In 1968, New York film critic Pauline Kael christened her "the great Ruth Chatterton."[1] High praise ... coming from the opinionated Miss Kael, the most influential film critic of her day. In 1957, producer and co-founder of Paramount Pictures Jesse L. Lasky had referred to Ruth Chatterton and her "voice" as godsends for his studio. "We gloated over our good luck," he said, "in having signed her even before sound reared its domineering microphone. She had proved an asset as a silent star, and now we were sure her talents would be doubly valuable."[2] Ruth's stage experience gave her confidence and poise. Many silent stars were in trouble. Due to a "bad case of mike fright," Paramount's Gloria Swanson was having her lines written on the front of her leading man's shirt.[3] All Ruth had to do was become friends with the camera. Her ascension into the Hollywood firmament was rapid. "She turned out marvelous performances," admitted Lasky. "Even the rural audiences began to appreciate her—after they got used to her faultless English."[4]

While at Paramount, Ruth garnered two Academy Award nominations for "Best Actress." She was hugely popular—being called "The First Lady of the Screen"—a moniker she hated. (Ruth undoubtedly preferred the sobriquet: "La Chatterton.") In truth, when she arrived in Hollywood in 1927, Ruth's reputable stage career was fading fast. "Talkies" needed voices. Ruth knew she had one. While no beauty, at age thirty-six, she discovered the art of allowing the camera to make love to her. "Youth and beauty never had such a fling as it did in the movies," Ruth commented in 1929. "But that day is gone. A pretty girl is easy to look at, but mighty hard to listen to for very long."[5] In spite of her successes, after three years at Paramount, Ruth bailed out in order to infuse Warner Brothers with a touch of "class"—all to the tune of "$647,000 per year."[6] (All this when labor was fighting for 40 cents an hour wages!) Warner Bros. Archive Curator Emily S. Carman stated, "Perhaps the most powerful female star that worked at Warner Bros. was Ruth Chatterton."[7] Carman's assessment was based on Chatterton's "lucrative contract which gave her a substantial amount of creative control. Earning $8,000 a week, she had co-star, director, and story approval."[8] With this kind of star power and control why is Ruth Chatterton largely forgotten today?

To answer this question, one must take into consideration the production quality, or lack of it, in Chatterton's films at Paramount and MGM. While audiences may have thrilled at "La Chatterton's" voice, early talkies themselves were hampered by cumbersome sound equipment. Lionel Barrymore, who directed Ruth in MGM's *Madame X* (1929), followed her around the set with a microphone attached to a fishing pole. That way, Ruth didn't have to stand still every time she had a line. Give credit to Barrymore for creating the first "sound boom." Even though *Madame X* brought her popular acclaim and an Academy Award nomination, the film creaks, as do most of Ruth's early films. You have to be a die-hard fan to sit through some of them. By 1932, when Ruth arrived at Warner Bros., the fluidity of film and sound emerged as a more "polished" form. However, in spite of Ruth's exorbitant salary, Warner Bros. made films as "quickly and as cheaply as possible."[9] While some films had grit, many were trifles derived from pulp fiction. This partly explains why Warner's "most powerful female star" departed from her studio after only two years. "I hated motion picture work," she firmly stated in 1958.[10]

With Ullrich Haupt in
Madame X (MGM).

Ruth's longtime friend, Los Angeles reporter and press agent Paul "Scooper" Conlon, observed years later, "Despite all her triumphs in Hollywood pictures, the trouble with Ruth Chatterton was that she was and is an honest woman. Much too honest for her surroundings and associates in those days. She was far too intelligent and too forthright in expressing her opinions. If she thought something was stupid she said so. That's taboo in Hollywood. You were not supposed to talk that way to studio moguls. But Ruth did."[11]

She had good reason to argue. Warner Bros. refused to invest in acquiring film rights to reputable plays or novels. Ruth's so-called "script approval" and "creative control" allowed her to filter through an array of poor choices. After rejecting one, she would blithely go on suspension and what Ruth rejected was handed over to her successor as "Queen of the Warner Lot," Kay Francis. Both women were relegated to what were referred to as "women's pictures." Amidst Ruth's sea of celluloid tears, film historian Mark Vieira paid homage to her Warner Bros. output, saying, "The best of these starred Ruth Chatterton, who brought her clipped elegance to some piquant proceedings. In *Frisco Jenny* she was an unwed mother, a prostitute, a madam, and a murderer."[12] *Frisco Jenny* was a box-office hit, but none of Ruth's work at Warner could be designated as an "all-time classic." It was producer Sam Goldwyn who offered Ruth Chatterton the best role of her career as the selfish, frivolous wife of Walter Huston in the critically acclaimed, Academy Award nominated *Dodsworth* (1936).

With Walter Huston in *Dodsworth* (Samuel Goldwyn–United Artists).

Another reason for Chatterton's obscurity is that she considered her film career finished by 1938. Unlike cinematic icons Davis, Crawford, and Katharine Hepburn, after 26 films (1928-38), Ruth had had enough of Hollywood. Apparently, Hollywood had had enough of her. Her friend and one-time beau, director Fritz Lang, was annoyed by the reception Ruth received when she returned to Hollywood as a successful novelist in December 1950. "Hollywood is so peculiar," said Lang. "I had a good friend in Ruth Chatterton, who was really a star. She was a literate woman. She came back to California... but not one person invited her out for Christmas. They use you as they would cardboard in the studio. [They are] only interested in you as long as you are in the limelight."[13]

Surprisingly, a remarkable passion for aviation had helped pull Ruth even further away from Hollywood. When her last film for Warner Bros. wrapped up in December 1933, she took up flying. She was serious about it. Within a year, she was the most noted aviator to come out of Hollywood, putting up $2,000-$5,000 to sustain the "only great amateur air race, from Los Angeles to Cleveland."[14] For two summers in a row, the Chatterton Air Derby made front-page aviation news. Ruth was well acquainted with the legendary pioneer aviator Amelia Earhart before her ill-fated "flight of the globe" in 1937. Ruth, along with Earhart, was among the few female "Fair-

1936 news photo of Kay Francis, Ruth Chatterton, Amelia Earhart at the 16th National Air Races, Los Angeles.

Haired Bastards" adopted by Dr. Margaret Chung, whose famous patriotic organization on behalf of allied forces was recognized in the 1930s and 40s.[15] Chung, a successful San Francisco physician and great friend, was Ruth's equal when it came to ambition. As a medical student in an all-male school, she adopted masculine dress and called herself "Mike," which is exactly what Ruth demanded to be called as a young girl. But we get ahead of ourselves.

❦

Upon learning that Ruth Chatterton was a popular novelist, I decided to begin her story by diving into the "final chapter"–the last decade of her remarkable life. Ultimately, Chatterton's four books reveal a compassionate woman connected to her fellow human beings. Authors usually have intent… a point to make. The challenge for Chatterton was to make her message subtle enough to reach into the thick-skinned prejudices of a self-proclaimed "free society." Chatterton accomplishes this, if not in spades, in hearts. She is a brilliant writer. I was easily enveloped in the characters and worlds she created on paper.

"I cannot remember being indifferent to any thing in my life," Ruth told *New York Times* reporter and playwright Harvey Breit following the release of her first novel, *Homeward Borne*.[16]   As you will discover, Ruth Chatterton was courageous in what she had to say and what she had to write.   To delve into issues such as anti-Semitism, McCarthyism, Civil Rights, what she referred to as the "nebulous world of religion," and offering rather circumspect views of war heroes in the late 1940s and 1950s was unusual as well as audacious.   Chatterton acknowledged the frailties of human experience and was forgiving… to a point.   Her protagonists inevitably released their shadows and fears to emerge, if not triumphant, more enlightened.   While she didn't have much hope for the dyed-in-the-wool prejudices of adults, she saw hope for the innate truth in children, who were perplexed by the failings of so-called "civilization."

Chatterton laid out her life, her plans, with no apologies and what followed spoke for itself.   "Ruth has the odd but compelling habit of looking a person straight in the eye when that person is talking to her," observed Scooper Conlon.   "It is either flattering or embarrassing, according to how much sense a person is making.   By the same token, she looks a person straight in the eye when she is talking, so they had better damn well listen."[17]   As Ruth's "voice" carries much of the narrative in the chapters that follow, gentle reader, I suggest that you "had better damn well listen."

Endnotes

1   Pauline Kael, *Kiss Kiss Bang Bang*, Little, Brown and Co., NY, c. 1968, pg 121.

2   Christopher Silvester, *The Grove Book of Hollywood*, Grove Press, c. 2002, pg 109 (excerpt taken from Jesse Lasky, *I Blow My Own Horn*, Doubleday, c. 1957; Chatterton starred in only one silent film: *Sins of the Fathers* in 1928).

3   Christopher Silvester, *The Grove Book of Hollywood*, Grove Press, c. 2002, pg 109.

4   Christopher Silvester, *The Grove Book of Hollywood*, Grove Press, c. 2002, pg 109.

5   "New Order in Hollywood," *Evening Post*, New Zealand, June 3, 1929.

6   Emily Susan Carman, *Independent Stardom: Female Stars and Freelance Labor in 1930s Hollywood*, University of California, Los Angeles, c. 2008, pg 42 (Contract dated February 27, 1931, Ruth Chatterton legal file, WBA, USC).

7   Emily Susan Carman, *Independent Stardom: Female Stars and Freelance Labor in 1930s Hollywood*, University of California, Los Angeles, c. 2008, pg 42.

8   Emily Susan Carman, *Independent Stardom: Female Stars and Freelance Labor in 1930's Hollywood*, University of California, Los Angeles, c. 2008, pg 82 (Contract dated September 9, 1931, Ruth Chatterton legal file, WBA, USC).

9   Mark A. Vieira, *Sin in Soft Focus*, Harry N. Abrams, Inc., NY, c. 1999, pg 76.

10   Cynthia Lowry, "Ruth Chatterton, Once A Bright Star, In Second Career As Serious Writer," *The Register-News*, ILL. August 27, 1958.

11   John McCallum, *Scooper*, Wood and Reber, Inc., Seattle, Washington, c. 1960, pg 183.

12   Mark A. Vieira, *Sin in Soft Focus*, Harry N. Abrams, Inc., NY, c. 1999, pg 118.

13   Barry Keith Grant, *Fritz Lang: Interviews*, University Press of Mississippi, c. 2003, pg 143.

14   John McCallum, *Scooper*, Wood and Reber, Inc., Seattle, Washington, c. 1960, pg 184.

15   John McCallum, *Scooper*, Wood and Reber, Inc., Seattle, Washington, c. 1960, pg 184.

16   Harvey Breit, "Success, It's Wonderful!" *New York Times*, December 3, 1950.

17   John McCallum, *Scooper*, Wood and Reber, Inc., Seattle, Washington, c. 1960, pg 185.

Ruth Chatterton penned four novels: *Homeward Borne* (1950), *The Betrayers* (1953), *The Pride of the Peacock* (1954), and *The Southern Wild* (1958).

1
NOVELIST

May 28, 1950. *Homeward Borne* hit *The New York Times* best-seller list and stayed there for 23 weeks. As a novelist, Ruth Chatterton had arrived. Critics were begging for more. She readily complied. Anger fueled her new ambition. "To write a good novel," she declared, "I need a theme that makes me angry."[18] Ruth's work on behalf of Jewish refugees had triggered her emotions and her typewriter. When her second novel, *The Betrayers*, hit the bookstores three years later, she was asked why she tackled another controversial subject. "I got *mad*," Ruth explained. She had watched people she knew and respected get raked over the coals by the House of Un-American Activities (HUAC) investigations. In the aftermath, Ruth's typewriter let off more steam. *The Betrayers* was a scathing exposé about the fanatics (Senator Joseph McCarthy in particular) behind what was being referred to by some as "Anti-Communist Witch-Hunts." Although it didn't hit *The New York Times* best-seller list, *The Betrayers* was brave territory to write about for someone in Ruth's position. Even so, she didn't stop there. There would be more anger, more books to come.

Before *Homeward Borne* (originally titled *As a Wren's Eye*) was released, Ruth, a fourth generation New Yorker, was in the midst of furnishing an apartment in the East Seventies. She anxiously waited for the reviews. "If people don't like this book," she said, "I'll probably crawl under a rock."[19] She didn't have to. It was considered a remarkable achievement for a first novel. "Miss Chatterton," stated one critic, "has … created a story which lands a hard punch on the glass jaw of complacency."[20] Jane Cobb of *The New York Times* complimented Chatterton's ability to tell a story "with unusual perception and wisdom." "It is pleasant news," she added, "that an actress of Miss Chatterton's standing should be sufficiently versatile to write a novel as good as this one."[21] Cobb pointed out that the problem of children whose lives had been spent in concentration camps hadn't received as much attention as it deserved. "She has perhaps stacked the cards against her characters a little too thoroughly," Cobb concluded, "but her climax is both plausible and terrifying. It is to be hoped that Miss Chatterton continues on her second career."

In an interview with playwright Harvey Breit, Ruth emphasized, "I felt very strongly about the ideas for my book. If there was one good thing to come out of World War II, it was that the minorities problem was brought out into the open."[22] W.G. Rogers, arts editor for the Associated Press, agreed. "*Homeward Borne* is serious, mature and worthwhile," he stated, "and the idea of it will anger you as much as it angered the author."[23] Ruth's anger found resolution. What had begun as an idea for a play evolved into a book when a friend, novelist Edwin Gilbert, told her that there was "too much for a play." "How do you write a novel?" she asked. "Just the way you told it," he replied.[24] "The first paragraph was hard," Ruth admitted. "It took me longer to write than it did the first three chapters. After that it wrote itself."[25] Ruth got completely wrapped up in her characters. "I would go to a party," she said, "and only be half-present. I would have one ear cocked for dialogue and bits of conversation, and I would sometimes drift off into my fictional world and not know what was going on at all."[26] After eleven months, the completed manuscript was handed over to a literary agent, Margot Johnson, who also represented novelist Patricia Highsmith. Johnson, after ripping off the title page bearing the name Ruth Chatterton, delivered it to the top editors of Simon and Schuster: Lee Wright and Max Schuster. She wanted their decision to be based solely on merit. The publisher liked the combustible theme and bought the story. They also requested to meet their new author. When Ruth showed up, she was greeted by two exclamations: "My God!" by Miss Wright and "We should have had the newsreels here!" by Schuster.[27] In July 1949, it was announced that Simon and Schuster would promote the Chatterton novel in its "big spring book."[28]

Chatterton's lead character in *Homeward Borne* is a young mother named Pax (French for "peace"). She grew up on the east coast, raised by an agnostic father, a literate and scholarly educator. Pax thrived in the Ivy League atmosphere. Or had she? Author Chatterton wastes no time in pointing out that, in one respect, academic isolation kept "real folk" at bay, hidden from view. Using flashback, we learn that Pax was head-over-heels in love with a young Jewish man. However, when she met his quaint, very traditional Jewish parents, she was unprepared, uncomfortable, and embarrassed to be seen with them. The author makes it clear that Pax is far from perfect. Pax's mentor, Phillip, a professor, chastises her: " ...honest to God, what I don't understand is your making no effort to find out what kind of people they were inside, that man and woman who conceived the boy you think you love."[29] It is Philip who expresses Chatterton's own worldview. The reader does not necessarily find Pax likeable. It was a risk that Chatterton was willing to take with her protagonist.

Years later, following WWII, we find Pax married to the college football hero, raising a young son, Tubby, and carrying a great deal of guilt from the way she had treated her former Jewish beau. She decides to redeem herself by adopting an orphan, Jan, whose parents perished in the Auschwitz-Birkenau crematorium. Early for her appointment to meet the boy, Pax goes to the cinema, where a newsreel shows Jewish refugees, "children standing … clinging with their little hands to the wire fence, gazing out like monkeys from behind a cage… their faces were hard and expressionless… The scene faded out to nothing and on the screen appeared one word: 'Cyprus.'"[30] World War II "wasn't over for everyone," Chatterton reminds us. Pax is in no way ready for such an undertaking. The boy, afraid of dogs and anyone in uniform, does not speak English. Understandably, he is a loner and has survived by lying and cheating. Jan is suspicious of everything that surrounds him. Pax struggles to connect, struggles to find Jan loveable. One day, she somehow justifies sending him away to a boarding school. We later learn that the school is supposed to be strictly for Gentiles. No one appears to be guiltless in this charade.

Chatterton appears to offer a glimmer of hope as Jan's English improves and he begins to question what is going on around him. Pax had shown him affection, then sent him away to school. A teacher who had favored him suddenly turned his back. "He was becoming conscious of the fact that they had given him something, then taken it away. Why?"[31] Chatterton allows Jan's mastery of a new language to create a turning point in the plot. Alan Rosen's 2005 book, *Sounds of Defiance: the Holocaust, multilingualism and the problem of English*, compliments Chatterton's *Homeward Borne* for "demonstrating a radical suspicion of the language in which she writes her novel." "Intriguingly," says Rosen, "her plot pivots around [Jan's] increasing skill with his new language, only to have his command of it implicated in his failure to fit in. Mastery of English brings not eloquence but rather a sense of despair."[32] Pax herself feels a shift in consciousness. It makes her uneasy. "She had taken on a responsibility and she was evading it," deduces Chatterton. "What was it she was afraid of? Anti-Semitism? In the people around her—or in herself?"[33]

The author complicates things even further. Robert, Pax's war hero husband stationed in Germany, returns home. He has become a bigot as far as Jews are concerned, bellowing, "We fought the wrong guys!... If it hadn't been for the damn Jews, there wouldn't have been this bloody war."[34] Pax is horrified when she learns his true feelings. It doesn't take long for Robert's attitude to rub off on Tubby. Some reviewers rejected the character of Robert Littleton, calling it "overdrawn," insisting that a war hero wouldn't harbor such prejudices.[35] In truth, Chatterton was exactly on target. An alarmingly large number of American service-men succumbed to the die-hard prejudices of their superiors as well as German-Nazi propaganda, "thus conveying to American soil the virus of Germany's anti-Jewish sentiments."[36] Joseph W. Bendersky's shocking 2001 study, *The Jewish Threat: Anti-Semitic Politics of the U.S. Army*, delves extensively into the issue.[37]

Jan, now designated as a "Jew" at boarding school, leaves campus. Sensing his inevitable expulsion from Pax's home, he tries suicide. During his recovery, Pax and her husband separate. Tubby opts to go with his father. In the aftermath, Pax is relentless as she tries to discover a place in her soul where she and Jan can connect. Chatterton likes making her reader uncomfortable and face realities. The ending allows just enough glimmer to stir the spirit. Pax realizes she can love Jan for his own sake and no other reason. Her son, Tubby, returns home, as if *he* had recognized the very thing that Pax was looking for: human connection. Quoting Shakespeare's "How far that little candle throws its beams...," Chatterton casts a light, a hope, in a dark and dangerous world. As far as happy endings go, we can ask for little more.

Chatterton's views become more explicit as one reads: i.e., the stock market disaster of '29 was generated by greedy men who had "no business selling apples" in the first place; the hatred of Jews is a blight on what we refer to as "civilization"; a child brought up by an agnostic has a becoming innocence. When Tubby asks Pax what religion Jan is, she answers, "I don't know his religion, Tubby. I think he's too small to have one."[38] Chatterton isn't exactly in your face with her opinions. She is no stranger to subtlety. Nevertheless, her "message" is clear. And no, not everyone liked her book. Among the naysayers was Hearst syndicated gossip columnist Dorothy Kilgallen. While the *Boston Globe* acknowledged Chatterton's "emotional insight and humanitarian understanding,"[39] Kilgallen railed, "Ruth Chatterton's novel struck me as tripe. If she wrote it herself she ought to go back to acting fast; if she hired a ghostwriter to do it for her, she ought to sue him for misrepresentation."[40] Kilgallen's column, "The Voice of Broadway," ultimately reflected "the voice" of her conservative publisher. Like other Hearst columnists, Kilgallen was on the lookout for Communists and supported the HUAC investigations. Perhaps Kilgallen didn't like Chatterton commenting on the "sour faces those Congressmen had" during the HUAC investigations. That was on page 8 of *Homeward Borne.* It could be that was as far as Kilgallen read to make her brusque assessment of Chatterton's first novel.

"Naturally," Ruth explained, "having a best seller has altered my life. It's opened up ambitions which are very exciting. I think the main gratification is that people treat me with slightly more respect than if I were simply an actress."[41] Following her newfound acclaim as a novelist, the Motion Picture Academy paged her to present the writing Awards at the 1950 Oscar ceremony. On March 29, 1951, at Hollywood's Pantages The-

March 29, 1951-Academy Awards Ceremony. In honor of her
new career as an author, Chatterton presented the writing awards.

ater, Chatterton, "Regally holding her spectacles before her, noted that a husband-and-wife team had been nominated in each of the three writing categories."[42] One couple won: Edna and Edward Anhalt for *Panic in the Streets*. Ruth also presented the Best Screenplay Award to Joseph L. Mankiewicz for *All About Eve*. She then handed Oscars to Charles Brackett and Billy Wilder for *Sunset Boulevard* (Best Story and Screenplay). Other Oscar presenters evoking nostalgia were Marlene Dietrich, Helen Hayes, and Ethel Barrymore. *Variety's* Army Archerd had the temerity to say, "The Academy Awards were very dull until these ancient creatures hobbled onto the stage."[43]

The HUAC investigations, which targeted Jews, among others, cast its shadow over the Academy Awards that evening. Judy Holliday won for Best Actress in *Born Yesterday*. The book *Red Channels* had listed Holliday (a Russian-Jew) as having alleged Communist leanings. Following this, the Catholic newspaper *Tidings* condemned *Born Yesterday*, calling it "Communistic." Catholic War Vets carried placards at theaters casting aspersions on Holliday's patriotism.[44] Such was the hysteria that fueled more Chatterton anger. In 1945, Chatterton had cast Holliday in a "dumb blonde" role for the 1945 Kay Francis stage tour of *Windy Hill*. Chatterton directed. One reviewer thought Holliday "the shining light of the production."[45] A few months later, Holliday was "shining" as another "dumb blonde" in Broadway's *Born Yesterday*. In spite of her success and her Oscar, the *Red Channels* debacle managed to blacklist Holliday from TV and radio, jeopardizing her career. Sponsors like Chesterfield Cigarettes didn't want to be associated with her.[46] As Ruth's anger reached a boiling point, she acquired the counsel of a Yale law professor who was well-versed in the tactics of Joseph McCarthy and the HUAC. Ruth began to formulate the plot for her next novel.

In 1951, Julius and Ethel Rosenberg, a Jewish-American couple, were convicted for conspiracy and sentenced to death. The charge: passing information about the atomic bomb to the Soviet Union—still classified as an ally. In 1953, the couple were the first civilians in US history to be executed for espionage. His sister-in-law testified that Julius, an electrical engineer, thought it only fair that the Soviets should be privy to atomic information. Ethel's conviction was based on "flimsy evidence to place leverage on her husband."[47] There were other scientists supplying Soviets with information from the Manhattan Project who, after conviction and imprisonment, were released. *The New York Times* editorial on the 50th anniversary of the Rosenberg execution stated, "The Rosenberg case still haunts American history, reminding us of the injustice that can be done when a nation gets caught up in hysteria." This hysteria was the basis of Ruth Chatterton's second novel, *The Betrayers*. Ruth attempted to show how people lose perspective and compassion if they lean "too far" politically toward the left or right. While she didn't overlook the danger of subversives, she focused on the harassment of liberal thought during the growth of McCarthyism. It was a risky thing for her to do considering the chill of blacklisting hovering over fellow artists in the world of entertainment.

Oddly enough, Ethel Rosenberg had read *Homeward Borne* while in prison. She wrote her husband, Julius, on December 3, 1951, commenting about "Ruth Chatterton's most unusual first book." "Here is a theme of the utmost importance and of the most far reaching implication," she said, "woven simply and sincerely into a story at once heart-wrenching and heart-warming. Furthermore, it is a theme that must have taken a good deal of personal courage and integrity to tackle, and congratulations to the author on this score alone are very definitely in order."[48] Undoubtedly, the Rosenberg case fueled further HUAC investigations as well as Chatterton's pen while writing *The Betrayers*. The ending reveals that the "victim" under investigation by the HUAC, a young nuclear physicist named Mike Prescott, is not innocent after all. His motives, his betrayal, resembled that of Julius Rosenberg.

While Chatterton may give short shrift to the misguided Prescott, she is utterly merciless in her portrayal of Senator Glavis in *The Betrayers*. Glavis, like Senator Joseph McCarthy, wasn't so much after justice as he was drunk on power, persecution, and guilt by association. She pulls out the old chestnut about the "idiot who burned down the barn to kill a couple of rats!"[49] Chatterton's story is a double indictment. The manipulations of both men got in the way of the FBI doing their job, which was catching traitors in action. Robert Kirsch, for *The Los Angeles Times*, emphasized the point Chatterton was making. "Miss Chatterton's new book is able to stand on its own merits," he praised. "It is a novel written in vehemence and anger, the point of which seems to be that it is the function of the FBI to root out subversives and that Congressional committees only interfere with this task."[50] After complaining about Chatterton's "angry and earnest mood," *The New York Times* reviewer, Nancie Matthews stated, "Miss Chatterton is nothing if not brave in her attempt to fathom the make-up [of Soviet spies]." Matthews assumed that Chatterton had drawn her own conclusions.[51] She hadn't. She acquired the help of the reputable Fowler "Chick" Harper, who taught law at Yale University. Ruth would dedicate her book to him. Within months of arriving at Yale (1947), Harper had persuaded a majority of the law school's professors to call for the abolition of the HUAC.[52] In 1947-48, while the HUAC subpoenaed film stars, Harper commented to the press, "It is hardly believable that members of Congress will uncover by holding a Hollywood performance on Capitol Hill, evidence of espionage that, has not been learned by responsible government officials."[53]

The Betrayers is centered in Washington, D.C. Our protagonist, Celia (a role that appears to be designed for Chatterton), is a lawyer who gave up her practice to relocate and support her husband, a newly elected Senator called to serve on the HUAC subcommittee. Chatterton's description of Celia could well have described herself: "Taken as a whole her face had no real beauty, but because it was so alive and mercurial it suggested beauty, and her personality was immediately vivid and endearing."[54] Celia's crush on Mike Prescott, the rising young physicist suspected of being a subversive, compromises her marriage. It is Prescott who provides the key to the *disillusionment* that Chatterton holds so dear.

Initially, Celia is more critical of individuals whose politics lean to the right, particularly Senator Glavis. Glavis, described as jowly, aggressive, magnetic, has only one saving grace: a closeted homosexual son, Dickie. (After all, this was 1952.) Dickie is a Washington, D.C., gadfly and gossip columnist, described as having the "face of an angel and the temper of Satan as a child." He also has an unrequited crush on Mike Prescott, who, at one time, had rejected Dickie's sexual advances. "You never seem to realize how much I like you, Mike," Dickie sobs in a drunken stupor.[55] Feeling spurned, Dickie tells his mother that Prescott was spreading "rumors" about him. She in turn tells her husband. When Senator Glavis announces that Prescott is a dangerous Communist and believed by many to be a homosexual, Dickie falls apart. "You told Pa, didn't you?" he wails to his mother. "I wish I could kill myself!" By the end of Chatterton's story, Dickie Glavis, a hero of sorts, manages to reveal important evidence on Prescott's behalf.

Doing the *real* work on behalf of the country is Johnny Hadley, a close friend of Prescott and, unbeknownst to most, an agent for the FBI. The FBI, Chatterton emphasizes, is after facts, not public attention. Add to this mix Celia's father, Gregg Worthington, a retired D.C. judge, and you have most of Chatterton's ensemble. Judge Worthington reminds his daughter that many good people, striving for Utopia, joined the Communist Party during the Great Depression. At that time, before the Stalin purges were made public, the Party's ideals were international. Now its former members' civil liberties were being suppressed.

Prescott works for the Atomic Energy Commission (one of the main targets of the HUAC). Celia snidely refers to it as "the bomb factory." In an unexpected twist, Celia takes on the assignment of defending Mike Prescott when he stands trial for contempt of Congress. One critic complimented Chatterton's "passionate sincerity... eloquently voiced through this most effective medium—interrogation and cross-examination."[56] Prescott is acquitted, but Celia is still troubled by Mike's "secret" and "solitary" life. The author pulls the readers' attention into a shroud of mystery while Celia does some risky detective work. Things begin to unravel when she visits an old mentor of Prescott, Professor Goodyear. Although he has a great deal of affection for his former pupil, Goodyear recognizes Prescott as a "great danger." He tells Celia, "Michael Prescott is a militant pacifist—if you will forgive the anomaly—and he would be entirely capable of destroying the world that he hates, if it were in his power to do so."[57]

Chatterton's conclusion surprised some. We get a hint of it early on when Celia's father reminds her that Justice Oliver Wendell Holmes cautioned: "—not only freedom of thought for those who agree with you, but freedom for the thought you hate."[58] An Australian critic thought Chatterton had weakened her story. "If she had allowed her scientist to remain what most of the book suggests he is—an innocent victim—it could have been a scathing indictment. She leaves the reader with the uneasy feeling that he has been kidded up that well-known gum tree."[59] The gum tree in question was nothing other than disillusionment. Chatterton's book had no hero. "Chatterton is more daring than most of her contemporaries," said author Roslynn D. Haynes in her 1994 book, *From Faust to Strangelove: Representations of the Scientist in Western Literature.* Haynes deduced that Chatterton's "hero," who is unambiguously a traitor, did not allow her to propose a "satisfactory moral solution."[60] Providing a snug "solution" for mature adults was not Chatterton's intention. One need look no further than the book's title for proof of this.

"Betrayers" is plural, as in the power-hungry Glavis and the equally terrifying Prescott, who is lost to the left of reasoning. The author purposely displayed the extremes of the liberal/conservative pendulum. Chatterton quotes from Jean-Baptiste Alphonse Carr, "*Plus ca change, plus c'est la meme chose*"—The more it changes, the more it's the same thing. She questioned any "difference between the totalitarian governing class and the proletariat masses." "They both want the world for themselves," declares the wise old Professor Goodyear. Chatterton concludes: "Utopia exists only in a man's soul."[61] Disillusionment does not have to compromise one's capacity for compassion. If you have an axe to grind, which Chatterton certainly did, speak up and be willing to "let be." "The rest is silence" (Chatterton quoting the last line of *Hamlet*).

"It's quite likely to become controversial," concluded one review for *The Betrayers.*[62] Critic James Burnham, a former Marxist turned conservative, fumed, "Its message is simply this: it is cruelly anti-liberal to ask men who are working on such projects as atomic defense whether they are agents of the Kremlin." Describing Chatterton's writing style as "pseudo-New Yorker sophistication," Burnham twisted her message. "The characters alternate between pouring drinks for one another and tossing off irresponsible nonsense," he huffed. "The villains are the men who want to bring Communism and espionage into the open and do something about them. It is this mixture of cocktails and blood that gives the book its peculiar air of moral indecency."[63] In her defense, the *Chicago Daily Tribune* rated *The Betrayers* "more than timely" and "a terrifyingly credible novel." "Miss Chatterton," said the review, "does indeed know Washington, D.C. She knows… its emotional atmosphere. And she knows Capitol Hill. Evidently she has attended committee hearings in person; only close observation could produce so impassioned a novel."[64] The *Saturday Review of Literature* was in agreement, adding that "*The Betrayers* is an exciting, highly entertaining novel. As the tension mounts, and as mystery about young Prescott deepens, you will find yourself turning the pages faster and faster."[65] Australian critic Murray Tonkin deduced, "Miss Chatterton appears to feel very deeply about the smearing of the innocent with the guilty, and the tactics which turn a Congressional inquiry into a three-ring circus."[66] It was this very same "three-ring circus" that had placed Ruth's vision for a film version of *Homeward Borne* in jeopardy.

⁂

The proposed Columbia film production of Chatterton's *Homeward Borne* fell victim to the HUAC. In July 1950, producer/writer Sidney Buchman, who had written the screenplay for the American classic *Mr. Smith Goes to Washington* and had won the Oscar for his screenplay *Here Comes Mr. Jordan*, acquired the screen rights. It was considered "the most important story acquisition of the year."[67] Chatterton's story was in skillful hands. The previous month, Louella Parsons had scooped, "Ruth is coming to California soon to work with Sidney Buchman on her best-selling novel, *Homeward Borne*! She will coauthor the script with him. In all the years I have known Ruth, I have never seen her so happy. She is ecstatic over having her good friend Margaret Sullavan play the heroine of her novel on the screen."[68] Ruth was adamant that no flutter-eyed blonde have the lead role and preferred a refugee in the role of the boy, a real one. Margaret Sullavan emphasized that her participation depended on a "good script." Ruth put everything else on hold. "I'm sort of on call at Columbia," Ruth stated in August, "and I can't do anything else."[69]

In September, Sullavan's agent confirmed that in six weeks, she would be filming *Homeward Borne.* In November, Buchman and his brother Harold (a screenwriter) held a conference to discuss production problems filming *Homeward Borne.* In January 1951, Ruth commented, "I've found myself in the perplexing position to cut the script and at the same time write in added scenes. One thing has made it a pleasant and worthwhile undertaking and that is Mr. Buchman's aid and integrity."[70] It was reported that the film had yet to be cast. Then, in March 1951, it was announced that Jane Wyman would play the lead in Buchman's production. Filming was postponed until September, the same month that Buchman, who was Jewish, was called before the HUAC. At a three-hour-long hearing in Los Angeles, he freely admitted having been a member of the Communist Party, but refused to name names. He was blacklisted. Jerry Bresler took over as producer. Dudley Nichols was then engaged to do another screenplay. In lieu of a screenplay, the writing was now on the proverbial "wall." Jane Wyman put the nail in the coffin of *Homeward Borne* when she told Columbia chief Harry Cohn that the story was "too somber."[71] The film project was dropped.[72]

In the aftermath of her disappointment, Ruth forged ahead with her writing and acting. She did occasional book reviews for *The New York Times,* wrote two more novels, and was working on her fifth when she passed away in 1961. Ruth had been a voracious reader since she was a child. How this privileged daughter of what was said to be wealthy New York aristocrats acquired her fame and her worldview... is another story.

Endnotes

18   W.G. Rogers, "Books and the Arts," *Sunday Times Signal*, OH, April 23, 1950.

19   "Ruth Chatterton's First Novel To Be Published," *Walla Walla Union Bulletin*, March 21, 1950.

20   Rosalie M. Raphael, "Ruth Chatterton Is Applauded In First Appearance As Author," *Delta Democrat-Times*, MS, April 30, 1950.

21   Jane Cobb, review of *Homeward Borne*, *New York Times*, June 11, 1950.

22   Harvey Breit, "Talk With Miss Chatterton," *New York Times*, August 27, 1950.

23   W.G. Rogers, "Books and the Arts," *Sunday Times Signal*, OH, April 23, 1950.

24   W.G. Rogers, "Book and the Arts," *Sunday Times Signal*, OH, April 23, 1950.

25   Harvey Breit, "Talk With Miss Chatterton," *New York Times*, August 27, 1950 ("After that it wrote itself" taken from interview with Jean Strouse, *Newsweek*, 1950).

26   Mel Heimer, "My New York," *La Cruces Sun-News*, October 15, 1950.

27   Howard Smith, "Chatterton's Advice to Writers Is Novel," *Miami News*, 9/26/54.

28   Erskine Johnson, "In Hollywood," (syndicated column) August 3, 1949.

29   Ruth Chatterton, *Homeward Borne*, Simon & Schuster, NY, c 1950, pg 120.

30   Ruth Chatterton, *Homeward Borne*, Simon & Schuster, NY, c 1950, pg 8.

31   Ruth Chatterton, *Homeward Borne*, Simon & Schuster, NY, c 1950, pg 301.

32   Alan Rosen, *Sounds of Defiance: the Holocaust, Multilingualism and the Problem of English*, University of Nebraska Press, c 2005, pg 60.

33   Ruth Chatterton, *Homeward Borne*, Simon & Schuster, NY, c 1950, pg 230-231.

34   Ruth Chatterton, *Homeward Borne*, Simon &Schuster, NY, c 1950, pg 258, 288.

35   Edmund Fuller, "Chatterton's Novel Fine—2/3 of the Way," *Chicago Tribune*, April 23, 1950.

36   Hasia R. Diner, *We Remember with Reverence and Love: American Jews and the Myth of Silence After the Holocaust, 1945-1962*, New York Press, c. 2009, pg 236.

37   Joseph W. Bendersky, *The Jewish Threat: Anti-Semitic Politics of the U.S. Army*, Basic Books, c. 2001.

38   Ruth Chatterton, *Homeward Borne*, Simon & Schuster, NY, c 1950, pg 313.

39   Review of *Homeward Borne*, *Boston Globe*, April 30, 1950.

40   Dorothy Kilgallen, "Voice of Broadway," *Charleston Gazette*, June 16, 1950.

41   Harvey Breit, "Success, It's Wonderful," *New York Times*, December 3, 1950.

42   Mason Wiley and Damien Bone, *Inside Oscar 10ᵗʰ Anniversary Ed.*, Ballantine, NY, c 1996, pg 208.

43   Armand Archerd, "It's Grandma Who's Grabbing the Bows," *Post-Herald* (WV), May 12, 1951.

44   Mason Wiley and Damein Bone, *Inside Oscar 10ᵗʰ Anniversary Ed.*, Ballantine, NY, c 1996, pg 204.

45   J.E.F. "Miller Comedy 'Disappointing,'" *Montclair Times*, August 16, 1945.

46   "The Chesterfield Memo" FBI file, from Louis B. Nichols to Clyde Tolsen, April 7, 1951 (only 9 days after she had won her Oscar).

47   Sam Roberts, "Father Was a Spy, Sons Conclude with Regret," *New York Times*, 9/16/2008.

48   Ethel Rosenberg letter dated December 3, 1951, from *The Rosenberg Letters: a Complete Edition of the Prison Correspondence of Julius and Ethel Rosenberg*, Taylor and Francis, c 1994, pg 269.

49   Ruth Chatterton, *The Betrayers*, Houghton Mifflin, Boston, c 1953, pg 77-78.

50   Robert R. Kirsch, "Chatterton: 'Betrayers' Stands on Own Merits," *Los Angeles Times*, October 25, 1953.

51   Nancie Matthews, "A Question of Loyalty," *New York Times*, September 20, 1953.

52   David J. Garrow, *Liberty and Sexuality: the Right to Privacy and the Making of Roe v. Wade*, University of California, c 1994, pg 149.

53   Dr. Fowler Harper, "So They Say," *Dunkirk Evening Observer*, September 14, 1948.

54   Ruth Chatterton, *The Betrayers*, Houghton Mifflin, Boston, c 1953, pg 3.

55   Ruth Chatterton, *The Betrayers*, Houghton Mifflin, Boston, c 1953, pg 127-128.

56   Rosalie Warne, "An Actress Puts American Politics on Trial," *The Argus* (Melbourne) August 28, 1954.

57   Ruth Chatterton, *The Betrayers*, Houghton Mifflin, Boston, c 1953, pg 264.

58   Ruth Chatterton, *The Betrayers*, Houghton Mifflin, Boston, c 1953, pg 39.

59   Murray Tonkin, "Ex-Film Star Cracks At McCarthyism," *The Mail* (Adelaide, SA) September 4, 1954.

60   Roslynn D. Haynes, *From Faust to Strangelove: Representations of the Scientist in Western Literature*, John Hopkins University Press, c 1994, pg 306.

61   Ruth Chatterton, *The Betrayers*, Houghton Mifflin, Boston, c 1953, pg 308.

62   Pat Edwards, "Case Against Investigating Committees Related in Book," *Avalanche-Journal*, TX, September 13, 1953.

63   James Burnham, review of *The Betrayers, The Freeman*, November 1953.

64   Marjorie B. Snyder, "A 'Terrifyingly Credible' Novel," *Chicago Daily Tribune*, September 13, 1953.

65   May F. Belden, "Senatorial Inquisition," *Saturday Review of Literature*, October 3, 1953.

66   Murray Tonkin, "Ex-Film Star Cracks At McCarthyism," *The Mail* (Adelaide, SA), September 4, 1954.

67   "Screen Rights For Chatterton Novel Acquired," *Brownsville Herald*, TX, July 9, 1950.

68   Louella Parsons column, *Lowell Sun*, MA, June 27, 1950.

69   Harvey Breit, "Talk With Miss Chatterton," *New York Times*, August 27, 1950.

70   Edward Schallert, "Movie Star-Novelist Now Script Writer," *Los Angeles Times*, January 7, 1951.

71   Louella Parsons, "Jane Wyman Has Role in Comedy," *Cedar Rapids Gazette*, April 30, 1952.

72   Louella Parsons column, "Jane Wyman Has Role In Comedy," *Cedar Rapids Gazette*, April 30, 1952 (In 1955, Columbia offered *Homeward Borne* to TV. A truncated version of Chatterton's novel, directed by Arthur Hiller, was filmed at Columbia for TV's Playhouse 90 in 1957. It starred Linda Darnell.).

73   "'Why Be Afraid?' Asks Ruth Chatterton," *New York Times*, March 17, 1912 (according to her passport and census records, the actual address of her birth was: 20 East 129th Street).

1894-Ruth and her mother Lilian. Photo taken
by Hiram C. Moore, a relative and photographer
in Springfield, Mass. (Ruth's personal collection-
courtesy of Brenda Holman).

2
THE CHATTERTONS
& THE REEDS

Ruth Chatterton is my real name," she told a reporter for *The New York Times*. "I was born right here in New York on 128th Street (sic). Nobody in my family has ever been on the stage and my getting on was really an accident."[73] It was 1912. Ruth was 19 years old and offering tidbits about her life via the telephone. She was practically an unknown in New York until she faced audiences at the Liberty Theatre. On stage, she was playing the daughter of producer/actor Henry Miller in his new play, *The Rainbow*. There were innumerable queries about who she was and where she came from. In her interview, Ruth told how her career started three years earlier while visiting a young girlfriend at the Columbia Theatre Stock Company in Washington, D.C. "I used to run in to see this friend in her dressing room during matinees," Ruth explained, "and I was awfully interested in the work. I was only sixteen years old then. One afternoon the stage manager grabbed me as I was leaving the theater and said,

'You're the very girl I'm looking for to play Polly in *Merely Mary Ann* next week.'

'Oh, but I can't act,' I said.

'That's why I want you,' he replied. 'Have you got the nerve to do it?'

'Yes, if my mother will let me.'

"At first Mother objected," Ruth added. "But later, she said she didn't mind."[74] Ruth would embellish the story over the years, saying *she* approached the stage manager on "a dare" from friends and relatives.[75] The simplicity of her 1912 explanation makes more sense. One thing is for certain. The opportunity to go on stage came at a crucial time. Until they could get their bearings, Ruth and her mother, Lilian, were staying in D.C. with Lilian's younger sister, Miriam Minuse. At 16, Ruth sensed an obligation to support her mother. Her parents had separated; something had to be done. Coming from generations of "old money" and a social status that "had been assured," mother and daughter were going from "riches to rags."[76] Apparently, Ruth would simply chalk it up as an experience. "Twice in my life I've been quite poor," philosophized Ruth years later. "Once… when my father suddenly lost everything and I had to support my mother on $10 a week. I had a fine time… so did she. It was never dismal and I've never regretted those days. They gave me something—a norm to go by."[77] It was undeniable that Ruth and "Tilly," as Ruth called her mother, were an inseparable team. Tilly accompanied Ruth to and from the theater. She was quick to admonish Ruth whenever the ingénue's language grew "somewhat extravagant."[78] Tilly also gave her daughter moral support—she helped her to dream. In turn, for decades to come, Ruth always made sure that Tilly was financially secure.

Lilian Reed Chatterton (born January 1, 1867 in New York City) was the daughter of a shipbuilder, Andrew Reed.[79] Aside from Miriam, she had two older sisters, Ida and Jane. Andrew Reed had the good fortune to marry Mary Jane Lugar, whose father, Rodney Park Lugar, amassed a sizeable fortune by 1869. Lugar had his own shipbuilding business on Avenue D, the city's dry dock section. After offering his son-in-law the

c.1888 Lilian Reed, by Hiram C. Moore
(Ruth's personal collection-courtesy of
Brenda Holman).

opportunity, the business became known as Lugar & Reed. Andrew Reed would retire at middle age to enjoy the life of a country gentleman. Life was uncomplicated for their family despite a few inconveniences, like the time Lilian's aunt, Estella Lugar West, was robbed of her jewelry while dining with relatives in St. Louis. She lost gems valued at $7,000, though it was a drop in the bucket for her millionaire husband, who news reports described as a "wealthy capitalist." Much to Estella's relief, the thieves had overlooked $23,000 worth of diamonds that always accompanied her. Detectives from all over the world were on the case. "Mrs. West's Egyptian jewelry collection," stated one report, "[is] second only to that of Sarah Bernhardt." After returning to New York, Estella convalesced from the ordeal at her permanent residence: the Waldorf Astoria.[80] Unlike her aunt, Lilian Reed fell in love with a young man who was financially unpredictable and not much of a provider.

When she was 25, Lilian married 18-year-old Walter Smith Chatterton. The ceremony took place in New York on January 20, 1891. Walter was born in Newark, New Jersey. His family claimed a connection to the tragic English poet Thomas Chatterton. The Chatterton Family Bible noted that Walter's great-grandfather was George Chatterton, a man of humble beginnings.[81]   George, a weaver, left England after textile companies began shutting down and arrived in New York in 1820. Among his eight children was John Carson Chatterton, a bookkeeper and theologian who found success as a minister.[82] John inherited exactly $1.00 from his father.[83] It was John's son, George H. Chatterton, who married into money. His marriage to Mary Carrie Smith took place in 1871. Carrie's father, Eliphalet C. Smith, Esq., a banker/realtor/surveyor in Newark, generously supplemented the Chatterton family coffers. This afforded George H. (Ruth's grandfather) to dabble as an inventor. George is listed as having several inventions with the U.S. Patent office: an illuminated advertising device, a cleverly designed folding beach-seat, and a duplex telegraph device.[84] Amidst all his creativity, he managed to declare bankruptcy. When the U.S. Census came around in 1880, Ruth's Grandfather George had recouped, listing his occupation as "Gentleman." Though they may tinker with inventions, gentlemen did not work. Nor did their sons attend public school. Ruth's father, Walter, age eight, and his brother, Halsey, age six, were designated as "Scholars." They were tutored at home, as was the rule for the privileged class. While Ruth was growing up, her father pursued his own hobbies of art, music, and architecture. Like his father before him, Walter Chatterton could not handle the money he married into.

When the Chattertons made the news, it was usually about financial or marital difficulty. Ruth's Grandfather George and Great-Grandfather John C. Chatterton joined in the "Debtors' Jubilee" in 1878, declaring bankruptcy before the current law was repealed.[85] Walter Chatterton also filed a couple of bankruptcies while Ruth was growing up. Marital woes plagued the Chattertons. In 1892, Ruth's eighteen-year-old Uncle Halsey eloped with a twenty-year-old neighbor, Jenny Manuel. Soon after they took their vows, the girl's father, a Wall Street banker, was seen "in hot pursuit," chasing the bride as well as the young couple's lawyer down West 56th Street, yelling, "Stop thief!" He did not approve of what the press designated as a "clandestine marriage." Neighbors crowded around as Jenny was overtaken by her father. Halsey, described as a slight man with plenty of pluck, placed himself between Jenny and her father. "Now you've got me to settle with!" he declared.[86] In the aftermath, a flustered Jenny threatened to reveal disparaging information about her father if he did not relent. The matter was closed. Mr. Manuel, it must be noted, was known as "the first man to draw a check for over $3,000,000 on a New York bank.[87] Halsey and Jenny went to live with Ruth's grandmother, Carrie Chatterton, and an "uncle" who the *New York Herald* referred to as "Mr. Earl." Exactly two years later (1894), Ruth's father, acting as Halsey's designated guardian, appeared at Superior Court. After a quarrel, Jenny had returned home to her father. Halsey was suing for divorce.[88] Halsey, a florist at the time, was still living with his mother and Mr. Earl.

Ruth's grandmother, Carrie Chatterton, preceded her son Halsey in creating a real scandal. Like her father-in-law George H., Carrie came up with her own invention: "Uncle Earl." He was actually Carrie's lover. Carrie, along with her teenage sons, had left George Chatterton to be with Edward Earle, a lawyer. In 1891, a year before Ruth was born, Clara Earle had asked husband Edward for a divorce, giving the cause: desertion. He had also run up $148,000 in mortgages using her money. In 1894, the *New York World* reported that divorce proceedings between Earle and his former wife had "been surrounded with the utmost secrecy."[89] Papers in the case were ordered sealed. The final judgment on which the divorce was granted "declared that Earle had been intimate with Mary C. [Carrie] Chatterton at various times between January 1, 1891 and August 15, 1891 at the Palisade House." News reports of the divorce also indicated that Mr. Earle simply got tired of his wife's "nagging" and went to live with Mrs. Chatterton and her two grown sons. Interestingly, it was also decreed that Mr. Earle could not legally remarry "during the present Mrs. Earle's life." In 1896, Carrie and Edward Earle somehow managed to marry, but were once again in court. The case involved a judgment based on non-payment of apartment rental fees. During the proceedings, Earle admitted that he and his new wife were "living on borrowed money."[90] Fortunately for Ruth, the Reed side of the family did not lend itself to such… disreputable behaviors.

1893-Ruth's first portrait by Jacque Joel of New York (Ruth's personal collection-courtesy of Brenda Holman).

Ruth was born on December 24, 1892, at the Manhattan home of her Grandfather Andrew Reed (20 East 129th Street–now considered East Harlem).[91] In that same year, Ellis Island Immigration Station opened just off the southern tip of Manhattan Island, processing 450,000 immigrants in the first twelve months. These new arrivals were generally required to have between $18-$25 on their person to make a fresh start. The new Chatterton "arrival" seemed far removed from the squalor and densely populated "melting pot" of immigrant neighborhoods on the Lower East Side. When Ruth turned two, Grandfather Reed acquired a second residence—an estate in Fordham Heights. It was here, surrounded by acres of forests and gardens, that Ruth spent most of her childhood. Described as a "roomy old mansion" by *The New York Times*, the Reed residence was just north of Webb Academy and Home for Shipbuilders on Sedgwick Avenue. Grandfather Reed supervised the Academy's construction and was resident manager for the institute from 1892-1902.[92] Webb Academy recruited from the heart. Its founder, W.H. Webb, the preeminent shipbuilder of his day, was attuned to the fact that many capable, bright young men were denied the opportunity to become shipbuilders due to a lack of funds. In 1896, Andrew Reed put forth Webb's ideas succinctly to the *New York Tribune*. "The boy must be able to show that his parents are not able to give him a collegiate education," said Reed. "Give the boy with brains and without money a chance in the race for an education with the sons of wealthy families. That is all there is to it. There is no institution of just this kind in America."[93]

c. 1898 -Webb Academy. Ruth's childhood playground.

Ruth's childhood memories were focused on the environs near the Webb Academy. "She had free run of the large estate," said reporter Dan Thomas in 1930. "The estate seldom housed less than a dozen dogs, and this number often was augmented by as many more mongrels that Ruth would find and bring home with her."[94] Ruth, her pet pony, and the family's young Italian gardener, Ferdinand, were her playmates. "I was spoiled," Ruth merrily admitted.[95] According to Thomas, Ruth considered other children "annoying interruptions." She would make her little guests feel welcome no matter how boring she found them, but her father's library was her sanctuary. "When I was a child," said Ruth, "I had no friends—except books. They were my first love."[96] She consumed the entire works of Charles Dickens before she was twelve. Little did she

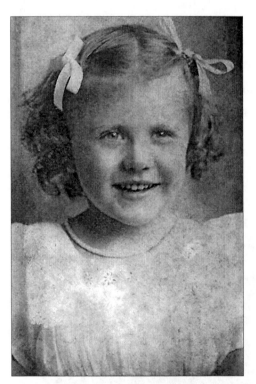

c.1898 - Ruth at age five (Ruth's personal collection–courtesy of Brenda Holman).

know that she would one day play the part of "Dora" in a Milwaukee stage production of *David Copperfield.*[97] Dora's uselessness in household chores was a shoo-in for Ruth. Her Grandfather Reed employed: three chambermaids, three house workers, two laundresses, four waitresses, and three cooks.[98] "I lived in blissful ignorance of all things culinary," Ruth confessed in 1916. "I did not know the first thing about cooking. I had a vague sort of idea that the kitchen was somewhere below-stairs, but I had never been there. I had not the faintest sort of idea how to get into an egg."[99]

At the core of Ruth's upbringing was the woman she referred to as her "Mammy." "She took me into her arms from the moment of my birth," recalled Ruth, "and was, in turn, my nurse, and cook, and private companion. I remember many things about her—like her method of awakening me. Softly, she'd come into my room—raise the blind an inch at a time, so that the light wouldn't pour in suddenly and awaken me rudely." Ruth admitted to having a terrible temper as a child, but her Mammy had a way of glorifying bad points until they became good. "Mammy had a daughter of her own—Daisy," said Ruth. "And when anyone would ask her, 'Which do you love more?' she would invariably answer: 'Daisy's awful sweet, but she ain't like my white child. Of course, my white child's got a temper, but who'd give anything for anyone without a temper?'" "Mammy didn't approve of evening clothes," said Ruth. "She'd look me over... screw up her face, and declare, 'Child, you're as naked as a buzzard—put some clothes on.' And this black woman—this adored Mammy of mine became a symbol of reality in my life."[100]

⚜

Ruth stated that her father had intentionally selected the name "Ruth," thinking it would not lend itself to nicknames or adding diminutives. In spite of this, at an early age, other children began calling Ruth "Mike." The name clung to her while she grew up.[101] "I don't know how I acquired that nickname," Ruth declared. "On the surface, one probably would say that I was a tomboy but I wasn't—at least I don't think I was."[102] During adolescence, "Mike" waded into Shakespeare, relishing the roles of Lady Macbeth and Juliet. "Strangely enough the perusal of these Shakespearean works did not arouse in me any desire for the stage," Ruth remarked. "My one big thought during those years was to enjoy life as much as possible and I read books purely for the enjoyment I got out of them."[103]

Lilian Chatterton was an accomplished pianist and daughter Ruth proved to be a natural. She could play anything by ear and when she was nine, she created "quite a sensation" at a recital in Carnegie Hall. There were plans for her to study music in Vienna when she was 16.[104] A career in music was Ruth's childhood dream. During her acting career, she continued to compose songs for the sheer love of it—improvising for hours "beautiful, soft things."[105] "The most satisfactory medium for beauty is music," Ruth stated in 1915. "It speaks of the inner self when the medium of speech is inadequate."[106]

In the summer of 1903, ten-year-old Ruth was mentioned in the *New York Tribune*. She was maid of honor at her aunt Miriam Reed's wedding to Alfred Minuse, a shipbuilder and '02 graduate of the Webb Academy. The ceremony took place at the Fordham Heights Estate. "The bride's sole attendant was her niece," stated the article. "Miss Chatterton's bouquet was of pink and white sweetpeas."[107] The following year, the *St. Nicholas* children's magazine placed Ruth in their "honorable mention" column for some prose she submitted.[108] At age 12, Ruth was sent to Mrs. Hazen's Private School for Girls at Pelham Manor on the Hudson. While there, she became well grounded in French, and English Literature. Ruth described it as "a sketchy education, but a very expensive one."[109]

Much of what was written about Ruth during her Hollywood heyday was filled with hyperbole. Aside from fiddling around with her age, she embellished the circumstances of her parents' separation. In March 1904, soon after Ruth turned eleven, both of her parents were in financial straits. They filed separate petitions for bankruptcy with no assets.[110] In June 1905, Grandmother Reed passed away. Andrew Reed, who had provided the only stability that Ruth had known, died the following year.[111] After only a brief respite, Lilian and Walter Chatterton found themselves faced with more problems during the summer of 1907. Walter was arrested on suspicion of burglary. He was dining in a café on 125th Street and Park Avenue prior to attending a board meeting of the Economic Power and Pump Company (which he owned). Detectives involved thought Chatterton resembled the notorious safe-blower Uly Burke. Amid much protesting by Walter's friends, who had accompanied him, detectives hauled Walter away. According to news reports, it was all a "monstrous mistake" for the "reputable businessman."[112] *The Evening World* put it bluntly, blaming the "mental density" of men assigned to the Detective Bureau. While Walter was locked in a cell, no one notified Lilian.[113] "Just imagine my anxiety," she told reporters, "as I watched the hours creep by waiting for my husband's return. When he did come home and told me of the indignities to which he had been subjected, it made my blood boil."[114]

Not long after this episode, Walter Chatterton once again became financially insolvent. Taxes for the Economic Power and Pump Co. were in default.[115] Adding to his woes, October brought the onslaught of the Wall Street Panic of 1907. The stock market neared collapse. Banks across the country folded. Complete disaster was averted when J.P. Morgan encouraged other prominent bankers to raise $23 million dollars in ten minutes, which they did. But it was too late for Lilian and Walter Chatterton. They separated. Ruth, at age fifteen, was sent to stay with Lilian's sister Miriam in Washington, D.C., until the trouble "blew over."[116] Instead of blowing over, the situation was augmented by further financial reversals. Lilian had unwittingly gone through the principal of her inheritance instead of the interest. A product of the age of gracious futility, her little fortune was now dissipated. She joined her daughter in Washington. In 1929, Ruth remarked that the men on the Chatterton side of her family were all "charming and entirely useless." As one reporter put it, "Her own father she resented as a child and enjoyed as good theater later on."[117]

⁂

May 17, 1909: Ruth's first stage appearance as Polly Trippett in the comedy *Merely Mary Ann.* In hindsight, it was a fortuitous moment even though Ruth's role was considered nothing more than an "attractive bit." "They must have been satisfied," said Ruth, "because they asked me to play the second-act Claudia of *The Prince Chap* the next week. Miss Julia Dean was the third-act Claudia, and she told me afterward that I had done very well. I stayed in the company eighteen weeks and the last eight weeks I played the leading ingénue parts."[118]   Ruth failed to mention the first-act Claudia was none other than little Helen Brown (who later became known as Helen Hayes). The review for the *Washington Times* commented, "To have three people cast as a growing child at the ages of five, eleven, and eighteen is likely to spoil the illusion. But the work of little Miss Helen Brown, of Miss Ruth Chatterton, and of Miss Julia Dean blended so well that the transition seemed most natural."[119]   In August 1909, Miss Dean scored a "triumph" in the humorous love story *Cousin Kate.* The *Washington Post* made note that "Ruth Chatterton made a charming house maid."[120] As one of the trio of girls in a revival of *Charley's Aunt,* the *Washington Herald* found her to be "altogether sweet and winsome."[121] The Columbia season closed with *The Girl From the Circus.* One review found it "hilarious," stating that Ruth "contributed effectively to the fun."[122] Ruth felt she had found her niche and she was winning scores of admirers. "I always get what I make my mind up to get," Ruth said when reflecting back on those days. She also admitted, "Sometimes I'm sorry for it."[123] In 1909, life had placed Ruth Chatterton in the glare of footlights. She resolved never to leave.

The importance of stage veteran Julia Dean at this juncture in Ruth's life cannot be underestimated. Here was a woman who was a full-fledged star with a maid to dress her and a star's dressing room. "Julia Dean helped me more than I can tell in my first baptism of footlights," emphasized Ruth. "She gave me part of her wardrobe and plenty of good, sound advice. It was she who warned me not to invade New York until I had garnered experience from at least three stock companies. 'You have the talent,' she told me, 'but you are so inexperienced and young. Avoid Broadway until you can overcome their cynical doubts with a strong list of past engagements.'" [124]

After rejecting an opportunity in Minneapolis, Ruth signed on for six months with a Milwaukee stock company whose players included Lowell Sherman, Pauline Lord, and Lenore Ulric. "We had much varied experience there," admitted Ruth, "and it all seemed like a prank, for the majority of the company was made up of actors and actresses so young that it was more like 'high school' dramatics." [125] When asked, Ruth would answer that her own favorite actresses were Gertrude Elliott and Julia Dean. Elliott had created the role of Cleopatra in Shaw's *Caesar and Cleopatra*. Dean, of course, was Ruth's advisor and would come to her rescue when needed. One of Ruth's roles required an evening gown, for which she lacked funds. She wrote Julia Dean, asking for one of her discarded frocks. Dean graciously supplied a trunk of costumes—a complete wardrobe for Ruth's fledgling "repertoire." The gift remained uppermost in Ruth's mind for years to come. In 1930, reporter Dan Thomas made the observation, "The friendship formed between these two when Ruth was starting out at the age of 14 (sic) is just as strong, if not stronger, now than it was then." [126]

While playing at Milwaukee's Shubert Theater, Ruth learned more about life than she had bargained for. A fourteen-year-old Polish girl,

Hattie Zinda, had been kidnapped. Her assaulted body was found later in an abandoned Milwaukee office building amid a pile of beer bottles. It was quite evident the girl had made a "desperate fight for her honor" and that two assailants were involved.[127] Detectives and patrolmen found very few leads. The city was in an uproar. The Chief Inspector stated that the only chance rested on a cash reward for information leading to their arrest. "Miss Chatterton gave one-half her share of the house one evening toward a reward for the capture of the slayer," recalled columnist Tom Lindsay. "Inspired by her charitable and laudable act, several business men contributed heavily to the fund as did the City of Milwaukee."[128] While the incident certainly disturbed the 16-year-old actress, it helped develop a conscience and compassion that stuck. The assailants were apprehended two weeks later. Amidst the ominous threat of a lynch mob, the two men were sentenced to life imprisonment.

After Milwaukee, Ruth and Tilly ventured to Worcester, Massachusetts. "I played every sort of part," Ruth admitted, "from a child to an old woman."[129] "The part I liked best with them was 'Flora Wiggins' in *A College Widow*."[130] Flora was described as an irresistibly droll waitress with some of the best lines in the play. Ruth's acting of Micah Dow, a ragged urchin, in *The Little Minister* was well received. By word of mouth, her performance was touted in newspapers as far as Washington, D.C. "I started at $5 a week," said Ruth, "felt I had arrived when I got $10 and that I was one to be vastly envied when I got $50. We had to do things for ourselves—had to make a good many costumes—had to learn a great deal more. We knew how to direct ourselves, how to get the most out of our lines. It was a hard school, but thorough, and it made actors."[131]

As the Worcester Stock Company folded its props for the summer season, Ruth decided it was time to brave the sacred offices of theatrical producers in New York. It turned out that she didn't have to walk far. Producer Henry W. Savage had seen one of her Worcester performances and "immediately took her under contract."[132] In October 1910, Ruth was back in D.C. playing the niece of star Gertrude Quinlan in *Miss Patsy*. Florence Nash, who originally played the role on Broadway, bowed out, allowing Ruth to take over when the play went out on the road. The drama editor for the *Washington Herald* found *Miss Patsy* "clean and wholesome, but rather stupid."[133] The *Washington Post* pointed out that Ruth played her role "well." It was several months before Ruth was back in New York playing the ingénue in the Henry Kolker starrer *The Great Name*. It was her Broadway debut. During the out-of-town tryouts in May 1911, a critic for *The Indianapolis Star* commented, "Miss Chatterton has not yet learned how to act her role flawlessly."[134] No specifics were given. Curiously, before the play reached Broadway, Ruth took a break one summer evening to perform in a concert held at the Catskill Mountains resort Mamakating Inn. Her piano rendition of Gounod's serenade, *Sing, Smile, Slumber* was "artistically rendered."[135] When *The Great Name* premiered in New York on October 4, *The New York Times* raved about Ruth, saying, "Ruth Chatterton did the sort of thing that contrasts the artist and mere actor of a part. She was thoroughly charming… and wholly natural at all times."[136] Sadly, *The Great Name* lasted less than three weeks on the Great White Way.

Following this disappointment, Ruth went to Chicago for the suffragette-themed *Standing Pat*. Expectations were high. At the premier, notables in attendance included Tyrone Power, Sr., and his wife. Onstage, Zelda Sears starred as a businesswoman running for mayor in rural Colorado. Ruth played Sears' 16-year-old sister. Percy Hammond, for the *Chicago Daily Tribune*, disliked the "ineffective drool" in the first two acts, but complimented Sears' eccentric characterization. He noted "several excellent performances in the play" and enjoyed the hotel scene in which Ruth is compromised by a brewery agent. "She did not so much as lose a libretto,"

Hammond snickered.[137] *Variety* thought the scene licentious and inappropriate. "The producers will do well to remove this dirt spot," it sniffed.[138] In need of a heavy rewrite, *Standing Pat* yielded to mixed reviews and closed

Ruth learned the risks, disappointments, and vagaries of her profession. When she and Tilly returned to New York, it was only to become familiar with second-class boardinghouses and twenty cent dinners on side streets. Between theater engagements, they got by on the $10 weekly annuity that Tilly managed to hold on to. Their domicile usually consisted of a single room, scantily furnished. There was also a little alley cat that Ruth took pity on. "Tommie" became part of the family. Ruth had no problem discussing her days of hardship. "During the weeks I searched New York for work," she said, "we evolved a midget budget system. I was given 20 cents a day for car fare and lunch, which was unvarying in its consistency—being always a chocolate soda at Huylers."[139] In Ruth's favor was her breeding and character—things money could not buy. Equally important was the influence that her Mammy had had upon her. "Her memory is shining and lasting," Ruth acknowledged years later. "Her love taught me what selfless loyalty, what honesty, what devotion meant. And it couldn't help but contribute to me as a personality—and therefore as an artist."[140] Ruth later revealed that her father was furious with her decision to become an actress. Tilly brought her daughter "vitriolic" letters from Walter filled with disapproval. All this from Ruth's father, who, along with her Grandfather Chatterton, toyed with business schemes and inventions while declaring bankruptcies. After reading his letters, Ruth never talked about her father or claimed to know his whereabouts.[141]

Ruth preferred keeping in touch with her aunts and cousins from the Reed side of the family. Her grandfather, Andrew Reed, the successful naval architect who drank his coffee out of a saucer, was the ancestor she liked best. "He was a self-made man … despite his handicaps," said Ruth. "I like to think I get my decent qualities from him."[142] One of Ruth's favorite cousins, the daughter of her Aunt Miriam, was Olive Minuse Wehbring. When I talked with Olive's daughter, Brenda Holman, she recalled her mother saying, "We didn't even know who this Walter Chatterton was!" Olive's father, Alfred Minuse, a shipbuilder like Ruth's Grandfather Reed, was also Vice President of U.S. Steel. "They lived comfortably, too," said Brenda, "but very low-key." Brenda had nothing but good memories about her famous relative. "Ruth was one of a kind," she told me. "Ruth was alive! She was just *in there*! And, she was consumed by politics, the world around her. To me, she was an authority on everything. She was very cosmopolitan and sophisticated. For not ever really having a formal education, Ruth was very bright. And, she could be really funny. My mother became executor of her estate when she died. Ruth was so gracious and loving to her. They were very close. My mother just loved Ruth to death."[143]

While Ruth may have faced hard times, she never saw any reason to abandon the gilded cage in which she grew up. When she reached Hollywood, her salaries at Paramount and Warner Brothers were exorbitant. "Money never meant much to Ruth," insisted Paul "Scoop" Conlon, her personal representative in the 1930s. "She was generous to a fault, as I found out after her picture career was finished and she was nearly strapped. She lived on a royal scale in Beverly Hills, yet she knew in her heart that most of her 'friends' were apt to turn up missing when the chips were down."[144] Ruth's family confirms Scoop's observation. "Ruth was very generous," says Brenda Holman. "After my mother graduated from Smith's College (Class of 1927) Ruth paid for her to go to Europe! To go to the Continent! How generous is that! And, how wonderful! Ruth lived very well. Even at the end, when she didn't have *any* money."[145] Though her bank account may have fluctuated, one thing never shortchanged Ruth Chatterton: ambition.

Endnotes

74   Magda Frances West, "Nobody Stars a Fat Woman," *Green Book Magazine*, August 1912.

75   Florence E. Yoder, "Henry Miller Appears in Comedy Success," *Washington Times*, April 9, 1916 (Some accounts say the stage director was a Mr. Thomson).

76   Adele Whitely Fletcher, "Beauty, Brains or Luck?" *Photoplay*, February 1930.

77   Molly Merrick, interview, *Milwaukee Journal*, October 31, 1932.

78   "Footlight Flashes," *Oakland Tribune*, June 2, 1912.

79   The US Census 1900 confirms the 1867 birth date. Her passports from 1913 and 1920 give her birth year as 1874 and 1875 respectively (Her passport signature indicates that she spelled her name "Lilian").

80   "Big Diamond Robbery," *Kansas City Journal*, February 9, 1898.

81   (Held at the Adriance Memorial Library in Poughkeepsie, NY)

82   *New Church Life – A Monthly Journal*, 1884 (devoted to the teachings of spiritualist Emmanuel Swedenborg) (records from 1852-55, show that John C. Chatterton was also connected to the Methodist-Episcopal Church) (the 1860 US census lists him as a "bookkeeper").

83   Betsy Cernosia, researcher and descendant of John Carson Chatterton. Email dated January 3, 2012.

84   Official Gazette of the U.S. Patent Office, June 29, 1889, pg 1479; The Commissioners of Patents Journal, August 13, 1878, and December 4, 1879.

85   "Debtors' Jubilee," *New York Evening Express*, August 31, 1878.

86   "In Chase of His Daughter," *New York Sun*, September 25, 1892.

87   Obituary for Horace Manuel, *New York World*, February 24, 1896.

88   "Marriages That Were Failures," *The Sun*, September 11, 1894.

89   "A Severed Marriage Tie," *New York World*, December 30, 1894.

90   "Edward Earle Examined," *New York Tribune*, June 23, 1896.

91   U.S. Passport Application (M1490), May 5, 1920.

92   "Good Use For His Wealth," *New York Times*, July 17, 1890.

93   "Here Youth And Age Meet," *New York Tribune*, March 22, 1896.

94   Dan Thomas, "The Life Story of Ruth Chatterton," *Charleston Gazette*, November 2, 1930.

95   Charles W. Collins, "The Girl Who Made Good," *Green Book Magazine*, August 1914, pg 417.

96   Harvey Breit, "Talk With Miss Chatterton," *New York Times*, August 27, 1950.

97   Wood Soanes, "Curtain Calls," *Oakland Tribune*, May 1, 1923.

98   US Census 1900, Reed residence, 269 Sedgewick Avenue.

99   "Ruth Chatterton Says She Never Could Cook," *The Sun*, NY, November 19, 1916.

100   Quote taken from Ruth Moesel manuscript held at the New York Public Library at Lincoln Center.

101   Frank Condon, "The Laughing Lady," *Saturday Evening Post*, November 28, 1931.

102   Dan Thomas, "The Life Story of Ruth Chatterton," *Charleston Gazette*, November 2, 1930.

103   Dan Thomas, "The Life Story of Ruth Chatterton," *Charleston Gazette*, November 2, 1930.

104   Adele Whitely Fletcher, "Beauty, Brains, or Luck?" *Photoplay*, February 1930.

105   From Ruth Moesel manuscript held at the New York Public Library at Lincoln Center (quote taken from interview with Ruth's tutor/friend Countess Ada De Lachau).

106   Ruth Chatterton, "Music As Beauty's Handmaid," *The Bee* (Omaha), April 2, 1915.

107   "Minuse-Reed," *New York Tribune*, June 7, 1903.

108   Mary Mapes Dodge, "St. Nicholas League-The Roll of Honor," *St. Nicholas Magazine*, October 1904.

109   Dan Thomas, "The Life Story of Ruth Chatterton," *Charleston Gazette*, November 2, 1930.

110   "Business Troubles," *The Sun*, March 1, 1904.

111   New York Census, June 1, 1905 (Andrew Reed, Shipbuilder, age 78 was listed as living with his daughter Ida, age 51, Lilian, Walter S. Chatterton, son-in-law, and Ruth Chatterton, age 12).

112   "Rich Man Held As Bank Burglar Despite His Proof," *The Evening World*, June 24, 1907.

113   "Detective's Grave Error," *Brooklyn Daily Eagle*, June 24, 1907.

114   "Blunder Stirs Bingham—Will Investigate False Arrest of Walter S. Chatterton," *New York Tribune*, June 25, 1907.

115   *Acts of the Legislature in the State of New Jersey*, Secretary of State, c 1910, pg 624 (includes report of default taxes from 1907).

116   Dan Thomas, "'If'—Maker of Stars," *Rhinelander Daily News* (WI), February 1, 1932.

117   Gladys Hall, "I Am a Renegade in Hollywood" (interview with Ruth Chatterton), *Motion Picture*, July 1929 (Hall was a reputable writer and founding member of the Women's Hollywood Press Club).

118   "Why Be Afraid Asks Ruth Chatterton," *New York Times*, March 17, 1912.

119   Review for *The Prince Chap, Washington Times*, June 1, 1909.

120   Review for *Cousin Kate, Washington Post*, August 3, 1909.

121   Review for *Charley's Aunt, Washington Herald*, August 10, 1909.

122   Review for *The Girl From the Circus, Washington Herald*, August 24, 1909.

123   Lee Shippey, A.L. Ewing, "Folks Ushud Know…" Kessinger Publishing Co., c 2004, pg 43-46.

124   Dan Thomas, "The Life Story of Ruth Chatterton," *Charleston Gazette*, November 2, 1930.

125   Magda Frances West, "Nobody Stars a Fat Woman," *The Green Book Magazine*, August 1912.

126   Dan Thomas, "The Life Story of Ruth Chatterton," *Charleston Gazette*, November 2, 1930 (Ruth was 16 when she made her debut).

127   "Gang Slays Girl in Vacant House," *Waterloo Evening Courier*, November 18, 1909.

128   Tom Lindsay, "Ruth Chatterton," *Long Beach Press-Telegram*, June 21, 1950.

129   "Along Came Ruth," *New York Times*, October 25, 1914.

130   Magda Frances West, "Nobody Stars a Fat Woman," *The Green Book Magazine*, August 1912.

131   Lee Shippey, "Folks Ushud Know," Kessinger Publishing Co., c. 2004, pg 45.

132   "Washington Girl in 'Miss Patsy,'" *Washington Times*, October 2, 1910.

133   Hector Fuller, review of *Miss Patsy, Washington Herald*, October 9, 1910.

134   C.J.B. review for *The Great Name, Indianapolis Star*, May 6, 1911.

135   "Mamakating Inn Guests Enjoy Fine Program," *Middletown Daily Times-Press*, August 29, 1911.

136   Review of *The Great Name, New York Times*, October 5, 1911.

137   Percy Hammond, review of *Standing Pat, Chicago Daily Tribune*, December 4, 1911.

138   HEBO, review of *Standing Pat, Variety*, December 8, 1911.

139   Dan Thomas, "The Life Story of Ruth Chatterton," *Charlestown Gazette*, November 2, 1930.

140   Quote taken from Ruth Moesel manuscript held at the New York Public Library at Lincoln Center (Ruth's Mammy also accompanied her during the 1917 tour of *Come Out of the Kitchen*).

141   Dan Thomas, "The Life Story of Ruth Chatterton," *Charlestown Gazette*, November 2, 1930.

142   Quote taken from Ruth Moesel manuscript held at the New York Public Library at Lincoln Center.

143   Conversation with Brenda Reed Wehbring Holman, January 16, 2012.

144   John McCallum, "Scooper," Wood and Reber, Inc., c 1960, pg 183.

Producer Henry Miller (c.1911). Early publicity shot of Ruth Chatterton (1912).

3
MR. MILLER &
"MISS PEACHES"

"I wonder if any other girl ever had a daddy like you?"

Ruth's first great success on Broadway, *The Rainbow*, was a tender-hearted tale about a young girl, Cynthia, who is reunited with her father after many years. Ruth's on-stage entrance was a heart-tugger. The daughter quietly steps into her father's Fifth Avenue bachelor apartment. She is anxious and alone. Garbed in a simple blue dress, a small blue cap accents the long chestnut-brown braid hanging down her back. On opening night, Ruth stood there for a moment in the sunlit doorway, her serious, inquiring blue eyes waiting for her cue. "A sudden ripple of applause started in the orchestra section, and in an instant the entire house was giving an unknown actress of nineteen an ovation before she even had spoken a line."[146] As *The Rainbow* unfolded, it was the daughter's "innocence" that created the dramatic conflict.

"Rain or shine," wrote Charles Darnton, the dean of New York drama critics, "you're bound to shed considerable moisture during *The Rainbow*... a comedy with a very human touch."[147] Darnton found Ruth both "pleasing... and irritating." He was alone in his assessment. Fellow critics and audiences were captivated by her performance. Miss Chatterton, "sweet and pure as drifting apple blossoms," was showered after the curtain fell with an ovation lasting ten minutes.[148] It was a foregone conclusion that she would become a star. After numerous curtain calls, actor/producer/director Henry Miller, who had played her father, graciously recognized how responsible Ruth was for *The Rainbow*'s success. He came forward, took her by the hand and shared with the audience that "he would feel desperately lonely if [Ruth] left him, and whimsically advised her not to expect a raise of salary on that account."[149] His feelings were genuine. The fact was, Henry Miller, an aging matinee idol, was completely smitten with his new discovery. In turn, Ruth gushed about her good fortune to be connected with producer Miller. She told a *New York Times* reporter, "You know that line, in the play, where I say, 'I wonder if any other girl ever had a daddy like you?' Well, that's how I feel about Mr. Miller off the stage."[150]

Prior to the opening of *The Rainbow* on March 11, 1912, Julia Dean was considered to be "Miss Chatterton's footlight godmother."[151] After the play opened to rave reviews, Ruth gave all praise to Henry Miller. "He has taught me everything I know," she said. "Everything I do in the play is nothing in the world but the things that Mr. Miller has taught me in the past month. He has never spoken an unkind word to me. And, when he told me in rehearsals to change the reading of a line, or some of the business, he always stopped to tell me the reason why." As far as curtain calls, Ruth insisted, "I don't deserve them. The credit is entirely due to [Mr. Miller]."[152] Eventually, Ruth would give herself some credit. She was very motivated. She enjoyed challenge and had ideas of her own.

In truth, it was actually Miller's son, Gilbert, who opened the door for Ruth. Henry Miller was in Europe while Gilbert Miller was casting *The Rainbow*. Gilbert was having a difficult time finding a young girl who was skilled at playing the piano, could sing well, and spoke French. Ruth arrived at his office one morning to inquire if there was anything for her. Young Miller soon recognized that she was the answer to his prayers. Ruth landed the role and a salary of $100 a week. Shortly thereafter, she learned that the play was to open at the "jinxed" Bijou Theater. It was the lore of the profession that Miller, as well as other producers, had nothing but failures at the Bijou. Ruth told Gilbert that she would not play the part unless the theater was changed. He was completely taken aback. Not knowing what else to say, he told her he "would let his father fire her upon his return" from Europe.[153] Ruth's first interaction with father Miller was over the phone. "Mr. Miller called me up," said Ruth. "He made me talk for a few minutes, and then said he had been studying my voice, that it was all right, and to report the next morning for re-hearsals."[154] Of course, Gilbert had already given his father a description and photographs of the lithesome and charmingly attractive Miss Chatterton. And yes, when the play opened it was at the ... *Liberty* Theatre.

The morning following the premiere, *The New York Times* sub-headed its review for *The Rainbow*, "Ruth Chatterton's Hit." It referred to her as "an exquisite little person, who knows how to express feeling and to radiate charm ... without a trace of affectation."[155] In conclusion, the review declared, "Miss Chatterton avails herself beautifully of her exceptional chance." That same day, as Miller's office was besieged with telegrams and telephone calls demanding photographs and facts about the "youthful unknown," Miller presented his new protégé with a five-year contract.[156] It offered a substantial annual increase in salary plus a share of the profits. And profits there were. Seating capacity at the Liberty Theatre could not accommodate the record-breaking crowds. Miller was ecstatic. He told the press that he would never again produce a play which did not "reach him below his collar button."[157] Miller clarified that statement, saying that any future success must appeal to the emotions of his heart. Con-

Publicity shot for *The Rainbow* (1912).

sequently, it wasn't long before Ruth and Tilly were happily situated in a new, sizable apartment at 431 Riverside, overlooking the Hudson River.

⚜

Ruth later admitted that she and Miller did, on occasion, lock horns. During rehearsals, Miller told Ruth, "It is wrong to tell anyone that she does a thing particularly well. After that she doesn't do it so well." "I knew what he meant," Ruth said. "The bits of business I had in *The Rainbow* I had introduced myself. I found myself after a speech of his shaking my head. He had said that was effective. I declined after that to shake my head. He insisted; I persisted. I said, 'But if I don't do it well it were better not done. We kept at it for a week. He won."[158] The whole company at the Liberty enjoyed working with Ruth. When Miller began calling her "Miss Peaches," everyone else followed suit.[159] "Miss Peaches" didn't really care for the character she played. "I never liked Cynthia," Ruth admitted. "That sounds ungrateful, but it really isn't, for there was no depth to the character—just honeyed sweetness from head to toe. It required no genius to present her to the public. She had no temperament; no emotional depth; no knowledge of life, and less idea of its sufferings. I didn't like her, and the fact made it seem very funny to me when the New York critics kept insisting that 'Cynthia' and I were one."[160]

At the end of June, *The Rainbow* took a hiatus. While he ignored Ruth's plea to play Puck in Shakespeare's *A Midsummer Night's Dream*, Miller, for some reason, decided to test her mettle in vaudeville. For the week of August 4, Ruth took on the one-act play *Susan's Gentleman*, about life in the slums. She played a 12-year-old "waif" who falls in love with a "fine gentleman" who turns out to be a crook. Her co-star for the week was House Peters. To follow Ruth, Proctor's Fifth Avenue Theater lined up comedienne Fanny Brice and George White's "Eight English Roses"— "an octet of pirouetting prettiness."[161] Ruth's voice did not carry well at Proctor's and she was not convincing. "She tried hard to be what she was supposed to be," summed up *The New York Herald*.[162] *Billboard* was just as blunt, saying the play would have a chance "with... another woman in Miss Chatterton's place."[163] After this embarrassment, Ruth toured with *The Rainbow* until the summer of 1913. At that point, Mr. Miller rewarded "Miss Peaches" and her mother with a voyage to Paris. Ruth was ecstatic. She and Tilly stayed in Montmartre, the artist "colony on the hill," and thoroughly enjoyed themselves. Both spoke French and easily adapted to their surroundings. In August, Ruth returned home to resume touring in *The Rainbow*. Traveling by train from town to town, she would settle down with a book and never look up until they disembarked. Cast member Louise Closser Hale recalled asking her, "Ruth, why don't you look out the window at the scenery?" Without hesitating, Ruth replied, "Why should I? It's all in the book."[164] Chatterton grew tired of playing Cynthia, but persevered. "I shudder to think," she complained, "that I should ever become inseparably identified with simpering, brainless young girl characters, whose prettiness and sweetness are their only appeal. Really I want to play ugly women."[165]

In spite of Ruth's disdain for her character, there appeared to be no end to Mr. Miller's success. From eastern Canada to San Francisco, theatergoers got to discover Ruth Chatterton for themselves. "Ruth Chatterton's promise of future splendor is a veritable rainbow," raved the *Oakland Tribune*. "She has about her an air of natural simplicity—has it in her makeup and has it in her art."[166] Commenting on the scene where father and daughter are forced to separate, the critic remarked, "Miller has never painted a more faithful picture of a broken heart." Literally shaking, Miller would break down in uncontrollable sobs. "Miller seems to have found himself," observed a reviewer from *The San Francisco Call*. "He seems to have discovered new acting power... and he certainly has discovered a most charming young actress in Miss Chatterton."[167]

Henry Miller was articulate to a fault. He minced no words. *The Rainbow* was his pot of gold and he guarded it vigorously. During a performance in Joplin, Missouri, Miller's anger was piqued. The strongest scene in the play is when Miller bids Ruth goodbye, knowing she's going for good. Just as he kissed her farewell, some "unappreciative curmudgeon" in the gallery puckered up and let loose with a loud "smack." At the close of the act, Miller came before the curtain. He "launched swiftly into a brief but blistering arraignment of the offender... pungently forceful, scathingly eloquent." The audience greeted it with "tempestuous applause."[168] Miller's dander was triggered not to defend his play, but the feelings he held for his leading lady—undoubtedly the source for his newfound "acting power."

In 1932, Broadway's flag-unfurling producer/playwright/composer George M. Cohan took on Hollywood (*The Phantom President*). He also gave his take on Henry Miller and Ruth Chatterton.

> Ruth was just a kid, and the prettiest little thing you ever saw in your life. I always had a warm spot in my heart for Ruthie. She was a dead ringer in looks for my sister Josie. I had a picture hanging on the wall of my office of Josie, autographed *'With all My Love,'* that looked so much like Chatterton it was funny.
>
> One day, Henry Miller, who was nuts about Chatterton, you know, dropped up to see me. My offices at the time were right above the theatre where Ruthie was scoring such a hit in *Come Out of the Kitchen.* Miller was sitting in my office, talking about this and that, when all of a sudden he saw the picture that looked so much like Ruth. Miller read the autograph *'With All My Love,'* and nearly hit the ceiling. He was so jealous he nearly jumped out the window. I guess he thought I had been sneaking down to the theatre between scenes to court his girl! After I explained about the picture of Josie he apologized profusely. He was crazy about Ruthie, Miller was.[169]

For obvious reasons, Henry Miller and his wife, former child star Helene "Bijou Heron" Miller, had separated. Married in 1883, the couple had been co-stars on stage. Bijou eventually retired to focus on raising their three children, Gilbert, Henry, Jr., and Agnes. Miller kept his family at a convenient distance in Europe.[170] All three children received their education and upbringing abroad. The fact that Miller was married and a father was rarely mentioned in the innumerable newspaper stories about him. Miller was not involved on a deep personal level in his children's lives. Author Margaret Case observed in 1944, "Henry Miller was not wholeheartedly a family man, and he seems to have regarded his children, especially Gilbert, with a quizzical detachment that occasionally flowered into insult."[171] During his attempt at an acting career, Case told of the time Gilbert, a juvenile lead, was surprised to see his father's face staring at him from the audience. "Your carriage has improved and so has your diction," Miller told his son afterward. "There are unquestionably many parts you can play. What I have just witnessed is not one of them."[172] To avoid future embarrassment, said Case, Miller removed his son from the stage "as a gardener might pick a bug off a rose" and put him to work as his business manager. Miller's other two children also attempted to establish themselves as actors. While Miller and Ruth were touring in *The Rainbow*, Mrs. Miller chaperoned daughter Agnes, who was touring in *Isle of Dreams*.

John Henry Miller

By 1912, Henry Miller had been on stage for over thirty-five years. Born John Henry Miller in London in1859, he was fourteen years old when he immigrated with his parents to Toronto, Canada, where he made his stage debut. By 1880, he was acting in New York. In 1882, Miller toured with Bijou Heron in *Odette*. They married on Miller's twenty-fourth birthday, February 1, 1883. A decade later, Miller was the popular leading man for the Charles Frohman Company. Few people knew that Henry Miller was never an American citizen. Ironically, he was considered "the American ideal of honest, sym-

pathetic, taciturn masculinity."[173]
Miller cut an extremely handsome
figure at the time. He had notably
portrayed Sidney Carton in *The
Only Way*, a stage adaptation of *A
Tale of Two Cities*. In 1905, Miller
left Frohman and took over Broadway's Princess Theatre, starring in
his biggest success as an actor, *The
Great Divide*. It wasn't long before
Miller, a formidable taskmaster,
was considered the dean of ac-
tor-managers. He launched the
careers of the Russian actress Nazimova and Laura Hope Crews.
Theater was Miller's religion. He
was hard on actors who failed to

Henry Miller (c. 1888).

give him full measure. After raking an actor over the coals, Miller, with a pit-
tance of sympathy, would mutter, "Thank God he is no worse!"[174]

Actor-producers met with a great deal of financial risk. Miller had
made and lost fortunes by the time Ruth came along. He was a grandfather—twelve years older than Walter Chatterton. As Ruth received
no real upbringing from her own father, Miller's nurturing presence and
guidance was something she appreciated. The thirty-three years in age
that separated them didn't seem to bother her. Although a bit portly, he
was still a handsome man. And he was in love with her. "He's really been
like a father to me," Ruth would say.[175]

In early 1914, Miller decided that it was time for twenty-one-year-old Ruth to "go it alone." He selected a story written by Mark Twain's niece, Jean Webster. Miller had picked up a copy of Webster's popular book *Daddy Long-Legs* at a newsstand, became completely absorbed in it, and before long had his son Gilbert contact the author about adapting the story for the stage. Webster laughed at Miller's idea.[176] As an author, Jean Webster combined writing with social activism. The story was inspired by her work on behalf of orphans. She drew her material from monthly visits to orphanages in New England. Despite her initial misgivings, Webster, with Miller's encouragement, discovered that she had no problem adapting *Daddy Long-Legs* for the stage. In fact, she toured with the play, which opened at the Apollo in Atlantic City, February 20, 1914.[177] *Variety* praised, "*Daddy Long-Legs* is a full-grown comedy in which the author has blended a laugh and a tear in almost every line."[178] On stage, Ruth played "Judy Abbott" the eldest girl at an orphanage. She had been refused the opportunity to find a home. The woman in charge used Judy as a drudge to raise the younger children. Judy is actually their protector. The play did not hold back on the orphanage's sordid conditions. Judy rebels one day in front of a wealthy trustee. She wants a chance to make it on her own. She says she wants to "escape" from the institution. The grim matron, embarrassed by Judy's pluck, calls her an ungrateful imp and demands an explanation. The trustee was all ears at this point, as was the audience. "There was consuming fire in Miss Chatterton's voice that opening night," commented drama critic Frank P. Morse. "But a world of artistic restraint, as she answered,

> I don't feel any gratitude because I have nothing to be
> grateful for. There is no charity about it. I have earned
> my living in the John Grier Home. I have worked from
> the time I was a tiny child. For three years straight I pol-

ished brass door knobs until you discovered that I was clever enough to do other things. And you haven't kept me all this extra time just for my own good. When I was eleven years old that lady wanted to adopt me. But you made her take another child instead, because I was useful. I might have had a home too—like other children—and you stole it away from me. And you call me ungrateful because I'm glad to go?"[179]

The trustee takes sympathy and anonymously affords Judy the opportunity to attend college—he becomes her shadowy benefactor, "Daddy Long-Legs."

Ruth made a thorough study of her role. "Judy fascinated me," she said. "I had read the book and thought about the character for a year and a half."[180] Ruth was pleased that Miller stayed out of her way during rehearsals. "He has left me pretty much alone to work out my own salvation, and that of the heroine of Miss

Ruth as "Judy" in
Daddy Long Legs (1914).

Webster's story," she said. "It has been a great delight, for 'Judy' is so human. She has a sympathetic understanding of what goes on in the hearts of other folk, and just as vital is her keen and genuine humor."[181] *Daddy Long-Legs*, with not a weak spot in the cast, drew big houses wherever it went—lasting eight weeks in Chicago before it tackled Broadway in September 1914.

On opening night at New York's Gaiety Theatre, Ruth was recalled again and again to the stage. "The play served to introduce Ruth Chatterton as a star to Broadway," said *The New York Times*.[182] "Her command is quite refreshing in so young a star," noted the *New York Tribune*. "She has a manner, coupled with her personal attractions, that puts her quite in the first rank."[183] American playwright Channing Pollock predicted that *Daddy Long-Legs* would "make a fortune for its producers," the main advantage being the "winning and winsome personality in Ruth Chatterton."[184] Theatrical critic John Briscoe concurred that "Henry Miller has a small sized gold mine in *Daddy Long-Legs*... with pretty Ruth Chatterton as the cast's chief magnet."[185] Indeed, for the next two years, *Daddy Long-Legs* played to full houses across the country. While the play had no big message, Jean Webster had a way of mixing whimsy into her activism. She was a suffragist and committed to social reform for both orphanages and prisons. It would be six more years before women would have the right to vote. Ruth's character, at one point, imposes the question,

> Don't you think I'd make an admirable voter if I had my rights? This is an awful wasteful country to throw away such an honest, educated, conscientious, intelligent citizen as I would be.

During the Broadway run of *Daddy Long-Legs,* Ruth was confronted with the adoration of a young British actor named Edmund Gorst. Gorst had come to the States from London and toured with the legendary George Arliss in *Disraeli.* Edmund was completely taken with Ruth and one night the neophyte actor, still in his teens, managed to blurt out a proposal of marriage. "She broke my heart and mended it again all in one evening," he told his wife a few years later.[186] Edmund treasured Ruth's compassion and understanding at a crucial moment. In October 1914, he left acting and the U.S. behind to join the Dorsetshire Light Infantry. England was at war.

Shortly before her twenty-second birthday, Ruth emphasized in the *Cosmopolitan* article, "Ambition's Daughter," that she wanted to be an actress, not a star. "An actress is competent to play anything," Ruth explained. "An actress can play comedy as well as she can play tragedy. A star may be a triumph of frills and personality, or of a manager's persistence." Ruth then zeroed in on the roles she had been playing.

> Would I, could I, be satisfied to go on doing this sort of thing? And if I were satisfied, could I call myself an actress? *Daddy Long-Legs* is a dear play and I love it. It has given me a wonderful opportunity, and I am grateful. But, I ask you, would it be right for me to be satisfied with that?[187]

During the summer hiatus, Ruth requested of Miller that she be allowed "special permission" to play Nora Helmer in Ibsen's *A Doll's House.* "He killed that dream then and there," said one reporter.[188] And, as for having her name "in lights" on Broadway, Ruth felt undeserving. "I thought I was too young for such an honor," she admitted. "I have felt weighed down by it. I am working to deserve what I have. I am studying, studying, studying.

I am working on my voice to enlarge and strengthen it, and I am importuning Mr. Miller to help me."[189] While diligently spending the best part of her day at the gymnasium (fencing and dancing), in the studio learning voice production, and at home reading dramatic poetry and working out pantomime, Ruth pleaded with Henry Miller to recognize her own artistic vision. He had hesitated when she decided on wearing black in the final act of *Daddy Long-Legs*. "Mr. Miller yielded," Ruth proudly stated. "Black in the last act will show [Judy's] development in quietude of spirit, in dignity. At the same time it expresses her… realization of the more serious aspects of life."[190] Ruth had taken time to select fabrics and colors that would reflect her character's growth as an individual. "Clothes make the greatest difference to an actress who thinks," she emphasized.[191] Marlis Schweitzer, in her book *When Broadway Was The Runway*, complimented Ruth's courage, saying, "Chatterton's success in persuading Miller… suggests one way that actresses used costuming to challenge male authority and define themselves as professional… Chatterton demonstrated her knowledge of emerging acting theories, which stressed the importance of understanding character motivation and psychology."[192]

When someone criticized Ruth's onstage slouch after "Judy" leaves the orphanage and enters college, Ruth rationally explained, "Nothing could completely eradicate what eighteen years of an orphan asylum have done to Judy's sensitive character. Something of that 'horizonless' institutional life must survive, and in Judy's case her mental attitude transforms it into her gait and her slight slouch… her sensitive nature has retained this little reminder of the time when four brick walls were all she saw of the world."[193] In spite of her "privileged" background, Ruth found herself completely capable of literally walking in her character's shoes.

Henry Miller was known for his uncontrollable temper. According to one of his biographers, Miller "was restless, utterly impatient, and subject to violent rages."[194] "I hate God! I hate God! I hate God!" he ranted during a rehearsal for the San Francisco opening of *The Rainbow*. An important prop, Miller's "beloved door" from which Ruth made her first entrance, was missing—still in transit. "My life is one continual apology," Miller would muse afterward. In private, Miller could be a gracious host, a brilliant conversationalist, charming—a welcome figure. His devastating sarcasm, however, was reserved for actors and stagehands. In January 1915, a critic from *Theatre Magazine* noted that Ruth's deep blue eyes looked like "overgrown forget-me-nots" when asked the question, "Is Henry Miller as severe a director as some actors with bruised feelings and painful memories would lead us to believe?" Ruth remained calm during her appraisal. She said Miller left actors alone who had brains and used them. "Persons with small minds resent him," she observed, "and he knows it and focuses his instruction upon them. I have learned more by acting with him and watching his methods than by his direction."[195] Her blunt assessment was grounded in her own truth. When she was asked to be guest speaker at a Washington, D.C., girls' club, she told her audience to acknowledge their faults and "turn them about" into assets. "Take the fault of talking all the time about yourself," Ruth suggested, "That is such a tiresome fault that before we realize it we have to keep alert to find any one who will listen to us." "Stop for awhile," Ruth advised, "collect some new facts about yourself which will compel attention." She concluded by saying,

> I want to tell you girls, and ask you to tell other girls, that the wrong way to succeed is to coddle yourselves and feel sorry that you have no chance in life. And the right way to succeed is to be honest with one's self. Then you can't help being honest with others.[196]

"Honesty" was a trait that never left Ruth. Her portrayal of "Judy Abbott" was redefining the modern heroine. Ruth argued that Judy was much, much different from the role she portrayed in *The Rainbow*. "I never, oh, never," she stated *very ferociously*, "wish to play any part again where I do not have to think. Every time I have acted Judy Abbott, eight times a week, I feel that I have grown spiritually. I have breathed in the forces which raise the little pale orphan to the wife of the fine Jervis Pendleton, and I cannot help being affected by it. I am always imbued with new desires, and if I do this long enough I am sure that I shall conceive a great and immortal purpose. It has awakened me to many of the social obligations of modern womanhood."[197] Feminist writer Doris Fleischman, the first woman to ever cover a prizefight, had also interviewed Theodore Roosevelt and social activist Jane Addams.[198] Upon interviewing Ruth, Fleischman pointed out that Chatterton's success was guaranteed from playing such characters as Judy. "I sighed with contentment," wrote Fleischman, "at the pathetic pluck of the little girl, who with instinctive courage and good taste pits her wits against wise school boards and haughty D.A.R.'s."[199]

While the phenomenal success of *Daddy Long-Legs* kept her on tour, Ruth cried real tears when her beloved companion, the little alley cat Tommie, saw his demise during a play date in Canada. In Tommie's place came Jim, a Boston bull terrier of distinguished pedigree. Jim took a leave of absence one afternoon while Ruth paid her taxi fare in front to the Hotel Biltmore. Ruth posted a $25 reward for his return. *The New York Times* stated, "Miss Chatterton believes that some unscrupulous dog fancier stole the dog, for she cannot understand how Jim could be impelled to run away. She has notified the police... detectives of the Second Branch Bureau are out looking for the dog."[200]

Before wrapping up the *Daddy Long-Legs* tour in 1916, Miller, satisfied that Ruth had established herself as the star of the production, joined the cast to become Judy's "Daddy Long-Legs." D.C. drama critic Florence

Publicity shot by Nalinger during
Chicago run of *Daddy Long-Legs* (1914).

Yoder told her readers, "That [Miller] would so far eradicate himself, and be presented merely as a member of the cast, is in itself a great tribute to the abilities of Miss Chatterton."[201] Yoder added, "The fact that *Daddy Long-Legs* is a comedy does not rob it of several fine moments of tragedy. Miss Chatterton rises to the occasion in all of them." While visiting Ruth in her dressing room, Yoder was impressed by the "calm, sensible, and intelligent" young actress. "She *sat still,*" Yoder marveled. "She talked and she listened, and when the time came to smile she smiled." Most young actresses were too busy giggling, wiggling, and smoothing their hair. While Ruth put on her "little black velvet suit" for the last scene, she prepped herself mentally to return to the circumstances "which affected the character." As Yoder got up to leave, Ruth turned to her and said, "Next year… I hope to do bigger and better work than I have ever done before. I am studying [a] part now and it is very complex."[202] Someone besides Henry Miller was now making a real difference in Ruth's outlook and how she presented herself.

Shortly after *Daddy Long-Legs* had opened on Broadway, Gilbert Miller remarried. His new wife, Margaret, showered attention upon Ruth. Ruth credited Margaret for any aesthetic quality she possessed as an individual and actress. "She was a brilliant, charming woman," Ruth recalled later. "I admired her keen voice… I wanted to be like her. I tried to speak as she did. She opened my mind to many cultural vistas. The graces which I admired so greatly in her, I made every effort to copy." "Her love," Ruth emphasized, "was a vital factor in my artistic growth."[203]

The role of "Judy Abbott" would prove pleasant foil for Mary Pickford in a 1919 silent film version of *Daddy Long-Legs* and for Janet Gaynor, according to one biographer, a "lackluster performance" in the 1931 talkie remake.[204] By 1955, the story seemed old hat, but Fred Astaire and Leslie Caron teamed for a charming musical version of the play, which introduced the Oscar-nominated song "Something's Gotta Give." Apparently something did. The orphanage's "cheery atmosphere" replaced Jean Webster's critical take on these institutions. The original play wasn't created purely for entertainment. Both Ruth and Jean Webster teamed with the State Charities Aid Society in its effort to place New York's 35,000 orphans into real homes. In January 1915, Ruth had put on a benefit performance of *Daddy Long-Legs* for the Charities Aid. She helped market "Daddy Long-Legs" dolls to help raise funds. Applicants and societies interested in dressing the dolls contacted Ruth directly at the Gaiety Theatre. [205] It wasn't long before there were so many requests for orphans coming in that a special committee was appointed to handle the influx of applications. As part of her activism, Ruth joined in with a throng of other suffragists in a tribute to Susan B. Anthony at the Hotel Biltmore in February 1915. At her table were Nazimova, Gladys George, and Mrs. Otis Skinner.[206] Ruth's association with Jean Webster no doubt triggered her own activist leanings. Tragically, Webster died following childbirth in June 1916. *Daddy Long-Legs* had just completed its long, successful run. Ruth folded up Judy's "little black velvet suit" for what she thought would be the last time.

Henry Miller had staked a great deal in featuring a new star in a new play by a new playwright. He had ignored Ruth's pleas not to be featured as a star just yet. "I felt as if I were taking something that did not belong to me, that I hadn't earned," said Ruth repeatedly. While feeling "fearfully lucky," she ended up relishing the role of Judy.[207] She had become an extraordinarily popular star with a huge personal following. "I have worked hard," Ruth admitted, "for the most bitter grief that I can imagine for myself would be to have Mr. Miller disappointed in me."[208]

Endnotes

145   Conversation with Brenda Reed Wehbring Holman, January 16, 2012.
146   Dan Thomas, "The Life Story of Ruth Chatterton," *Charlestown Gazette*, November 2, 1930.
147   Charles Darnton, "The Rainbow a Comedy With a Very Human Touch," *The Evening World* (NY), March 13, 1912.
148   Road tour review of *The Rainbow*, Trenton Evening Times, October 17, 1912.
149   Review of *The Rainbow*, New York Times, March 12, 1912.
150   "'Why Be Afraid?'–Asks Ruth Chatterton," *New York Times*, March 17, 1912.
151   "The Theater," *Indianapolis Star*, May 4, 1911.
152   "'Why Be Afraid?'–Asks Ruth Chatterton," *New York Times*, March 17, 1912.
153   Dan Thomas, "The Life Story of Ruth Chatterton," *Charlestown Gazette*, November 2, 1930.
154   "'Why Be Afraid?'–Asks Ruth Chatterton," *New York Times*, March 17, 1912.
155   Review of *The Rainbow*, New York Times, March 12, 1912.
156   Frank P. Morse, *Backstage with Henry Miller*," E.P. Dutton & Co., NY, c. 1938, pg 114.

157   Ralph Graves column, *Washington Post*, March 10, 1912.

158   A.P. "'Judy' On and Off the Stage," *Theater Magazine*, January 1915, pg 50.

159   Magda Frances West, "Nobody Stars a Fat Woman," *Green Book Magazine*, August 1912.

160   Julia Chandler Manz, "Confessions of a New Luminary," *Washington Herald*, March 1, 1914.

161   *New York Sun*, August 4, 1912.

162   Review of *Susan's Gentleman, New York Herald*, August 6, 1912.

163   Review of *Susan's Gentleman, Billboard*, August 17, 1912.

164   Cal York (pseudonym for various *Photoplay* columnists), "Monthly Broadcast From Hollywood," *Photoplay*, June 1932.

165   "Society," *Lima Daily News*, December 12, 1915.

166   Review of *The Rainbow, Oakland Tribune*, November 21, 1913.

167   Review of *The Rainbow, San Francisco Call*, November 4, 1913.

168   "An Henry Miller Incident," *Joplin Globe*, April 11, 1926.

169   Nancy Pryor, *Yankee Doodle Dandy Is In The Movies Now, Movie Classic*, September 1932.

170   Lillie West Brown, *Some Players: Personal Sketches*, H.S. Stone & Co., c. 1899, pg. 422.

171   Margaret Case, *Take Them Up Tenderly*, Alfred A. Knopf, NY, c. 1944, pg 8.

172   Margaret Case, *Take Them Up Tenderly*, Alfred A. Knopf, NY, c. 1944, pg 10.

173   Frank P. Morse, Don. B. Wilmeth, *Cambridge Guide to American Theatre*, Cambridge Univ. Press, c. 1993, pg 441.

174   Frank P. Morse, *Backstage with Henry Miller*, E.P. Dutton & Co. NY, c. 1938, pg 9.

175   "'Why Be Afraid?' Asks Ruth Chatterton," *New York Times*, March 17, 1912.

176   "Henry Miller–The Last Iron Man and Daddy Long-Legs," *Washington Times*, March 26, 1916.

177   "Jean Webster Doesn't Know What Inspired Her To Write *Daddy Long-Legs*," Syracuse Herald, 3/1/1914.

178   Review of *Daddy Long-Legs, Variety*, February 27, 1914.

179   Frank P. Morse, *Backstage with Henry Miller*, E.P. Dutton & Co. NY, c. 1938, pg 161-162

180   A.P., "'Judy' On and Off Stage," *Theatre Magazine*, January 1915, pg 50.

181   Julia Chandler Manz, "Confessions of a New Luminary," *Washington Herald*, March 1, 1914.

182   Review of *Daddy Long-Legs, New York Times*, September 29, 1914.

183   Review of *Daddy Long-Legs, New York Tribune*, September 29, 1914.

184   Channing Pollock, review of *Daddy Long-Legs, Green Book Magazine*, December 1914.

185   Johnson Briscoe, "Plans for the New Season," *Green Book Magazine*, October 1914.

186   Theresa de Kerpely, *Of Love and Wars*, Stein and Day, NY, c. 1984, pg 132 (Gorst later became a British diplomat, dying in 1935; his wife Theresa was a novelist and poet. She was also influential in the career of singer Buffy St. Marie).

187   "Ambition's Daughter," *Cosmopolitan Magazine*, December 1914, pgs 328-329.

188   Charles W. Collins, "The Girl Who Made Good," *Green Book Magazine*, August 1914.

189   A.P. "'Judy' On and Off Stage," *Theatre Magazine*, January 1915, pg 50.

190   Marlis Schweitzer, *When Broadway Was The Runway: Theatre, Fashion and American Culture*," University of Pennsylvania Press, c. 2009, pg 161.

191   Florence E. Yoder, "Ruth Chatterton Ambitious To Be More Than One Part Actress," *Washington Times*, April 15, 1916.

192   Marlis Schweitzer, *When Broadway Was The Runway: Theatre, Fashion and American Culture*," University of Pennsylvania Press, c. 2009, pg 161.

193   Hector Turnbull, "Plays and Players–Ruth Chatterton's Slouch," *New York Tribune*, November 1, 1914.

194   Frank P. Morse, *Backstage With Henry Miller*, E.P. Dutton, Inc., NY, c. 1938 (book jacket).

195   A.P., "'Judy' On and Off Stage," *Theatre Magazine*, January 1915, pg 50.

196   "Make Capital of Your Faults," *The Washington Times*, May 30, 1914.

197   Doris Fleischman, "On Personality," *New York Tribune*, February 7, 1915.

198   Anne Bernays, "Doris Fleischman," *Jewish Women, A Comprehensive Historical Encyclopedia*, March 1, 2009, Jewish Women's Archive, <http://jwa.org/encyclopedia/article/fleischman-doris>.

199   Doris Fleischman, "On Personality," *New York Tribune*, February 7, 1915.

200   "Actress Seeks Her Pet," *The New York Times*, June 20, 1915.

201   Florence E. Yoder, "National Greets Daddy Long-Legs," *Washington Times*, April 11, 1916.

202   Florence E. Yoder, "Ruth Chatterton-Ambitious To Be More Than One-Part Actress," *The Washington Times*, April 15, 1916.

203   Quote taken from Ruth Moesel manuscript held at the New York Public Library at Lincoln Center.

204   Sarah Baker, *Lucky Stars: Janet Gaynor and Charles Farrell*, BearManor Media, c. 2009, pg 141.

205   "Daddy Long-Legs Benefit," *The Sun*, December 4, 1914.

206   "Suffragists Honor Susan B. Anthony," *New York Tribune*, February 10, 1915.

207   Charles W. Collins, "The Girl Who Made Good," *Green Book Magazine*, August 1914.

208   Julia Chandler Manz, "Confessions of a New Luminary," *Washington Herald*, March 1, 1914.

1918 portrait of Ruth by Lewis-Smith (Chicago).

4
ACTRESS-MANAGER

Ruth Chatterton in *Come Out of the Kitchen,* played to the biggest receipts of her career, according to *Variety.*[209] For over a year, the comedy, attracting S.R.O. crowds, proved to be the third smash hit in a row for Miller and Chatterton. However, their relationship was going through a transition, especially for Ruth. She was motivated and had ideas of her own. Concerned about being pigeonholed in lightweight comedies, Ruth wanted to take more risks. Miller had to accept this—a man in love has no choice. Together, they signed a five-year contract with the booking agent Klaw & Erlanger. Ruth was now designated an actress-manager. While developing her art as an actress, she acquired a manager's point of view. She learned the financial risks involved. It would put her at odds with her fellow actors during the landmark Actor's Equity strike in 1919.

San Francisco, August 14, 1916. Playing what one critic described as a "vivacious, coaxing, insinuating little puss," Ruth received a warm welcome at the Columbia Theatre for her debut as Olivia in *Come Out of the Kitchen.* It was all about a contemporary Southern household, dead broke, trying to make ends meet by renting out their sizable home to a rich Northerner. Unexpectedly, the family finds themselves having to masquerade as servants (Olivia was the designated Irish cook). It was a comical farce with Olivia constantly chasing suitors out of the kitchen and shedding an occasional tear into the boiling pots and pans on the stove. "Miss Chatterton has created a character that will live in the memory of all who see her," praised Walter Anthony for the *San Francisco Chronicle*.[210] "The capacity to make a character live and move is given to but few. Miss Chatterton is one of the few." When the play arrived on Broadway, *The New York Times* found the storyline "none too convincing," but gave kudos to the playwright A.E. Thomas, director Henry Miller, and the leading lady. "The greatest of these is Ruth Chatterton," insisted the reviewer. "[Her] delightful performance as Olivia Daingerfield is the best and most persuasive reason for going to see the new play at the Cohan."[211] It was Ruth's false Irish brogue that got most of the laughs. Upon meeting her new "employer," she reassures him regarding her culinary skills.

> T'is meself can take the sole of your honor's shoe and
> turn it out so's it'll melt in your honor's mouth.

Nation magazine found the play to be "well adapted" to Ruth's talent and applauded the scene where everyone has been "fired" except Olivia, who "with a quivering lip and a tearful eye is taken into the lap of her comforting black mammy."[212] Ruth made good use of her vocal talent to introduce the "hit song" "Li'l Liza Jane," also made popular by Earl Fuller's Jazz Band on the Victor label. While *Come Out of the Kitchen* enjoyed its successful seven-month run in New York, Ruth displayed a new talent for slamming doors. She found herself directly in the line of fire during one of Miller's tantrums. He was a precisionist when it came to the timing of his plays. One evening, he arrived at the Cohan Theatre shortly before the final curtain. Ruth had unknowingly slowed up the play's tempo. Fellow players followed her lead. As a result, *Come Out of the Kitchen* ran ten minutes over. For Miller, this was unpardonable. His general stage manager, Bertram Harrison, witnessed "the last hot words between the youthful star and her irate manager. The slamming of the dressing room door put a period to [Miller's] dramatic peroration."[213]

Robert Ames, who would portray Ruth's husband in Paramount's *Tomorrow and Tomorrow* (1932) played her rebellious brother in *Come Out of the Kitchen*. Ames, along with other stage stars such as Julia Dean, Billie Burke, Laura Hope Crews, and the Barrymores, would occasionally dabble in making silent films. In 1918, producer Myron Selznick offered Ruth a $300,000 contract for six pictures. His company would follow her around on tour and film only between the hours of 9am and 4pm. Henry Miller encouraged Ruth to accept the generous offer.[214] There was one clause that troubled her: no story approval. "I returned it unsigned," said Ruth.[215] She was also offered contracts from Universal and Famous Players-Lasky. Ruth focused solely on theatrical ventures. Although she never mentioned it, Ruth was part of the supporting cast in the 1914 silent film *Wildflower*.[216] The production, directed by Allan Dwan, starred the soon-to-be-popular film favorite Marguerite Clark. Clark would star in the silent version of *Come Out of the Kitchen*. In 1919, Ruth would sign on with the Stage Women's War Relief for a film version of Rachel Crothers' story, *A Mite of Love*. The day before filming began, Ruth had to back out. She was replaced with Mabel Taliaferro.[217] Most likely, Ruth was attracted to Crothers' narrative of an orphan girl who resolved the selfishness of her new family.

The closest Ruth came to Hollywood was on stage. She played All Aloney, "Queen of the Movies," in a tryout (1917) of the British fantasy

Anthony in Wonderland. The *San Francisco Chronicle* called it a "distinct triumph" for both Miller and Chatterton.[218] Miller, as Anthony, falls in love with Aloney (Ruth, adorned in Mary Pickford curls) while under the influence of a "harmless opiate." During his drug-induced delirium, they sing a duet. Aside from his "unusually promising" play, *The New York Times* reported that Miller arrived in New York with a "tidy sum of California gold" from Ruth's tour of *Come Out of the Kitchen.*[219] *Anthony* lasted five days on Broadway—without Chatterton. "In view of Miller's past achievements," said one review, "it is only charitable to say as little as possible about *Anthony in Wonderland.*"[220]

***

While many insisted that Ruth was a natural as Olivia in *Come Out of the Kitchen,* such roles began to pall on her. She complained, "To be eternally good is deadening after awhile for an actress. I wondered every night before the curtain arose how in the world anybody could enjoy the characterization."[221] Ruth enjoyed a brief respite in some of the smaller Miller productions, such as her five-minute role in John Galsworthy's *A Bit O' Love.* Here, her character runs away from her husband to live in an unconventional manner. "The point I make," Ruth emphasized, "is that the actress after many months in the same role has touched its top and struck the bottom of it. She has explored every angle of the creature she is supposed to be." Ruth felt that characters such as Olivia were missing something—were "not true to the facts of life." "If there is a dash of the original evil which resides in us all," said Ruth, "then the character becomes human and the player can suffer with her." Langdon Mitchell's satire on divorce, *A New York Idea,* was another tryout that Ruth liked. Critics found it "fabulously human." San Francisco critic Walter Anthony said that while he did not want to see Ruth as a divorcee, he changed his mind after seeing the play and remarked, "She revealed an emotional energy which has not heretofore been observed."[222]

While Ruth contemplated her career, Henry Miller took advantage of the financial boon that her success had afforded him. In 1907, Miller had bought eight acres of farmland he called Sky Meadows north of Stamford, Connecticut. The country air relaxed him. Not until the success of *The Rainbow*, however, was he able to perfect his plan… as a producer…

1914 publicity for *Come Out of the Kitchen*.

of Grade-A milk. Box office profits allowed extraordinary and costly improvements at Sky Meadows. First was a stable, a veritable stone castle for his cattle, at the tune of $40,000. "Electric push buttons measured out scientific portions of oats and corn" which were deposited in hygienic troughs.[223] "It was *The Rainbow*," says Miller's biographer, "that financed the electrical kingdom… when Henry Miller appointed himself the big milk and cream man of his Connecticut neighborhood."[224] Sky Meadow Farm dairy products invaded the New York market. Miller enjoyed his healthy bank accounts, but his surplus flesh nagged at him. He spent another small fortune on physical apparatus and medicine balls to help him lose weight. (They ended up being merely props). "My principal exercise," Miller admitted, "is to swear at the laborers on the farm."[225]

Daddy Long-Legs broke all house records and poured more gold into Miller's dream. This time, a new stucco mansion was built at Sky Meadows. Twin power plants heated the interior. It cost an enormous sum, as did the elaborate swimming pool and palatial bathhouse. As long as Ruth was around, Miller's bank balances bulged. And *Come Out of the Kitchen*? Profits from her third phenomenal success afforded her mentor to erect the ideal monument to himself: the Henry Miller Theatre. In 1917, philanthropist Elizabeth Milbank Anderson bankrolled the land on which the 950-seat theater was to be built. Architect Paul R. Allen, who designed Miller's Sky Meadow estate, began razing buildings on West 43rd Street. True to form, Miller changed his mind weekly, altering the construction plans for New York's first air-conditioned theater. There were costly delays. The price of steel escalated after the U.S. was dragged into WWI. Refusing the advice of experts, Miller placed his order too late— more added expense. Miller's theatre progressed satisfactorily whenever he left town. On opening night, April 1, 1918, it was the *theater* that received rave reviews. A critic from *The New York Times* felt "lapped in luxury." As for the play, *The Fountain of Youth*, in which Miller played a rubber magnate, the *Times* critic felt it "lacking."[226]

A name from the past made news in 1918 when Walter Smith Chatterton married a Miss Anna Moran. The ceremony took place in the chambers of Washington, D.C.'s new Chief Justice McCoy. The puzzling thing was that Walter claimed to be a widower.[227] Was it his third marriage? Several months later, Chatterton was in the news again under "Business Troubles." True to form, he had filed a petition in bankruptcy showing liabilities of $84,896 and no assets.[228] Unsurprisingly, Ruth made no comment on these affairs; she was too busy preparing for her debut at the Henry Miller Theater. In *Perkins*, which opened October 23, she impersonated a character similar to Olivia Daingerfield—an heiress, impersonating a servant, who was obligated to marry a Canadian rancher (Henry Miller). Despite the prolific smooching of Miller-Chatterton on stage, the play ranked as yet another failure, lasting twenty-three performances. Critics barbed that Ruth, as the title character, looked as if she had just "come out of the kitchen."

To the rescue of Mr. Miller's theatre came a "triumphant" two-week run of *Daddy Long-Legs*. "Ruth Chatterton's Best," cheered *The New York Times*. The revival was a healing of sorts for theatergoers. The World War that had permeated the air with a feeling of despair was over. The play opened just five days after the armistice was signed "on the eleventh hour of the eleventh day of the eleventh month." "For the public of late," said the *Times* review, "graceful romance [is] proportionately welcome. Ruth Chatterton … always an artist of extraordinary subtlety and authenticity of charm, her technique has gained precision, authority."[229] Ruth was still receiving letters from children addressed to "Judy Abbott" or "Judy Abbott Chatterton." "The funny part," laughed Ruth, "is that the children who wrote to me, and there are literally hundreds of them—are absolutely convinced that I am still Judy."[230] After she resuscitated the Henry Miller Theatre with a shot of *Daddy Long-Legs*, Ruth resumed her tour in *A Marriage of Convenience*, based on a story by Alexandre Dumas. Dressed in a series of stately Louis XV gowns, she played the wildly impulsive Comtesse de Candale. Ruth dazzled her audiences with silk brocades as well as her wit. Henry Miller co-starred in the revival. In Washington, D.C., all the applause focused on Ruth. "Of Miss Chatterton," said one review, "one needs a moment or two to analyze the great delight of her work,

> As the countess, it is an effort to conceive how the enthralling sweetness of this girl managed to bubble up through the towering wig, the powder, and the Pelion of dry goods that swathed the role, but bubble it did… to the everlasting satisfaction of everyone. It is conceivable that this young woman could make a gunnysack or a barrel a fascinating costume.[231]

Another critic raved, "Never, perhaps, has Miss Chatterton appeared to better advantage. If first honors are to be given to anyone, they belong to her." Henry Miller didn't seem to mind the praise showered on his co-star. When the play reached San Francisco, Miller stood before the curtain one evening, reminiscing back twenty years when he first played the role of Comte de Candale. With a hint of sadness, he felt he was "nearing home." He then countered his melancholy and snapped, "But, I don't use crutches yet!" Miller then paid graceful compliments to Ruth, who, in turn, flattered him by saying she could not "understand Henry Miller's talk of so many years. No man can tell." No man, that is, excepting Mr.

Miller's hairdresser. Bay Area critic Ben Macomber complimented the "exquisite actress," insisting that Ruth had "a grace so delicate that one wonders if the bloom can last the evening."[232]

Billie Burke, the glittering good-witch "Glinda" in 1939's *The Wizard of Oz*, had played Comtess de Candale with Miller prior to Ruth taking it out on the road. Miss Burke (wife of Florenz Ziegfeld) wasn't exactly thrilled when Ruth, knowing she would be taking over the role, offered advice about costumes. "Mr. Miller," whimpered Burke, "gave me carte blanche, never sniffing at expenses, not even when I spent one hundred and twenty-five dollars for a lace handkerchief. But Miss Chatterton... there were several interesting arguments."[233] Burke goes on to say that she and Ruth were "not the same type," but she thought Miller to be an "elegant actor" and an "astute producer." Burke also commented on Miller's success as an amateur dairy farmer. She said his "milk ought to be good. It cost me two dollars and fifty cents a glass."

❦

On July 4, 1919, Ruth was asked by San Francisco Mayor Rolph to convey the "Peace Message" from General Pershing, who was in Paris. It was part of the city's "Celebration of the Victory Fourth" to be held at the Civic Center. Standing outside the balcony of the mayor's office, Ruth's voice was transmitted by a new invention called "Magnavox." Through this pioneer loudspeaker, Ruth, wearing a sporty white hat with a bandana, read: "This independence day has a new significance. By the valor of our soldiers and the loyalty of our people we have demonstrated our right to liberty and those kindred qualities which we hold most dear." Men's hats swept off instantly from more than a block away, giving "evidence that she was heard."[234] Earlier in the year, Ruth had hosted a matinee performance

Ruth and Lucille Watson in a scene from *A Marriage of Convenience* (1918).

of her new play, *The Merrie Month of May,* for convalescing soldiers at Walter Reed Hospital. Washington, D.C.'s New National Theatre also welcomed wounded marines from nearby Quantico as Ruth's guests. Dozens of ambulances from the Red Cross Motor Corps assisted in transporting men confined to wheelchairs. The theater filled to capacity.[235]

In *The Merrie Month of May* (soon re-titled *Moonlight and Honeysuckle*), Ruth's character, Judith, is the daughter of a U.S. Senator. The flirtatious type, Judith accepts proposals from three men, who all happen to show up at her doorstep on her twentieth birthday. Judith decides to test their sincerity by admitting she had once "dallied in the honeysuckle" with a former beau. Utter chaos follows. Her foolish "yarn" is eventually recognized for what it is: pure fabrication. It was a daring theme for the time. *The Boston Globe* called it original, "if not of conventional propriety." A snub from *The Woman Citizen* magazine huffed, "The man at the box office said it was a clean play. If to be clean dramatically connotes inanity, by all means let us be wicked."[236] Ruth not only tackled the lead in this tom-foolery, she was the director. During rehearsals for *Moonlight and Honeysuckle*, Henry Miller cabled Ruth from Europe, telling her to take charge. New York critic Charles Darnton wrote, "Of most importance in the play is Ruth Chatterton. At last, she seems grown-up. She has 'manner'; she wears her clothes as if she had been born in them. Miss Chatterton makes Judith altogether desirable."[237] Darnton was less fascinated by the play. Registering ninety-seven performances at the Henry Miller Theatre, it just missed the coveted box-office "hit" mark of one hundred.

The summer tour of *Moonlight and Honeysuckle* drew large audiences and lasted two months in Chicago. A reviewer on the west coast swooned, "Ruth Chatterton... carries us along breathlessly from act to act, and before she is through with us has got us in the same hopeless state that belongs to her three suitors."[238] James Rennie received his share of kudos as the suitor who wins Ruth's hand. Rennie would marry Dorothy Gish, of filmdom's famous Gish sisters. When her sister, Lillian, who never married, went to England on business, Dorothy told Ruth that she was worried. There was an Englishman there who insisted he was Lillian's husband. Dorothy wanted James to accompany Lillian in case something untoward happened. Ruth, in her simplicity, asked, "Why does anyone need to know she's there?" "Dorothy, of course," said Ruth later, "howled at my naiveté. But in the theater no one cares about your personal life."[239] Surely, this incident gave Ruth pause. Was the notoriety of a screen star something she would even consider?

Ruth admitted that she enjoyed being on the road. She thought it a mistake, professionally, to be confined to the big cities. "It gives me such an adventurous feeling," she said. "You never know just what will happen to you... in a new town that you never even heard of. You stand at the head of a street and look down and see the queer side streets that lead you don't know where, and it's fascinating."[240] Ruth, as actress-manager, was less fascinated when the cast of *Moonlight and Honeysuckle* reached Salt Lake in August 1919. She faced a real dilemma. Actors Equity was on strike, threatening alignment with the American Federation of Labor.

Ruth and Henry Miller had formed a 5-year alliance with Klaw & Erlanger, the booking agents. As an actress-manager, Ruth felt that art and labor were antithetical. When asked about a possible merger, she told a reporter, "I shall leave the stage, change my profession or, much against my inclination as an American citizen, go to London or Paris to continue my career."[241] Being out on the road, Ruth had little chance to study the real situation, excepting the telegrams she received from Miller or Klaw & Erlanger, who had established a monopoly and were known for their ruthless tactics.[242] On July 1, Equity had asked for better rehearsal pay and an eight performance week. Producers resisted. On August 7, the casts of twelve Broadway shows refused to go on. The Ziegfeld Follies closed when Eddie Cantor refused to show up. Joining Equity's fight were Ethel and Lionel Barrymore, Lunt and Fontanne, Marie Dressler, and Lillian Russell. Producers and managers began to tremble, especially those working on small margins—high rollers who could be wiped out. They all sat around New York's Lambs Theatre Club pontificating while producer Al Woods handed out expensive cigars, chuckling, "Here, smoke yourself to death, sweetheart."[243] Millions of dollars were, in fact, "going up in smoke."

By the end of August, twenty-one theaters had closed in New York. Ruth was still adamant that "art" could not be unionized. "Mind you," she declared, "some of my dear associates and friends are among the strikers. I am in the greatest sympathy with those who have not had fair play from managers, but I am sure if the stage does come under the control of the federation it will put the American theatrical interests back years... I am unwilling to break my word of honor in regard to contracts." Salt Lake audiences were unaware of the strain the troupe of players was operating under. A walkout would mean closing down the show and returning to New York. "We are just agreeing to disagree and let matters take their course," Ruth announced. One reporter called her a "brave little actress manager who is willing that the whole world shall know her stand." The 30-day strike was resolved in a landmark decision, September 6, 1919. Despite Ruth's feelings, Actors' Equity was finally recognized as a legal bargaining agent. Ruth's "dear associates" would now be paid higher wages and work under better conditions. Equity membership rapidly increased from 2,700 to 14,000. Ralph Bellamy understood Ruth's position. Mandatory membership in Equity became a given in order for an actor to work. "I resented this," said Bellamy, who was a teenager at the time. "It was, in effect, comparing actors with bricklayers."[244] Bellamy also understood the attempt to resolve many years of inhumane abuse of actors by management and would one day become President of Actor's Equity.

In protest, George M. Cohan, who refused to sign the Equity contract, founded the Actors Fidelity League, of which he was elected President. Billie Burke, Helen Hayes, Fay Bainter, Charles Coburn, Miller, and Chatterton, all of whom received substantial salaries, sided with Cohan and his "founded by managers" rival organization. [245] None of them could see themselves as discontented laborers. Their efforts were unsuccessful. Billie Burke and Helen Hayes (apologetically) would join Equity in 1924. The Fidelity League, for which Ruth was treasurer, dissolved shortly thereafter.

Occasionally, Ruth removed herself from career and pending issues by going horseback riding. "I love riding," she admitted. "It makes me

**1919- Ruth on horseback, by White Studios,
New York (Ruth's private collection–
courtesy of Brenda Holman).**

forget the theater. Give me a dog, or a horse and a rural setting painted by Nature herself, and I'm happy. I love acting, too, but I don't like the theater. That sounds a bit peculiar. But theaters are walled in, and I would rather be in the great outdoors."[246] Commenting on her fellow players, the opinionated Miss Chatterton had this to say: "It makes me smile to hear some of our comrades-in-arms discuss 'The Philosophy of Life,' and… topics which they know nothing of. They go on and on and on, and they go to sleep. They never get out-of-doors. Instead they get in a rut, and make the theater their entire life. I do not want to be like that." *Moon-*

light and Honeysuckle wrapped up its successful tour and Ruth cheerfully looked forward to a holiday in London. "I am going to run across the sea and back," she laughed. There was talk of her playing Shakespeare's Juliet in an elaborate Henry Miller production upon her return.

In May 1920, Ruth and Tilly sailed on the French liner *Leopoldina* for England and France. Both women's passports listed their address as 100 West 59th Street on Central Park. While abroad, Ruth visited the home of author James Barrie. "I searched the French theater and the English theater for plays," Ruth reported. "I spent a season in Paris and went to everything given; I did the same thing in London. And out of all that I saw, *Mary Rose* was the only play I wanted. The charm of it, the beauty of it, simply captured me. I felt I must have the play."[247] On July 24, mother and daughter arrived home on the *S.S. Baltic*—James Barrie's *Mary Rose* in hand. Ruth was ready to produce, direct, and perhaps play the lead.

Ruth knew that there would be some flack about her taking on a role written by James Barrie. Barrie was considered Maude Adams territory. Adams was famous for her portrayals in Barrie's *The Little Minister* and *Peter Pan*. In fact, *Mary Rose* had been written for her. Quite possibly, the Frohman Company, who owned rights to the play, favored Ruth and offered *Mary Rose* to Maude Adams under the condition she give up her exclusive rights to Barrie's other plays, which they knew she would refuse to do. After this upset, Adams quit Frohman altogether.[248] Miller was against Ruth taking on *Mary Rose*. He had contracted A.E. Thomas, author of *Come Out of the Kitchen*, to create something especially for Ruth. The result, *Just Suppose*, was a charming trifle about the Duke of Windsor (or someone like him) having a dalliance with a southern girl during his recent visit to the U.S. Ruth objected to the idea and was set on doing James Barrie. "I won't play bedroom farces and silly comedies," Ruth stated in an interview. "Henry Miller tells me that I'm too highbrow, but

I can't help it. I'd much rather be thought too particular."[249] Ruth got
her way and *Mary Rose* achieved the "hit" mark with a five-month run at
Broadway's Empire Theatre.

Before the opening, Ruth attended a performance of *Bab* starring
Helen Hayes. Reviews hadn't been kind to Hayes' portrayal. Ruth made
a point of inviting Hayes and her mother to an after-theater party at Henry
Miller's apartment. "I needed cheering up," recalled Hayes. "Since I respected Ruth Chatterton as an actress as well as a friend, I asked her what
was wrong with my performance. Ruth was a bluff and candid woman.
She rarely minced words." Ina Claire stood close by, listening to what
Ruth had to say. "O.K., Helen," began Ruth. "I've always thought you
had talent. That's obvious, and absolutely no credit to you. It's something
else." She measured a tiny space in the air with her thumb and forefinger,
explaining, "You don't have *that* much technique."[250] Ina Claire nodded
in agreement. The two women insisted that Hayes make an appointment
with Frances Robinson Duff, who had coached them and been very helpful. "The Misses Chatterton and Claire saved my professional life with
their happy recommendation," Hayes admitted. Hayes used Duff as a
drama coach for many years and *Bab* went on to last 88 performances.
Duff was also influential in the career of Katharine Hepburn and was
paged by producer Irving Thalberg to coach wife Norma Shearer for her
lead role in the film *Romeo and Juliet*.

Mary Rose was one of the shortest star parts ever written. Ruth had
little dialogue. But the whole development of the play is intimately connected to her *mystical*, ghost-like character. Even when she is not on
stage, her presence is felt. As a young woman, Mary Rose is mysteri-
ously whisked away to a tiny island in the Hebrides—one of Barrie's
trademark "lands that never were." She returns home twenty years later,
unchanged, youthful. The other characters, her husband, her parents,

have aged while weathering earthly realities. Mary Rose is puzzled by what surrounds her. She is unable to recognize her own son, who is now a grown man. The mix of shadow and substance ends as the son consoles his mother until she finds the peace that enables her to return to her "island." The play was an echo from James Barrie's own childhood. "The only ghosts, I believe, who creep this world," wrote Barrie, "are dead young mothers, returned to see how their children fare."[251] After Barrie's older brother died at age thirteen, their mother, now emotionally unavailable, took to her bed and became a ghostly figure in her younger son's life. For Barrie, *Mary Rose* had less to do with enchantment than it did with healing old wounds. Still, it carried Barrie's soft humor and an occasional tug at the heartstrings. American author Montrose J. Moses put it thusly, "The philosophy is a little hazy, and theatergoers have been divided as to what Barrie was aiming at. But, as it is Barrie, one swallows it whole—a delicate morsel."[252]

When Ruth met James Barrie in England, he only offered a "whimsical smile" when she asked him the meaning behind *Mary Rose*. Ruth had her own idea.

> I think that Barrie was trying to tell people what he believed to be better than the spiritualism that pictures the dead as returning to earth and their old associations. He saw England caught in a wave of emotional intensity [WWI] and through *Mary Rose* he tried to show how much more kindly and truly comforting it can be to think of those we have lost as somewhere in a place where everything is beautiful, rather than being forced back to revisit an earth that perhaps they were not sorry to leave. To me, the crux of the whole play is in that line spoken by Mary Rose's father. 'Should she have come

As Mary Rose (**1921**).

back?' he asks, and there, I believe, Barrie puts the question of his play.[253]

A surge of "spiritualism" had indeed taken England by storm following WWI. The prolific Sir Arthur Conan Doyle, an adherent, was constantly searching, a la Sherlock Holmes, for evidence confirming "the
return of the dead." As Ruth toured in this blend of mysticism and reality, one sure-fire way to upset her during an interview was to ask exactly
where Mary Rose went at the play's finis. "What does it matter where she

went?" she would snap. "I don't know, and I'm not so sure that Barrie knows. She went away, that's all. I'm so sorry for people that have to have things explained to them."[254]

Theatre Magazine editor Arthur Hornblow (father of the film producer) felt that Chatterton's *Mary Rose* paled in comparison to the English stage production. He compared it to a flower that could not be transplanted into American soil. "New York's mood," observed Hornblow, "is not—well not exactly, spiritual."[255] Hornblow recommended the play, but felt that Chatterton did not quite "convey... the illusion." Author/critic Kenneth MacGowan described the play as "Barrie at his worst" and Ruth "simply unbelievable."[256] A few reviewers wondered how Maude Adams would have been in the role. Some audiences were "surcharged" by the play's theme, admiring Ruth's "grace... dramatic instinct and whimsical originality."[257] In spite of mixed reviews, Ruth enjoyed a successful tour. "I have never played a part that I loved so," she said. "Really, [Mary Rose] has become almost a religion with me, and I find myself using her unconsciously as a test for other people. If they like Mary Rose, I like them, if they don't, or if they insist on asking questions about her, well, somehow I can't feel anything but sorry for them."[258]

After almost a year on the road, the play reached Boston's Hollis Theatre. The *Boston Daily Globe* praised, "The illusion of ghostly, mystical atmosphere is amazingly well sustained. Miss Ruth Chatterton portrays the extremely exacting role of Mary Rose with intelligence."[259] In the New Year, 1922, *The Indianapolis Star* raved, "No more brilliant performance has been given here this season... none is likely to pass it. Miss Chatterton rings true on every note. *Mary Rose* is the best thing she has done."[260]

Staged as recently as 2007 at New York's Vineyard Theatre, *Mary Rose* received a facelift from director Tina Landau. She cast Keir Dullea to narrate Barrie's "evocative" stage directions. Cast as Mary Rose was director Ron Howard's daughter, Paige, in her professional debut. The *New Yorker* called it "clever and stimulating."[261] The revival was more than just a James Barrie curio. His line regarding the "dear departed" remains relevant: "Mary Rose belongs to the past and we have to live in the present."

⁂

While on the road, Ruth wrote a one-act play based on the life of her distant relation, the tragic English poet Thomas Chatterton, who died by his own hand in 1770. Her play dealt with the last few days of Chatterton's life. Ruth planned to impersonate the young poet herself. For five years, Ruth had collected authentic data as well as a rare first edition of Chatterton's work.[262] A production of her play was never realized. Ruth's energy as author-translator also focused on finding something new for her and her mentor to co-star. Her gratitude to Henry Miller would culminate in a translation of the French play *La Tendresse.*

Among Ruth's own disciples was the American poet George Sterling, who was part of San Francisco's Bohemian Club and a close friend of author Jack London. Sterling doted on Ruth whenever she visited his "cool, grey city of love." Found in the 1921 correspondence between Sterling and fellow writer H.L. Mencken was this eye-opener: "I've been to luncheons and suppers with Ruth Chatterton this week and last, and have written another poem to her, in which I refer to her 'seraph-tempting mouth'—not such an exaggeration as you think. (But I forget: you're not strong for labial stuff.) In return, she gives me tickets to *Mary Rose.*"[263] Henry Miller was (conveniently) back in New York putting together a fundraiser for Actors Fidelity League during this round of Chatterton-Sterling tête-à-têtes. Sterling archivist Alycia Hesse told me, "I am always adding to the list of Sterling's lady companions and I would not be surprised if he and Ruth

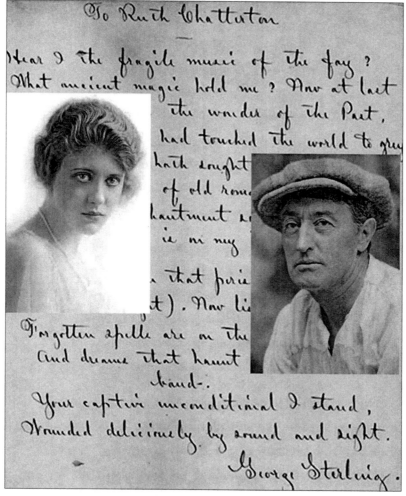

Original hand-written poem (from Ruth's private collection). San Francisco poet George Sterling adored Ruth and wrote several poems to her. Ruth shown in 1917 Seattle portrait. George Sterling (c. 1920).

hit it off."[264] Hesse emphasized that Sterling combined wooing and art and that his language was "not to be trusted entirely. He tends to do a lot of 'bar talk' with Mencken."[265] Although Sterling was prone to drink and a womanizer, his flame for Ruth unleashed profound feelings:

To Ruth Chatterton

Hear I the fragile music of the fay?
What ancient magic holds me? Now at last
I seem to find the wonder of the Past,
Known before Time and touched the world to grey.
Some vanished star has found me with its ray,
That once in seas of old romance was glassed;
A shadow of enchantment softly cast
By some lost moon is on my heart today.

Yours is the charm that perished long ago
(Or so we thought). Now listening, I know
Forgotten spells are on the air to-night,
And dreams that haunt me in an irised band.
Your captive unconditional I stand,
Wounded deliriously by sound and sight.[266]

Ironically, Sterling joined the ranks of Thomas Chatterton. He carried
a convenient vial of cyanide with him at all times. When asked about it, he
replied, "A prison becomes a home if you have the key." So Sterling, consumed with love and suffering for art's sake, swallowed the "key" and left
"home" in November 1926. Apparently, his feelings for Ruth went back a
few years. In 1919, Sterling had written Mencken, saying, "I'm sorry that
you were not able to use the Chatterton sonnets. She will be out here soon,
and I'll give them to some newspaper. I don't imagine I can steal her from
Miller anyway."[267] The implication was obvious. Theater scholar Gerald
Bordman stated that Ruth was "openly bruited" to be Miller's mistress.[268]
However, by the end of 1924, even Henry Miller would be out of the picture. A number of witnesses held their collective breath as Miller stormed
toward the theater exit one day and out of Ruth Chatterton's life forever.

Endnotes

209   *Variety*, January 11, 1918.
210   Walter Anthony, review of *Come Out of the Kitchen*, *San Francisco Chronicle*, June 10, 1917 (commenting on her performance from the previous summer).
211   Review of *Come Out of the Kitchen*, *New York Times*, October 24, 1916.
212   F., review of *Come Out of the Kitchen*, *Nation*, November 2, 1916.
213   Frank P. Morse, *Backstage with Henry Miller*, E.P. Dutton & Co. NY, c 1938, pg 216.
214   "Early Screen Offer Scorned By Chatterton," *Schenectady Gazette*, November 10, 1931.
215   Dan Thomas, "The Life Story of Ruth Chatterton," *Charleston Gazette*, November 2, 1930.
216   *Washington Times* article, November 19, 1914 (Ruth was billed 5th in this film, which was released on October 14, 1914. The story was about two brothers in love with the same girl.).
217   "Cuts and Flashes," *Film Daily*, January 17, 1919.
218   Review of *Anthony in Wonderland*, *San Francisco Chronicle*, July 15, 1917.
219   "Broadway Wig-Wags," *New York Times*, July 29, 1917.
220   "Henry Miller's New Play," *Brooklyn Daily Eagle*, October 24, 1917.
221   Walter Anthony, "Ruth Chatterton Enjoys Change In Her Assignments," *San Francisco Chronicle*, June 24, 1917.
222   Walter Anthony, "*The New York Idea*, Vital Drama," *San Francisco Chronicle*, June 19, 1917.
223   Frank P. Morse, *Backstage with Henry Miller*, E.P. Dutton & Co. NY, c 1938, pg 155-156.
224   Frank P. Morse, *Backstage with Henry Miller*, E.P. Dutton & Co. NY, c 1938, pg 157.
225   Frank P. Morse, *Backstage with Henry Miller*, E.P. Dutton & Co. NY, c 1938, pg 156.
226   Review of *The Fountain of Youth*, *New York Times*, April 2, 1918.
227   "Bridegroom is Father of Ruth Chatterton," *Washington Times*, June 3, 1918.
228   "Business Troubles," *New York Tribune*, February 5, 1919.
229   Review of revival of *Daddy Long-Legs*, *New York Times*, November 18, 1918.
230   "Ruth Chatterton Can't Shake Judy," *Evening Public Ledger*, PA, October 27, 1917.
231   Review of *Marriage of Convenience*, *Washington Times*, September 3, 1918.
232   Ben Macomber, "Henry Miller Scores Hit in Old Play," *San Francisco Chronicle*, June 17, 1919.
233   Billie Burke, *With a Feather on My Nose*, Appleton, c. 1949, pg 195.
234   "Thousands Join in Celebrating Holiday in SF," *San Francisco Chronicle*, July 5, 1919.
235   "Reed Boys To See Ruth Chatterton," *Washington Times*, March 20, 1919.
236   M.H.F. "Stage Reflections-'Moonlight and Honeysuckle,'" *The Woman Citizen*, Vol 4., December 20, 1919.
237   Charles Darnton, review of *Moonlight and Honeysuckle*, *Evening Herald* (NY), October 4, 1919.
238   H.M.L., "Memory Lingers On Comedy Hit," *Oakland Tribune*, July 22, 1919.
239   Katherine Albert, "That Old Devil, Camera," *Photoplay*, May 1929.
240   "Concerning Clothes On The Stage," *Boston Globe*, January 25, 1920.
241   "Ruth Chatterton Carries Role On Veritable Volcano in Playing Present Production," *Deseret Evening News*, (UT), August 23, 1919.
242   John N. Ingham, *Biographical Dictionary of American Business Leaders*, Greenwood Pub., c. 1983, pg 725.
243   Lewis Hardee, *The Lambs Theatre Club*, McFarland, c. 2006, pg 143.
244   Ralph Bellamy, *When The Smoke Hit The Fan,*" Doubleday, c. 1979, pg 41.
245   "Winter Garden Succumbs to Actors' Strike," *New York Tribune*, August 25, 1919.
246   Thomas W. Baily, "Star Believes In Utilization Of Spare Time," *San Francisco Chronicle*, July 6, 1919.
247   Marjorie C. Driscoll, "Girl Who Plays Specter Role Tells of Work," *San Francisco Chronicle*, June 12, 1921.
248   Armond Fields, *Maude Adams: Idol of American Theater*, McFarland, c. 2004, pg 261.
249   Marjorie C. Driscoll, "Girl Who Plays Specter Role Tells of Work," *San Francisco Chronicle*, June 12, 1921.
250   Helen Hayes, *On Reflection*, M. Evans and Co. (NY), c. 1968, pg 116-117.
251   J.M. Barrie, *The Little White Bird*, Charles Scribner's (NY) c. 1920, pg 40.
252   Montrose J. Moses, review of *Mary Rose*, *The Independent*, July 9, 1921.
253   Marjorie C. Driscoll, "Girl Who Plays Specter Role Tells of Work," *San Francisco Chronicle*, June 12, 1921.
254   Marjorie C. Driscoll, "Girl Who Plays Specter Role Tells of Work," *San Francisco Chronicle*, June 12, 1921.

255   Arthur Hornblow, "Mr. Hornblow Goes to the Play," *Theatre Magazine*, March 1921.

256   Kenneth MacGowan, review of *Mary Rose*, *Theatre Arts*, April 1921.

257   Paul Fredrix, "Ghosts, Ghosts," *Des Moines Daily News*, May 10, 1921.

258   Marjorie C. Driscoll, "Girl Who Plays Specter Role Tells of Work," *San Francisco Chronicle*, June 12, 1921.

259   Review of *Mary Rose*, *Boston Globe*, November 8, 1921.

260   Robert G. Tucker, review of *Mary Rose*, *Indianapolis Star*, January 6, 1922.

261   John Lahr, "Trapped in Time," *New Yorker*, March 5, 2007.

262   "Life of Young Poet Forms Theme for Play," *San Francisco Chronicle*, May 22, 1921.

263   George Sterling, Letter to H.L. Mencken dated June 2, 1921, *From Baltimore to Bohemia: The Letters of H.L. Mencken and George Sterling*, c. 2001, pg 129.

264   Email from Alycia Hesse, February 29, 2012.

265   Email from Alycia Hesse, March 4, 2012 (see: http://george-sterling.org/).

266   George Sterling, "To Ruth Chatterton," *Sails and Mirage and Other Poems*," A.M. Robertson, San Francisco, c. 1921.

267   George Sterling letter to H.L. Mencken dated May 1, 1919, *From Baltimore to Bohemia: The Letters of H.L. Mencken and George Sterling*, c. 2001.

268   Gerald Martin Bordman, *American Theatre: a Chronicle of Comedy and Drama, 1914-1930*, Oxford University Press, c. 1995, pg 110.

1922 portrait (Ruth's private collection–courtesy of Brenda Holman).

5
LA TENDRESSE

"The frankness of the French Theater is much preferable to the suggestiveness of the American Theatre."
Ruth Chatterton, 1922

Following her sojourn to France in 1920, Ruth translated the Henri Bataille play *La Tendresse.* It was about a young cinema star, Marthe, whose relationship with Paul, a much older married playwright, is abruptly terminated when he learns that she has been (oddly enough) "unfaithful." By the final act, Marthe and Paul manage to reinvent a companionship founded on tenderness. In 1922, Chatterton and Miller reunited on stage to enact this May-December relationship. The play was both applauded and panned. Some critics insisted it was too frank for American audiences. In spite of an admirable run on Broadway and a lengthy tour, Ruth, as co-producer, met with a heavy financial loss of $40,000. "But no one ever heard her utter one word of complaint," revealed one source.[269] Was there an underlying motive for Ruth's keen interest in *La Tendresse*? It would seem that, for her, art was reflecting life. The question was: did Miller recognize this? Did he even want to?

During an interview, Ruth pointed directly to a scene in *La Tendresse* that inadvertently offered insight into her relationship with Miller. After the coquettish Marthe leaves Paul, he finds himself in the company of an older actress. "She bores him to death," said Ruth. "It is not what he seeks." Ruth herself had matured. She felt she could no longer provide what Miller sought. His age, weight, and health issues were also concerns—in reality, he had only a few years left. Ruth was no longer interested in the physical side of their relationship. And, as in the play, she did not want to risk losing his companionship—the deep affection... *la tendresse.* Unfortunately, all her fears were realized—a worst case scenario. For the "great" Henry Miller, there could be no other man in Ruth's life.

After Ruth purchased the rights, the piquant tale of *La Tendresse* was first produced in San Francisco. Like Ruth, the character of Marthe adores her aging lover and appreciates his contribution to theatrical arts. While her adoration never wavers, Marthe feels the pangs of deception when she meets someone else, a hot-blooded young actor. "The performance of *La Tendresse*," said a Bay Area critic, "revealed Ruth Chatterton in a new light. She gave a remarkable performance, a real characterization, away from anything she has done before."[270] The review pointed to the "tense tragedy" Ruth displayed in the powerful scene where Marthe and Paul separate. After Paul learns of her betrayal, he is out for revenge. He hires stenographers to hide behind curtains to capture Marthe's conversations. When he gets the "scene" he is after, he traps her into reading it along with him as if he were rehearsing a new play. Another critic described the scenario as "ripe grapes for us onlookers, knowing, as we did, that the shorthand reporters were taking down the hot though innocent remarks."[271] "Of Miss Chatterton," noted the review, "only words of admiration can be uttered. She was so pitiably and eloquently human... that we almost forgot to notice the glaring price labels which someone had forgotten to remove from her pretty coat."

Ruth wanted to change the ground rules with Miller and, like Marthe, she wanted to establish her independence. Burns Mantle, Chicago critic, found *La Tendresse* offensive and sniveled that it was "quite out of harmony with American taste."[272] In New York, Alexander Woollcott felt no pity for the character Miller played. "You can almost hear the steady drip-drip-drip of his sympathetic tears," Woollcott complained. "The lady who thus tears his heart… [is] capitally played by Ruth Chatterton."[273] Charles Darnton, for *The Evening World,* thought Ruth "put herself into the changing moods so humanly that she did by far the finest work of her career."[274] Reviews concurred that Ruth's exit scene was prolonged to the point of being irritating. Percy Hammond put it succinctly, "The prejudice against delayed and prolonged departures impedes the sweep and storm of Miss Chatterton's renunciation. She has said that she is going, and since she is unhappy you wish her to go. She stays and stays and stays."[275] A revision was in order. It never happened. Ruth claimed that she had not read a newspaper critique in five years. As a producer, she rationalized that criticism after a metropolitan opening was "futile and dangerous." The company had reached the ultimate destiny of New York's Empire Theatre and there would be no further changes. She voiced her opinions thusly,

> Five years ago, Emma Dunn told me that I should never become emancipated until I learned not to read criticism. She advised me to [only] listen to criticism at dress rehearsals and at out-of-town performances to modify my conception of the role. I have found the emancipation that Emma Dunn promised me.

Ruth was adamant that she was not interested in "commercial" theater or acting only in "money-makers." She was still defensive of *Mary*

Rose and argued that the more intellectual theatergoers were opting for the symphony and opera for the stimulus they used to find in theater. The idea of an American conservatory of the theater was important to her. "We seem so lethargic here," complained Ruth, "that I am afraid there will be no conservatory like the Conservatoire in France. The frankness of the French theater is much preferable to the suggestiveness of the American theater. Here things are suggested over and over again until they simply become nasty."[276] No doubt Ruth had also translated a few cuss words into French for her own personal use as well as Tilly's. American poet Langston Hughes, who as a black expatriate had enjoyed a brief spell in Paris, recalled: "As Ruth Chatterton's Mother said when she tripped over the rug in the foyer on West 55th Street, '*Merde, alors!*'"[277]

Not to be overlooked, the role of Alan Sergyll, Ruth's hot-blooded younger lover in *La Tendresse*, was played by none other than Ronald Colman. Colman, a recent arrival from his native England, was down on his luck. He was about to toss the acting profession aside and become something more stable: a steamship clerk. "Luckily, while I was still out of work," recalled Colman, "I received an offer from Henry Miller to play opposite Ruth Chatterton in *La Tendresse*. The world lost a good clerk."[278] Colman had been touring in *East is West* with Fay Bainter when he met Ruth. It began a friendship which was a real turning point in his life. It was thanks to Ruth that Miller cast Colman in the role.[279] By another stroke of luck, film director Henry King saw the production, was impressed with Colman, and approached him about traveling to Italy and playing opposite Lillian Gish in *The White Sister*. Colman was reluctant, but it was *The White Sister* which secured his future as a leading man in films. After *La Tendresse* left New York, the role of Alan Sergyll ended up in the hands of another future Hollywood leading man, Warren William.

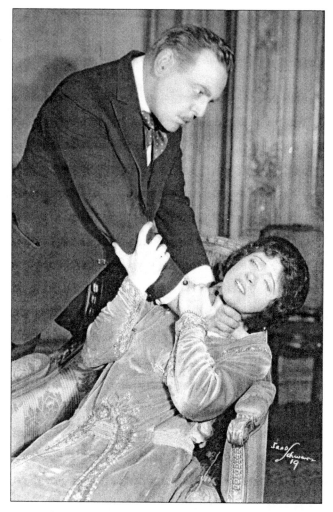

A vengeful, jealous Miller, and Miss Chatterton in *La Tendresse*.
Life would begin to reflect art. (Courtesy of Wisconsin Center
for Film and Theater Research)

Ruth stayed in touch with her mother's sister, Miriam Minuse, and
Miriam's daughters, Olive and Elva (who went by "Judy"). In a letter
to her cousin Olive (c. 1922), who wasn't feeling well, Ruth sent good
wishes and a few comments about her first visit to the South:

Knoxville, Tennessee

Olive, darling:

I'm distressed beyond words, to hear that you too, are ill and in bed. You poor little dear! I suppose you've worried about our precious little Judy, until you were ready to take anything that came along. I had it once, so I know exactly what you are going through. I'm so sorry, dear. I hope when this letter arrives from this wretched South that you will be well on the road to recovery.

This is the first time I've been South, and its an education! The people are like a different race. Lazy, no 'count white trash, for the most part—as my Mammy used to say. As I was driving up from the station yesterday in Lexington, I asked the taxi driver what the town's principle occupation was. He said, "Well, Miss, I don't guess they do nothin' in the winter time. In the summer they grows tobacco, and in the fall and spring there's horse-racin.'" And they look it. I haven't found a house that has been painted since the War! Very few motors—and they're so dirty you couldn't tell what color they were once—mostly mules drawing wobbly little carts. They have one train a day and that leaves at dawn. No one goes anywhere. There isn't a classified telephone book! So if you want to find a hairdresser or a tea-room… you walk 'til you find it. However, I'm making for New Orleans and we expect to be there for Mardi Gras. And that is one of the most fascinating cities in the world.

I'm chatting away about nothing to you, dear, quite forgetting that it is nearly two o'clock, and that I'm very tired. I'm hoping for better news of you both tomorrow. Do get well and take good care of your poor Mummy.

Love and Kisses, darling,

Ruthie[280]

Thirty-five years later, author Ruth Chatterton dug beneath the surface of her first impressions of the South. Her book, *The Southern Wild*, boldly injected her own theories regarding the mental and physical paralysis—the stuck-ness of Southern states. In a brew of murder, mobs, and a lynching, she exposes the tenacious hold tradition had on blacks and whites alike—prohibiting the progress of civil rights and integration.

⚜

While Ruth invested her heart and soul in *La Tendresse,* Ina Claire reigned at the Henry Miller Theatre in the classic comedy *The Awful Truth*. It was a role which Ruth had originated in San Francisco and scored a notable success. "Even Henry Miller in a curtain speech declared that it was 'the most perfect first night performance' he had ever seen," noted *Variety.*[281] Ruth couldn't care less about being in another comedy, hit or no hit. Yet somehow, Miller convinced her to join the cast of *The Changelings* (September 1923), a story of marital mix-ups that had an equally successful run at the Henry Miller. Burns Mantle selected it as one of the season's "10 Best." *Theatre Magazine* editor Arthur Hornblow greeted *The Changelings* as perhaps the "first genuine comedy of American manners."[282] *Nation* magazine simply called the play "immoral." *The Changelings'* improbable situation revolved around Ruth's mismatched parents and in-laws as they engage in a bit of wife-swapping. Ruth's character, with her ultra-modern views on morality, dabbles in an extra-marital affair herself. She receives a sobering jolt when she discovers her own mother in the arms of her father-in-law. The characters come to realize that these liaisons are but temporary. As Percy Hammond put it, "Though there have been many changes, there is little change."[283] Making the best of imperfect marriages was a sobering, if dubious, punch-line for theatergoers. No matter, Hammond said that the play provoked "much laughter and deep thinking."

Dramatist Thornton Wilder (*Our Town*) penned a letter after seeing *The Changelings*. "Oh, how bad it was," he lamented. "Even Laura Hope Crews was bad." Wilder found the "jumbled" play to be a "quilt of contrasted intentions." He was put off when Blanche Bates, who played Ruth's mother, made a curtain speech saying how "they all loved Henry Miller." Bates touted that it was Miller that led the way for the "best things" in theater. "…and Stanislavsky and Reinhardt both in town!" scoffed Wilder.[284]

⁂

On a personal level, Ruth was focused on something other than the mundane complexities of love. "Achievement," said Ruth, "is the most important thing in life to a woman. Beauty fades. Riches slip through your fingers. Fame is a fickle affair. Love is apt to die. Achievement—that's something inside of you. Something no one can take away."[285] A San Francisco reporter asked for Ruth's opinion on what poet Amy Lowell (sister of President Lowell of Harvard) had recently stated about women. Lowell insisted that the most important activity of a woman's life "must be to attract man through every means in her power." Lowell found women's careers "vacuous" and "causing unrest." Ruth burst out laughing. "Why look at me?" she asked. "I've been on the stage since before I was sixteen and I don't feel—vacuous. Why if all the women were to put into practice what Miss Lowell advises, we'd turn into a nation of flappers. The granddaughters of this generation wouldn't be equipped for anything but long-distance dancing!"[286] Ruth felt that her own life refuted Miss Lowell's theories, as well as those of extreme feminists. "Intelligent people, men or women, keep to the middle of the road," said Ruth. She had never felt the urge to marry and her life was crowded with many "beautiful interests" that were in no way connected with men. "It's hard to believe," Ruth insisted, "that the hope of the race rests with some of the little persons we see hastily applying the rouge and then contentedly sitting back to wait for some young man in the corridor of a hotel lobby. I would prefer the hope of the race to rest, for instance, on the young lady in the public library who knows all the nooks and crannies of the best-loved books and who'd just as lief show them to me as to the best-looking young man who ever put his foot in the library."

Ruth pointed to an article written by Professor Burton, President of the University of Michigan. Burton had said that regardless of sex, the only real differences, as far as intelligence, were social differences. As far as a career being a sacrifice, Ruth simply shook her head. "I feel just like anybody else inside and outside! I haven't sacrificed any earthly thing to my career." Surprisingly, Ruth remained out of touch with the rights of fellow actors. Acting as treasurer for the Actors Fidelity League, she sought an injunction against the current Actors Equity contract, which required that eighty percent of every cast be equity members. Fortunately, New York Justice Platzek handed down a refusal.[287] It was the last gasp for the Fidelity League.

At this point, something had to fuel the Miller-Chatterton bank accounts. They decided to revive *Come Out of the Kitchen* and call it *The Magnolia Lady*. It was Ruth's idea to create a musical-comedy version of the play as she had been studying dance and taking voice lessons. *The Magnolia Lady* offered Ruth the opportunity to strut her stuff. An avalanche of adverse criticism followed her decision, but she was determined and began scouting around for a suitable leading man. When Ruth saw a young English actor, Ralph Forbes, in the play *Havoc*, she was impressed. The 6-foot,

165-pound, ash-blonde, blue-eyed Forbes had already pulled a publicity stunt to convince everyone that he was a dead ringer for the Prince of Wales. Forbes' publicist, Bernard Sobel, inadvertently acted as matchmaker for Ralph and Ruth. It was he who suggested that Forbes was "just the man" for the lead in Ruth's new play.[288] "I had no intention of doing [Magnolia Lady]," said Forbes, "but I did agree to go have tea with the star. It was late one afternoon when I called on… Miss Ruth Chatterton."[289] "For Forbes," said columnist Dana Rush, "it was love at first sight. He worshipped Ruth."[290] The smitten Forbes took on the non-singing role of the wealthy English gent who falls for Ruth's character (rechristened Lily Lou Ravenel). At first, Ruth was oblivious to Forbes' adoration.

After *The Magnolia Lady* debuted in Pittsburgh on November 7, it was touted as having "earmarks of success." Ruth, Ralph Forbes, and Skeets Gallagher were the draws. *Commonweal* magazine thought it had a "real charm" and "a touch of distinction."[291] No one else was impressed. One critic complained that Ruth's "small, sweet voice was a shade studied."[292] *Time* magazine put it bluntly. "Ruth Chatterton is not a good musical comedienne. She sings only mildly and dances doubtfully."[293] New York drama critic Arthur Pollock was also hard on Ruth. He found her efforts "depressing," her voice "uneventful," and argued, "*The Magnolia Lady* would be no worse without her."[294] In her eagerness to tackle a new medium, Ruth made a mistake by playing down to her audience. Her gaiety and charm were self-conscious. Pollock felt that Chatterton, along with Fay Bainter, who had recently failed to "coo" her way through the operetta *The Dream Girl*, would "do well to leave the business of playing musical comedy to the fetching young ladies who know nothing of acting." Had Bainter at thirty-one and Ruth almost thirty-two reached the point of no return when it came to playing sweet young things on stage?

Writer Leonard Hall witnessed *The Magnolia Lady* during its six-week run at the Shubert Theater. "It was another night to wish for sudden death," said Hall. "Ruth was pretty and charming—but it was just all wrong. It didn't work. Ruth fell down dancing off on one of her exits—and we all went into the night shaking our heads. Poor Chatterton! This obviously was the last of her."[295] Ruth Gordon was also among first-nighters. Gordon wrote about it later, saying she, along with many others, was rooting for Chatterton after her breakup with Miller. "Everybody who worked for him had to look out," wrote Gordon. "Everybody took a lot of trouble not to get Mr. Miller upset." Gordon wanted to see Chatterton "come in with colors flying."[296] "They not only didn't fly," said Gordon, "but in the dance with her new husband Ruth slipped and fell." Gordon hoped that no one had ever told Miller. *The Magnolia Lady* would be revamped with a much improved libretto for the 1930 Fox film *Honey* starring Janet Gaynor. But even Gaynor paled in comparison to the fourth-billed Lillian Roth, who belted out the hit tune, "Sing You Sinners."

During Ruth's search for a leading man in *The Magnolia Lady*, sixty-five-year-old Miller, in an attempt to rekindle Ruth's waning interest, had had a facelift.[297] Dyeing his hair was no longer enough to maintain the illusion of youth on or off stage. After his procedure, he assisted in staging *The Magnolia Lady*—until he realized something was amiss. The *Oakland Tribune* talked about his "withdrawal in a huff." During a rehearsal in Washington, D.C., Ruth was seated in the director's chair while Ralph Forbes looked on adoringly. In a 1931 article, Dana Rush clearly described the scene, saying, "Ruth didn't understand at first. But the older eyes of Henry Miller saw and feared the younger man. As the seat next to Ruth was occupied, Ralph Forbes in order to be near her, had been forced to seat himself on the floor—at her feet. Miller stormed and raised a scene—and for the first time Ruth turned to look at the boy—for the first time saw him as a man."[298] Some news columns apologized for Miller, saying that he was experiencing "personal difficulties." "During rehearsals he was taken suddenly and seriously ill," reported the *New York Evening Post*, emphasizing that only Miller's close friends "understood his personal troubles."[299] Another column put a more pungent spin on the situation, saying that gossips in the theatrical district were held captive as Ruth and Ralph's relationship stirred up an intensity "more congenial to a sizzling drama than the frolicsome musical comedy in which they currently are appearing."[300]

Miller was also preparing for his role in a play that Ruth had translated from the French *Un Homme en Habit* (*The Man in Evening Clothes*). It was a depressed Miller, sporting his new face, who showed up at his theater for the December 5 premier. The play failed to click with audiences and critics. Arthur Pollock felt the play "sputtered" and "deserved to fail." His blistering commentary concluded that Miller was "beyond the age when a man, particularly one who looks his age, can hope to remain a matinee idol. Audiences are interested more in younger men."[301] Pollock was annoyed that Miller seemed "unable to resist the temptation to cry." *The Man in Evening Clothes* lasted eleven performances. A week later, Ruth and Ralph Forbes were married.

Ralph Forbes had proposed to Ruth while *The Magnolia Lady* was playing tryouts in Baltimore (mid November). Off stage, they had been seen together frequently. The wedding ceremony took place on the afternoon of December 20 at the Church of the Beloved Disciple. Reverend Dr. George Van De Water presided. On the marriage license, Ruth gave her age as 28 (she was four days away from being 32) and Forbes said he was 24 (he was 28). Thirty of their friends attended. English actress

December 20, 1924–Ruth marries actor Ralph Forbes at the
Church of the Beloved Disciple in New York. Mother Lilian gave
the bride away and the Best Man was Reginald Venable.
Ruth's absentee father sent her a box of candy for the occasion.

Auriol Lee was Ruth's maid of honor and Fay Bainter's husband, Navy Commander Reginald Venable, was best man. Mother Lilian gave away the bride. Ruth and Ralph promptly returned to the Shubert Theatre to resume their roles in *The Magnolia Lady.* After the performance, the cast showered the couple with rice.[302] It came as a complete surprise when Ruth received a large and very festive box of candy honoring the occasion. It was from her father. She later stated that she regretted that it was perishable, feeling that it should be "preserved for posterity."[303]

Henry Miller's "fit" continued to garner considerable coverage in the New York press. Theatrical critic Burns Mantle referred to Ruth as Henry Miller's "chief concern" and that rumors of her proposed marriage added significantly to Miller's unhappiness. Both Ruth and Forbes denied any disagreement between themselves and Miller. However, following the wedding, Miller announced his decision to retire and leave the stage for good. Columnists, knowing the real scoop, tended to scold Miller for his rash decision. "Miller has been having an unpleasant time," wrote Bay Area drama critic Wood Soanes. "It is hoped he cools down. The American theater will suffer a severe loss if Miller adheres to his idea."[304] It would be over a year before Miller resumed his stage career. Author Adela Rogers St. Johns wrote that Miller "was never his own man after he met Ruth. That he loved her completely and absolutely for many years no one has ever thought of denying."[305]

The new Mr. and Mrs. Forbes teamed for a revival of James Barrie's *The Little Minister* at Broadway's Globe Theatre. It proved a big mistake. Critics, many of them still holding a grudge against Ruth's involvement with the Actor's Fidelity League, were merciless in their assessment of her impersonation of "Lady Babbie," which Barrie described as "a wild thing made mad by the moon." "This Lady Babbie," wrote Percy Hammond, "was maddening rather than mad." As Ruth twirled and skipped through the play, Hammond found her performance to be filled with "monotonous devices… noisy subtlety… showy and deliberate." "It was acting plus," concluded Hammond. "At times it resembled a factory more than a characterization."[306] Critic George Gene Nathan, who popularized the saying "I drink to make other people interesting," obviously forgot to imbibe before seeing Ruth's performance. "Miss Chatterton's gipsy Babbie," mused Nathan, "is a musical comedy figure as Miss Chatterton's *Magnolia Lady* was not." He then requested that the actress, instead of acting with her "powdered tootsies" and "pirouettes," "hustle back to Mr. Henry Miller's direction as fast as her legs can carry her."[307] Reviewers found Forbes engaging as the minister who loves Babbie, but the consensus was that Ruth, with her engine relentlessly purring, lacked the fragile wistfulness of Maude Adams' original portrayal. Ruth's Babbie lasted sixteen performances. In the fall of 1926, Forbes reflected back on this misadventure, saying, "My wife and I did several plays together, all of them quite awful. We did, for instance, *The Little Minister*, but I won't linger on that."[308]

To recoup from the critics' lambaste, Ruth and Ralph opted to try out a couple of plays before tackling Broadway again. First up was another French offering, *Women and Ladies*, wherein Ruth played a peasant girl fascinated by the love life of her nobleman employer (Forbes). It opened at Washington, D.C.'s Belasco in May. The *Washington Post* thought Ruth's peasant girl, "a thing of beauty, a work of art."[309] "An interesting little play," said the review, no more, no less. Ruth wanted more. Next up, her troupe of players (which included her bridesmaid Auriol Lee) headed to Philadelphia to debut Mrs. Wallace Irwin's *The Siren's Daughter*. The *New York Times* called it "anything but successful." Ruth's third attempt to find a vehicle for herself took her to Newark for the opening of *The Man With a Load of Mischief* by British playwright Ashley Dukes. Dukes' play, in which Ruth had heavily invested, had been received favorably in London and had logged in over 100 performances. Ruth and Ralph's version, however, "met with disaster" according to *The New York Times.* Why had it failed? Mr. and Mrs. Forbes sailed to London to find out.

Sailing on the *Leviathan* on July 25, Ruth and Ralph arrived in England to stay at the London home of his mother, actress Mary Forbes (currently Mrs. Quatermaine). The couple attended performances of *The Man With a Load of Mischief,* which was still enjoying a successful run in city's West End. Ruth's confidence was at stake as much as her career. She had lost most of her money with her recent flops. Leaving Ralph behind, she sojourned briefly to France before boarding the *Majestic* for

"Yodeling" for Ralph Forbes in *The Man With a Load of Mischief* (courtesy of Wisconsin Center for Film and Theater Research)

New York—arriving on August 18. Among her fellow passengers were Leslie Howard and Noel Coward, who later commented on the voyage, saying, "Leslie was vague and amiable... Ruth Chatterton was still and reticent."[310] For whatever reason, Ralph arrived in Toronto on October 4. By then, it was old news that he had lost the lead role in his wife's play. He was replaced by Robert Loraine—a much older British actor who had made a great success as a swashbuckler for Dumas' *The Three Musketeers* back in 1889. Forbes appeared to be in limbo... but not for long.

Ralph Forbes Taylor

Ralph Forbes Taylor was born to E.J. and Mary Forbes Taylor in London on September 30, 1896.[311] E.J. Taylor was a concert singer, his wife an actress. By 1913, Ralph's mother was managing London's Ambassadors Theatre. Ralph had two younger sisters. The eldest, Brenda, also took to the stage, won a scholarship at the Old Vic Theatre, and enjoyed a long career in character roles. In his youth, Ralph contemplated a more spiritual path. "Once I had that fatal malady, idealism," offered Forbes in a 1926 interview. "I was to become a priest and save the world. Strange, isn't it, how many actors once aspired to the priesthood and how many priests... but then, let us leave that there."[312] His family instructed him to study law. His main achievement at Denstone College in Staffordshire was the acquisition of a permanent scar on his cheek while playing football. Accused of being more interested in his friends at Denstone than the dead masters of Greece, one instructor informed him that the school could struggle along without him. So Ralph left the halls of academia to become an actor. He took his mother's maiden name and made his film debut in *The Fifth Form at St. Dominic's* (1921). "I knew absolutely nothing about acting," confessed Forbes, "so I got away with it. I grew enthusiastic about myself."

Forbes' London stage debut was a juvenile role in *Three Wise Fools.* "I

spent a year touring little English vil-
lages and drinking good English beer,"
said Forbes. "Then I felt equipped to
come to America." Ralph's modesty
precluded him from boasting about
his applauded stage performance as
Hugo Blantyne in *The Flame* (1924).
British theatre critic James Agate
thought Forbes gave Hugo "precision, and depth of emotion." "Mr.
Forbes strikes me as being the best
juvenile lead in the country," Agate
raved.[313]   After this success, Forbes
was offered the role in Broadway's

Ralph Forbes (c. 1930).

short-lived *Havoc.* He then mesmerized, married, and toured with Ruth
Chatterton. In the meantime, his actress mother had made mention of her
blonde, good-looking son to Hollywood producer Louis B. Mayer. While
The Man With a Load of Mischief met disaster the second time round, Ralph
made a screen test, which led to his American film debut in *Beau Geste.*
From then on, Forbes' screen career was a *fait accompli.* Years later, accord-
ing to close friend Paul Conlon, Ralph summed up his life as simply being:
"Hag-ridden, my boy. Hag-ridden from the cradle to the grave."[314]

After his return from England, Ralph acquiesced to a supporting role in
Ruth's production of *The Man With a Load of Mischief.* Her new leading
man, Robert Loraine, had already begun rehearsals. Opening October 26
at Broadway's Ritz, the tongue-in-cheek affair cast Ruth as a singer from

Covent Garden in the early nineteenth century. To her credit, she had composed an appropriate ballad, which she sang while playing a spinet piano. Percy Hammond approved, saying, "And so I bend my knee to Miss Chatterton for orchestrating, singing, and playing…at a critical point in the second act."[315] The play itself, however, met with mixed reviews. After watching Ruth avoid the adoration of a foppish nobleman (Loraine) and his man (Forbes), *The New York Times* called playwright Ashley Duke's work "drivel, gibberish and claptrap," but admitted it was "thoroughly delightful"—the performances "resplendent."[316] John Anderson, for the *New York Evening Post*, felt differently, saying the play's message was blurred by the "cloying sweetness" of Forbes' portrayal. Chatterton, argued Anderson, had a tendency to "yodel" the final syllable of her lines and provided nothing more than a "tinkling echo" of Fay Compton's London performance. Loraine was targeted by *American Mercury Magazine*, which claimed he "groaned and grunted his way through the comedy like a man being wheeled through a long hospital corridor."[317] *Theatre Arts Monthly*, of which Ashley Dukes himself was associate editor, felt that Ruth and Ralph "killed" his satire. Ruth was "brittle" and "obvious," said the review, and Forbes "unsuited."[318] The play closed after sixteen performances.

Completely discouraged, Ruth decided to chuck it all and quit, but only after offering herself to vaudeville in a condensed version of *Come Out of the Kitchen* for $3,500 a week. No one was interested. She consoled herself and her pocketbook in the New Year 1926 by joining operetta diva Grace Moore at the Palace Theatre—Moore offered a recital; Chatterton selected a one-act play by Vincent Lawrence, *The Conflict*. (Lawrence would write the screenplay for Ruth's 1931 Paramount release *The Magnificent Lie*.) Ralph had taken an important role in the Italian tragedy *Stronger Than Love*, starring Nance O'Neil at the Belasco. *The New York*

Times thought he excelled as the illegitimate son. "Forbes brings a power of seeming always near the breaking point, yet mostly and gallantly not breaking," said the review. To make matters worse (for Ruth), critic Burns Mantle wagged that Forbes "is a lot better actor when his wife was not in the cast."[319] Ruth, having reached her own breaking point, succumbed to touring the Orpheum circuit. She opened in *The Conflict* at the Albee on January 11. One critic thought the comedy adapted itself "very easily to the whimsical moods of Miss Chatterton."[320]

When Ralph's play closed in February, fate stepped in. D.W. Griffith persuaded him to do a screen test at Long Island.[321] Paramount was impressed with the result and cast Ralph for an important role in *Beau Geste*—a French Foreign Legion adventure. It was a coup that would eventually turn around the lives of both Mr. and Mrs. Forbes. The film was being touted as one of the most prestigious productions of the year. Ruth's former co-star Ronald Colman had the lead. Ralph packed his bags and headed west for two months' location shooting near the Mexican border. Then, unexpectedly, while Ruth stuck it out in vaudeville, her former lover and mentor, Henry Miller, died.

Miller had recently returned to the stage in *Embers*, which closed February 27. In his review for *The Washington Star*, Philander Johnson wrote, "No such portrayal of majestic grief has been seen for many a year."[322] Financial anxieties had nagged at Miller. He had considered selling his theater. Instead, he arranged a merger with Klaw & Erlanger. After *Embers*, he plunged immediately into his last production, *A Stranger in the House*. Miller relocated across the street from The Lotus Club (strictly for gentlemen of the arts) on East 66th Street. His former residence on 55th Street, according to biographer Frank Morse, was haunted by unhappy memo-ries. After a tryout in Baltimore, *A Stranger in the House*, a light comedy in which Miller played the father of a flapper, was scheduled for The Henry Miller Theatre. Suffering from a severe cold the night of the opening, Miller struggled from bed and managed to reach his dressing room before curtain time on April 5. The effort brought on a violent hemorrhage. By the time his son Gilbert arrived at the hospital, Miller was barely con-scious. Gilbert was joined at his father's bedside by producers Walter Wanger and Arthur Hornblow, Jr. Miller passed away of pneumonia at 11:32 pm on Friday, April 9.

Mrs. Miller was in France. Their second son, J. Heron (now going by Henry Miller, Jr.), attempted suicide the day his father's play was can-celled. He had been sentenced in Los Angeles for narcotic violations. Miller, Jr. had no idea of his mother's whereabouts or whether or not she was alive and wept to reporters, "I killed him! He told me once that he felt like turning on the gas for being responsible for my coming into the world. I decided to kill myself. I am sure that my plight hastened the death of my father."[323] Not completely merciless, Miller, Sr. had faithfully forwarded his son a monthly remittance check. Henry Miller's daughter, Agnes, who had married western film star Tim McCoy, left her home in Wyoming to attend the funeral on April 13.

The memorial service for Henry Miller, held at New York's Little Church Around the Corner, required police reserves to control the crowds of onlookers. Hundreds of mourners filled the church. Dean Randolph Ray officiated. Opera singer Alma Clayburgh (grandmother of actress Jill Clayburgh) sang Gounod's "Ave Maria." Son Gilbert and daughter Agnes were the only two family members present. Mrs. Miller was still en route from Europe. Among the theatrical folks attending were Lionel Atwill, Charles Coburn, Laura Hope Crews, Ina Claire, Al Woods,

David Belasco, Grace George, and ... Ruth Chatterton. She slipped into the church shortly before the service began and placed a small bouquet of violets on the coffin.[324]

Shortly after Miller's demise, journalist W.B. Seabrook theorized in his nationwide column that the sixty-seven-year-old actor/producer had died of a broken heart—that he was a "victim of lost love." "At one time," wrote Seabrook, "the beautiful Ruth Chatterton, much younger than Henry Miller, was his star and leading lady. She suddenly left his company and his management and married a young actor. After this, Mr. Miller, great actor though he was, never scored another outstanding success—nor did she."[325] One only had to read between the lines of Seabrook's brash assessment. It was a wonder that Chatterton had put up with Miller's infatuation as long as she did. The pangs of gratitude.

Miller's assets at the time of his death totaled a mere $35,000. After providing his wife a $3,000 annuity, the remainder was bequeathed to his four grandchildren and son Gilbert. Henry Miller had continued taking financial risks to promote what he really believed in: "Theatre." In 1919, Miller reminisced during an interview at San Francisco's Columbia Theatre. Puffing on a cigar, he looked up at the portrait of his former mentor and employer Charles Frohman. "That photograph makes me think of some of the wonderful sacrifices made by those managers of by-gone years," Miller pondered aloud. "Frohman died broke; Augustine Daly died broke; A.M. Palmer died broke; and Lester Wallack died broke. They made money at some times during their careers. But they didn't keep it all to themselves: they distributed it among the profession. Those men were creators who gave their lives to the theatrical work."[326] Miller, in many respects, had described his own epitaph.

Following her melodramatic split with Henry Miller, Ruth employed a more practical attitude about the men in her life. Actor Christopher Plummer, who toured with Ruth in *The Little Foxes* (1952), mentioned visiting her New York apartment. Ruth took Plummer on a tour of what he called her "very posh... eagles nest." "By God!" he said, "she had the gift of making you feel you were the only man in the world."[327] When they entered the master bedroom, she breezily announced, "Those are all my husbands on the wall." Plummer described the elaborate picture frame above the headboard which had portraits of Ralph, George Brent, and her current husband, Barry Thomsen. "In the center," wrote Plummer, "dominating all three, her original mentor and lover—the Broadway impresario, Henry Miller—seemed to be glowering downwards in general disapproval."[328] The current "Mr. Chatterton" lay sick in same bed with a raging cold as Plummer looked on. "Poor Barry," he thought, "what a horrible fate to be constantly haunted like that in bed. Under such critical surveillance, how could he ever possibly perform?!"

Following his death in 1926, Henry Miller was no longer on Ruth's conscience. She found herself grieving less for her glowering benefactor than she did her own foundering career.

Endnotes

269   Adele Whitely Fletcher, "Beauty, Brains or Luck?" *Photoplay*, August 1930.

270   Geo. C. Warren, "After-Thoughts," *San Francisco Chronicle*, June 4, 1922.

271   Review of *La Tendresse*, *New York Tribune*, September 26, 1922.

272   Burns Mantle, "Difficult to Share Mr. Miller's Enthusiasm for *La Tendresse*," *Chicago Tribune*, October 1, 1922.

273   Alexander Woollcott, "Second Thoughts on First Nights," *New York Times*, October 1, 1922.

274   Charles Darnton, "The New Plays," *The Evening World*, September 26, 1922.

275   Percy Hammond, "Oddments and Remainders," *New York Tribune*, September 20, 1922.

276   "Criticisms Do Not Exist For This Actress," *New York Tribune*, October 1, 1922.

277   Langston Hughes, Carl Van Vechten, Emily Bernard, *Remember Me to Harlem: The Letters of Langston Hughes and Carl Van Vechten*, Vintage, c. 2002, pg. 194 (letter from Hughes to writer/photographer Carl Van Vechten, October 30, 1941—*merde alors* translates as "Shit, then!" or "Oh, Shit!").

278   Ronald Colman, "Ronald Colman, Clerk!" *Piqua Daily Call*, August 21, 1931.

279   Gladys Hall, "Romantic Recluse," *Photoplay*, February 1939.

280   Letter from Ruth Chatterton to her cousin Olive Minuse (from Brenda Holman collection) written from Knoxville (c. January 1922).

281   Review of *The Awful Truth*, *Variety*, May 26, 1922.

282   Gerald Bordman, "The Changelings," *American Theatre: A Chronicle of Comedy and Drama*, pg 213.

283   Percy Hammond, review of *The Changelings*, *New York Morning Papers*, September 18, 1923.

284   *The Selected Letters of Thornton Wilder*, Harper, c. 2008, pg. 167.

285   "Do Women Exist Solely to be Loved?" *San Francisco Chronicle*, May 27, 1923.

286   "Do Women Exist Solely to be Loved?" *San Francisco Chronicle*, Mary 27, 1923.

287   "Actors' League is Denied Injunction," *Morning Herald*, July 8, 1924.

288   Bernard Sobel, *Broadway Heartbeat: Memories of a Press Agent*, Hermitage House, NY, c. 1953, pg 154.

289   Jean Millet, "The Blond Boy from Bond Street," *Photoplay*, December 1926.

290   Dana Rush, "The Unknown Ruth Chatterton," *Silver Screen*, September 1931.

291   Review of "Magnolia Lady," *Commonweal*, December 1924.

292   Gerald Bordman, "The Magnolia Lady," *American Musical Theatre*, Oxford University Pr., c. 2010, pg 448.

293   "Theatre: New Plays," *Time*, December 8, 1924.

294   Arthur Pollock, review of *The Magnolia Lady*, *Brooklyn Daily Eagle*, November 30, 1924.

295   Leonard Hall, "The Destiny Fighter," *Photoplay*, July 1930.

296   Ruth Gordon, *Myself and Others*, Atheneum, NY, c. 1971, pg 364.

297   Wood Soanes, "Exits and Entrances," *Oakland Tribune*, November 21, 1924.

298   Dana Rush, "The Unknown Ruth Chatterton," *Silver Screen*, September 1931.

299   "Two on the Aisle," *New York Evening Post*, December 11, 1924.

300   "Ruth Chatterton Now Mrs. Forbes," *New York Evening Post*, December 20, 1924.

301   Arthur Pollock, review of *The Man in Evening Clothes*, *Brooklyn Daily Eagle*, December 14, 1924.

302   "Ruth Chatterton Weds Ralph Forbes," *New York Times*, December 21, 1924.

303   Gladys Hall, ""I Am A Renegade In Hollywood," *Motion Picture*, July 1929.

304   Wood Soanes, "Curtain Calls," *Oakland Tribune*, December 26, 1924.

305   Adela Rogers St Johns, "The Men in Ruth Chatterton's Life," *Liberty*, January 20, 1934.

306   Percy Hammond, "Percy Hammond's Letter," *Ogden Standard Examiner*, March 29, 1925.

307   George Gene Nathan, "The Theatre," *American Mercury Magazine*, May 1925 (Nathan's remark about drinking was penned in an April 1923 issue of *The Smart Set*).

308   Jean Millet, *The Blond Boy from Bond Street*," *Photoplay*, December 1926.

309   John J. Daly, review of *Ladies and Women*, *Washington Post*, c. May 1925.

310   Noel Coward, *Present Indicative*, Doubleday, c. 1937, pg 216.

311   "Ralph Forbes," *Motion Picture Almanac*, 1929 (other sources give: 1898, 1901, 1902, and 1905).

312   Jean Millet, "The Blond Boy from Bond Street," *Photoplay*, December 1926.

313   James Agate review of *The Flame*, from *The Contemporary Theatre*, 1923.

314   John McCallum, *Scooper*, Wood and Reber, Inc., c. 1960, pg 191.

315   "Percy Hammond's Letter," *Ogden Standard Examiner*, November 8, 1925.

316   Review of *The Man With a Load of Mischief*, *The New York Times*, October 27, 1925.

317   George Gene Nathan review of *The Man With a Load of Mischief*, *American Mercury*, January 1926.

318   Review of *The Man With a Load of Mischief*, *Theatre Arts Monthly*, 1925, Vol. 10, Part 1, pg 6 & 36.

319   Burns Mantle, "New York Stage Sidelights," *Salt Lake Tribune*, January 3, 1926.

320   Review of *The Conflict*, Brooklyn Daily Eagle, January 12, 1926 (playwright Vincent Lawrence would later write Hollywood screenplays such as the MGM hit *Test Pilot* (1938)).

321   *Motion Picture News Blue Book 1930*, pg 80 (Ralph's screen test done before February 1926).

322   Frank P. Morse, *Backstage with Henry Miller*, E.P. Dutton, NY, c. 1938, pg 274.

323   "'I Killed Him,' Sobs Miller Jr.," *Oakland Tribune*, April 10, 1926 (Henry Miller, Jr., died of a drug overdose in Mexico City on April 1, 1927).

324   Randolph Hay, *My Little Church Around the Corner*, Simon & Schuster, c. 1957, pg 234.

325   W.B. Seabrook, "New Scientific X-Ray on Broken Hearts," *Hamilton Evening Journal*, OH, May 15, 1926.

326   Thomas W. Baily, "Henry Miller Favors State Theater Club," *San Francisco Chronicle*, June 22, 1919.

327   Christopher Plummer, *In Spite of Myself: A Memoir*, Knopf (NY) c. 2008, pg 101.

328   Christopher Plummer, *In Spite of Myself: A Memoir*, Knopf (NY) c. 2008, pg 118.

Publicity shot for *Doctor's Secret* (Paramount).

6
From Brand X to *Madame X*

Beau Geste: location shooting outside of Yuma, Arizona, covered miles of undulating sand dunes which Paramount had enhanced at a cost of $17,000. A mammoth tent served as the dining hall for cast and crew and hundreds of smaller tents as desert living quarters. Corrals for a thousand horses and a hundred camels contributed to the Hollywood oasis. Ralph brought along his collection of revolvers to shoot rattlers for evening entertainment. His tent-mate was actor Neil Hamilton. Along with Ronald Colman, the trio played onscreen brothers. "The bugle awakened us at five thirty," recalled Hamilton. "Taps were sounded at ten thirty." Despite the military regulations, there was time for fun. When the "Geste brothers" weren't shooting film (or rattlesnakes), they kept busy pulling pranks on the rest of the cast, which included William Powell and Victor McLagen. The camaraderie translated well on screen. *Beau Geste* would prove a tremendous hit. After two months away, Ralph returned to Ruth and began a west coast tour of Michael Arlen's stage success *The Green Hat*. However, when Louis B. Mayer caught the rushes of Forbes' performance in *Beau Geste*, Hollywood beckoned once more. A contract was signed. Ruth lost her leading man and was about to lose a husband in one fell swoop. Publicist Paul Conlon reminisced years later, "How well I recall when the young woman, whom I had learned to admire and respect as a great stage actress, arrived in Hollywood flat broke. Walking quietly in the shadow of her husband, she found herself unknown in a town of blonde ingénues. Out of the crash of her stage career she had saved only her talents, an indomitable spirit and a divine sense of humor."[329]

Before Ralph signed with MGM, *The Green Hat*, an adult offering filled with love, sacrifice, and suicide, had a record run at Hollywood's El Capitan Theatre. Sadie Mossler's review commented on the audiences' "unrestrained enthusiasm" that first night—the theater filled with celebrities. She found Ruth's portrayal of Iris March to be "poignantly touching." "Ruth Chatterton gives a most creditable performance," wrote Mossler, "rising to remarkable emotional heights in her big scene."[330] In London, Tallulah Bankhead smoked and drank the role of Iris and the play didn't go. On Broadway, Katharine Cornell didn't want to "do" things, she wanted to *be* Iris.[331] Ruth followed her friend Cornell's cue in creating her own interpretation. Although Iris may have snapped her fingers at conventional morality, as Ruth played her, Iris came from the heart. Her guilt over her husband's suicide (after he reveals he has syphilis) keeps Iris drifting from one man to the next. After the miscarriage of her illegitimate child, she speedily ends all the gloom and doom by colliding her luxury sport car into a tree. *The Los Angeles Record* also pointed to Ralph Forbes' "finesse" as Napier, the man Iris had loved and lost.

Ralph's exit from stage to film meant a long separation from Ruth, who continued on tour with *The Green Hat*. "Isn't it a silly predicament?" Ralph sighed to reporters, "But, we are both excited about it. Strange this life of the theater!"[332] Ruth received only praises from Bay Area critics, who welcomed her back with open arms. "Her interpretation of Iris March… was indeed a revelation… a masterful document of reality," remarked

Wood Soanes.[333] Upon resuming his screen career in Lon Chaney's *Mr. Wu*, Ralph and Ruth unknowingly purchased what was considered Hollywood's haunted house. It had been the former residence of director William Desmond Taylor (who was murdered) and actor Max Linder (who committed suicide). John Gilbert and Leatrice Joy lived there temporarily, then the house stood idle until Mr. and Mrs. Forbes arrived. For them, ignorance was bliss—at least, until the divorce rumors began.

After Ruth wrapped up her tour in January 1927, she was paged for a screen test in New York. Before heading east, she had good reason to be optimistic about joining the ranks of filmdom when she attended a party given by director Fred Niblo. Niblo was directing Ralph and his leading lady Lillian Gish in the anti-war film *The Enemy.* Those invited included such popular luminaries as Antonio Moreno, Norma Talmadge, Conrad Nagel, and directors George Fitzmaurice and Sidney Franklin. Still, Ruth was somewhat apprehensive about appearing on screen. When her good friend, actress/scenarist Elsie Janis, encouraged her to go into moving pictures, Ruth laughed, "What! With my nose!"[334] Ruth went to New York a few days later.

Accompanied by her maid, she arrived on the set at Cosmopolitan Studio to discover a frustrated Barbara Stanwyck attempting to cry before the camera. Stanwyck was testing for the lead as a cabaret dancer in *Broadway Nights.* The director was using onions and a weeping violin to induce a few tears. "Ruth Chatterton tittered," said one witness, "and in a voice that would have frozen a Boston butler began talking to her maid— asking her to imagine anyone on the stage resorting to onions."[335] Barbara hissed, "Shut up!" "The two gals had quite a scene afterward," reported Paul Harrison, "and the elder one is probably lucky to have escaped with her scalp."[336] A few minutes after this embarrassment, Ruth began her own test. "I was quite bad," she frankly admitted. "They told me I screened abominably and I agreed."[337]   During their reign in Hollywood, the two actresses never uttered a word to each other. When Stanwyck was asked about the long-standing coolness between them, she replied tersely, "Oh, it's nothing—nothing at all."[338]

While back east, Ruth hobnobbed with her stage friends. On February 27, into the wee hours of the morning at the home of her longtime friend Lenore Ulric, Ruth fraternized with Ethel Barrymore, Jeanne Eagels, Beatrice Lillie, and Gertrude Lawrence. From the diaries of writer/photographer Carl Van Vechten, we learn of a similar affair on March 10. The all-women's party, filled with strange games and no menu, was immortalized in Isa Glenn's novel *East of Eden* (not to be confused with Steinbeck). Glenn, in attendance, chatted with Ruth and her mother. Of course, there were plenty of cocktails, prepared by host Van Vechten (the only male), who had his own bootlegger.[339] Van Vechten noted one "very gay" party in which "everybody [took] off their clothes."[340] Ruth wasn't invited, but not to worry. At the end of March, she attended a gathering at the residence of playwright Lawrence Langner, where she mixed with Scott and Zelda Fitzgerald, feminist writer Rebecca West, radical journalist Louise Bryant, Harlem Renaissance writer Nella Larsen, African-American singer/composer Nora Holt, the extravagant Stettheimer sisters (known for their disdain of marriage, romance, and children), and critic Percy Hammond, among others.[341] After this plethora of stimulus, Ruth was ready to tackle another play. As far as their respective screen tests, Stanwyck ended up with a small, non-crying role in *Broadway Nights*. Chatterton ended up with nothing.

A Los Angeles producer contacted Ruth about starring in *The Devil's Plum Tree* by John Colton. It was reputed to be an adaptation of a Hungarian play. Colton had previously taken Somerset Maugham's shocker *Rain* and turned it into a Broadway triumph for Jeanne Eagels. Ruth was encouraged. Ralph's mother, Mary Forbes, joined the cast for moral support. After a tryout in Santa Barbara, the play premiered at San Francisco's Curran Theatre. Despite Ruth's strong following there, the beautifully staged production lasted less than three weeks. Her portrayal of Mara, a Croatian nymph whose sexual indiscretions are hampered when she is betrothed to a pious priest, failed to impress. After atoning for her sins, Mara becomes a saint who heals lepers. The bizarre story carried little conviction and was accused of being a product of Colton's preposterous imagination. The Los Angeles run, according to Burns Mantle, appealed only to "oversexed women and curious girls."[342] Ruth had hoped *The Devil's Plum Tree* would revive her New York stage career. It eventually did reach Broadway in 1933. Colton renamed the play *Saint Wench* with Helen Mencken in Ruth's role. Critics called it "bilge" and "an unconscionable bore." It lasted one week. Fortunately for Ruth, Emil Jannings, one of the greatest actors of his generation, came to her rescue with a film offer.

※❀❃❀✧

While Ruth was in Los Angeles with *The Devil's Plum Tree*, she and Ralph decided to separate. "Our divergent interests caused our separation," explained Forbes, "with Mrs. Forbes on the stage in New York for months at a time and I working in Hollywood, we could not lead a normal married life."[343] It was an odd assessment considering that it had been almost two years since Ruth had set foot on a New York stage. In January 1928, it was announced that Ruth signed with Paramount to play opposite Adolphe Menjou in a comedy with a Parisian setting, *His Tiger Lady*. She had leased a bungalow from actress Marie Prevost. Menjou delayed his honeymoon to start the film, but Ruth had already made a prior commitment:

covering the infamous William Hickman Trial for the Los Angeles press. Most likely, there was a conflict between her schedule at Paramount and the trial, which ran from January 26–February 10. Ruth lost her film role to Evelyn Brent. Ruth was so absorbed in the trial that she was caught speeding on Melrose Avenue—32-miles-per-hour. Ironically, she ended up in court herself on February 6 for traffic violations.[344]

As a news investigator, Ruth was in unusual company. Author Edgar Rice Burroughs, of *Tarzan* fame, was also contracted to write numerous columns during The Hickman Trial. The case involved one of the grisliest murders on record. In December 1927, nineteen-year-old William Hickman was accused of abducting Marion Parker, the 12-year-old daughter of his former employer, a banker. The girl attended school in Beverly Hills. Following a series of ransom notes, $1,500 was delivered at night, but Mr. Parker was not allowed to get close to the car. The driver then drove down the block and pushed the girl out of the passenger side. She had been murdered; her arms and legs amputated; her internal organs missing. Only a towel stuffed inside of her had kept the body upright in the car. Her eyes had been sewn open. A $100,000 reward was announced for Hickman's capture. He was arrested in Oregon. On trial, Hickman made use of the new California law and pleaded insanity. His account of the planning and execution of the crime was confused. Even so, the jury found him guilty and he was taken to the death house in San Quentin, where on October 19, he was hanged. The glaring and sensational methods employed by reporters during the trial were typical of the American press. But did the hysteria get in the way of the truth?

During the trial, Ruth reported that as she was watching Hickman (a.k.a. "The Fox") a woman's scream from another courtroom made the youth wince.[345] Ruth was captivated as psychologists invaded the court bearing portfolios with data on brain reactions. Their intent was to prove, or disprove, that "The Fox" was normal. But was Hickman "The Fox"? Or was he a stooge? This brings us to an extraordinary account told by Hollywood set designer Laurence Irving. Irving was brought to Hollywood in 1928 by Douglas Fairbanks to work on his film *The Iron Mask*. Irving's daughter also attended school in Beverly Hills. Irving's close friend, art director William Menzies, had daughters attending Beverly Hills High. Both men were aghast at the hysterical insistence of patriotic Americans that Hickman was guilty. A few years after the trial, Irving attended a dinner party at which Ruth was a guest. He never forgot what Ruth had to say when the conversation turned to the subject of "crime."

> Miss Chatterton remarked that she had covered the [Hickman] trial for a Los Angeles newspaper. She told me that she and other journalists had circumstantial evidence, based on the time and place at which certain relevant telegrams were filed, that Hickman was innocent. Further enquiries led her to believe that the murderer was the psychopathic son of a high official in the Californian judiciary. She deduced that the mentally deficient Hickman had been persuaded by the offer of a large sum of money to surrender himself and plead guilty.

Ruth and other journalists felt that Hickman had been convinced that he would be released from prison after the trial. "The wretched dupe," wrote Irving, "was of course, left to his fate. I did not find [Chatterton's] suppositions incredible."[346]

⚜

In the aftermath of the trial, Ruth was considered for the lead in *The Eas-*

iest Way.[347] Plans for the film were dropped. Not long afterward, Paramount suggested that Ruth test for the role of a tough bar-hopper who murders her husband in the waterfront saga *The Docks of New York*, starring George Bancroft.[348] Although Ruth and Ralph were separated, he encouraged her to make the test. She felt instinctively that it would be a failure. As predicted, she was turned down and reported back to Ralph, "I told you so." Still, the rejection bothered her. This silent classic was under the helm of master director Josef von Sternberg. It was von Sternberg himself who was not impressed. He thought Ruth unsuitable and she never let him forget it. A year later, they crossed each other's paths frequently on the Paramount lot. Ruth had become a hot property. Occasionally, she would stop von Sternberg, smile at him, and ask, "So you didn't like that test very well, Josef?"[349]

With virtually no income coming in, Ruth was desperate. "I had been out here for months hunting work," she reported later. "I was so broke that I had to borrow money from my manager to live. In fact, I would have returned to Broadway... if it had not been for his faith in me." With the coming of sound pictures, Ruth's agent and champion, Myron Selznick, who years before had offered her a film contract, assured her that it would only be a matter of a few months.[350] He advanced her $7,500.[351] Ruth was also consoled by an adoring fan... silent matinee idol Ramon Novarro. The two were introduced to each other by Elsie Janis. Many evenings, Novarro showed up at Ruth's humble home (part of the floor had fallen into the cellar) and serenaded her to her heart's content. She would sit in a high back chair, her head thrown back, and listen to the gallant troubadour, who was adored by millions of women and desired none. Ruth understood completely.[352]

Emil Jannings, who had been impressed with Ruth's performance in *The Devil's Plum Tree*, was searching for a leading lady for *Sins of the*

With Emil Jannings in *Sins of the Fathers* (Paramount).

Fathers. Although other men directed his pictures, it was Jannings who decided the fine points and more or less ran the show. For his previous work, he was about to receive the first Academy Award for Best Actor. In June, while Jannings watched Paramount film tests of several women, Chatterton's old test was finally projected. "Ach!" he cried, arising in the darkness emitting guttural sounds of approval. "I am told," Ruth related, "Jannings arose from his seat and walked slowly down the length of the

room. Stretching out his arms, he embraced the shadow on the silver
sheet and kissed it. A day or so later, I received a letter from Mrs. Jannings
inviting me to have dinner… asking me to excuse the unconventional-
ity of not having been formally introduced. Of course I went." When
Ruth arrived at Jannings' home, he simply stared at her while other guests
milled around the room. "He slowly advanced toward me without saying
a word," said Ruth. "Then he went down on his knees and said, 'This vo-
man I vill'. And I was as good as chosen for the part."[353]

Sins of the Fathers was Paramount's final release for 1928. Ruth played
Gretta, a hard, calculating woman and a home wrecker. Her affair with
an emigrant saloonkeeper (Jannings), who rises to fabulous wealth as a
bootlegger during Prohibition, inadvertently has dire consequences for
his family. His loyal wife (ZaSu Pitts) dies of a broken heart and, after
he marries Gretta, he throws his daughter (Jean Arthur) into the street.
His beloved son (Barry Norton) goes blind from his dad's poison wood
alcohol. Jannings' character ends up in the state penitentiary.

Jannings coached Ruth patiently and contentedly with impressive results. She was an astute listener. "I don't know whether she is greater as
an audience or as an actress," he marveled.[354] Ruth nursed a second-de-
gree California sunburn and swollen lips as she faced the camera on July
16, 1928.[355] It didn't get in the way of impressive results. Welford Beaton,
editor of *The Film Spectator*, raved, "This picture introduces Ruth Chatterton to us. The young woman has come among us to stay… she contrib-
utes a gem of a performance that matches Jannings' in artistic finish."[356]
Beaton felt that Jannings' tremendous range of expression outshone his
previous performance in *The Patriot*. "He never quite loses our sympathy,"
said Beaton. "He makes us grasp his point of view, something that all actors should do, but which few can." "His excellent acting," wrote another
critic, "is mirrored in that of Ruth Chatterton who is … fiery, sneery, alive

and tempestuous."[357] Mordaunt Hall for *The New York Times* thought *Sins of the Fathers* was slow in the telling, but pointed to Ruth, saying, "Miss Chatterton does well as the harsh, loud, calculating Gretta."[358] *Photoplay* also found the film slow, lacking the emotional tug of Jannings' previous work, but admired it as "an eminently distinguished parade of prohibition and its evils." "Be sure and see this film," stressed the review. "Ruth Chatterton makes a vivid screen appearance in an unsympathetic part and her work is intelligent and forceful. She is excellent."[359] The magazine put Jannings and Chatterton among the best performers of the month for December 1928.

"Jannings meant a great deal to my screen career," commented Ruth in 1930.[360] "In Henry Miller I believe I had the finest director the stage has known. In Jannings I had the finest actor the screen has known. Both wanted to help me, because they saw I wanted to help myself. Jannings

With Emil Jannings and ZaSu Pitts in *Sins of the Fathers* (Paramount)

figuratively led me by the hand through the kindergarten of my new schooling."[361] Ruth admired Emil Jannings as an artist and, in one instance, reached him emotionally where others failed. "He was just like a child," said Ruth. "One day he had a heart attack at the studio. Everyone was trying to get him to take a little brandy. He waved them all away. Finally I went over to him, and said, pleadingly, 'Won't you take a little brandy for Ruth?' He waved me away. Then I said, 'This nonsense has got to stop. You take this right now.' And he took it without another word."[362] Sadly, following his return to Germany in 1929, Jannings used his acting craft to make Nazi films.[363]

Sins of the Fathers was Ruth's only silent film, although dialogue sequences had been announced. In December 1928, the release version was synchronized with music, sound effects, and Jannings' whiskey baritone singing an aria from *Der Trompeter von Sakkingen*. Ruth listened to Paramount executives praise her work. She asked Jannings if she had done well enough to support him in his next film. "You will never support anyone," Jannings smiled.[364] In early October, she signed a long term contract and began filming an adaptation of James M. Barrie's *Half-an-Hour*—an all-talker. Ruth was then scheduled to play with Jannings in his first all-talkie, *The Concert*, but his heavy accent, along with a falling out with Paramount, brought his Hollywood career to an abrupt end. In 1929, Jannings made the inevitable journey home to Germany. "The king of them all is gone," declared Los Angeles critic Edwin Schallert.[365]

Once her contract was signed and her career secure, Ruth and Ralph reconciled. Ruth managed to tolerate her husband's fastidiousness (he now posed for Arrow starched collars). His reputation for formality apparently had been a problem. While Ruth enjoyed relaxing in silk pants at home, Ralph insisted on dressing for dinner. Photographer Ruth Harriet Louise, head of MGM's portrait studio, told a columnist of Ralph's declaration, "I would not think of sitting at my desk unless I were dressed for letter writing."[366]   It was a mutual interest in film acting that provided a new bond for Mr. and Mrs. Forbes. Ralph had made ten films in Hollywood and Ruth listened and learned. "I take Ralph's advice," she explained. "He knows many of the tricks of acting before a camera about which I know nothing."[367]   Besides Lillian Gish, Ralph had played opposite Dolores del Rio and twice with Norma Shearer. He had so heavily doted on Shearer (wife of producer Irving Thalberg) that Louis B. Mayer had to pull him into his office. Mayer warned that bringing Norma ice cream and engaging in lengthy tête-à-têtes between takes were out of order. Ralph apologized. Still, he waxed enthusiastic whenever Shearer's name was mentioned and gave her credit for his comedic timing in *The Latest from Paris* (1928). "Norma made me feel wonderfully at ease," enthused Ralph. "I feel she opened new avenues of acting work for me."[368]   Sadly, it wasn't much longer before the "new avenues" led to dead ends. Ralph's career as a leading man had peaked. MGM did not pick up his option at the close of 1928. It was revealed that "Forbes just didn't get over in pictures despite opportunities in *The Trail of '98* and other films."[369]

With a steady income, Ruth made a point of seeing that her young cousin, Olive Minuse, newly graduated from Smith College, traveled to Europe. Upon Olive's return, Ruth invited her out to Hollywood to spend the summer. "Can you imagine being twenty-three years old and spending the summer with Ruth? In Hollywood?" marveled Olive's daughter, Brenda, in 2012. "Ruth would call somebody up and say, 'I'm sending my niece over.' Mother would talk about playing tennis with Mary Astor. Going to various events, and so forth." Olive admired her famous cousin and was frank in her opinions about her. Olive thought Ruth too independent for Hollywood. Brenda emphasized, "My mother often stated, 'Ruth certainly would not spend time with people she thought were not

With H.B. Warner in *The Doctor's Secret* (Paramount).

interesting. People saw Ruth as part of the smart, intelligent set. They exchanged opinions. They talked about more than the weather and the job.'"[370] Olive's observations were decidedly spot on.

⁂

Ruth's next film, re-titled *The Doctor's Secret,* secured her position at Paramount.   Columnist Leonard Hall declared Chatterton "one of the outstanding emotional actresses of the audible screen." [371] Ruth was hardly a bubbling ingénue. At thirty-six (she admitted to anywhere between thirty and thirty-two) and with a scent of intellectuality (which Middle America abhorred), Ruth was honest with Hall when he asked her about her "ability." "Perhaps it is because I am older," Ruth admitted. "We learn things from life. But it is more than just that. I feel things more deeply. I rely less on technique than I once did." Hall understood. His assessment of Ruth was simply, "Soul has been added to technique, and that is truly great art."[372]

Film Daily's review for *The Doctor's Secret* confirmed, "Miss Chatterton jumps to the top of the class for talking screen stars. Her voice is perfect; she screens well, and knows her acting angles."[373] James Barrie's one-act play *Half-an-Hour*, a London society drama, had been exactly that on stage: 30 minutes. Padding it out to 61 minutes was risky. Notices were respectful, but scarcely enthusiastic. Audiences weren't used to a screen star finishing a complete sentence. Silent films moved at a clipped pace. "It simply does not move," complained Harrison Carroll for the *Los Angeles Examiner*. "Ruth Chatterton's voice is marvelous... but the talking hampers the action."[374] On the east coast, critics and audiences responded more favorably to the spoken word on screen, although one reviewer complained that Ruth's voice sounded like it came through a drainpipe. Recording apparatuses picked up everything. During production, the nylon knocked-knees of bit player Hazel Flint emitted scratching noises which the microphones picked up. "A bow-legged girl got her part," smirked one columnist.[375]

The Doctor's Secret was the first film to be held over at the Paramount Theatre since it opened in 1926. It did well at the box office. Ruth's on-screen character, Lady Lillian Garson, deals with an abusive husband (H.B. Warner) whom she was forced to marry (he gave her parents $20,000 for the privilege). Lillian attempts to escape to Egypt with the man she loves (John Loder). Feeling a surge of hope and happiness, she barely leaves her house before tragedy strikes. Loder's character is killed by a car. A physician on the scene, convinced Lillian is a prostitute, suggests that she commit suicide. She rushes home in a panic to destroy an incriminating note and later that evening discovers said doctor among her husband's dinner guests. Her only recourse is to conceal her anguish. The physician, while amusing guests with what he had witnessed that day, keeps Lady Garson's identity a secret—but for how long? New York critic Freddie Schader raved, "You don't have to worry about Miss Chatterton. The ease with which she handles herself and the manner in which she utilizes her voice... of the women who, to date, have tried delivering in the "talkies" she stands first and foremost."[376] Syracuse critic Chester Bahn concurred, "Lady Lillian Garson is hardly an easy character to delineate and delineate truthfully. You scan Miss Chatterton's portrayal for flaws in vain."[377] John Loder later recalled that Chatterton literally pulled him through his first talkie.[378]

The Doctor's Secret was Paramount's second all-talking release. Producer Jesse Lasky issued orders that no more silent films were to be made. Construction for four new soundstages went full speed ahead. As the first one reached completion, a fire destroyed the building. Shooting schedules were at night when silence was still golden. Ruth reported to work at 9 p.m. for an old crooks-and-kidnappers play, *The Dummy.* The yarn focused on the adventures of a tough messenger boy (Mickey Bennett) planted in a nest of criminals by a detective bureau. Fredric March, in his film debut, and Ruth played an estranged couple whose daughter is kidnapped. The film didn't take itself too seriously. With lovable and sympathetic kidnappers such as Jack Oakie and ZaSu Pitts, laughs abounded. In fact, it was Ruth who suggested ZaSu for the role of the whining, timid kidnapper.[379] Pitts was given the opportunity to utter a phrase that became her trademark for years to come. "I was directed to wring my hands for effect," Pitts recalled. "In disgust, I cupped my hands over my forehead and let out a doleful, 'Oh dear!' Everyone on the set went into convulsions of laughter."[380] "ZaSu Pitts steals the honors away from Miss Chatterton," said *Motion Picture News.*[381] "Jack Oakie and ZaSu Pitts give perhaps the most outstanding portrayals of the picture," agreed the *Los Angeles Record.* Bay Area critic Wood Soanes pointed out that Chatterton

With Fredric March in *The Dummy* (Paramount).

and March had their roles whittled down to practically nothing by the scenarist (Herman Mankiewicz) and director (Robert Milton). Soanes felt that it made it all the easier for ZaSu to "romp off with the picture."[382] Indeed, the roles of Chatterton and March were undemanding and peripheral at best. The film had all the earmarks of a "quickie production." There were complaints that the sound quality was badly synchronized and frequently unintelligible.

Photoplay grumbled that *The Dummy* looked like a convention of faces imported from the stage. Chatterton and March were joined by stage veteran Robert Milton, directing his first film. Broadway's John Cromwell, who would direct Ruth in *Unfaithful* (1931), was making his film debut as an actor. There was a hint of resentment toward the influx of stage talent invading Hollywood. On the heels of Chatterton and March came Ann Harding, Leslie Howard, Claudette Colbert, Basil Rathbone, Kay Francis, and Sylvia Sidney.

March came across as photogenic and well-spoken. He was given a five-year contract. Many silent stars simply didn't have what talkies demanded. Cleverly lit close-ups were no longer enough. Fans were now demanding voices that matched their fantasies. Ruth Chatterton was at the right place at the right time. The phenomenal success of her next film placed Ruth as the premier star of what the film industry referred to as "the woman's picture."

Madame X was successful turf for Sarah Bernhardt, Dorothy Donnelly, Pauline Frederick, and dozens of lesser-known actresses by the time MGM offered Ruth the much sought-after leading role. Alexandre Bisson's French tear-inducer had been a sensation in Europe before reaching the U.S. in 1910. The plight of Jacqueline Floriot was a tour de force for any actress. After leaving her husband and young son for another man, Jacqueline is forbidden from seeing her child. She literally tramps around Europe finding consolation in drugs, booze, and easy virtue. Twenty years pass. In a moment of desperation, she shoots her paramour/blackmailer to keep scandal from touching the life of her son. Refusing to divulge her name, she goes on trial for murder as "Madame X." The audience is held captive as the young attorney for the defense is (unbeknownst to him) defending his own mother. Until a climactic moment, she is equally oblivious as to *his* identity. The film had success (twice) as a silent release and the talkie version was no different. *Madame X* was among the "10 Best Pictures of 1929" (third place) in *The Film Daily Poll* solicited from over four hundred of the nation's top critics. Both Ruth and Lionel Barrymore (as director) were contenders for Academy Awards.

Watching the film today, Ruth comes across as being excessively theatrical in the early scenes when she confronts her ex-husband (Lewis

Stone). While her propriety and aristocratic intonation provide contrast to what follows, it feels over-the-top. Her performance turns into an astounding achievement when she descends into the slangy, husky-voiced woman—an addict, entangled with the wrong kind of man (Ullrich Haupt). Film historian Jerry Vermilye, in *The Films of the Twenties* (1985), stated, "Chatterton's... drunk scenes with the subtly villainous Ullrich Haupt can only represent 1929's screen-acting art at its finest. Chatterton even helps us believe *Madame X*'s incredible courtroom climax, blending sentiment, irony and coincidence beyond all logic."[383] In 1968, Pauline Kael had written, "Chatterton... knew how to get into a broken-down old vehicle and get some mileage out of it."[384] *Film Daily*'s review put it thusly, "The sympathetic and consummate work of this comparative newcomer to talking pictures will remain fixed in your mind. Her artistry is inescapable."[385] *Theatre Arts Magazine* stated, "Chatterton has emerged more powerfully on the screen than she did on the stage."[386]

Not everyone was ecstatic. Playwright Robert E. Sherwood found the dialogue by Willard Mack "trite" and Ruth, in the earlier scenes, "embarrassingly bad," but confessed, "She is superb at the finish—and it is the finish that counts in *Madame X*."[387] Sherwood added, "Miss Chatterton had a hard-boiled audience choking and sniveling at everything she did."[388] Mordaunt Hall, for *The New York Times*, complimented director Barrymore, but said, "Without a doubt the acting of Ruth Chatterton in the title role is the outstanding achievement of the picture."[389] Hall also blamed the dialogue director for the actors declaiming rather than conversing. ("Stop it! Stop it, I tell you!" Ruth warns an amorous young sailor.) "Willard Mack ought to have avoided utterances that savor of old Drury Lane days," cautioned Hall, "for such lines may result in creating laughter rather than tears." It was noted that Ruth fought with Mack on the set.[390] She had spent time translating dialogue from the original

French. It was obvious that Mack wasn't interested in her suggestions. Even so, the real problem might have been Barrymore himself.

Between "takes" on the big sound stage at Metro, a reporter from *The New York Times* interviewed Chatterton while she and Lewis Stone were shooting the early sequences. Ruth commented on film-making, "It's so different from the stage—just as the people themselves are. Lionel, of course, I knew on the stage, and it's wonderful to have him for a director. He's so much like his sister Ethel it sometimes amazes me." Barrymore, wearing earphones, did his "directing" by listening from a sound-proof monitor room above the set. Over the loudspeaker, he roared at Ruth, "Put a little tone in it this time, please." "All right, Mr. Barrymore," she replied succinctly. A bell rang twice and Barrymore clanged shut the great sound-proof doors. The reporter noted a moment of intense silence—then,

> "Louis, no matter what I have done," intoned the actress, repeating a stock sentence. This time the scene finished. Barrymore descended from the sound-proof monitor room. "You hate to come out of that cubbyhole up there, don't you?" asked Miss Chatterton. "I stay up in the monitor room and hear every word," Barrymore explained. "My assistant stays on the floor and watches the action. I guess I'm the ear director... but that's the best way to get perfect speech recording."[391]

"Perfect speech" enunciated to the point of distraction was exactly what makes the early portions of *Madame X* difficult to watch. Apparently, Barrymore liked what he heard. The next take was more of the same. "I'm only asking for what the suffering souls in purgatory ask!" Ruth begged Stone after he refuses her one last look at their son. Barrymore emerged from his booth, yelling, "Miss Chatterton! I wish I could

Intoning "perfect speech" for director Barrymore...
with Lewis Stone in *Madame X* (MGM).

plead like that when I talk to my creditors. It's great, every word." Unfortunately, it was Chatterton who had to live with the legacy of every over-enunciated syllable that Willard Mack and Lionel Barrymore elicited from her mouth. Still, Ruth had great admiration for her director, especially the day he restored the confidence of an elderly Italian actor playing a bit part who kept going up on his lines. Controlling the famous Barrymore temper, Lionel kept blaming the retakes on the sound equipment until the actor got it right. "The patience of Lionel Barrymore never faltered once," observed Ruth. "To me, he was Christ-like."[392]

Barrymore later admitted, "I gave [directing] up. It was too much for me, working all day and worrying all night."[393] Sound technicians protested Barrymore's clever idea for a sound boom. It allowed actors to walk and talk simultaneously. Others would claim credit for the invention, but Barrymore always responded with, "All I can say is that in 1929 I recorded Miss Ruth Chatterton's voice with a fishing pole."[394] Filming *Madame X* wasn't easy. Barrymore was often late on the set; the assistant director ended up rehearsing the actors; shooting the courtroom scenes took place between 7 p.m. and 6:40 a.m., which brought Ruth and Raymond Hackett, who played her adult son, to the point of collapse.[395] While dealing with the heat and lack of air, Ruth turned on the tears at the witness stand, mascara running down her cheeks. She commented on her difficulty "getting out of the mood" after the final "take." Talkies demanded day and night concentration until the last "shot."

When Marie Dressler, an old acquaintance of Ruth, visited scenarist Frances Marion at MGM, she was adamant that they visit the *Madame X* set. "Come on over and meet Ruth," said Dressler. "You'll like each other. You're both so nuts about books, the theatre, symphonies, and all that kind of stuff." The cameras were rolling when they reached the sound stage. "A small crowd had gathered behind the battery of lights," recalled Marion, "and those who had criticized [Ruth's] clipped British accent must have wondered what had become of it when they watched her act, for even the most critical could not withhold their tears during one of her dramatic scenes."[396] Afterward, Dressler rushed forward to embrace Ruth and greeted her with, "Nothing can stop you from being a tremendous movie star." On their way out of the studio, Marion remarked to Marie, "Miss Chatterton floored me! She must have had a brilliant education. Did she go to school in England?" Dressler was frank. "Broadway was her alma mater," she said. "Let me tell you what a kid and her mother go through to reach success. I remember one hot summer day when the sidewalks were melting, I came out of a store and met Tillie. She had Ruth with her, a pale sickly little tad. 'How are you, Tillie?' I asked. 'Simply exhausted, Marie. I've been tramping up and down for days in this heat, going from one agency to another, trying to get Ruthie a job.' That's a theatrical mother for you."[397] Although Chatterton never told her story in exactly those terms, Dressler's account tells another side to the story. Chatterton and Frances Marion became lifelong friends.

Ruth complained that censorship got in the way of telling *Madame X*. "The greatest enemy of any art is the censor," she observed. "The arts are not intended primarily for children. Censor the children, if you like, but not the pictures."[398] Case in point was the murder scene in *Madame X*. "It would have been immoral for me to pull the trigger," said Ruth. "This man had to be shot by Madame X or there wouldn't have been much point to the incident." On screen, Ruth reaches for the gun. In the next frame, a shot rings out and the man falls. "So far as actually witnessing the thing," added Ruth, "you couldn't prove I did it. Apparently the man died just to help the plot." A crucial, emotionally charged frame of Ruth aiming and firing the gun was not to be. Over at Paramount, Jeanne Eagels had pulled the trigger and fired several times into the camera for *The Letter*. The same action posed a problem at MGM. Nonetheless, Chatterton is riveting. Aghast at what she has done, Jacqueline's body literally shakes as she tells herself, "I was worse than I am!" Unfortunately, Barrymore's *Madame X* moved at a snail's pace. The action felt drawn out, the script overstated. Luckily for Ruth, filming had gone over schedule and she was spared playing in *The Studio Murder Mystery*, which was panned for its hokum and endless talk.

When the Motion Picture Academy (brainchild of Louis B. Mayer to discourage unionism in Hollywood)

Madame X (MGM).

selected the top performances for 1928-29, Ruth was a shoo-in for Best Actress. Competing with her were: the recently deceased Jeanne Eagels for *The Letter*, the always competent Betty Compson in her comeback *The Barker*, Bessie Love for *The Broadway Melody*, and Mary Pickford's uneasy performance in *Coquette*.[399] The women were all seasoned veterans. Eagels and Pickford were slightly older than Ruth. Compson and Love were in their early thirties. There were definite problems with the awards: favoritism and an absurd voting procedure. One could say that Ruth Chatterton lost "over a cup of tea." Pickford, a founding member of the Academy, invited all five (voting) members of the Central Board of Judges to high tea shortly before the gala occasion.[400] Of course, she won.

Hubbard Keavy, future chief editor for the Associated Press, stated diplomatically that it was Ruth Chatterton that "gave Pickford a close race."[401] According to Keavy, the actresses who had received the most nominations before voting closed were: Chatterton, Love, Pickford, Joan Crawford, Nancy Carroll, Phyllis Haver, and Greta Garbo.[402] On April 3, 1930, the Awards Ceremony was held at the Cocoanut Grove of the Ambassador Hotel. The host and presenter was William C. DeMille (older brother of Cecil B.), who had directed Ruth in *The Doctor's Secret*. This private party wasn't filled with all the brouhaha for which it became known and received no more press coverage than had the first awards ceremony (1927-28). Film publications were indifferent. *Motion Picture* magazine referred to the winners as "The Prize People in Hollywood." "The Academy's awards," scoffed the editorial page, "were little gold statuettes. Press notices were proportionately small."[403] *Film Daily* didn't mention the awards at all. In all likelihood, Ruth was indifferent about winning the "little gold statuette."

In the aftermath of this fiasco, the Academy rules were changed. The Central Board was dissolved. From then on, the entire Academy membership voted. Film critic and scholar Richard Watts, Jr.'s assessment of Pickford was, "her audible debut on *Coquette*, to put it mildly, wasn't very good."[404] One columnist wrote that Pickford's victory proved "that the Academy is handing out its cups on a political or social basis," and on merit alone, the Award should have been given to Ruth Chatterton or the late Jeanne Eagels.[405] Ruth commented that Eagles was a "strange, intense little creature—so alive that she still must be persisting somewhere. Anyway, I like to think so."[406] Eagels' uniquely raw, destructive portrayal in *The Letter* was uncannily self-revealing. The role would also prove perfect turf for Bette Davis in 1940. As for *Madame X*, a revamped and mercilessly twenty-three minute shorter version would elicit more tears when the consummate Gladys George played the role in 1939. In 1966, a lavishly gowned Lana Turner pleased her fans in a glossy Ross Hunter remake.

⁂

When asked if her abandonment of the stage had left a gap which couldn't be filled, Ruth offered a skeptical smile,

> No one is indispensable. This is one of the great truths
> of life. At present I am very busy with talking pictures,
> and very happy in making them. The talkies have hit the
> theatre business hard … My prediction is that fewer poor
> plays will be shown and that fewer plays in the aggre-
> gate will be produced, but they will be of greater artistic
> value. Against the competition of Hollywood, only good
> plays can survive. Talking pictures and stage plays are
> different, and it is futile to try to decide which is better.
> It is like trying to decide which is right, the person who

prefers a cream colored car or the person who prefers black.[407]

As far as being indispensable, Ralph proved Ruth's point. His career at MGM was quashed after only two years. He returned to the Los Angeles stage in a production of *The Swan*. Before the release of *Madame X*, Ruth had shoveled in enough indispensable dough to buy herself a new roadster as well as a lovely home on North Palm Drive in Beverly Hills. Though she stated that it was futile to decide which is better, stage or screen, Ruth rested her case for the latter. "I have no desire to return to the stage," she admitted.[408] The money, the California sunshine, the challenge of a new medium had turned her whole life around. And she wasn't going to complain, not yet.

Endnotes

329   John McCallum, *Scooper*, Wood and Reber, c. 1960, pg 182.
330   Sadie Mossler, review of *The Green Hat*, *Los Angeles Record*, August 10, 1926.
331   Ruth Gordon, *Myself Among Others*, Atheneum, NY, c 1971, pg 235.
332   Leonard Boyd, "Studio Contract May Part Ralph Graves and Ruth Chatterton," *Los Angeles Examiner*, September 12, 1926.
333   Wood Soanes, review of *The Green Hat*, *Oakland Tribune*, November 2, 1926.
334   Elsie Janis, "Chatterton, the Charmer," *New Movie*, July 1932.
335   Ella Smith, *Starring Miss Barbara Stanwyck*, Crown Publishers, NY, c. 1985, pg 5-6.
336   Paul Harrison, "Around Hollywood," *Bakersfield Californian*, September 19, 1940.
337   Malcolm H. Oettinger, "Another Lady!" *Picture Play*, June 1931.
338   Robbin Coons, "Screen Life in Hollywood," *Joplin Globe*, February 25, 1924.
339   Carl Van Vechten, *The Splendid Drunken Twenties: Selections from the Daybooks, 1922-30*, University of Illinois, c. 2003, pg 157.
340   Carl Van Vechten, *The Splendid Drunken Twenties: Selections from the Daybooks, 1922-30*, University of Illinois, c. 2003, pg 165.
341   Carl Van Vechten, *The Splendid Drunken Twenties: Selections from the Daybooks, 1922-30*, University of Illinois, c. 2003, pg 159.
342   Burns Mantle, *Burns Mantle Yearbook*, Dodd Mead, c. 1927, pg 26.
343   "Film Actress and Hubby Kept Apart Agree to Separate," *Logansport Herald* (IN), December 14, 1927.
344   "Court In Orbit of Film Stars," *Los Angeles Times*, February 1, 1928.
345   "Celebrities See Fox Drama Unfold," *San Antonio Light*, February 9, 1928.
346   Laurence Irving, *Designing for the Movies: the Memories of Laurence Irving*, Scarecrow Press, c. 2005, pg 71.
347   Chester B. Bahn, "Up and Down the Rialtos," *Syracuse Herald*, March 25, 1928.
348   Chauncey L. Carr, "Ruth Chatterton," *Films in Review*, January 1962 (Carr states that Olga Baclanova got Ruth's role—a third billed supporting role. Other references say Ruth was considered for the wife of Bancroft, a role that went to Betty Compson.).
349   Frank Condon, "The Laughing Lady," *Saturday Evening Post*, November 28, 1931.
350   Alberto Rendon, "Los Mercaderes de Estrellas," *Cinelandia*, February 1932.
351   Dan Van Neste, "Ruth Chatterton," *Films of the Golden Age*, Fall 1997.

352   Adela St. Rogers Johns, "The Men in Ruth Chatterton's Life," *Liberty*, January 20, 1934.
353   "Chatterton and Brook," *New York Times*, September 29, 1929 (Interview was taken on the set of *The Laughing Lady*, which co-starred Clive Brook.).
354   "Ruth Chatterton Divorce Catches Gossips Napping," *Pittsburg Press*, March 15, 1934.
355   Louella Parsons column, *Los Angeles Examiner*, July 12, 1928.
356   Welford Beaton, review of *Sins of the Fathers*, *The Film Spectator*, December 1, 1928.
357   D.E. review of *Sins of the Fathers*, *Waterloo Evening Courier*, (IA), February 8, 1929.
358   Mordaunt Hall review of *Sins of the Fathers*, *New York Times*, January 29, 1929.
359   Review of *Sins of the Fathers*, "The Shadow Stage," *Photoplay*, January 1929.
360   "The Girl on the Cover," *Photoplay*, February 1930.
361   "They Said Ruth Chatterton Was Through," *The American Magazine*, June 1931.
362   "The Girl on the Cover," *Photoplay*, February 1930.
363   Robert S. Wistrich, "Who's Who in Nazi Germany," Psychology Press, c. 2001, pg 129
364   Frank Condon, "The Laughing Lady," *Saturday Evening Post*, November 28, 1931.
365   Edwin Schallert column, *Los Angeles Times*, April 28, 1929.
366   Cal York, "Gossip of All the Studios," *Photoplay*, January 1928.
367   Donald H. Clarke, "Her Voice A Boon," *New York Times*, May 5, 1929.
368   Lawrence J. Quirk, *Norma – The Story of Norma Shearer*, St. Martin's Pr. NY., c. 1988, pg 98.
369   "As We Go to Press," *Photoplay*, December 1928.
370   Conversation with Brenda Holman, January 16, 2012.
371   Leonard Hall, "The Destiny Fighter," *Photoplay*, July 1930 (Hall was managing editor).
372   "The Girl on the Cover, " *Photoplay*, February 1930 (Leonard Hall interviewed Ruth for a subsequent article; as no credit is given, it is also possible that Cal York or editor John Quirk interviewed Ruth for this issue).
373   Review of *The Doctor's Secret*, *Film Daily*, February 10, 1929.
374   Harrison Carroll, review of *The Doctor's Secret*, *Los Angeles Examiner*, January 25, 1929.
375   "In Hollywood," *Piqua Daily Call*, (OH), January 10, 1929.
376   Freddie Schader, review of *The Doctor's Secret*, *Motion Picture News*, February 9, 1929.
377   Chester B. Bahn, review of *The Doctor's Secret*, *Syracuse Herald*, February 10, 1929.
378   Harrison Carroll, "Behind the Scenes in Hollywood," *Evening Independent*, November 25, 1940.
379   Obit for ZaSu Pitts, *New York Times*, June 8, 1963.
380   Charles Stumpf, *ZaSu Pitts: The Life and Career*, McFarland, c. 2010, pg 40.
381   Review of *The Dummy*, *Motion Picture News*, March 9, 1929.
382   Wood Soanes, review of *The Dummy*, *Oakland Tribune*, March 16, 1929.
383   Jerry Vermilye, *The Films of the Twenties*, Citadel Press, c. 1985, pg 240.
384   Pauline Kael, *Kiss Kiss Bang Bang*, Little, Brown (NY), c. 1968, pg 121.
385   K A N N, review of *Madame X*, *Film Daily*, April 25, 1929.
386   Review of *Madame X*, *Theatre Arts Monthly*.
387   Robert E. Sherwood, "Take Your Handkerchief," *Hollywood Daily Citizen*, May 4, 1929.
388   Robert E. Sherwood quote from "Screen Silhouettes," *Winnipeg Free Press*, May 18, 1929.
389   Mordaunt Hall, review of *Madame X*, *New York Times*, April 25, 1929.
390   Charles Higham, *Merchant of Dreams: Louis B. Mayer*, D.I. c. 1993, pg 141.
391   "Making Scenes For A Talking Film," *New York Times*, April 7, 1929.
392   Gladys Hall, "I'm a Renegade in Hollywood," *Motion Picture*, July 1929.
393   "Patriarch of U.S. Actors Lionel Barrymore is Dead," *Racine Journal Times* (WI), November 16, 1954.
394   James Kotsilibas-Davis, *The Barrymores*, Crown (NY), c. 1981, pg 81.
395   Charles Higham, *Merchant of Dreams*, Donald I. Fine (NY), c. 1993, pg 139.
396   Frances Marion, *Off With Their Heads*, MacMillan (NY), c. 1972, pg 189.
397   Frances Marion, *Off With Their Heads*, MacMillan (NY), c. 1972, pg 189.
398   Jessie Henderson, "Censors Are Enemies Of Films, Avers Star," *Ogden Standard Examiner*, February 23, 1930.
399   (Note: the contending 5 actresses were announced on October 31, 1929. In 1994, Corinne Griffith received a belated nomination for her portrayal in *The Divine Lady*. See Robert Osborne's *65 Years of the Oscar*).
400   Mason Wiley, Damien Bona, *Inside Oscar-10th Anniversary Edition*, Ballantine (NY), c. 1996, pg. 17.

401   Hubbard Keavy, "High in Achievements," *Charleston Gazette*, July 13, 1930 (Keavy became the Bureau Chief for the Associated Press).

402   Hubbard Keavy, "Screen Life in Hollywood," *Sandusky Register*, September 3, 1929.

403   "Talking Pictures," *Motion Picture*, July 1930.

404   Richard Watts, Jr., "Critic Ridicules Idea of Film Star Walkout," *Oakland Tribune*, August 31, 1930.

405   Mason Wiley, Damien Bona, *Inside Oscar-10th Anniversary Edition*, Ballantine (NY), c. 1996, pg. 18.

406   John L. Haddon, "Lest We Forget," *Motion Picture*, June 1933.

407   Jessie Henderson, "Censors Are Enemies Of Films, Avers Star," *Ogden Standard Examiner*, February 23, 1930.

408   "The Girl on the Cover," *Photoplay*, February 1930.

1930 portrait by Russell Ball (Ruth's private
collection – courtesy of Brenda Holman).

7
The Lady is a Tramp

"I am a tramp. I like to bum around in strange places."
Ruth Chatterton, 1929

It seems odd that Ruth Chatterton, a cultivated woman noted for her splendid voice, achieved popularity on screen by playing a home wrecker, a murderess, a divorcee, a dance hall girl, and other genres that were miles away from her bookish, intellectual self. "But you've got to un-inhibit yourself," insisted Ruth. "You must shake off embarrassment. What you play on the stage or screen has nothing to do with the sort of person you, yourself, are."[409] Chatterton brought a ripe maturity to her onscreen suffering. She took her work seriously by personally observing life at its rawest. One male columnist offered a few tidbits about Ruth to Frank Conlon before his *Saturday Evening Post* interview with the star. "Miss Chatterton," he said, "has a decided personality, strong determinations, pays no attention whatever to the conventions, and at any moment may obey some strange, whimsical impulse." Conlon's curiosity was piqued. "Such as what?" he asked. "Well, for example," the gentleman replied, "she is as likely as not to step into her limousine, drive down town to one of the penny dance halls and there dance with a sailor." "An ordinary sailor?" Conlon queried. "Right off the fleet," came the answer.[410] Conlon wondered how he could politely lead up to the subject of Ruth's whimsical impulses and ... sailors. He never got up enough nerve.

In truth, Ruth had already declared her penchant for the unconventional to writer Katherine Albert. When Albert asked Ruth how she had acquired the reputation of being "ritzy," Ruth thought it absurd. "That I'm not," she laughed. "I'm a tramp. I like to bum around in strange places. Put on old clothes and go down to Harlem. And I adore people of every calling. As a rule, I like men better than women."[411] While Ruth absorbed herself observing others, there was one thing she made clear to Albert: "I've never had my life pried into." This didn't mean she was anything less than cordial during interviews. Seattle reporter Richard Hays found Chatterton to be gracious, charming—she completely won his admiration. Hays told her that he had recently seen Ruth's "understudy" in a film. "She seemed to try so hard to be like you," he said. "Oh, you mean Miss Tobin," Ruth replied. "Really, if there is a resemblance or similarity I think it is quite unintentional." Gently rebuked, Hays secretly admired Ruth's reply, finding it a generous gesture. Ruth knew that the word "understudy" was being used facetiously by the press in comparing the two actresses—with the added sting of Tobin's "youth" thrown in for good measure. Two days later, Hays waited for Genevieve Tobin, who was doing a photo shoot. Tobin begrudgingly acknowledged him with a strained smile. Hays told her that he was glad she was now making films. "Thank you," she uttered with a slight nod. He then complimented her on her performance in *A Lady Surrenders.* Offering another slight nod, she sighed, "Thank you." He turned to the studio host and said, "Well, let's go." "I found that I was mistaken," said Hays in summary. "Miss Tobin was not at all like Miss Chatterton."[412]

Charming Sinners, an engaging frolic amongst London's upper-crust, was based on W. Somerset Maugham's *The Constant Wife*. The play was a success for Ethel Barrymore. The film secured Ruth's position as the "First Lady of the Screen" (which is exactly how MGM billed Norma Shearer). As Kathryn Miles, Ruth effortlessly delivers Maugham's witticisms while dealing with her selfish, errant husband, Robert (Clive Brook). Kathryn opts for the single standard herself in the hope of getting him back. Enter William Powell (as Karl), a former beau. An exquisite interlude has Ruth seated at the piano. Her light soprano wraps around a wistful melody while Karl pours his heart out. Kathryn dismisses his ardor with an appreciative laugh. The two stars create a special simpatico on screen. As he catches on, Robert begins to have second thoughts about his involvement with a flirtatious blonde (Mary Nolan).

Laura Hope Crews (as Ruth's mother) is delightfully dismissive of her son-in-law's extracurricular activity, saying, "I've never been able to attach any importance to the philandering of men—it's their nature." Maugham puts his own foot in his mouth when Robert declares, "philandering is the most overrated amusement ever invented." The irony is, of course, that Maugham created an engaging piece of work on the subject and allows the wife to be very much in control of the outcome. Chatterton lends poignancy to the wife's resolve to take a six-week holiday in Italy by herself. "I have longed for some time to be in a position," Kathryn informs Robert, "where I could, if I felt inclined, tell you with calm courtesy, but determination, to go to the devil!" Chatterton's depth of understanding carries *Charming Sinners* to a winning, though revamped, conclusion. The stage version had Barrymore and the former beau venture together to Italy. On screen, Chatterton reclaims Brook's adoration by the time she boards the train. There was no point in her indulging in "overrated amusement." It was an effective, thoughtful finish.

The decidedly highbrow, airy attitude in *Charming Sinners* reflected

With William Powell and Laura Hope Crews
in *Charming Sinners* (Paramount).

Ruth and Ralph's own belief in having an occasional vacation from marriage. Ruth was optimistic about the appeal of a sophisticated film. "All this talk about not being able to make high-class pictures because they won't be accepted in small towns is a lot of bunk," she declared. After the film was released, Hollywood concurred. Some felt that Ruth seemed more at home in sophisticated comedy than melodrama, comparing her favorably to Barrymore. "Miss Chatterton's performance dominates the picture," raved Chester Bahn. "She is, I tell you in all sincerity, one of the screen's finest artists."[414] In 1937, Ruth would make her British stage debut in *The Constant Wife*.

Charming Sinners was something new for the cinema. It was not about action. It was about words—expertly delivered by a well-seasoned cast who deliver just enough tension amid all the flippancy to make it work. Ruth and Laura Hope Crews had worked together for years in the Henry

Miller Company. Clive Brook, Montagu Love, and William Powell were all stage veterans. Robert Milton directed and Dorothy Arzner blocked the scenes for camera with good results in spite of the fact that it had to be shot at night.[415] Crews commented she found it a bit difficult to be funny at 4 a.m. The tragic Mary Nolan, a former Follies girl who would end up broke and drug-addicted, is excellent as the pampered schemer with whom Brook, as the husband, is smitten. Always thinking and plotting, she turns her distasteful character into something peculiarly fascinating. She proved that some silent stars didn't need to fear the influx of stage veterans to Hollywood.

As with most films of the period, faulty recording hampered *Charming Sinners*. Ruth's voice had been known to blow out as many as three microphone tubes on the set. She laughed, "I talk into the thing with an ordinary conversational tone and they say, 'Softly, Miss Chatterton, softly.' But it's pioneering. It's because it's new that it's exciting." For a number of silent stars, the transition to sound continued to be anything *but* exciting. Clara Bow, the hugely popular "It" girl of the 1920s, was on the verge of a nervous breakdown. She told fellow actress Louise Brooks, "Schulberg sent Ruth Chatterton up to my house on Thursday... and I beat it out the back door because they make me feel so terrible I can't talk."[416] In May 1930, an article by New York critic John S. Cohen headlined, "Ruth Chatterton Passes Clara Bow in Popularity." Chatterton's fan mail and drawing power at the box office had soared. "Miss Chatterton is a first rate actress in the talkies," wrote Cohen, "and Miss Bow is a first rate vision to look at, and a second rate actress. Technique, therefore, is beginning to count for something—and the fact that Miss Chatterton has surpassed Miss Bow at the box office means a great deal. And, it should."[417] The news was a real eye-opener for Paramount. "Now that the movies have grown up and begun to talk," explained Ruth, "people want to listen to something more than calf-love patter."[418] The Chatterton hold on popularity polls and box-office wasn't nearly as long-lasting as Bow, but she generated a new "type" for the screen that encouraged audiences to demand more from actors they doted on.

※⊰⊱⊰⊱⊱

During a break from film-making, Ruth and her longtime friend from Actor's Fidelity, Fay Bainter, flew to New York in September 1929. Bainter had just spent a month with Ruth at her Malibu rental. Ruth was godmother to Bainter's six-year-old son Reggie, who never quite broke the silver cord. In the 1950s, Bainter insisted Reggie be hired as publicity assistant for her tour in *Long Day's Journey into Night*. His acting career had reached a permanent standstill.[419] Bainter herself was in a career slump in 1929. It would be four years before she had another success in the stage version of Sinclair Lewis' *Dodsworth*. And she wasn't exactly thrilled two years later when Ruth got the coveted role of Fran Dodsworth in the Sam Goldwyn film version.

Ruth was in New York a few days when her vacation came to an abrupt halt. She was called to replace Jeanne Eagels in a trifle called *The Laughing Lady*. Filming would begin immediately on Long Island. Reports stated that due to an eye infection, Eagels was unavailable.[420] She died two weeks later. Ruth didn't return to Hollywood until the end of December. It was another "vacation from marriage" for her and Ralph. While in New York, Ruth visited her mother Tillie and prepared to film another Ethel Barrymore stage role. As a result, Paramount abandoned plans for Ruth's scheduled remake of *Zaza*—which was postponed until 1938 with Claudette Colbert as the French chanteuse.

Director/composer Victor Schertzinger created an affable, if uneven,

With Clive Brook in *Laughing Lady* (Paramount).

piece of work in *Laughing Lady*—another tale of high-class philandering. The film boasts one of the earliest musical underscores. Schertzinger's composition "Another Kiss" waltzes in and out of the scenes, adding romantic punch. Ruth is the lady in question who laughs at fate. As Marjorie Lee, she finds herself laughing at the most inopportune moments— in a courtroom where the custody of her daughter is at stake. She loses the case and is cut off from her social circle. "Well, well, well," Marjorie says with some bite, "this is getting more like a funeral every moment." The stiff, unbending prosecuting attorney, Daniel Farr (Clive Brook), becomes her target for revenge. Marjorie sees to it that he falls hopelessly in love with her. She wants to ruin his career. She laughs again when her plans go astray. *Laughing Lady* picks up nicely when the flirtation between Marjorie and Daniel starts tongues to wag. Here, Chatterton and Brook make an attractive team. The odd choice of Raymond Walburn as her husband, however, was unfortunate. It was difficult to believe this annoying, witless man would have ever charmed Chatterton, let alone have a mistress. Even so, it was the husband's philandering that allowed Marjorie to regain custody of her daughter.

As a rule, critics responded favorably to *The Laughing Lady*. Bay Area critic Wood Soanes felt that the film had a "dash of smartness." "Miss Chatterton is particularly fine in the lighter moments," he stated, "and acceptable as she rises to emotion, although she is always inclined to overact in the *Madame X* manner."[421] The script may have hampered Ruth's tear-stained scenes, but she managed to glide with natural ease through mostly preposterous situations and a contrived ending. While other actors were parroting lines, she and Brook gave the film momentum. Los Angeles critic Doris Denbo commented, "Ruth Chatterton triumphs over a poor story. It is interesting only because of the artistry of the glorious Miss Chatterton and the smooth acting."[422] Freelance critic and wit Thornton Delehanty perhaps was right, however, when he reported, "The picture would have been pleasanter with the laugh left out."[423]

Shortly after she returned home from New York, Ruth wasn't laughing. She explained why to Kenneth R. Porter, a Los Angeles writer whom she welcomed into her boudoir for an interview. Ruth was nursing a stiff neck after completing *The Laughing Lady*—her fifth picture within a year. The first scene in the film, where she is rescued from drowning, was shot last. It was mid-winter. "No one knew the true temperature of the water," Ruth complained. Her rescue also proved to be an arduous task for former wrestler Nat Pendleton, who played the lifeguard. Pendleton had nosed out Olympic swimmer Johnny Weissmuller for the role. He would joke later, "Johnny got even with me by nosing me out of Tarzan."[424] During her bedside chat with Porter, Ruth complained about finding suitable stories that could be crammed into the time allotted for a movie. At one point, Ralph entered into the conversation, insisting he offer their guest a glimpse of his gun room. "Their beautiful Beverly Hills home can

well afford such a corner for firearms," wrote Porter. Ralph accused Ruth
of not being appreciative of his collection. "Did you see the bullet hole
in the door of the gun room?" she inquired sharply upon their return.
"That came while Ralph was experimenting." After a pregnant pause, she
added, "Dodging bullets… may be fun in Chicago, but it really doesn't fit
in with the peacefulness one might expect in a home."[425] Ralph's arsenal
was obviously a sore point in their relationship.

A housewarming celebration for Ruth and Ralph's Beverly Hills home
on Palm Drive had been postponed. The stylish English country house,
furnished with antiques, soon began a round of social gatherings for their
small circle of friends, which included: Mr. and Mrs. Clive Brook, Ramon Novarro, actress/screenwriter Elsie Janis, author Louis Bromfield,
Ronald Colman (who told intimates that Ruth was the only woman who
had ever won his confidence), Fay Bainter, actress/director Auriol Lee,
theatrical legends Guthrie McClintic and Katharine Cornell, screen vet-

Ruth's residence at 704 North Palm Drive, Beverly Hills
(Ruth's private collection–courtesy of Brenda Holman).

eran Lois Wilson, Helen Hayes, and husband Charles MacArthur. Ruth and Helen liked to drive up to Santa Barbara to enjoy the beaches and sea while putting the world in order.[426] Lois Wilson, often seen chatting with Ruth in the more private Paramount studio café, would occasionally pop up as an extra or have a small role in Ruth's films. Ruth's gatherings were organized by her secretary, Hazel Gray. Hazel had been with her for almost two years. She took care of the servants, the marketing, and planning of events.[427] After visiting California in the summer of 1929, Lilian Chatterton decided to join her daughter in Beverly Hills. She now resided close by on Palm Drive with her Filipino houseboy.

Ruth preferred the intimate setting of her home and rarely ventured out. She and Ralph never entertained more than ten at dinner, often less. Their guest of honor was usually a visiting stage celebrity such as Irving Berlin. Dinner parties were filled with conversation that lasted far into the night around the fireplace in Ruth's upstairs library. Guests were inevitably people who enjoyed strong coffee and liked to talk. Columnist Marquis Busby (onetime lover of director Edmund Goulding) wrote that Ruth had "the faculty of drawing about her the most interesting people. Perhaps she comes the nearest to holding what is termed so grandly, a salon."[428] Ruth liked to entertain at the piano and sing one of the numerous songs she had composed (but refused to have published). On one occasion, a hit tune was conceived during one of Ruth's "salons." Concert pianist Jack King was seated at her piano when a tune came to him. Ruth joined in and sang the melody. "How Am I to Know" became the theme song for the film *Dynamite* (1929).[429]

Ramon Novarro adored Ruth. According to biographer Allan Ellenberger, she accepted Novarro's attraction to men. "We talk music together, listen to music," said Ramon, "and argue for hours over ascetic questions."[430] He was introduced to Ruth by Elsie Janis. Both women helped bring Novarro out of his shell—using him as an escort to various social affairs.[431] Ramon and Ralph acted as Ruth's escorts when the trio saw "La Argentina," the South American dancer who was the first to mix the notion of castanets with dancing. Mr. and Mrs. Forbes preferred the arts—particularly the German opera company's performance of *Tristan and Isolde* (Ruth loved the Wagnerian Ring Cycle). Occasionally, they were seen at a film premier, such as *All Quiet on the Western Front* or *Morocco*. More rarely, Ruth and Ralph would join in the Hollywood crowd. Not to be missed was Kay Francis' novel evening in honor of Louis Bromfield. The women wore lounging pajamas and the men white flannel sporting attire. Among Kay's guests were Humphrey Bogart, John Gilbert, Helen Hayes, Katharine Cornell, Billie Burke, and Edmund Goulding. Mr. and Mrs. Forbes officially "arrived" into the Hollywood elite when they were summoned to Pickfair by Mary Pickford and Douglas Fairbanks. The gala event was in honor of Doug, Jr.'s birthday. The dinner-dance celebration included Doug and wife Joan Crawford mingling with Gloria Swanson, Charles Farrell, Gary Cooper, Ann Harding, Ben Lyon, and wife Bebe Daniels, among others.

In the fall of 1930, Ruth had her own round of farewell courtesy parties when she announced she was planning a vacation to Europe. Musician Jack King and his mother gave a supper in Ruth's honor at their Hollywood home. Columnist Louella Parsons, who often dined with Ruth and Tillie, was there, accompanied by her urologist, "Docky" Martin. Docky was also Louella's husband. He brought along his reputation for hitting the bottle, which always left him semi-comatose. Parsons told guests, "Oh, let him rest. He has to operate in the morning."[432] To Ruth's dismay, her much anticipated holiday was not to be. Paramount demanded that her marathon of movie-making continue. Louella sympathized, "Ruth Chatterton has been trying to get away to London for two months. Every time she has been ready to go, Paramount would say, 'Another picture.' Being a star isn't all milk and honey."[433]

For Ruth's first release in 1930, she received her second Academy Award nomination. Dorothy Arzner, who had assisted with *Charming Sinners*, was her director for *Sarah and Son*. Paramount placed almost all phases of the production in the hands of women. Arzner directed, Zoe Akins adapted the screenplay, Verna Willis edited, Henrietta Cohn was the unit business manager, designer Edith Head was on board, Elsie Janis helped supervise, and Chatterton starred as Sarah Storm, the naïve immigrant

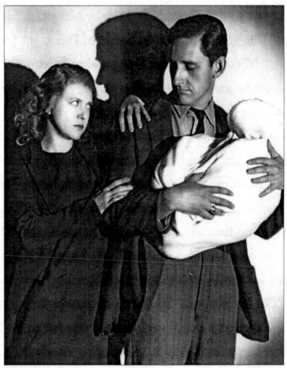

With Fuller Mellish, Jr. in *Sarah and Son* (Paramount).

who made her way from vaudeville to grand opera. Like Chatterton, Sarah was ambitious and determined. In 2004, film critic/author Molly Haskell wrote, "In *Sarah and Son*, a hugely successful 'weepie' when it opened in 1930, Ruth Chatterton's Oscar-nominated German refugee hoofer and singer is surrounded by weaklings, first, the loafer-husband who gives her a child and then sells it before skipping town, and a well-meaning, but dim-witted lawyer (Fredric March). The main purpose of the movie seems to be to give heartbroken Ruth Chatterton a chance to emote in German-accented English while looking for her child: 'Vat vorse could happen to me!'"[434]

Haskell was correct, but Chatterton sustained the broken accent and her character's English progressed along with the story. Mordaunt Hall for *The New York Times* praised, "This is quite a remarkable feat, especially before the microphone with constantly changing scenes spread over a period of six weeks or two months." Hall thought the agony was piled on a little heavily (which it was), but felt Arzner's direction "praiseworthy," the performances restrained, and recommended the film, stating, "Ruth Chatterton gives another splendid performance."[435] "Miss Chatterton's greatest effect," wrote Los Angeles critic Elizabeth Yeaman, "is achieved more by what she fails to say rather than by what she utters."[436]

Sarah and Son had no real villain, no hero or heroine. It was filled with real flesh-and-blood, credible people. The men are manipulative and weak, the women intuitive and strong. This was Arzner's point of view. In telling the story, she tempered the not-so-pleasant aspects of human nature with compassion. A wealthy couple, the Ashmores (Gilbert Emery and Doris Lloyd), desperate to have a child, "buy" Sarah's son illegally. After she locates them, they threaten to declare her insane. Their relative/lawyer Howard Vanning (Fredric March) is an unwitting accomplice in this charade. Sarah has no resources to fight. Years pass. Sarah, now a famous prima donna, returns to fight for her son and succeeds. In a nutshell, that's the story. It was *Madame X* in reverse. The reconciliation between mother and son was handled with care by Arzner. At a lakeside setting, Sarah converses with the boy, not knowing who he is. He invites her for a ride in his motor boat. There is a mishap—the two are rescued, the boy hospitalized. By this time, Sarah knows the score. When the bedridden boy begins calling for his mother, Sarah looks at the adoptive mother and says sadly, "It's *you* he wants." "We'll both go," she replies. As the son comes to, he extends his arms to Sarah, not the adoptive mother, who acknowledges, "He knows. He *knows*, somehow." It was a stretch, but *Film Daily* called it a "dramatic masterpiece," saying, "Rarely does the screen offer that deep sincerity that makes of *Sarah and Son* something fine and beautiful."[437] Chatterton's versatility, coupled with Arzner's ability to show human frailty on screen, turned *Sarah and Son* into something rare. Another review raved, "Miss Chatterton seems more praiseworthy here than at any other time in her cinematic career."[438]

Audiences were spared Chatterton tackling an aria, but she did quite well with Brahms' "Cradle Song" sung in both German and English. She was coached by the celebrated contralto Ernestine Schumann-Heink, who also advised Ruth's accent. The two had known each other since the summer of 1917. While *Come Out of the Kitchen* played in San Diego, Schumann-Heink gave a luncheon in Ruth's honor. Old radio broadcasts of the Grande Dame sound uncannily like Ruth's portrayal of Sarah Storm.

As the only woman director under contract to a motion picture studio, the alert and unassuming Arzner made every frame count. "A woman has to be twice as good as a man in any new field before she wins recognition, or even a chance," she said. Dressed in tailored suits and sporting what was called a "mannish" bob, Arzner quietly and calmly guided her productions. She saw human beings as nothing more or less than the life force behind the world and the thought force inside the world.[439] "A woman's viewpoint is important for certain pictures and scenes," Arzner emphasized. She felt women were capable of reaching the right conclusion through intuition before men reached the same conclusion through logic. Ruth's own intuition, along with a dash of hope, prompted her to take interest in the deaf, mute boy who had a small role in the film. She chartered an airplane to see if a sudden dive would restore his hearing. It didn't.

Philippe De Lacey, who played Ruth's son, commented on Arzner in 1985, saying, "She was extremely capable, quiet, and she had to deal with a very forceful and temperamental actress in Ruth Chatterton."[440] Arzner guided Ruth through two of her biggest screen successes. When asked about Chatterton's career in the 1970s, Arzner replied, "[Ruth] was a good actress. Yes, I certainly affected [her career]. When I made… *Sarah and Son*, it broke all box-office records at the Paramount Theatre in New York. Chatterton became known to the press as 'The First Lady of the Screen.'"[441] Contrary to De Lacey's recollections, one visitor on the set found Ruth "tractable" and commented:

> I watched her in a scene from *Sarah and Son*. It was one of those apparently simple, but extremely difficult sequences. The scene had been taken and retaken. At last it seemed right. Ruth played with deep emotion. The stage was as silent as a tomb. And then, at the most emotional point, someone coughed. It must have blown out six tubes. With tears still in her eyes, Ruth smiled at the offender. Not a word of blame. She lit a cigarette and waited for a new set-up.[442]

During production, Arzner visited Chatterton at home and found her in the middle of an interview. "Why shouldn't women work together?" Ruth asked the reporter. "The men are always handicapped by catering to their own ego, but women forget that and just apply themselves to the task at hand."[443] When asked if there was any trouble on the picture, Ruth answered in the affirmative. "Of course we had trouble. It's always a terrible job to make a picture. Everybody's nerves are worn to a frazzle, but every time I thought things had come to the breaking point, this rascal Dorothy would pipe up with that little girl voice and say something that would send me into fits of laughter."[444] "The feminists have surely come into their own," declared Louella Parsons after seeing the film, "without any needlessly futile sentiment."[445]

One would think that Ruth would include Arzner on her list of top ten film directors. She did not. When asked, she quickly jotted down her friend Sidney Franklin, who would direct her in *Lady of Scandal*. Next in line were: George Fitzmaurice, Ernst Lubitsch, Rouben Mamoulian, Richard Wallace (who directed Ruth twice), William Wellman (who directed her three times, uncredited in *Female*), King Vidor, Harry D'Arrast, Lewis Milestone, and Jacques Feyder. Ruth admitted numerous times that she would enjoy directing. She thought most films to be pretty feeble affairs—"one good and twelve bad, because they are manufactured by business men," she emphasized, "who use ingredients for business purposes."[446] Ruth believed that Noel Coward would excel at film directing. Audiences would have to wait until the 1940s before Coward produced a number of award-winning films. He admitted that he found it too much of a chore.

***

It wasn't long before Ruth's accent turned decidedly French. Along with Elsie Janis, she concocted a scenario, "The Montmartre Girl," for the studio's all-star hodgepodge for 1930: *Paramount on Parade*. At 101 minutes, the film, seen today, seems never-ending. Three dozen stars played in twenty different numbers. Maurice Chevalier, along with Evelyn Brent, provided the musical bright spot with a racy rendition of the Apache Dance directed by Ernst Lubitsch. Too bad Ruth wasn't able to work with one of her favorite players and directors in this lively number. Seven Technicolor sequences (that most reviews complained were blurred and scarcely discernible) featured dozens of

In *Paramount on Parade* (courtesy of Photofest).

stars, among them: Kay Francis, Gary Cooper, Fay Wray, Virginia Bruce, Jean Arthur, Mary Brian, and Chevalier. Midway through the film, Skeets Gallagher, who had co-starred in Ruth's *Magnolia Lady,* knocks on her dressing room door and the two have a little chat before her number. The film segues to a Paris bar where we discover Ruth, a lovelorn French streetwalker. A couple of wisecracking doughboys, Fredric March and Stuart Erwin, take pity as she sings "My Marine"—a tale of woe about a guy who promised to take her "back home" to Idaho. Like the audience, what these two guys *really* wanted was a good time. One film scholar commented that the number nearly stopped the film cold.[447] Part of the problem was the song composed by Richard Whiting. It was easily among the film's worst. A New York critic gibed, "Clara Bow comes in for her share of the spotlight, and if she fails to impress here as being either much of an actress or a song plugger, the same may be said of Ruth Chatterton, whose skit misses its mark widely. But let's not be carping, for these are only drops in an immense bucket."[448] The comparison was unfair. Bow's number, "True to the Navy," could have easily sunk a battleship. While Ruth's number put a damper on the proceedings, you believed her as she powdered her nose in the aftermath of her song and prepared to hustle the streets of Montmartre. No doubt this was something Ruth had witnessed herself in Paris while bumming around in "strange places."

In the winter of 1929-30, there was much to-do about Ruth signing on with MGM to play Nancy Sykes in an elaborate production of Charles Dickens' *Oliver Twist*. Lionel Barrymore, cast as Fagin, had signed on to direct. Tests for the title role had begun when the project was called off. In its place, MGM selected *The High Road*, a play by Frederick Lonsdale in which Herbert Marshall and wife Edna Best had teamed successfully. As a box office concession, it was re-titled *The Lady of Scandal*. Basil Rathbone, fresh from co-starring with Norma Shearer in Lonsdale's *The Last of Mrs. Cheney*, was chosen to play opposite Ruth. MGM used the same director, Sidney Franklin, and many members of the *Cheney* cast. The new mixture of romance and comedy made a profit and according to *New York Times'* Mordaunt Hall, "captured the moods and movement of the original work."[449] In spite of its staginess (it was filmed scene for scene), *The Lady of Scandal* was at least a change of pace from the dramatics of *Sarah and Son*. Ruth plays Elsie Hilary, a musical comedy star who is engaged to John, a young nobleman. Elsie is faced with the not-so-subtle insults of her fiancé's family—a bunch of dour Lords and Ladies and well-to-do snobs. Before Elsie realizes she is out of her element (the family demands that she leave the stage) and not in love with John, she falls for his cousin, the Duke of Warrington (Rathbone).

The Lady of Scandal turns to champagne that has ceased to bubble after Elsie suggests that Lord Trench (Frederick Kerr), the teetotaler of the family, have a cocktail. He begrudgingly downs a "gullet-washer" and his reaction is amusing... for about five seconds. The camera dotes on Kerr's mugging while he drinks an endless stream of "gullet-washers"—even in his tub. This, coupled with unconvincing declarations of love between Chatterton and Rathbone (who lack chemistry), leads to a somber finish. Under Sidney Franklin's direction, the joke is lost and the cardboard characters become tiresome. *Film Daily* felt the play lacked possibilities for the screen to begin with and called *The Lady of Scandal* a "fair programmer." The reviewer enjoyed Ruth's "lively characterization," but emphasized that its success would depend on her popularity. In her musical numbers, Chatterton proves that dancing was not her strong point. However, she does nicely singing "Say It With a Smile," a song written especially for her by Jack King (music) and Elsie Janis (lyrics). One critic put it succinctly, "Miss Chatterton

With Ralph Forbes in
The Lady of Scandal (MGM).

is charming in her musical comedy costume and her singing is fully up to the requirements of the character, as good as that of the average star of such a show."[450]

Filling the shoes of Elsie's nobleman fiancé, MGM selected Ralph Forbes. It would be Ruth and Ralph's only screen teaming. Forbes, who had recently been reduced to filming the Poverty Row release *Mamba* (1930), was grateful to be back on track. Bay Area critic Wood Soanes wrote, "Ralph Forbes gives better account of himself than ever before." Forbes does excellent work—sincere, real, and forceful when necessary. His struggle with Hilary's change of heart is genuine. Their farewell scene is quite touching—one of the film's best. Soanes' review felt that Ruth was competent, but that her performance was the "weakest link in the histrionic chain."[451] Another critic felt Rathbone inadequate, saying, "The final scenes are weak, due largely to the failure of Rathbone to measure up to the Chatterton standard."[452] Chatterton has her moments, but *The Lady of Scandal* is one of her weaker films.

Frederick Kerr, who played Lord Trench, connected Ruth to three generations of actors in the one family. Kerr's son, Geoffrey, was Ruth's co-star from the Henry Miller Company (*The Changelings*). Geoffrey would also play her husband in Paramount's *Once a Lady* (1931). In 1940, Geoffrey's son, John, was cast as Ruth's son in a Cape Cod production of *Tomorrow and Tomorrow*. Ruth never forgot the connection. In 1952, she urged director Guthrie McClintic to see young John's performance in *A Sleep of Prisoners* near Boston. Impressed, McClintic cast Kerr in *Bernadine*, his Broadway debut for which he earned critical raves, a Theatre World Award, and a bright future. John Kerr is remembered for his roles in *Tea and Sympathy* and *South Pacific*.

On November 5, 1930, the third annual Academy Awards took place. Ruth's neighbor, Conrad Nagel, was master of ceremonies. Competitors for Best Actress included Ruth for *Sarah and Son*, Norma Shearer's emancipated woman in *The Divorcee*, and Garbo's woman with a past in *Anna Christie*. Under Edmund Goulding's direction, two more nominees were added to the list: Nancy Carroll in her first dramatic effort, *The Devil's Holiday*, and Gloria Swanson in *The Trespasser*. Shearer won. The results had people asking more questions. How was it that Norma Shearer posed with her little statuette two days before they were handed out? An October 22 news release stated that the honor for Best Actress would be decided between Ruth Chatterton and Nancy Carroll.[453] Was it just a rumor that MGM employees had been sent a memo to vote for Norma Shearer? According to Metro director Robert Z. Leonard, Shearer worked hard for it. "I wasn't surprised when she won," said Leonard. "She drove us all crazy wanting rehearsals, then endless takes. She would sit with me in the cutting room muttering to herself."[454]

AP columnist Robbin Coons took exception to the Shearer verdict and stated that many felt that Chatterton deserved better than "honorable mention." "*Sarah and Son* was her best without a doubt," he insisted.[455] Syndicated NEA correspondent Gilbert Swan complained, "We are unable to agree that Norma Shearer in *The Divorcee* proved herself the best actress. We could think of half a dozen performances we liked better: Ruth Chatterton in almost anything; Greta Garbo in *Anna Christie*; or Ann Harding—or a lot of others. I can't quite see how Miss Chatterton's work in *Sarah and Son* can be dismissed so lightly in favor of Miss Shearer."[456] Before the awards, Cecil B. DeMille, while admitting he had "profound admiration" for Chatterton, defended Shearer. "Look at Norma Shearer," he said. "I have never seen a finer performance than she gives in *The Divorcee*. No stage actress could compare with her technique, her charm and the manner in which she speaks her lines. Norma has never had five minutes of stage training."[457] DeMille, who had been directing films since 1913, had a natural bias toward the silent players. And Shearer, as she held tight to the little statuette, deserved recognition. Of the five competitors, Ruth had faced the most challenging characterization and was most likely just as satisfied to receive what Louella Parsons called an "interesting statue" given to her by Madame Schumann-Heink at the completion of *Sarah and Son*.[458]

⁂

"The First Lady of the Screen" opted to star in *Anybody's Woman*—a very popular release, which drew an "Adults Only" decree from the censors in Chicago. It was Ruth's third and last teaming with director Arzner and co-star Clive Brook, who took on the unsympathetic role of a divorced socialite/lawyer named Neil Dunlap. While on a drinking spree, Dunlap marries Pansy Gray (Chatterton), a cynical chorus girl whom he had once defended on charges of indecent exposure (on stage). Arzner included a number of atmospheric touches. They had grit. In the opening shot, we see Pansy with a ukulele, her leg swung over a chair, belting out a blues song to take her mind off the heat. In the next scene, she and her landlord (dancer Tom Patricola) offer a crude burlesque of the Apache Dance. The two were coached by Joyzelle, who would alarm censors in 1932 with her provocative lesbian dance in DeMille's *Sign of the Cross*.

Pansy sees marriage as a chance to turn her life around. She is determined to make good, although Dunlap's friends, even the servants, snub her attempts. Dunlap himself is not exactly crazy about Pansy, even though she rescues him from depression and drink and saves his career. When a wealthy client, Gustave Saxon (Paul Lukas), takes overt interest in Pansy, she is outraged and slaps his face. Dunlap, however, is more concerned about the money he might lose if she isn't "compliant." After the mismatched couple separate, things are resolved by the long arm of coincidence. The viewer is supposed to suspend disbelief as an electric fan, set at a certain angle, purportedly carries Dunlap's confession of love across a hotel courtyard and through an open window to where Pansy is sitting.[459]

In New York, Mordaunt Hall found the climactic scene disappointing and "absurdly unconvincing." Another astute critic commented, "It is only the excellent work of Miss Chatterton and Clive Brook which saves this concluding episode from becoming altogether absurd."[460] Hall acknowledged Arzner's ability, but found the film "preachy." A number of critics made a point of saying that men made a poor showing in Arzner's films and that her work had a "feminine feeling." At one point, Pansy herself declares that she never had any reason to look up to men and frankly

As Pansy Gray in *Anybody's Woman* (courtesy of Photofest).

didn't see much difference between the male species and insects. Arzner, anticipating critical flack for being a woman, had refused screen credit earlier in her career. Now she defended her work. "Try as a man may," she said, "he will never be able to get the woman's viewpoint. Many stories demand treatment at the hands of a woman, not only from the script side but also in the direction, and here a woman should be allowed to direct in all cases."[461]

Chatterton's portrayal of Pansy is tough, restrained, and combustible when necessary. She's entirely believable. She *is* Pansy. It's as if Chatterton took a pill and disappeared. *Anybody's Woman* easily ranks as one of her best performances. The film's most powerful scene has Pansy, the uneasy hostess of a fashionable dinner party, getting a little too tight for everyone's comfort. Dunlap's client (Lukas) has encouraged her drinking. Another "gentleman" maneuvers his hand under the table and onto her lap. Pansy rips into him—demanding that Dunlap do something about it. It is a riveting, drunk scene that Chatterton gives us and makes the viewer shrink with humiliation. She is painfully real, out-of-control, and rightly so. Both men fill the bill as loathsome predators. Arzner brings her point of view home and scores. If Chatterton's empathy for such women as Pansy was a result of "bumming around in strange places," it had certainly paid off.

Critic Norbert Lusk found *Anybody's Woman* "trite" and "incredible," yet "intensely interesting." Many felt that Chatterton had a way of making something ordinary seem extraordinary. "Miss Chatterton is the *ne plus ultra* of actresses," Lusk wrote, "and once more reminds us that she is the most compelling of all the wayfarers from the stage."[462] A Pittsburgh reviewer concurred with Lusk, saying, "it is certainly the most shoddy story this brilliant star has received, but... Miss Chatterton lends a certain distinction to anything in which she appears. She has always been interesting and not infrequently positively brilliant. Here she is equally at home as an uneducated, tactless burlesque queen, and not once does she slip out of the character."[463] Drama editor Chester Bahn hailed Chatterton as the successor to Jeanne Eagels after he saw *Anybody's Woman*. He admitted to the glaring weaknesses in the scenario. "But, honestly," wrote Bahn, "they are forgotten in the living portrayal of Miss Chatterton."[464] In New York, *Anybody's Woman* broke Paramount's one-week policy and played two. The film also broke records in Los Angeles, San Francisco, Salt Lake, and Omaha.[465] Paramount quickly signed Ruth to a new contract. Her next release was an even greater success. Then began a downward spiral from which Ruth Chatterton's film career never fully recovered.

Endnotes

409   Katherine Albert, "That Old Devil, Camera," *Photoplay*, May 1929 (Albert co-wrote the script for the Bette Davis film *The Star*).
410   Frank Condon, "The Laughing Lady," *Saturday Evening Post*, November 28, 1931.
411   Katherine Albert, "That Old Devil, Camera," *Photoplay*, May 1929.
412   Richard E. Hays, "Ruth Chatterton Interview Wins High Admiration," *Seattle Times*, December 7, 1930.
413   Ruth Gordon, *Myself Among Others*, Atheuneum (NY), c. 1971, pg 326.
414   Chester B. Bahn, review of *Charming Sinners*, *Syracuse Herald*, October 6, 1929.
415   Karyn Kay and Gerald Peary, "An Interview with Dorothy Arzner, *Cinema*, 1974.
416   Barry Paris, *Louise Brooks – A Biography*, University of Minnesota Pr., c. 1989, pg 265 (from a 1977 interview with Kevin Brownlow).
417   John S. Cohen, "Ruth Chatterton Passes Miss Bow in Popularity," *Oakland Tribune*, May 11, 1930.
418   "Elocution Campaign," *Evening Post* (New Zealand), June 3, 1929.
419   David John Clive, *Theatre Tales: Pre Andrew Lloyd Webber*, iUniverse, c. 2001, pgs 125-127.
420   "Chatterton Replaces Eagels," *Film Daily*, September 19, 1929.
421   Wood Soanes, review of *The Laughing Lady*, *Oakland Tribune*, February 17, 1930.
422   Doris Denbo, review of *The Laughing Lady*, *Hollywood Daily Citizen*, February 14, 1930.
423   Thornton Delehanty, review of *The Laughing Lady*, *Evening Post* (NY), January 6, 1930.
424   Irene Cavanaugh, "Nat Pendleton's Tough Days Are Over, Or So He Hopes," *Los Angeles Illustrated Daily News*, January 28, 1933.
425   Kenneth R. Porter, "Art Claims Toll, Even From Artist," *Los Angeles Examiner*, January 12, 1930.
426   Frank Condon, "The Laughing Lady," *Saturday Evening Post*, November 28, 1931.
427   Fanya Graham, "Their Private Secretaries," *Screenplay*, September 1931.
428   Marquis Busby, "Hollywood's 'Dignified Set,'" *Silver Screen*, September 1931.
429   Robbin Coons, "'Themic' Tale," *New Adams Transcript* (MA), August 28, 1929.
430   Allan R. Ellenberger, *Ramon Novarro- A Biography on the Silent Film Idol*, McFarland, c. 2009, pg. 118.
431   Andre Soares, *Beyond Paradise-The Life of Ramon Novarro*, St. Martin's Pr., c. 2002, pgs. 128-129.
432   Otto Friedrich, *City of Nets: A Portrait of Hollywood in the 1940's*, Harper & Row, c. 1986, pg 92.
433   Louella Parsons, "Movie-Go-Round," *Los Angeles Examiner*, November 31, 1930.
434   Molly Haskell, "Wild Girls," *The Guardian*, January 8, 2004.
435   Mordaunt Hall, review of *Sarah and Son*, *New York Times*, March 13, 1930.
436   Elizabeth Yeaman, review of *Sarah and Son*, *Hollywood Daily Citizen*, April 18, 1930.

437   Pelegrine, review of *Sarah and Son, Film Daily*, March 16, 1930.
438   Harold W. Cohen, "Ruth Chatterton Scores Again in *Sarah and Son,*" *Pittsburgh Post-Gazette*, March 25, 1930.
439   Jesie Henderson, "Intuition Held Help to Women in Labor," *Ogden Standard Examiner*, April 14, 1930.
440   Anthony Slide, *Silent Players*, University of Kentucky, c. 2002, pg 98.
441   Karyn Kay and Gerald Peary, *Women and the Cinema*, E.P. Dutton (NY), c. 1977, pg 160.
442   "The Girl on the Cover," *Photoplay*, February 1930.
443   Florabel Muir, "All-Women Film Breeds Nary a Scrap," *Sunday News*, January 19, 1930.
444   Florabel Muir, "All-Women Film Breeds Nary a Scrap," *Sunday News*, January 19, 1930.
445   Louella Parsons review of *Sarah and Son, Los Angeles Examiner*, March 21, 1930.
446   Frank Condon, *The Laughing Lady,*" *Saturday Evening Post*, November 28, 1931.
447   Richard Barrio, *A Song in the Dark: Birth of the Musical Film*, Oxford Pr., c. 1995, pg 180.
448   C.L.M. review of *Paramount on Parade, Rochester Democrat and Chronicle*, April 28, 1930.
449   Mordaunt Hall, review of *The Lady of Scandal, New York Times*, June 14, 1930.
450   A.R.D., review of *The Lady of Scandal, The Evening Independent* (FL), May 31, 1930.
451   Wood Soanes, review of *The Lady of Scandal, Oakland Tribune*, August 11, 1930.
452   A.R.D. review of *The Lady of Scandal, The Evening Independent* (FL), May 31, 1930.
453   "They're Voting On Best Picture," *Reno Evening Gazette*, October 22, 1930.
454   Lawrence J. Quirk, *Norma-The Story of Norma Shearer*, St. Martin's Pr., c. 1988, pg 114.
455   Robbin Coons, "Movie Awards of Honors Not Fully Popular," *Oakland Tribune*, November 26, 1930.
456   Gilbert Swan, "In New York," *Niagara Falls Gazette*, November 29, 1930.
457   Louella Parsons, "DeMille Views on Success," *San Antonio Light*, June 29, 1930.
458   Louella Parsons column, *Los Angeles Examiner*, January 1, 1930.
459   (Note: A fan throwing voices was a plot gimmick also used in the 1936 serial *Ace Drummond*).
460   Review of *Anybody's Woman, Brooklyn Daily Eagle*, August 16, 1930.
461   "Woman's Point of View Emphasized," *Schenectady Gazette*, August 27, 1930.
462   Norbert Lusk, review of *Anybody's Woman, Picture Play*, November 1930.
463   Harold W. Cohen, review of *Anybody's Woman, Pittsburgh Post-Gazette*, September 13, 1930.
464   Chester B. Bahn, "Ruth Chatterton Hailed as Jeanne Eagels Logical Successor," *Syracuse Herald*, September 7, 1930.
465   "Dramatic Rage of the Hour," *Film Daily*, September 4, 1930.

The Magnificent Lie (Paramount).

8
The Magnificent Lie

"If it's a Paramount Picture—It's the Best Show in Town"

C hatterton's favorite Paramount film, *The Right to Love*, was completed after signing her new contract. She relaxed at Malibu Beach afterward, garbed in duck trousers and a sweater. She didn't miss the rush of New York. "Out here I have time for tennis and swimming," Ruth said. "I never want to live anywhere else. I have no desire to return to the stage."[466] West Coast exhibitors now placed Chatterton in the number two spot (behind Norma Shearer) as the biggest female box office draw.[467] An annual cinema poll at Princeton University had Chatterton and Shearer tied for second as the Senior class favorite. Garbo landed the number one spot.[468] British cinemagoers voted Chatterton the talking screen's most beautiful voice. The poll, taken by *Film Weekly*, Britain's leading film publication, had over 21,000 replies—Ruth won by an overwhelming majority.[469] Ronald Colman was first among the gents. It was no surprise when Ruth was asked to accompany Alister MacDonald, a British cinema architect and son of the Prime Minister, on a tour of the Paramount lot. Ruth had every reason to be content. Then, in an abrupt turnabout, she shocked the film industry by announcing her parting-of-the-ways with Paramount Pictures. Ruth, along with William Powell and Kay Francis, were the chosen triumvirate in the infamous Warner raid on the studio. Chatterton, being the stellar favorite, sweetened the deal. In what some critics called revenge, Paramount rushed her through a quartet of what many considered to be her worst pictures.

✦

Ruth realized that her popularity wasn't based solely on talent or voice. "In the theater they come to witness a performance," she said. "They admire your work and go home and forget about you. In the movies they come to see your work and take you home with them, figuratively. You become one of the family. And they don't want any one in the family whom they don't love. If I've been successful, it's only because I've either succeeded in making the public feel sorry for me in my pictures, or because I've made them love me."[470] Journalist Radie Harris chatted with Ruth one afternoon in Malibu about *The Right to Love*, which would turn out to be her last critical and financial success for Paramount. Ruth had dropped out of *The Royal Family of Broadway* with Fredric March and suggested that Paramount adapt Susan Glaspell's 1928 novel *Brook Evans* for the screen. Re-titled *The Right to Love*, the film provided her a rare opportunity to essay two roles—mother and daughter—a difficult undertaking for "talkies." "It will be potter's clay in the hands of Miss Chatterton," Harris predicted.[471] She was right.

The Right to Love, adapted by Zoe Akins, captured the spirit of the Glaspell novel—that nothing should stand in the way of love. Taking place in a rural setting, we discover a farm girl cheated of happiness by the death of her young lover. She is forced to marry a bitterly religious man, who is aware she is with child. Years later, she struggles to make

With David Manners in *The Right to Love* (Paramount).

sure that her own daughter is assured the romance that she was denied. But when the daughter learns the truth of her parentage, she turns against the mother.

The Right to Love was praised not only for the excellent performances, but for the cutting-edge "Dunning process" which allowed Ruth, as the mother in the story, to walk behind Ruth the daughter and fasten a locket around her neck. Both faces were visible and the conversation perfectly recorded. One critic observed, "It is interesting to watch Miss Chatterton, as the mother, steal scene after scene from Miss Chatterton, as the daughter."[472] The breathtaking camerawork by Charles Lang received an Academy Award nomination. *The Right to Love* was actually a triple role for Ruth. She plays Naomi Childers at eighteen and later the middle-aged Naomi and her daughter Brook. The challenge was to adjust her voice to the separate ages and personalities of her portrayals. "Ruth Chatterton is doing a superb piece of virtuosity with her opportunity to play virtually three roles, and make each one a triumph of characterization," praised the

Los Angeles Record. "The film is one of the most striking of the year."[473] Reviewers felt that the remarkable ease of Chatterton's performance defied adjectives. The shrewdly critical Elizabeth Yeaman, columnist for the *Hollywood Daily Citizen,* had to admit, "Miss Chatterton gives a dual characterization which probably reaches the height of her emotional prowess. [She] can sound the depths of emotion with more power than any other actress on the screen"[474] *Motion Picture News* agreed, "Miss Chatterton enacts both parts so expertly that the audience, forgetting that the star is playing both roles, finds its sympathies divided."[475] Director Richard Wallace was reported to have needled Ruth while previewing footage in the projection room. The lights went on, Wallace turned around, saw Ruth, and said, "Go on, get out of here, all three of you!"[476]

Ruth credited cinematographer Charles Lang for helping her achieve the visual of the mother role. This was their third of six films together. Ruth liked his work so much that Paramount gave Lang a contract. "Lighting can place deep shadows beneath the eyes and lines about the mouth," she explained. "These lines are accentuated by grayish make-up, traced so that the lights will pick up the shadow effect. But you will have to think yourself old to put across the feel of your part."[477] The performances were also enhanced by the new Western Electric "noiseless recording system." Ruth's influence and input in the production was substantial. She encouraged the studio to cast Irving Pichel as Caleb, the cold, God-fearing husband. Pichel had directed Ruth's west coast tour in *The Devil's Plum Tree.* An author and drama instructor, Pichel was initially hired to be dialogue coach for *The Right to Love.* For his first time before the camera, Pichel made a strong impression. *The Right to Love* was on several critics' "Top 10 Lists for 1930."[478]

David Manners, as the young lover who is killed in a turbine accident, considered the role a career break. "Now that Ruth Chatterton has taken him up," said one interviewer, "his social success is assured. He greatly admires Chatterton and his apartment is plastered with photographs of her."[479] Manners' biographer, Donald McMurchy, wrote, "The movie began a firm friendship with Chatterton whom David described as adorable. 'I went to her home a lot,' he said, 'she was quite a lady.'"[480] As a frequent visitor, Manners was introduced to interesting guests such as Auriol Lee. Auriol had acted with Ruth during the Henry Miller days. By 1931, she was focused on directing and aviation. Auriol was the first woman to fly across the equator (1927) en route to Kenya. Covering an area of over 1,000 miles, she received a medal for her unusual feat. She would be influential in developing Ruth's own passion for flying. Auriol was staying with Ruth while advising (uncredited) the production of her next film, *Unfaithful*, based on a story by playwright John van Druten. No amount of input, however, could rescue van Druten's poor excuse for a story.

With Paul Lukas in *Unfaithful* (Paramount).

John Cromwell, who would helm Bette Davis' breakthrough performance in *Of Human Bondage,* directed *Unfaithful.* It was Chatterton's
eighth film centered on the hot box office topic of philandering. *Unfaithful* is absorbing at first. We are introduced to an American woman, Fay
Kilkerry (Chatterton), who discovers that her husband, a British Viscount
(Paul Cavanagh), has been cheating on her with her sister-in-law. Concerned that her emotionally delicate brother, a shell-shock victim, might
commit suicide if he knew the truth, Fay keeps quiet. "You've got me
trapped," she angrily tells her husband, before engaging in a steady stream
of cocktails. "You won't know me from now on!" Without any solid explanation as to why, we then witness Fay's self-induced degradation.

Fay careens out of control in an array of gorgeous Travis Banton gowns
as well as tights and a high hat while seeking flirtations and implausible
diversions. She's a female Pagliacci hiding her sorrow with a mask of gay-
ety. To say that author van Druten has far-fetched ideas is an understate-
ment. As one critic put it, "When Miss Chatterton got up at a party and
endeavored to sing a southern blues, a real dirt number ["Mama's in the
Doghouse Now"] she fell down dismally. She endeavored to coon shout,
and she can't, we must leave that to Ethel Waters."[481] On another occasion,
Fay brings home two American sailors. Her dinner guests look on with
horror as the trio shoots craps under the drawing-room piano. Chatterton
throws the dice and whoops, "Come on you little black-eyed babies. Roll
over on your flat backs and laugh up in yo' Mammy's eyes!" A typical review complained, "It is so improbable as to be positively ridiculous." Even
author Theodore Dreiser made a point of complaining, "Ruth Chatterton
has done very sympathetic work, but along comes Marlene Dietrich, or
someone wearing a high hat and tights, and so they compel this serious actress to imitate that sort of thing ... and she can't do it."[482] Dreiser, recently
returned from Hollywood, was fuming about what they had done to *An*

American Tragedy—his treatise on America's obsession with money and social status. He called movies an "opiate" filled with hokum and insincere "sexy stuff." He felt that instead of her studio finding important vehicles for her, Chatterton was being used.

Unfaithful finds resolve when Fay's husband is killed in an automobile accident while running off with said sister-in-law. Still determined to save her clueless brother's hopeless marriage, even though he's told her she's "just plain rotten," rebel Fay concocts a story that the guilty duo were out looking for *her*. She was being unfaithful—spending the night with an artist (Paul Lukas). Despite her utterly British accent, Chatterton captures this dispirited character as written, but one can only wonder what she thought of the convoluted plot. "It is difficult to see any excuse for so trashy and palpably artificial a story," wrote Tom Delehanty for the *New York Sun*.[483] A Los Angeles critic added, "The whole business takes on an entertainment value beyond its just deserts. Miss Chatterton gives her part a restraint and a pathetic gallantry worthy of a more carefully constructed tale."[484] The happy ending with Chatteron and the perpetually somber Paul Lukas enjoying a carefree spin around London feels perfunctory. As far as her singing, Ruth told one columnist, "For the millions involved, I'm afraid I should do almost anything."[485]

Creighton Peet, for *Outlook and Independent*, nailed it when he complained, "I couldn't get the slightest bit interested in Ruth Chatterton and her troubles in *Unfaithful*. A few more movies like this one and I'll be off love for life and go round snarling at people and popping little children over the head with gin bottles."[486] The aura of sacrifice displayed by Chatterton's character is especially irritating. Another critic stated, "Personally, we believe that there are limits to enjoying a tale of martyrdom. One hopes that Paramount didn't put Ruth Chatterton into *Unfaithful* as a punishment for her sin in accepting a million dollar bid to desert them."[487] Columnist

Mollie Merrick agreed. "If Paramount wanted adequate revenge on Ruth Chatterton for going over to Warner Brothers, they have it in *Unfaithful*."[488] Word was out. From January through November 1931, the press coverage of Ruth's signing with Warner Brothers, and that studio's ensuing battle with Paramount, received an inordinate amount of attention.

⚜

In Emily Susan Carman's 2008 study *Independent Stardom: Female Stars and Freelance Labor in 1930's Hollywood*, she explains the process of "star raiding," which is basically an actor's ability to negotiate for a better salary upon receiving an offer from a rival studio. There were no regulations preventing it. Using a counter-offer allowed the actor to break the old contract if he or she chose. "Perhaps the most powerful female star who worked at Warner Bros. was Ruth Chatterton," wrote Carman. "[Her] lucrative contract gave her a substantial amount of creative control… she had costar, director, and story approval, sole star billing, and maintained control over the [commercial use] of her image."[489] Talent agent Myron Selznick initiated star raiding by bargaining a deal for Chatterton and two other Paramount clients, William Powell and Kay Francis, to move to Warner. Ruth's contract offer, dated February 27, 1931, outlines her salary as follows: "Paid $675,000 per year for a period of two years in which the artist will make three pictures a year. Artist paid $35,000 upfront after signing contract, and rest of $640,000 will be paid in eighty weekly installments (approximately $8,000 a week)."[490] William Powell was on board for $6,000 a week and Kay Francis $4,000.

Outraged, Paramount sued. "They were stolen from under my nose," recalled producer Jesse L. Lasky.[491] Columnist Hubbard Keavy surmised, "The loss of Powell and Miss Francis didn't bother Paramount officials

Ruth confers with Buddah, 1930 (Paramount).

much, but the expected loss of Chatterton, the money maker, caused them some dismay."[492] Warner Brothers appeased their rival by allowing Francis to return for Ernst Lubitsch's sparkling *Trouble in Paradise* (1932). Chatterton stayed to make three more pictures for Paramount. Her final contract for Warner was signed September 9, 1931. In the heart of the Depression with a two-year salary in excess of a million dollars, Ruth had no room to complain. As far as Selznick's plundering of Paramount, he felt he was obligated to get "the maximum within the possible."[493]

Thanks to Selznick, film stars also had more versatile contract options. Aside from her "paltry" $2,500 a week at Paramount, Ruth may have had other reasons for leaving.[494] Film historian and educator Dale McConathy noted, "When Paramount began to spend huge sums to promote Dietrich, Chatterton perceived a threat to her position as queen of the lot, so she switched to Warner Brothers."[495] Chatterton's popularity gained her bargaining power, which Selznick maneuvered to her advantage. The Warner contract, however, included an ironclad pact that did not permit Chatterton to be loaned out to another studio.[496] When asked to comment in April 1931, Chatterton put it plainly,

> I have had no battle with Paramount. I have none now. They have been marvelous to me. They have given by courtesy what Warner Brothers gave me by contract. All except money. I mean I have sat in on every story conference—helped produce my own pictures... I cannot understand all the excitement of this move! They made me an offer. I turned it down. I took an offer twice as much. Is there anything wrong with that? As for the gamble Paramount took on me: of course, they took a gamble. A tremendous one. And I appreciate it, but appreciation does not make me independent. Money does.

At the end of two years more I can really live without working... It has hurt more than I like to say that people have said I am ungrateful to those who believed in me... I want to make my last three pictures for Paramount my best to date.[497]

Sadly, Ruth's final films for Paramount weren't worth the effort. When filming wrapped on *Unfaithful* at the end of January, Ruth went to New York for three weeks. Aside from attending the new plays, Ruth enjoyed her hobby of people-watching: hoboes, old women flower vendors, and newsboys. She listened to what they had to say. Walking through the crowded East Side, she paused to talk to women on doorsteps, a secondhand clothes dealer, and lost souls along the waterfront. Her motive wasn't philanthropy, although she often left money and an encouraging word to those she met. Ruth was always supplied with bags of candy for tenement children who surrounded her with their hodgepodge of languages.[498] While in New York, Ruth also took time out for business. She visited Dorothy Arzner at the Long Island studio. The two were planning on filming a story based on the semi-autobiographical novel *Not So Quiet: The Stepdaughters of War* by Helen Zenna Smith. It was a feminist view of the issues explored in Erich Maria Remarque's *All Quiet on the Western Front*. Ruth's friend from the Henry Miller troupe, Josephine Lovett, had completed a scenario which detailed the experiences of two women ambulance drivers during WWI. The stage version, starring Katherine Alexander and Warren William, had lasted only twenty-four performances. While playing at Broadway's Empire, one review stated that the play "never quite succeeded in becoming itself."[499] Literally speaking, the same can be said of the film.

Upon Ruth's return to the coast, she and Lovett conferred further on the project. Filming began in May 1931.[500] Ruth was assigned the role

Publicity for the uncompleted
Stepdaughters of War (Paramount).

of Kit Smith, an ambulance driver who witnesses the horrific effects of war, its futility, and the nationalism that fuels it. She begins to resent her mother bragging about her brave daughter's sacrifice. War-shocked and hardened, in a moment of emotional need, Kit turns to Geoffrey (a role assigned to Gary Cooper).[501] By the story's end, Geoffrey is literally and figuratively emasculated and Kit is left spiritually sterile. Soon after filming began, it was suspended. Footage from two scenes was included in the July 1931 Paramount release *The House that Shadows Built* (a twentieth-anniversary celebration of the studios past and future). In one excerpt, Chatterton is confronted about a letter she had written home to her sister. "You ought to know better than to write such things!" her commanding officer barks. "Well, it's true," Chatterton answers. "I'll tell lies to my aunt and my mother, they expect 'em. 'Such fun behind the lines!' 'So splendid to be really in it!' But, I want Trix to know the truth, not a lot of mush about this life out here." The letter is ripped up and Ruth gets latrine duty for her insubordination. In the second scene, Chatterton returns to headquarters to report that an ambulance driver named Newman, who had been missing, was outside. Before she is allowed to explain, her superior interrupts, "Send her in to report! There has been enough slacking in this unit. I'll have no more of it!" We next see Chatterton carrying in a dead body. "I brought Newman back to report!" she announces bitterly. When asked about the film in 1974, Dorothy Arzner stated, "There was a wonderful script called *Stepdaughters of War*. I'd worked on it for months for Chatterton, but when she signed with Warners it had to be called off. Warners offered her everything an actress could desire. Much later, we were planning it again with Dietrich. It was a big antiwar picture."[502] Arzner failed to explain the footage shot after Chatterton signed her first Warner contract. In June 1931, it was announced that *Stepdaughters of War* was postponed for six months.

⁂

The House that Shadows Built was frequently double-billed with Ruth's summer release for 1931, *The Magnificent Lie*, which proved to be a critical and box office disappointment. Ruth considered it the worst film she ever made. As far as the studio punishing Ruth for leaving, Paramount executive Ben Schulberg countered, "It would all react on us, and why should we take such a foolish revenge?"[503] Ruth felt differently. She later commented, "Once I was passing a theater which had in big letters over the marquee that famous slogan, 'If it's a Paramount Picture, it's the best show in town.' Right under it was, *The Magnificent Lie*." Before leaving Paramount, Ruth made it clear that the original story, *Laurels and the Lady*, purchased at her request, had been bastardized. "All that was retained was the one situation of a woman impersonating a French actress to fool a blind man," she fumed. "The motivation for her deception was perverted and all sympathy for the character and the beauty of her sacrifice lost in the picture *The Magnificent Lie*."[504] Chatterton was justified in what she had to say.

Laurels and the Lady, a poignant love story set in South Africa, tells of a young unpublished poet, Willy Childers, who loses his sight shortly after seeing an inspiring performance by the French stage star Rose Duchene in Dumas' *La Dame aux Camelias*. A young woman, Poll Patchouli, who runs a *parfumerie* and known for her precise impersonations of Duchene, is persuaded by Willy's friends to impersonate the actress to pick up his spirits. She obliges. By doing so, Patchouli falls in love. Willy is convinced that she is Duchene. The two become inseparable. The remainder of the story tells of Patchouli's sacrifice to keep the illusion alive. She reads Willy bogus reviews praising his (unbeknownst to him) unpublished poetry. In the years to come, the two live quietly together as man and wife, even though that, too, is a fiction.

On screen, *The Magnificent Lie* was an apt title. *Laurels and the Lady* was lost in the telling. Set in the Deep South, it's basically an ensemble piece about a cabaret singer, Poll (Chatterton), impersonating a French actress as a prank on a blind WWI veteran, Bill (Ralph Bellamy). Participating in the charade are Bill's buddy (Stuart Erwin), two French actors (Charles Boyer and Tyler Brook), and the French star herself, Rose Duchene (Francoise Rosay). Counter to the original story, Poll eventually tells Bill the truth—the magnificent lie about herself. We are then led to believe that as a result of an automobile accident, his sight is restored.

It was preposterous stuff—miles away from the intent of *Laurels and the Lady*. This may explain the extra punch Ruth put into her best line, "Gee, what a sucker I was to get mixed up in this!" The svelte hand of Ernst Lubitsch's favorite screenwriter Samson Raphaelson (who did not get along with the film's director, Berthold Viertel) failed as well as the input of Ruth's own favorite writer, Vincent Lawrence.[505]

Critics found little to like about *The Magnificent Lie*. Even so, the film does have a sense of fun that is infectious. The actors, while not taking the story too seriously, are a joy to watch. In his first American film, Boyer in particular displays magnetism. A hint of chemistry between Boyer and Chatterton plays nicely into a couple of scenes. It's a pity they never teamed in something worthwhile. Boyer was anxious to impress Chatterton and wanted her to like him. His unfamiliarity with the language prompted him to ask for advice from men on the set. They promptly set him up. He walked up to Ruth and said, in his most polished charming way, "How I could go for you, baby!" Boyer shuddered every time he recalled Ruth recoiling from him with obvious dismay. "When he found out how brash he had been he hid for a week." It was freely rumored that Ruth found Boyer most attractive. "During his first few months in Hollywood he was an attentive cavalier to the charming Chatterton," wagged one columnist.[507]

Time magazine thought *The Magnificent Lie* "un-magnificent"; Viertel's direction "perfunctory"; Ralph Bellamy "wooden"; and did not spare Ruth. "The role of the cabaret girl," it stated, "was perhaps selected for Ruth Chatterton because it gave her a chance to display her overestimated versatility."[508] The *New York Times* agreed as much, saying that the film was "apparently designed to its leading actress's abilities in filling several parts all at once."[509] *Film Daily* noted the poor direction, the aimless story, and Chatterton, "swamped in a part that gives her little chance."[510]

Wood Soanes' critique championed the star and praised, "The histrionic ability and resource of Ruth Chatterton lifted an impossible story... into something resembling credibility."[511] A Los Angeles critic agreed, saying, "Even though her role is not up to the standard of many of her former ones, Miss Chatterton makes the café singer an impressive character."[512] Bellamy's only recollection of the film was the plastic shell cap he wore to disguise the large gap between his two front teeth. "It worked fine, except for *s*'s and *f*'s," he wrote in his autobiography. "In a two-shot scene with Ruth, I was suddenly aware that my cap wasn't there. I stopped the scene. All of us, cast and crew, cautiously searched. In the midst of our bent-over quest, Ruth looked up and I saw my two front teeth stuck to her forehead."[513] Music from a violin or portable organ engulfed the set following each take. "This, I was told," explained Bellamy, "was designed

With Ralph Bellamy in *The Magnificent Lie* (Paramount).

to keep a calm and harmonious atmosphere on the set"—an antidote to soothe the Chatterton temperament, no doubt. After the final frame of *The Magnificent Lie* was shot, Ruth headed for Biltmore Beach in Santa Barbara to recover.

In Chatterton's cabaret act for *The Magnificent Lie,* she introduced the new Bing Crosby hit "Just One More Chance"—no one was complaining. Canadian writer, Joseph Worrell, compares Chatterton's deep vibrato to such French chanteuses as Frehel and Damia—singers who Ruth, no doubt, saw in person during her sojourns to Paris. "It's a testament to Ruth's skills as a modal actress," says Worrell, "and that she wasn't only about clipped English diction." Still, one can see why critics thought Ruth was stretching her versatility a bit thin. From the crap-shooting, blues-warbling Lady Kilkerry in *Unfaithful* to the cabaret singer who does spur of the moment death scenes from *Camille* in *The Magnificent Lie,* one could paraphrase the old cliché: "she brought everything but the kitchen sink" into her performance.

⁂

"Don't take any notice of the script, darling," Ruth told British theatrical legend Ivor Novello. "We'll build that part up!" She was coaxing him to co-star in *Once a Lady.* He balked at the idea after reading the scenario. "I hated the part," said Novello, "but one look into Ruth's eyes and, against my better judgment, I said I would do it."[514] Novello would provide a more lasting contribution to Hollywood as a contract writer. He provided dialogue for *Tarzan, the Ape Man.* "Me Tarzan. You Jane." Such is fate. And fate, as Anna Keremazoff, Ruth's character in *Once a Lady,* reminds us over and over again, is what life is all about. "What can I do? It ees de fate!" she declares. By the end of the film, it is obvious that it isn't fate after all; it must be the story, the dialogue, the direction, or all of the above that's the real problem.

Chatterton had met Novello at a Clifton Webb after-theatre party in Manhattan. "Someone pushed me to the piano, and I played Isolde's *Liebestod*," recalled Novello. "As I sounded the last few chords I happened to look where Ruth was sitting… there were tears running down her face. She came over to the piano and, putting an arm around my shoulder, softly whispered: 'You poor little boy. You play the *Liebestod* like that and you're going to Hollywood!'" Hollywood was the furthest thing from Novello's mind. He was enjoying success on Broadway with his play *The Truth Game*. Doug Fairbanks, Jr. and wife Joan Crawford, also visiting New York, were completely taken with the British star, as was Irving Thalberg, who bought the rights to *The Truth Game*. Surprisingly, Novello accepted the producer's offer to be a writer for MGM.

The secret of Novello's appeal was best put by his good friend Noel Coward, who described Novello as "violently glamorous" and "a little

With Ivor Novello in *Once a Lady* (Paramount).

vulgar."[515] Novello would become part of Chatterton's gay coterie of male friends which included Coward, Ramon Novarro, and David Manners. He arrived in Hollywood expecting to work on the scenario for *The Truth Game*, but Thalberg was satisfied with what two of his staff writers had already come up with. Instead, Novello undertook the task of creating a screenplay for *Tarzan*. "I never wrote such rubbish in my life," he later admitted.[516] Ruth sensed Novello's frustration. He was vocal in expressing his disappointment about having no film acting offers. So Ruth secured him a role in *Once a Lady* as the Parisian artist with whom she has an affair. Novello was attracted to the idea of working with the reputable Guthrie McClintic, who was directing. On screen, Novello was seen briefly, but his relaxed, natural performance stood out, even while mouthing the naughty nonsense that scenarist Zoe Akins concocted. "What a funny little pink tongue you have!" he declares while pouring Anna a cup of tea.

Once a Lady was a rehash of the Pola Negri silent film *Three Sinners* (1928), which *The New York Times* had declared a "totally unbelievable piece of work." The *Times* felt the same way about *Once a Lady*. Why Ruth opted to take on the role is puzzling. Shades of *Madame X* hover over this hackneyed tale that revolves around Anna, a Russian émigré. Immediately after a Paris honeymoon, Anna and husband Jimmy Fenwick (Geoffrey Kerr) arrive in London. Mournfully trilling every "r," she warns him, "This marriage of ours is a great mistake!" She reassures him, "There is always vodka when one is unhappy, and if one is too unhappy there are rivers everywhere." On that cheery note, she meets her new in-laws. They are highly affronted when she blithely announces, "Very soon now, we are going to have a leetle bah-bee." One look at their faces and Anna suggests, "A cup of tea with some cognac would be so nice!" Her exotic temperament vs. her husband's priggish family inevitably finds Anna thrown out of her London mansion, the husband taking custody of their daughter. These early scenes are "high camp" at its best and Chatterton, oddly enough, seems to be having a good time

Years later, we find Anna in Paris, a hardened, peroxide blonde who could double for Mae West. She refers to herself as a *coquette*—a kept woman. At a crucial moment, there is a chance meeting between Anna and her long-lost daughter (Jill Esmond), who believes her mother dead. Without divulging her true identity, Anna maneuvers the girl from a reckless life toward a stable marriage. The scenes between Chatterton and Esmond (wife of Laurence Olivier) are easily the film's best. *Once a Lady,* designed as another Chatterton tear fest, has moments when her genius as an actress surfaces through the preposterous muck for a glimpse into something compelling.

New York critic Mordaunt Hall found the dialogue in *Once a Lady* "awkward," but admitted, "Miss Chatterton handles her Russian-English accent with marked ability and her acting is good."[517] Although critics commented that Ruth looked dazzling and photographed beautifully, not everyone felt she was at her best. John S. Cohen for the *New York Sun* wrote, "[Chatterton] never makes a false move, being the sure-footed thespian that she is, but she goes through it a bit listlessly. She probably wasn't very interested in the story. Neither was I."[518] Pittsburgh critic Karl Krug lamented, "It grieves me painfully to see this outstanding First Lady sold down the river in such nincompoop talking screen fare. Miss Chatterton's once large following will dwindle to nothing, I fear, if this keeps up. It is hoped that when the actress reports on the Warner lot there will be something worth while in the bag for her."[519] Krug was not alone when he blamed the "none too fertile imagination" of Zoe Akins' scenario. Los Angeles critic Harrison Carroll pointed to Akins' "agenda," arguing that she was "afraid of diverting sympathy from the heroine." "There is not, in fact, a single male character who is really sympathetic," he wrote. "But come to think of it, isn't this characteristic of Zoe Akins' plays?"[520] Others blamed director McClintic for allowing the insipid dialogue. Carroll added, "The much heralded Ivor Novello comes dangerously near to being coy." As for Novello, his father's death provided the perfect excuse to back out of his MGM contract and return to England, where his talents were more appreciated.

⁂

It was an open secret that Ruth was not pleased with her last few pictures. Before her final film was released, she was asked about *Once a Lady* and whether or not she had made a mistake in making three dramas in a row. Ruth seemed perturbed. "I don't know," she snapped. "Right now I'm too tired to know anything. I've worked so hard up to the last moment doing one picture after another with only a few days in between. So until the time comes I'm not going to think about anything in connection with business. I'm going to the mountains, where there are no telephones or postmen; where the studio can't reach me and where I can just be a bum. Just loaf when I want to loaf, rest, sleep, play—do whatever I please and not think. It's almost too heavenly to believe."[521]

Before she left town for Lake Arrowhead, Ralph accompanied Ruth to a concert given by the African-American tenor Roland Hayes. Europe allowed Hayes the opportunity to establish himself as a professional concert singer before America would take notice. He paved the way for Paul Robeson, and Marian Anderson. Ruth, no doubt, was moved by the depth and richness Hayes brought to spirituals and the transcendent beauty he gave German lieder, like Schubert's "Nacht und Traume." The balm of music prepared her for several weeks of rest in the mountain air. "My blood pressure is down to 90 and my temperature is one degree subnormal," Ruth informed critic Harrison Carroll. "I want to walk in the woods and be outdoors all day. I'm taking a lot of books along and want to spend hours reading. Perhaps by the time I come back I will have regained my sense of judgment. Then I can intelligently plan for my next picture."[522] Ruth didn't entirely blame Paramount for the poor choices in which she had submerged her talent. On her vacation, she was accompanied by a female friend and one maid. "It will be a regular hen party," she said. Ralph stayed behind to focus on his polo game and would practice daily on a large wooden horse ensconced in a huge cage in their backyard.

By the time Ruth arrived on the Warner lot, her final Paramount release, *Tomorrow and Tomorrow*, a variation on Eugene O'Neill's Pulitzer Prize-winning *Strange Interlude,* hit theatres. Ruth personally selected the 1931 Philip Barry stage success, which had played the Henry Miller, with Zita Johann and Herbert Marshall. Paramount bought the rights for $85,000.[523] *Tomorrow and Tomorrow* was a play of subtle psychology. Any romance involved was incidental. Like *Strange Interlude*, it had no open conflict. Critics were skeptical that it would translate to film and felt Ruth was taking on too much. "The result of the picture," said Louella Parsons, "will be upon her head."[524]

The verdict on *Tomorrow and Tomorrow* was mixed. *The New York Times* thought it excellent screen fare. Mordaunt Hall's review praised the grace and understanding of Ruth's "restrained portrayal" of Eve, a frustrated, childless wife. The husband, played by Robert Ames, is obsessed with horses and conveniently dozes off whenever she brings up the subject of babies. Paul Lukas played a brain specialist who recognizes the wife's malady, then provides her with the necessary biological component. Chatterton wasn't exactly keen on having Lukas in the film. Aside from having trouble learning his English lines, Lukas' wife and Ruth weren't speaking to each other. Ruth wanted to avoid having an "atmosphere" on the set.[525] Apparently, she was correct. "Paul Lukas in the part of the eminent surgeon," cautioned Hall's review, "weakens the narrative for those who saw Herbert Marshall in the same role on stage."[526] At the end of one difficult shoot, Ruth was to slap Lukas across the face. She gave him such a wallop that the actor's ears were ringing. Lukas lost control, grabbed Chatterton and "shook her until all her dignity, and most of their mutual indignation was gone."[527] Witnesses said that following the flare-up, their mutual apologies were "very superficial." This undoubtedly riveting scene was deleted from the film. It would be five years before they worked together again.

When a child is born to Eve, the husband, completely clueless, develops a paternal instinct which finally bonds the couple. The audience at the Times Square Paramount was sympathetic to this unusual and ab-

Paul Lukas advises making a baby "quick" in *Tomorrow and Tomorrow* (courtesy of Photofest).

sorbing triangle. On the west coast, Los Angeles critic W.E. Oliver was surrounded by football fans who were there to see "In Person" the All-American half-back Ernie Pinckert. Oliver said that the audience was mystified by what was on screen. When Paul Lukas advised Ruth to have a baby and "Have one quick!" the gridiron crowd was "moved to mirth." Oliver felt the warmth of the stage play was missing in the film. "Miss Chatterton," he wrote, "sets the dramatic pitch at a more intense level. She plays the tempted wife like a high priestess [with] her bell-like vowels, and lingering consonants."[528] Oliver thought Robert Ames as the husband a "talking ghost of a person" on screen. Ames had died shortly after the film was completed. Years earlier, Henry Miller had taken interest in Ames, who had his first real Broadway success playing Ruth's brother in *Come Out of the Kitchen.* His untimely death on November 27, 1931, was a tragic mix of sleeping powders, large quantities of whiskey, a kidney ailment, medication for alcohol withdrawal, and desperate phone calls to his current love interest, Ruth's friend Ina Claire. [529] Claire was in the process of divorcing actor John Gilbert. Four times divorced, Ames' own matrimonial muddle and propensity for alcohol found resolve at the age of forty-two.

    "If I played in *Tomorrow and Tomorrow* back in 1885," said Ruth, "Anthony Comstock would have run me out of New York. But times have changed. The modern generation will understand the plight of the wife."[530] A review from *Nation* magazine quipped that Barry's play was plagiarized from the Old Testament story of a childless Shumanite woman promised a son by the prophet Elisha. Put in that context, it is surprising that the Bible was not among the 15 tons of objectionable books that Comstock destroyed during his career as United States Postal Inspector. (Comstock's causes and methods were admired by the young law student J. Edgar Hoover.) MGM would tackle similar cerebral cinematic fare with its 1932 release, *Strange Interlude*. Doctor Clark Gable facilitated patient Norma Shearer's pregnancy so she could avoid the dose of insanity in her husband's gene pool. In 1936, Chair of the Department of English at Rutgers, Charles Huntington Whitman, stated, "The likeness of *Tomorrow and Tomorrow* to O'Neill's *Strange Interlude* has often been remarked, and the comparison is not usually favorable to Barry."[531] Chatterton insisted that *Tomorrow and Tomorrow* was one of her favorite roles. Apparently this was true, as she revived it on stage in 1940.

⚜

Ruth's farewell to Paramount concluded with a quartet of undistinguished box office disappointments. Among movie fans, a Chatterton film was gaining a reputation as a "must to avoid." Ruth had no regrets about leaving the studio and stated philosophically, "There are very few incidents in my life that I would change. If I removed the experience of deep sorrow and despair, it would be like washing out important colors in a character portrait."[532] Nonetheless, Ruth was deeply concerned about her first Warner Brothers film. "The new responsibility is sobering," she admitted. "If it was my own money, I'd take a chance. I did it many times in the theater. But with Warners assuming the risk, I feel I have to be cautious. I am so afraid of picking a story that would not give them a financial success."[533]

Endnotes

466 "The Girl on the Cover," *Photoplay*, February 1930.

467 *Los Angeles Times*, November 23, 1930.

468 "Princeton's Favorites," *Film Daily*, May 22, 1930.

469 "Ruth Chatterton Prize Winner for Voice," *Reno Evening Gazette*, July 5, 1930.

470 Samuel Richard Mook, "They've Hit the Bulls-Eye," *Picture Play*, May 1930.

471 Radie Harris, "Star Gazing," *Chester Times* (PA), September 26, 1930.

472 Frederick James Smith, review of *The Right to Love*, *The New Movie*, April 1931.

473 Llewellyn Miller, review of *The Right to Love*, *Los Angeles Record*, December 26, 1930.

474 Elizabeth Yeaman, review of *The Right to Love*, *Hollywood Daily Citizen*, January 23, 1931.

475 Don Ashbaugh, review of *The Right to Love*, *Motion Picture News*, December 6, 1930.

476 B. Atlass, review of *The Right to Love*, *Decatur Daily Review*, January 26, 1931.

477   Alice L. Tildesley, "It Pays to be Homely-And How," *Oakland Tribune*, August 9, 1931.

478   In 2009, *The Right to Love* received a full restoration. The print is owned by Universal and at this writing is still waiting for release on DVD.

479   Edward Nagle, "David to His Mother—Perhaps," *Picture Play*, March 1931.

480   Donald McMurchy, "A Perfect Gentleman," *Classic Images*, 1999.

481   Don, review of *Unfaithful*, *The Gleaner* (Jamaica), June 9, 1931.

482   "Theodore Dreiser Blows Up...," *Syracuse Herald*, April 12, 1931.

483   Tom Delehanty, review of *Unfaithful*, *New York Evening Post*, March 9, 1931.

484   Llewellyn Miller, review of *Unfaithful*, *Los Angeles Record*, March 6, 1931.

485   Malcolm H. Oettinger, "Another Lady!" *Picture Play*, June 1931.

486   Peet Creighton, review of *Unfaithful*, *Outlook and Independent*, Jan-April 1931.

487   Ethel Max, review of *Unfaithful*, *Capital Times* (WI), March 23, 1931.

488   Mollie Merrick, "Stars and Talkies of Hollywood," *The Spokesman-Review*, March 6, 1931.

489   Emily Susan Carman, *Independent Stardom*, University of California, Los Angeles, c. 2008, pg 82.

490   Emily Susan Carman, *Independent Stardom*, University of California, Los Angeles, c. 2008, pgs 42-43.

491   Jesse L. Lasky, *I Blow My Own Horn*, Doubleday, c. 1957.

492   Hubbard Keavy, "Screen Life in Hollywood, *San Antonio Express*, May 17, 1931.

493   Alberto Rendon, "Los Mercaderes de Estrellas," *Cinelandia*, February 1932.

494   "Chatterton Status Not Determined," *Motion Picture Daily*, August 11, 1931.

495   Dale McConathy, *Hollywood Costume*, Harry N. Abrams, NY, c. 1976, pg 122.

496   "Ruth Stays at Warner Under Ironclad Pact," *Motion Picture Daily*, August 3, 1931.

497   Dan Van Neste, "Ruth Chatterton: 'Without a Trace of Affectation,'" *Films of the Golden Age*, Fall 1997.

498   Elizabeth Stephenson, "Hobbies of the Stars," *Key West Citizen*, August 19, 1931.

499   John Mason Brown, review of stage production *The Stepdaughters of War*, *New York Evening Post*, October 1, 1930.

500   "McClintic Assigned," *Film Daily*, May 24, 1931 (article implies that *Stepdaughters of War* was currently in production).

501   "Cooper Selected as Chatterton's Lead," *Moberly-Monitor Index*, May 23, 1931.

502   Karyn Kay and Gerald Peary, *Interview with Dorothy Arzner, Cinema*, 1974.

503   Louella Parsons column, *Los Angeles Examiner*, January 29, 1931.

504   "R. Chatterton Tells All the Para. Inside," *Motion Picture Daily*, August 25, 1931.

505   Barry Sabath, *Ernst Lubitsch and Samson Raphaelson: a Study in Collaboration*, New York University, c. 1979.

506   Jay Robert Nash and Stanley Ralph Ross, *The Motion Picture Guide L-M*, Cinebooks, c. 1988, pg 1808.

507   Elsie Randall, "Ruth Marries George And Everybody's Happy," Movie Classic, October 1932.

508   Review of *The Magnificent Lie*, *Time Magazine*, August 3, 1931.

509   Review of *The Magnificent Lie*, *New York Times*, August 2, 1931.

510   Review of *The Magnificent Lie*, *Film Daily*, July 26, 1931.

511   Wood Soanes, "Expressions Obtained On Relative Rating of Players and Directors," *Oakland Tribune*, August 9, 1931.

512   Dick Hunt, review of *The Magnificent Lie*, *Los Angeles Evening Herald*, July 24, 1931.

513   Ralph Bellamy, *When The Smoke Hit The Fan*, Doubleday NY, c. 1979, pg 118.

514   Paul Webb, *Ivor Novello: a Portrait of a Star*, Stage Directions, c. 1999.

515   William Mann, "Just Say Novello," *The Advocate*, April 2, 2002.

516   Geoffrey Macnab, "Homme Fatal," *The Guardian*, January 10, 2004.

517   Mordaunt Hall, review of *Once a Lady*, *New York Times*, November 9, 1931.

518   John S. Cohen, Jr., review of *Once a Lady*, *New York Sun*, November 7, 1931.

519   Karl Krug, review of *Once a Lady*, *Pittsburgh Press*, November 14, 1931.

520   Harrison Carroll, review of *Once a Lady*, *Los Angeles Evening Herald*, November 6, 1931.

521   Harry Mines, "Ruth Chatterton Rests," *Los Angeles Daily Illustrated News*, November 4, 1931.

522   Harrison Carroll, "Chatterton Moves Over to Warners," *Los Angeles Evening Herald*, November 7, 1931.

523   Brendan Gill, *States of Grace: Eight Plays by Philip Barry*, Harcourt, Brace, Jovanovich, c. 1975, pg 43.

524   Louella Parsons column, *Los Angeles Examiner*, September 24, 1931.

525   Cal York (pseudonym for various *Photoplay* columnists), "Cal York's Monthly Broadcast," *Photoplay*, December 1931.

526   Mordaunt Hall review of *Tomorrow and Tomorrow*, *New York Times*, January 30, 1932.

527   Jay Brien Chapman, "Does Gable Mean it When He Wallops the Heroine?" *Motion Picture*, May 1932.

528   W.E. Oliver review of *Tomorrow and Tomorrow*, *Los Angeles Evening Herald Express*, January 28, 1932.

529   "Career of Robert Ames – Colorful Even to Death," *The Bee* (VA), December 11, 1931.

530   "Actress Pauses to Discuss Own Favorite Plays," *Los Angeles Times*, January 31, 1932.

531   Charles Huntington Whitman, *Representative Modern Dramas*, Macmillan Co., c. 1936, pg 962.

532   Alice L. Tildesley, "If I Could Live My Life Over," *Oakland Tribune*, September 20, 1931.

533   Harrison Carroll, "Chatterton Moves Over to Warners," *Los Angeles Evening Herald*, November 7, 1931.

Mr. & Mrs. Brent sporting that "honeymoon look"
after the wedding (August 1932).

9
At Warner Brothers: Co-starring George Brent

"Where has he been all my life?"
(Ruth Chatterton, December 1931)

Christmas Eve 1931 found Ruth and Ralph at home in Beverly Hills. They spent the evening (her 39th birthday) with their mothers Tilly and Mary. Ruth was pleased with her newly remodeled five-room Spanish bungalow on the Warner lot (previously the roost of silent star Colleen Moore) and enthused about her career transition. However, she was concerned about "Rafe" (the British pronunciation for "Ralph"). His screen career was foundering and she was determined to help him. Their friends thought Ralph a grand fellow, but felt he wasn't for Ruth. "She mothered him too much," as one wag put it.[534] When Ruth was asked to write a syndicated article on the joys of marital bliss, she predicted, "During the ensuing decade divorce will decrease and marriage will increase."[535] Ruth believed that women's ability to support themselves would "sift materialism" from love affairs, making matrimony more enduring.[536] Before the "ensuing decade" was half over, Ruth chalked up two divorces of her own. Her second marriage to newcomer George Brent rescued his career. Chatterton's unbridled enthusiasm for him, coupled with her clout at Warners, afforded Brent the opportunity for stardom.[537]

❧❀❦

In the fall of 1930, Ruth reconnected with the theatrical world. Her adaptation of *Monsieur Brotonneau* premiered in London. She had worked diligently on the project. The French play concerned a banker who puts a twist on an old theme by living with his mistress while providing his wife a comfortable flat—the three of them a happy, congenial trio. Fellow Parisians, however, disapprove. They call him a Mormon. His reputation suffers; the bank suffers. Drama critic Charles Morgan found the play "extremely amusing," but felt that the original ironic mood resisted Chatterton's "attempt to transfer it from one language into another."[538] It was Ruth's third and last effort to translate from French. Her following theatrical project early in 1932, a British play, was designed to help Ralph out of his acting slump and show him to his best advantage. They had purchased the American rights to *Counsel's Opinion* soon after Ruth left Paramount. Re-titled *Let Us Divorce*, she produced, staged, and directed while working on her first two films at Warner.

Opening in Santa Barbara on April 8, *Let Us Divorce* moved to San Francisco's Geary Theatre (formerly the Columbia Theatre) on April 11. Critic Wood Soanes thought the frothy farce "a delightful evening's entertainment thanks to many agencies blended by Miss Chatterton."[539] Ruth sat in the middle of a packed house, the same theatre where she and Henry Miller had many of their successes. Soanes mentioned that Miller's ghost must be wearing a contented smile in the "upper reaches of the Geary ceiling." *The San Francisco Chronicle* commented, "Miss Chatterton offered a production that is the last word in beauty. Every detail of the three settings is complete... even Logan's law office in Temple Court taking on the richness and dignity of the law's majesty."[540] As to be expected, a hefty chunk of Ruth's paycheck created an eyeful for playgoers. Ralph's role, as a priggish barrister who falls in love with a very unconventional female, fit him like a glove. Rose Hobart co-starred as Forbes' love interest, making a favorable impression in a red velvet dress and enormous ostrich-plumed hat. Ruth had Adrian at MGM design the ensemble. Hobart got a kick from a critic's comment, "The costume was much more effective than Miss Hobart."[541] When *Let Us Divorce* premiered at the Los Angeles Belasco, Ruth, who was filming, slipped into a back seat next to Laura Hope Crews to catch the last act. After the curtain, Ralph brought her out on stage in response to repeated calls from the audience. While well-received, the play failed to reestablish Forbes as leading man in film except at poverty row studios. Occasionally, he landed supporting roles at MGM, where his resonant voice was used to advantage in important pictures like *The Barretts of Wimpole Street* starring Norma Shearer. *Let Us Divorce* yielded a $22,500 loss for the couple. "We take our chances," admitted Ralph. "Why should anybody yell when he gets hurt? We simply accepted our loss and said, 'What of it?'"[542] Ruth shrugged that the play was "too jolly English for Hollywood. I should have known better."[543]

***

Ruth aptly described her marriage, saying, "My husband and I congratulate ourselves that we can have a quiet evening at home together. We're really more like good friends than married people. We always find each other interesting."[544] Accompanied by their Aberdeen Terrier, Belinda, the couple had the habit of retreating to their second-floor sitting room to eat dinner on card tables before the fire. They would listen to music or find a topic to discuss until 4 or 5 in the morning. But all that was about to change. Shortly after Ruth arrived on the Warner lot, she took on the task of finding a new leading man for *The Rich Are Always With Us*. After watching numerous screen tests, Ruth's heart skipped a beat when she saw a young actor named George Brent. "Where has *he* been all my life?" she cried. He literally lit up the screen. Brent later admitted that he had a shot of whiskey to relax him before the camera rolled. Gladys Hall, a reputable and founding member of the Hollywood Press Club, asked Ruth if it was love at first sight. "I'm afraid it was," Ruth laughed. "I have always been a cynic, not believing overmuch in anything or anyone. Certainly not… 'love at first sight.' I was not at first attracted to George because of his physical appearance, glad as I am now that he is so satisfactory to look at. No, it was *an inside thing* that caused me to fall in love with George."[545] While Ruth rendezvoused with leading man George Brent, "good friend" and husband Ralph Forbes tagged along. They made an odd, if happy, trio.

In 1972, Fred Watkins interviewed George Brent for Leonard Maltin's *Film Fan Monthly*. Brent reflected back on his Warner screen test. "I was supposed to help out another guy who was making the test. I was living out of one suitcase in those days. You went out for every job that came your way. Anyway, screen tests are cold potatoes, so I downed a shot of whisky before I left the apartment. I didn't care, it wasn't my test. Just before we shot it—Dieterle directed it, I think—I started to get a glow on. I stopped shaking. It was the steadiest performance I ever gave."[546] It wasn't long before Brent received orders to visit the Chatterton bungalow. Once there, he got the once-over. "Talk about embarrassing moments!" he said. "I felt like take-me-home for $1.98. We talked a little, but to tell the truth the first thing I remember her saying is, 'I suppose they want me to have a look at you.' I tried to be nonchalant and said, 'Ha-ha I supposed so, too.' The next few seconds seemed an awfully long time, but finally:

'Well, you look all right to me!'"[547] Chatterton approved and Brent signed a seven-year contract at $250 weekly. "I was flat broke," said Brent. "It was a heaven-sent deal."[548] Brent got the jitters again when he began filming *The Rich Are Always With Us*. "First day on the set I spilled a cup of coffee, Ruth knocked a prop cordial into her lap, and between us we upset a glass of water. When a couple of troupers indulge in such shenanigans, there's something unusual afoot. This time it was love. And it hit me hard. I had an idea that Ruth felt a little the same way. During the rest of the picture we were both in the clouds. It wasn't hard to play the romantic scenes. There weren't enough of them to suit us."[549] When the first day of shooting wrapped, a reporter cornered Ruth, who gushed, "[Brent] is the best leading man I have worked with in Hollywood. He gave me the most perfect day I have had since coming to the screen."[550]

Ruth's fans had waited five months for the release of her Warner debut. *The Rich Are Always With Us* allowed the actress to bring depth and

**Chatterton and Brent during a famous cigarette scene
from *The Rich Are Always With Us* (Warners).**

shading to a snappy, modern, if unimportant, story. Her scenes with Brent have the warm chemistry one would expect under the circumstances. The story was originally purchased for Kay Francis. Columnist Jimmy Starr put it this way, "'Tis said around the studio, that if Miss Chatterton likes the yarn and thinks it is suited to her requirements, she will win, being the stellar favorite of the film plant at present."[551] Playing the richest woman in the world who is faced with a philandering husband and conflicting love interests placed Chatterton in familiar territory. The un-hackneyed treatment of trite situations made for diverting screen fare, which included the fresh-faced talents of George Brent and young Bette Davis, who was also being groomed for Warner stardom.

Davis, a longtime fan of Chatterton, said she was terrified of playing with her and never forgot the first day of shooting. "Miss Chatterton swept on like Juno," Davis recalled. "I had never seen a real star entrance in my life. I was properly dazzled. Her arrival could have won an Academy Award nomination. Such authority! Such glamour! She was absolutely luminous. And radiated clouds of Patou and Wrigley's Spearmint."[552] Columnists often commented that Ruth, in spite of her on screen hauteur, snapped spearmint gum with disconcerting informality. In their first scene together, Davis appears agitated as she enters a restaurant where Chatterton and Brent are having an intimate tête-à-tête. In truth, Davis was so flustered she couldn't get her lines out. The cameras stopped. She looked at Chatterton and blurted, "I'm so damned scared of you I'm speechless!"[553] This broke the ice and Davis was surprised to find Chatterton sympathetic. "She was most helpful in her scenes with me after that," recalled Davis.[554] "Miss Chatterton and I were friends from then on. I will always consider her one of the great actresses of her day."[555] When asked about Chatterton's box-office flops, Davis would come to her defense. "You happen to get a poor picture," she remarked. "It's not your fault and you do your best in it. That's what they did to Ruth Chatterton when she was getting bad pictures at Paramount. As a matter of fact, she never was better in her life."[556]

Davis hadn't been as fortunate with Barbara Stanwyck on the set of Warners' *So Big*, which was being filmed simultaneously. In the middle of a scene, Davis forgot her lines and complained to director William Wellman, "It all makes me so jittery, the pace of this scene." Stanwyck fired back, "You make *yourself jittery*! Try to fit into things!"[557] Their chilly relationship would mirror that of Stanwyck and Chatterton. Brent, also in the cast of *So Big*, would offer effusive praise to Stanwyck. Of all his leading ladies, he stated, "She was the most human, the most unassuming person in the world."[558] Newcomer Brent received second billing in *So Big*. Ruth was using all her influence at the studio to push his career forward.

In *The Rich Are Always With Us*, Ruth played Caroline Grannard, a woman struggling to remain faithful to her unfaithful husband (John Miljan). Her struggle includes afternoon teas and strolls through moonlit gardens with novelist/news correspondent Julian Tierney (Brent). After a speedy Paris divorce, Caroline begs Julian, "Please kiss me into needing you." He obliges. They face a series of obligatory misunderstandings before being reconciled in holy matrimony inside a hospital. It was a happy, if over-the-top, finish. Bette Davis, in her trademark, edgy performance, played Caroline's best friend, Malbro. Malbro wants Julian for herself, but can't get to first base with him. Life was reflecting art. Davis had seen Brent on stage in New York and developed what she called an "all-time crush."[559] She remembered watching helplessly as he fell in love with Chatterton during the filming of *The Rich Are Always With Us*. Davis consoled herself by marrying a former school chum, Harmon Nelson, soon after the film's release.

Frank Daugherty, a future story editor at Warner, tried to interview Ruth on the set. He arrived on time and her "attractively impersonal blue eyes" gave him *that look*. She abruptly announced, "No leading questions, mind. They embarrass me. I won't answer them. I'll run out on you." "And with that bit of unnerving news," observed Daugherty, "[came] the Chatterton smile, a little crooked, a little wry, but contagious and disarming." Ruth let Daugherty know that George Brent was one of the "finds" of the year. She abruptly changed the subject to Emile Zola's novel *Therese Raquin*—the role she coveted most. It concerned a woman and her lover who kill her husband, then plot to kill each other. "Not Bovary, no," said Ruth. "Therese is more interesting. Someday I shall make it and it will be my best picture."[560] Pausing to get a recalcitrant eyelash, Ruth conversed with director Al Green before finishing up a scene with Brent. She returned to her bamboo-backed chair, laughing. "This is a good picture," she told Daugherty, who nodded—didn't say a word—it might *lead* to something.

Al Green's direction and the polish of Ernest Haller's photography helped compensate for shortcomings in the plot of *The Rich Are Always*

With George Brent in *The Rich Are Always With Us* (Warner).

With Us. Still, it wasn't enough to elicit rave reviews. "Miss Chatterton gives a graceful and easy portrayal," said *The New York Times.* "George Brent, who portrays Julian, does capitally." The critic found the film mildly diverting, but commented, "Miss Chatterton, according to all reports, now has the choice of all her stories, and it is therefore surprising that she should have picked this one."[561] In Los Angeles, Elizabeth Yeaman acknowledged that the story was "rather conventional," but filled with clever dialogue, besides being "the best picture that Miss Chatterton has made in many, many months." Yeaman shared Ruth's enthusiasm for Brent and cheered, "This new screen actor justifies all the advance 'raves.' As an actor, he is far more polished and subtle than Gable ever dreamed of being. Furthermore, Miss Chatterton responds to his charm noticeably and her best scenes are with Brent."[562] Yeaman had trouble accepting Bette Davis as a close friend and "social equal" to "nicely bred people" such as Brent and Chatterton. "Bette Davis is prone to overact," smacked Yeaman. "She appears cheap because of her manner more than anything else."

Davis comes across as anxious. It may have fit the character, as Julian complains that Malbro is "always making a nuisance of herself" and needs to "think before she speaks." Midway into the film, Davis appears to be having more fun during a snappy 3-way phone conversation in which she reassures Caroline, who is calling from Paris, that Julian only stays home and smokes opium. Any charm that Davis lacks is compensated for by the natural chic of Chatterton and Brent. Their flirtatious give-and-take during a balcony scene is one of the film's delights. Ruth tells Brent that he must be out of practice as a home wrecker since he isn't getting anywhere with her. He persists in trying to kiss her.

"Haven't you any morals at all?" she asks after rebuffing him.

"Well," he answers, "they began to ache when I was 16. So, I had them pulled out."

After gushing about "new screen rave" George Brent, the review in *Screenland* magazine added, "Ruth Chatterton has acquired a new sparkle. Watch their love scenes—very hot! It's La Chatterton's best one for a long time."[563] Released in the heart of the Depression, it is a stretch to imagine poor folk lining up to see what troubled the rich—who, after all, helped create the economic mess in the first place. Perhaps it was therapeutic to watch millionaires suffer. *The Rich Are Always With Us* should also be remembered for the scene in which Brent and Chatterton spend a long, hard night on a chaise lounge. He puts two cigarettes in his mouth, lights them—one for Chatterton and one for himself. While they enjoy a smoke, she tells him about a woman who kept her lover hidden in an attic for two years. "That's how I feel about you," she says playfully. "Don't want anyone to look at you, or know anything about you." "Would you mind if I took a walk now and then?" he asks. "You might get run over," she answers. "Of course, I could take you out on a leash." After a pause, Brent smiles, "Yes! I'd like that!" The catchy cigarette idea was duplicated ten years later between Paul Henreid and Bette Davis in *Now Voyager*.

❧⊛☙

Much to Ruth's disappointment, Will Hays and censorship put thumbs down on her doing John Colton's *Shanghai Gesture*.[564] Warner decided to capitalize on the "steam" generated by the Chatterton-Brent duo and put them in *Children of Pleasure*, based on a Larry Barreto novel. Once again, the story revolved around the lives of money-obsessed individuals and the Wall Street tumble of '29. It was re-christened *The Crash* shortly before release. Ruth was adorned in twenty-two Orry-Kelly gowns as she portrayed Linda Gault, a woman who seduces wealthy men for stock market tips. Her husband, Geoffrey (Brent), uses her as bait. He's little more than a pimp who seems fonder

With George Brent in *The Crash* (Warner).

of liquor than he does of his wife. "What's the matter with us anyway?" he asks her. "The more money we make, the more wretched we are." Unable to solicit a desired "tip" at a crucial moment, Linda makes up a lie to tell Geoffrey. As a result, they lose everything. Afraid of poverty, Linda goes to Bermuda and tries to drink herself to death, but falls for an Australian sheep rancher (Paul Cavanaugh) instead. Director William Dieterle, or perhaps Ruth, had the idea of showing a closeup of a book the sheep rancher is reading, Aldous Huxley's *Antic Hay*, all about the self-absorbed elite. The book was highly controversial; considered immoral; banned in Australia; burned in Cairo. *The Crash*, with its own set of selfish, unscrupulous, characters, concludes with Linda and Geoffrey reuniting for a happy, if unlikely, conclusion. If nothing else, the bold, pre-Code flavor of this film makes it worth watching.

Critic Elizabeth Yeaman referred to the husband-wife team in *The Crash* as "human parasites… cautious cheaters on the fence, ready to jump on whichever side seems most profitable."[565] Chatterton and Brent offered convincing performances of unsympathetic characters, but was the story a good choice? Brent wasn't given much to do. Ruth's maturity belied dialogue that emphasized her youthful charm. Yeaman deduced that *The Crash* was an "ill chosen" vehicle. She was right. *The Crash* failed with critics and audiences. *Photoplay* said it was "too stupid to synopsize." *Variety* called it, "a weak sister... Nothing happens to pique interest." Critics mentioned the lack of spontaneity and tempo in the 58-minute feature, blaming Dieterle. Perhaps he hadn't consulted his astrological chart. The white-gloved director let the stars rule over all his productions, usually with good results.[566] *Film Daily* suggested to theater owners: "Ballyhoo the Chatterton-Brent romance, and go light on the picture."[567] The suggestion was based upon *off*-screen romance. A few weeks before release, Chatterton and Brent got married. But not before Ruth had a fling in Spain with a prominent American newsman.

***

Ruth left for Europe shortly after completing *The Crash*. When asked why she was going alone and if she and Ralph were separating, she stated matter-of-factly, "No. I just want to go abroad. I need a change and a rest. Ralph likes polo, outdoor things. He'll be happier here while I go about some of my old haunts on the continent. If Hollywood is going to talk, it will have to talk. I can't be bothered."[568] By the time Ruth sailed, it was predicted that the primary purpose of her trip was to secure a divorce. When asked, Ruth, in exasperation, blurted out, "I don't even bother to deny any more that I'm divorcing Ralph. I've been doing it for three years now."[569] She boarded the train for New York on June 2 and sailed June 6 on the *S.S. Bremen*, eluding reporters along the way. Ralph headed for the High Sierras and established residence in the "Divorce Capital of America," Reno, Nevada.

"I am as devoted to Miss Chatterton as if she were my sister," Ralph stated following their separation.[570] "Rafe and I have been like brother and sister far more than like husband and wife," Ruth concurred after the divorce. "That seemed to me, then, to be sufficient. I was very far from being unhappy."[571] The split between Ruth and Ralph was, unsurprisingly, a congenial one. Reporter Jack Smith, who had known Ruth since 1916, wrote a reliable piece on the Chatterton-Brent-Forbes triangle. Before the separation, the trio had spent time together in public and private. Brent, in his characteristic bluntness, informed Rafe one morning, "I can't come to your house any more. I'm falling in love with your wife." Rafe responded with, "You exhibit the best of taste."[572] When Ralph realized that Ruth felt the same, he simply stepped aside. It was a graceful exit.

Publicist Scoop Conlon represented both Ruth and Ralph at the time. Scoop and his wife Lilian joined Forbes in Reno. They spent a lot of time playing poker. Scoop noted that Ralph was in his element standing before a campfire by the lake, reciting ribald yarns and excerpts from Shakespeare and Kipling while an appreciative group of widely assorted Americans yelled for more.[573] The six-week stay required for a divorce went by quickly. News reports compared the Chatterton-Forbes split to the recently publicized "friendly divorce" of cinema star Ann Harding and actor/husband Harry Bannister. Nothing could have been further from the truth. Bannister spent years blackmailing Harding for the custody of their daughter. In 1960, Conlon confirmed that of all the movie-star divorces, Chatterton-Forbes was "the nicest one." Ralph Forbes and Ruth Chatterton would remain lifelong friends and professional partners, co-starring on stage during the 1940s.

While Ruth was in Europe, Brent and co-star Loretta Young left on an East coast promotion for their Warner feature, *Weekend-Marriage*. Brent arranged his schedule so that when Ruth's boat docked in August, he would be there to meet her. Unbeknownst to Brent, or anyone else,

Ruth's pleasure trip included a previously arranged rendezvous with a reporter covering the political crisis in Spain. His name was Rex Smith.

⚜

In 1931, Rex Smith attended a party at Ruth and Ralph's sumptuous home. Smith was recently designated as Bureau Chief in Madrid for the Associated Press. He would cover the politically unstable country until the Franco uprising in 1935. Ruth brought up the subject of rendezvousing in Madrid. Rex liked the idea. "All right," Ruth had told him, "I'll meet you in the Trocadero [one year] from tonight."[574] They promised not to mention their secret plan again. Smith's third wife, actress Jesse Royce Landis, mentioned the Trocadero incident in her 1954 autobiography. Landis said that Rex and Ruth had been friends for a number of years. "This friendship, believe it or not, *was* platonic," wrote Landis, "—even I, with all my jealousy, was convinced of that. Despite the fact that she had traveled from Hollywood to Spain to keep a dinner date with him."[575]

Rex thought it impossible for Ruth to really get away from Hollywood and when the designated date arrived, he went to a fiesta instead. But he hadn't forgotten. "Ruthie," reported Landis, "was furious at not finding him there, traveling incognito about six thousand miles to keep the date. She phoned his office." Once located, Rex showed up as promised. "Many people know this story," said Landis. "In fact, it was taken as the basis of a film in which Irene Dunne and Charles Boyer starred." She was referring to director Leo McCarey's *Love Affair* (1939). McCarey never mentioned the Chatterton-Smith connection and claimed the inspiration for the story came from seeing the Statue of Liberty as he was returning from Europe in 1938.

Rex Smith could spend hours drinking and arguing on any subject.

The well-built, red-haired, attractive, thirty-four-year-old Virginian had subtle charm, was selfish, and, according to Landis, "completely unreliable"—except when it came to Ruth Chatterton. After Ruth returned from Europe on August 11, she felt that marriage was the right thing for her and Brent. She had had her fling. She was ready. When reporters asked her to comment, Ruth obliged. "I remember once we were talking over this divorce, and Mr. Forbes said, 'Well, what grounds is there for it?' I said, 'Incompatibility.' He said, 'No sir-ree. I'll never say we were incompatible.' Now wasn't that sweet of him?"[576]

Ruth created a smokescreen explaining her rendezvous with Smith, saying that he had invited her to Spain *three* years prior. There waiting for her, at the designated time, "was the whole Smith family," Ruth smiled.[577] Smith, who considered himself the world's worst husband, was divorced at the time and his family resided in Virginia. Chatterton's story was a convenient fabrication. Writer Adela Rogers St. Johns confirmed that Ruth had practically turned the studio upside down in order to keep her engagement with Rex. "One day we were sitting in her bungalow on the lot," recalled St. Johns. "She suddenly smiled at me with that almost impish twinkle of hers and said, 'You see, I planned to go to Spain this summer and so I made a dinner engagement in Madrid on the twenty-second of June with a great friend of mine. And I couldn't disappoint him.'"[578] Ruth and George would end up visiting Rex in Madrid during the summer of 1933. On that visit, Ruth and Rex planned yet *another* rendezvous for the summer of 1935, which she also kept. She obviously enjoyed his company. Shortly after Ruth's death in 1961, syndicated columnist Leonard Lyons mentioned the Chatterton-Smith pact and paid tribute to their "memorable romance in Spain."[579]

There was a big to-do in the press on August 13, 1932, when Ruth and George married less than twenty-four hours after her divorce. The divorce was finalized in Minden, Nevada, and for witnesses, Ralph had lined up Ken Foster, manager of JC Penney in Reno, and Helen Gundy, hostess of the Hotel Riverside.[580] "It was five o'clock in the morning after Rafe had phoned me to say that our divorce was final and to give me his blessing," said Ruth. "I phoned George, woke my friends and my Aunt Ida, who were stopping at the hotel with me, and we motored up to Westchester and were married at high noon." Justice Winfred C. Allen presided in a ceremony at the Town Hall. Brent gave his real age of 28 and Ruth, wearing a light silk frock and small tilted hat, lopped off five years to instantly become 34. Three days earlier, screen idol John Gilbert had no problem admitting to his thirty-five years vs. his new bride Virginia Bruce's twenty-one. For Ruth Chatterton, an eleven-year difference was cause for discretion. A major shift in social conventions would come decades later.

Two of Chatterton's actress friends, Frances Starr and Virginia Hammond, were witnesses. Hammond had a supporting role in *The Rich Are Always With Us*. The wedding party celebrated at the home of actor William Courtenay in Rye, New York. "Too happy for words," was all the actress bride had to say as she and Brent headed for New York City in the late afternoon.[581] Tilly Chatterton told Louella Parsons about the ecstatic cables she had received from Ruth saying she was "very, very happy."[582] "I was more excited this time," Ruth said afterward. "I was more frightened. The more we know of life, I think, the more we fear it: the things it can give—the things it can take away."[583] On August 15, the honeymooners attended the wedding of Frances Starr to banker R. Golden Donaldson at Starr's posh Savoy-Plaza Hotel apartment. On the 17th, Mr. and Mrs. George Brent and a retinue of servants, traveled aboard a private car attached to a westbound train for Hollywood.

Ruth and George on the Warner set (courtesy of Brian Reddin).

The honeymooners stayed in Ruth's swanky bungalow on the Warner lot. It was there they threw their first big party—a southern dinner with fried chicken prepared in the smart kitchenette; a table set for ten in the green carpeted dining room; the atmosphere enhanced by the glow from two blazing fireplaces. Guests included: Tilly Chatterton, Elsie Janis, Helen Hayes and husband Charles MacArthur, and Ruth's new director, William Wellman. Ruth was well aware of Brent's unhappy first experience with marriage. "He was thoroughly disillusioned about women," she admitted, "disliked them, distrusted them." Ruth felt that a second marriage had made no fundamental change in her. "I am a very self-sufficient person," she said. "Right now, I believe with all my heart that we have something sound and permanent for as long as we both shall live. Neither one of us wants, or expects, to stay indefinitely on the screen. We both love to travel… he wants to show me the Ireland that is his. We both love music. A large part of our evenings now, either at home in Beverly Hills or here in the studio bungalow, we listen to symphonies and opera on the radio or the phonograph. Neither of us wants children. I never have felt the maternal urge—an offshoot, perhaps, of my original shrinking from things that tie. We both care for solitude and neither of us cares for parties—George even less than I. We are the same kind of people."[584] Gladys Hall put it succinctly when she commented that Ruth "stepped as smoothly... from first marriage to second as she might step in her own drawing-room, from one rug to another."[585]

George Brendan Patrick Nolan

In the summer of 1932, George Brent told Gladys Hall that only three people in the world were "really significant and important" to him: his sister Kathleen, her husband Victor Watson, who was the editor for *The New York Daily Mirror*, and Ruth. Brent was reticent when talking about his past. Studio publicity usually filled in the rest. Stars would play along with all the hype in order to avoid leading, uncomfortable questions. "People," said Brent, "never really care about you. When you are down, there is no one to help or to care. When you are up, there are—back-slappers. Next to being pitied, back-slapping is the most odious thing that can be done." [586] In 1931, an eye specialist had told Brent that he was going blind. "My first instinct was—suicide," said Brent. "I kept thinking, 'Have I worked so hard all these years—for *this*?' You achieve a certain philosophy if you survive the first shock of the thing. You retreat to your mind and find that you have scenes and faces to live with." Brent went to the east coast, had a risky operation to save his eyesight, and convalesced at the home of his sister. "For weeks while I sat there in bandaged darkness... I knew the feelings of a blind man." Brent, born George Patrick Nolan on March 15, 1904, in Ballinasloe, Galway, Ireland, offered details of his childhood from a blind man's point of view.[587]

> I seemed to 'see' mostly the days when I was a boy back home in Ireland. An unhappy kid, living with relatives

who didn't seem to understand the kind of kid I was, painfully shy and painfully sensitive, trying my best to hide it. My father, a newspaperman, had died when I was two. I 'saw' myself as a boy running barefoot over the bogs in the early morning. My memory... *had eyes.* I could 'see' the Autumn mornings when we went out, my Uncle and I, to round up the sheep who were lambing in the fields. I could smell the sweet, warm smell of the milk I fed the babies out

George Brent (c. 1932).

of nursing bottles—forgetting, then, that I was a shy and not very happy little boy, conscious only that I was doing the best I could for creatures in distress.

Faces and memories in the darkness start a train of thought. I thought of the different kinds of love. And it is *not* the kind based on sex appeal. There is too much stress laid on physical attraction. I should say that at least seventy-five per cent of love should be mental, should be companionship and sympathy. It is the most devastating thing in life—this physical attraction and the havoc it brings. I know—because I went through that sort of thing, too. I married it. And I went through Hell for nearly two years, although the marriage itself lasted less than six months.

I came to America for the first time when I was eleven. And that memory remained with me, too, though I hadn't thought about it for many years. I could see the dark waters and the averted and voiceless faces of my fellow-passengers, watching for the deadly periscope.

George Nolan was accompanied by his older sister Kathleen on the voyage, which departed Liverpool on September 11, 1915. England was at war. Germany had begun submarine warfare. The British liner *Lusitania* was sunk by a German U-Boat. George and Kathleen had every reason for panic. They arrived safely in New York on the *S.S. Philadelphia* on September 20. Although Brent never mentioned his mother, Mary McGuinness Nolan, who had abandoned him as a baby, census records from 1920 show that George was living with her on West 77th Street in Manhattan. At that time, George was attending school. Kathleen acquired a job as New York's first female news photographer for the *New York American*, and went by the name Peggy Nolan. In 1922, she ventured to Hollywood, where she married the French film director, Marcel De Sano. The couple had a son, but divorced in the summer of 1926. Kathleen would marry Victor Watson in 1928. Interestingly, it was De Sano who would be scheduled to direct Ruth Chatterton in Paramount's aborted project, *Zaza*.

Irish Filmmaker Brian Reddin contacted this author in 2012, clearing up the mystery and Hollywood spin surrounding George Brent's heritage. Reddin was shooting a documentary on the actor. Brent offered different versions of his youth, obviously a time he wasn't particularly fond of recalling. Reddin revealed,

Locals from Ballinasloe told me that George Brent's father, John Nolan, worked as a shopkeeper at the time of
Brent's birth. He then worked for the postal service. He
didn't die when George was two. Certainly he was alive
and living in Ballinasloe in 1911 according to the Irish
census. Locals tell me he was alive when George left for
the United States in 1915, but nobody seems to know
what happened to him after that. I imagine they did not
have a good relationship. I think his father was a heavy
drinker and the family fell apart. Brent's mother left with
three of his siblings to live in New York [c. 1905] and let
George and Kathleen stay with relatives in Ireland before
sending for them in 1915.[588]

When I contacted Brent's daughter from his fifth marriage, Suzanne
Brent, she had this to say:

Our father had a very diverse… exciting… and at times
mysterious life. His family included three sisters and
one brother. We never knew our grandparents, only that
grandmother is buried on Long Island, and grandfather
died in Ireland. His sister Kathleen… passed away April
2000 at nearly 100 years old. Her son, Patrick, our first
cousin, just passed this January 2012.[589]

At 16, young George returned to Ireland on January 29, 1921. He
sailed second class on the *Carmania*, arriving in Liverpool on February
7.[590] On board, he claimed to have met Father Dan, who was en route to aid
the Irish Republican Army. In some interviews, Brent mentioned having
an education at the National University in Dublin. Filmmaker Reddin
confirms that Brent would have been too young and "would never have

been accepted into a third level college."[591] And there was no Father Dan on the ship's passenger list. As reporter Herbert Cruikshank said about Brent, "You're never quite certain whether or no this Ballinasloe laddy-buck is passing out the Blarney."[592] It does appear, however, that young Nolan was drawn to Dublin's Abbey Theatre. "I was just a kid," George admitted, "but they let me have little parts and it got into my blood."[593]

The story goes that George Nolan descended from a long line of Irish-men who served with the British Armies. The closest that George got to the British Army was fighting it. His return to native soil coincided with the height of Ireland's War of Independence. Guerilla leader Michael Collins used the services of the teenager to be a dispatcher for the revolution. There were stories of young Nolan's last-minute escape, that there was a price on his head, but a truce was signed by the time he left. Whatever the case, George was back on U.S. soil on August 22, 1921, after sailing on the steamship *Bilbster* to St. Albans, Vermont, via Montreal.[594] He lied about his age, stating that he was twenty-two and listed his profession as "Seaman." The seventeen-year-old declared that he was headed to New York, where he would live permanently with his sister, Kathleen.

By December 1921, young Nolan found his niche and was signed by theatrical legend Guthrie McClintic for a minor role in *The Dover Road* by A.A. Milne. The comedy premiered on Broadway and set a record at the Bijou Theatre. Publicity hyped that George Nolan "hails from Dublin University." *The Dover Road* then went on tour until 1923. In 1924, "George B. Nolan" (George had replaced "Patrick" with "Brendan") had joined a road company to play the title role in the popular *Abie's Irish Rose*. "George B. Nolan handled his part in excellent fashion," said a review from Hutchinson, Kansas.[595] Jazz saxophonist George Johnson remembered playing golf with the twenty-year-old actor in the summer of 1924. They were lodging in the same private home in Indianapolis. Johnson recalled his shock, nine years later, when he went to the movies and saw Brent up on the screen. "I often wonder," said Johnson, "if he enjoys life as much as he used to when he made $150 a week."[596]

While touring with *Abie...* George saved his money to start his own theatrical group in Pawtucket, Rhode Island. This dream was realized, but George returned to New York with $1.47 profit in his pocket.[597] There would be other stock companies, over 300 roles, and a rewarding stay with Denver's Elitch Gardens. "I've played mining towns and little hillbilly dumps where the audiences catcall, throw things, and spoil your best emotional scenes," recalled Brent in 1932. "But after that you go on acting, even if the roof falls in."[598] The roof fell in on October 20, 1927, when George married Helen Louise Campbell (an older actress who went by Helen Louise Lewis on stage).[599] By January, the newlyweds were co-starring in the comedy *Up in Mabel's Room* with the Plaza Players in St. Petersburg, Florida. "George Nolan was at his best last night," raved a local review.[600] Although his first marriage only lasted six months, Brent waited to obtain a Los Angeles divorce in 1929/30.[601] By then, he was romantically linked with shimmy queen Gilda Gray, who, at one point, literally shimmied herself into a coma. Brent was at her hospital bedside and sent flowers daily. In December 1930, it was reported that the two were to marry.[602] Months later, Gray followed Brent to Hollywood, denying any romance and saying that she and George were "merely good friends."[603]

By the fall of 1928, George was using the surname Brent. A lucky break came a year later with the Broadway opening of *Love, Honor and Betray* starring Alice Brady. The cast included Clark Gable. Brent found Brady "grand to work with, if she likes you."[604] She liked George. When a scout from Fox studios saw the production, he suggested Brent for the lead in *The Man Who Came Back* to be directed by Raoul Walsh. Brent immediately headed west. Before meeting Walsh, George was asked to grow a heavy beard and stand in among a cast of "20,000 others" for the director's epic Western *The Big Trail*—John Wayne's first starring role. Brent agreed. Soon afterward, Brent learned that Charles Farrell got the lead in The *Man Who Came Back*. Fox gave Brent a role in a George O'Brien western instead. Before long, Brent was dropped. Louella Parsons then reported that Brent was "Universal's new leading man."[605] Erich von Stroheim offered him the lead in a remake of the director's 1918 hit *Blind Husbands*. When that project bit the dust, Brent was told that he literally *was* going blind and needed to undergo delicate eye surgery. From July until mid-October 1931, he convalesced at his sister Kathleen's in New York. "A hell of a mess," observed Brent, who had to limit his reading even after recovery.[606] "I was broke, though," he said, "so I barged out here to Hollywood again." Arriving on the west coast, Brent submerged his talent into becoming an action hero in a twelve-part serial co-starring Rin-Tin-Tin. *The Lightning Warrior*, filmed at Poverty Row's Mascot Pictures, included a scene where Native Americans perform a death dance around Brent, who is tied to a stake. Taking this as a forewarning, George had one ear to the ground for the chance to return to Broadway.

All it took was one look from Ruth Chatterton and a wave of her stellar wand to turn things around for George Brent.

Ralph Forbes continued to be part of the Chatterton-Brent equation after their marriage. He dropped in frequently to dine with Ruth and George and would join them for an occasional theater outing. The trio became a much talked-about triangle. Adela Rogers St. John referred to them as a "modern version" of *ménage a trios*.[607] Dismissing Ralph's passions for hunting, fishing, and playing polo, Ruth insisted how similar they

Ralph and George—became pals as well as ex-
husbands of Miss Chatterton. In 1940, the duo would
team up for a month-long voyage to Hawaii.

were. "Ralph and I are as alike as though we were close relatives. The
same tastes, ideas, dislikes—everything. It becomes monotonous after a
while. Marriage needs differences in reactions."[608] The irony was that her
divorce from Ralph was granted on grounds of "divergence of tastes."[609]
Ruth would discover, sooner than she expected, that she had traded in
comfortable monotony for dead silence.

Endnotes

534   Cal York, "Hollywood Goings On," *Photoplay*, October 1932 (York wasn't a real person, but a moniker for *Photoplay's* editorial offices in California and New York.).

535   Dan Thomas, "Nothing Important, But Much Interesting," *Capital Times*, January 9, 1931.

536   "The Talkie Ticker," *Southtown Economist* (ILL), January 20, 1931.

537   Ralph Wilk, "A Little from the Lots," *Film Daily*, December 27, 1931 and January 6, 1932 (Ruth had seen Brent's screen test by mid-December 1931. Following her approval, he was immediately signed to a contract and put in both *So Big* and *The Rich Are Always With Us*, which were filmed simultaneously.).

538   Charles Morgan, "Miss Chatterton Adapts," *New York Times*, October 5, 1930 (originally in the London press September 18, 1930).

539   Wood Soanes review of *Let Us Divorce*, *Oakland Tribune*, April 13, 1932.

540   George C. Warren, review of *Let Us Divorce*, reprinted in *The New York Times*, April 17, 1932.

541   Rose Hobart, *A Steady Digression to a Fixed Point*, Scarecrow, c. 1994, pg 79.

542   Jack Jamison, "Hard Times in Hollywood," *Modern Screen*, January 1933.

543   Nancy Pryor, "Contented and How!" *Motion Picture*, August 1932.

544   Lee Shippey, *Folks Ushud Know Interspersed with Songs of Courage*, A.L. Ewing, c. 2004, pg 44.

545   Gladys Hall, "Ruth Chatterton's Own Story of Her Second Marriage," *Motion Picture*, January 1933.

546   Fred Watkins, "George Brent," *Film Fan Monthly*, October 1972.

547   Cruikshank, "The Inside Story of the Ruth Chatterton-George Brent Romance," *Modern Screen*, October 1932.

548   James Robert Parish, "George Brent" from *The Debonairs*, Arlington House, NY, c. 1975, pg 26.

549   Cruikshank, "The Inside Story of the Ruth Chatterton-George Brent Romance," *Modern Screen*, October 1932.

550   Ralph Wilk, "A Little From the Lots," *Film Daily*, February 8, 1932.

551   Jimmy Starr column, *Los Angeles Evening Herald Express*, January 22, 1932 (Francis was mentioned for the role as early as July 26, 1931, in *The New York Times*).

552   Bette Davis, *The Lonely Life*, Putnam, c. 1962, pgs 124-125.

553   James Spada, *More than a Woman: An Intimate Biography of Bette Davis*, Bantam, c. 1993, pg 90.

554   Bette Davis, *The Lonely Life*, Putnam, c. 1962, pgs 124-125.

555   Whitney Stine, *Mother Goddam*, Hawthorne Books, c. 1974, pg 28.

556   Dena Reed, "Girl Who Played Wise," *Picture Play*, November 1932.

557   James Spada, *More than a Woman: An Intimate Biography of Bette Davis*, Bantam, c. 1993, pg 90.

558   Nancy Anderson, "Brent, Still Debonair, Coaxed Back to Work," *Tonawanda News*, June 2, 1978.

559   James Spada, *More Than a Woman: An Intimate Biography of Bette Davis*, Bantam, c. 1993, pg 90.

560   Frank Daugherty, "'No Leading Questions,'" *Brooklyn Daily Eagle*, June 19, 1932.

561   Mordaunt Hall, review of *The Rich Are Always With Us*, *The New York Times*, May 16, 1932.

562   Elizabeth Yeaman, review of *The Rich Are Always With Us*, *Hollywood Citizen News*, May 13, 1932.

563   Review of *The Rich Are Always With Us*, *Screenland*, July 1932.

564   Chester B. Bahn column, *Syracuse Herald*, March 22, 1932.

565   Elizabeth Yeaman, review of *The Crash*, *Hollywood Citizen News*, October 21, 1932.

566   Michael Barson, *The Illustrated Who's Who of Hollywood Directors*, Noonday Press, c. 1995, pg 114.

567   Review of *The Crash*, *Film Daily*, September 9, 1932.

568   Muriel Babcock, "Ruth Chatterton Finds Husband Useful Actor," *Los Angeles Times*, May 1, 1932.

569   "News and Gossip of the Studios," *Motion Picture*, September 1932.

570   Mark Dowling, "They Name Their Next Mates Before They're Free From Ex-Mates," *Motion Picture*, November 1932.

571   Gladys Hall, "Ruth Chatterton's Own Story of her Second Marriage," *Motion Picture*, January 1933.

572   Jack Grant, "Why the Chatterton-Brent Love Died," *Movie Mirror*, June 1934.

573   John McCallum, *Scooper*, Wood and Reber, c. 1960, pg 188-190.

574   "Ruth Chatterton Marries George Brent on Same Day She Hears of Divorce," *Syracuse Herald*, August 13, 1932.

575   Jessie Royce Landis, *You Won't Be So Pretty*, W.H. Allen, London, c. 1954, pgs 121-123.

576   "Ruth Chatterton Marries George Brent on Same Day She Hears of Divorce," *Syracuse Herald*, August 13, 1932.

577   "Ruth Chatterton Weds George Brent on Same Day She Hears of Divorce," *Syracuse Herald*, August 13, 1932.

578   Adela Rogers St. Johns, "The Men in Ruth Chatteron's Life," *Liberty*, January 20, 1934.

579   Leonard Lyons, "Ruth Chatterton Made Promise And She and Rex Smith Kept It," *Lawrence Journal World*, December 2, 1961.

580   "Film Actress Loses No Time In Remarrying," *Nevada State Journal*, August 14, 1932.

581   "Ruth Chatterton Weds George Brent," *The New York Times*, August 14, 1932.

582   Louella Parsons column, *San Antonio Light*, August 17, 1932.

583   Gladys Hall, "Ruth Chatterton's Own Story of Her Second Marriage," *Motion Picture*, January 1933.

584   Gladys Hall, "Ruth Chatterton's Own Story of her Second Marriage," *Motion Picture*, January 1933.

585   Gladys Hall, "Ruth Chatterton's Own Story of her Second Marriage," *Motion Picture*, January 1933.

586   Gladys Hall, "They Told George Brent That He Was Going Blind!" *Movie Classic*, September 1932.

587   Brent's birth certificate #4666252. Born: George Patrick Nolan, March 15, 1904, to John and Mary McGuinness Nolan, Ballinasloe.   Brendan was added later on.

588   Brian Reddin, email, May 27, 2012.

589   Suzanne Brent, email dated November 10, 2012.

590   UK Incoming Passenger List, New York to Liverpool, February 7, 1921- George lists his age as 22.

591   Brain Reddin, email, May 27, 2012.

592   Herbert Cruikshank, "The Inside Story of the Ruth Chatterton-George Brent Romance," *Modern Screen*, October 1932.

593   Alice L. Tildesley, "Best Slappers Become Rivals of Clark Gable," *Oakland Tribune*, August 14, 1932.

594   U.S. Petition for Naturalization #55766, District Court of U.S. at Los Angeles 1937 (Brent designated the August 22, 1921, date as his last entry into the U.S. for permanent residency).

595   "Laugh a Minute in Midland Play," *Hutchinson News* (KS), March 12, 1925.

596   Ralph De Toledano, *Frontiers of Jazz*, Pelican, c. 1994, pg 129.

597   Fred Watkins, "George Brent," *Film Fan Monthly*, October 1972.

598   Alice L. Tildesley, "Best Slappers Become Rivals of Clark Gable," *Oakland Tribune*, August 14, 1932.

599   "Marriages," *Variety*, October 26, 1927.

600   "Plaza Scores Big Last Night," *The Evening Independent* (FL), February 7, 1928.

601   "Ruth Chatterton Marries George Brent, Film Actor," *Pittsburgh Press*, August 14, 1932.

602   "Gilda Gray to Wed," *Capital Times*, December 13, 1930.

603   Walter Winchell, "On Broadway," *Port Arthur News*, July 11, 1931.

604   Charles Grayson, "Is George Brent Another Gable?" *Motion Picture*, June 1932.

605   Louella Parsons column, *Pittsburgh Post-Gazette*, April 1, 1931.

606   Charles Grayson, "Is George Brent Another Gable?" *Motion Picture*, June 1932.

607   Adela Rogers St. Johns, "The Men in Ruth Chatterton's Life," *Liberty*, January 20, 1934.

608   Jerry Bannon, "Ruth Chatterton Divorces Forbes To Marry Brent," *Movie Classic*, September 1932.

609   "Ruth Chatterton Weds George Brent," *St. Petersburg Times*, August 14, 1932.

Ruth and George at home on North Palm Drive.

10

"Richly Tired"

Upon signing with Warner Brothers, Ruth was asked if she would retire after her two-year contract expired. "Very likely," she replied. "By that time, the public ought to be richly tired of me."[610] In the summer of 1932, Warner backed out of Ruth's option to dictate on story, cast, and direction. As her films weren't the big hits they had expected, they felt her choices had worked to the studio's disadvantage.[611] Upon receiving the ultimatum, it was said she was considering a contract offer from MGM.[612] Warner Brothers refused to loan Chatterton to Universal, who really wanted her for the now-classic *Only Yesterday* (1933). *The New York Times* reported, "her displeasure has been said to be acute." Production head at Warner, Darryl Zanuck, decided that high-brow stories were "out" for Chatterton. *Frisco Jenny* would prove to be Chatterton's biggest box office hit at Warner, making a substantial profit. She carried the film on her own drawing power sans George Brent. In another year, she would have to carry on with her life without Mr. Brent completely.

Exorbitant salaries of film stars had become an issue. Chatterton's in particular. Due to the Depression, ticket sales were declining. Warner Brothers' net loss for 1932 totaled over $14,000,000.[613] After *Frisco Jenny* premiered, Zanuck cut employee salaries for eight weeks. It was reported that Ruth and William Powell steadfastly refused to take a salary cut even though someone like James Cagney, who was making $1,750 a week, surpassed their drawing power. Other studios were offering to buy Cagney's contract.[614] Ruth was accused of being money-mad. "I can't see why my salary should be singled out for such marked attention," said Ruth. "I am not so blind or so hopelessly insensible to what goes on in the world as not to recognize a change in conditions. That would be pitifully narrow-minded and materialistic, not to say stupid, of me, and I could not look myself in the face were it true. But it isn't. I'll admit I have never taken a cut in salary, though possibly some other stars have seen fit to do so. All I can say is that I was never *asked* to take a cut."[615] In fact, Ruth stated that she was overpaid while character actors were underpaid.[616]

Frisco Jenny had the acclaimed director William Wellman. The question was … could Wellman maintain the strength of his convictions in the presence of someone like Ruth Chatterton? Screenwriter Wilson Mizner, who had spent time as a gambler, scam artist, saloon singer, and opium aficionado in the Klondike, absolutely adored Ruth. "If I had her in Alaska in the boom days," he said, "she would have made the hairiest, unbathed miner feel he was a Valentino."[617] Mizner helped pen the classic *One Way Passage* for Warner and supplied the script for *Frisco Jenny*. Director Wellman, Mizner's close friend, immediately questioned the prospect of Ruth playing a tough Barbary Coast prostitute, mainly because of her cultured voice—her use of broad "A's." "She'll play Frisco Jenny," argued Mizner, "like she shoveled dirt to make her. She can make Mary Magdalen look like a sinner again."[618] When Ruth got wind of Wellman questioning her ability, she minced no words when she ran into him. "When I play a slut, I'm a slut!" she informed him.[619] Mizner was delighted. After a few more run-ins with Wellman, Ruth's imperious attitude subsided. She called a

Louis Calhern looks on as Ruth escorts a Bible-thumper (Frank McGlynn, Sr.) out of her dad's saloon in *Frisco Jenny* (Warner).

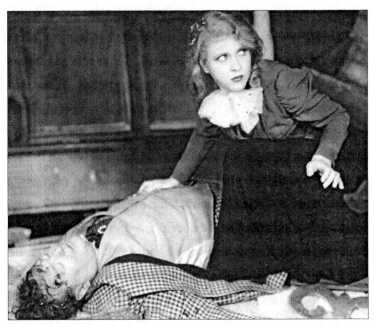

The '06 Quake puts Ruth's dad (Robert Emmett O'Connor) permanently out of business in *Frisco Jenny* (Warner).

truce. "And from that moment we became nothing but pals," Wellman stated. "We made a helluva picture together!"[620]

"Ruth loved Mizner," recalled Scoop Conlon in 1960. "They would sit up all night and talk about life and mankind, not excepting themselves. She was Mizner's favorite among all the women in Hollywood. 'She is my kind of people,' he would say, 'she could charm a pawnbroker out of his store.'" Not long after *Frisco Jenny* was released, Mizner lay on his death-bed in the hospital. When a clergyman tiptoed into his room, Mizner, one of the great raconteurs, is reported to have told him, in a hoarse whisper, "Don't bother, Father. I've just been talking to your Boss."[621]

The flavor of Mizner's world translates into enjoyable Pre-code cinema. Playing the title role in *Frisco Jenny*, Ruth finds herself unmarried and pregnant in the aftermath of the '06 Quake. The quake scene (for which Ruth refused to use a double) is remarkable film-making and occurs immediately following a tense situation between Jenny and her father. In so many words, she informs him that she is in love and with child. "I'm not sorry," she says. "I'm not ashamed. I love him more than anything in the world." Her father slaps her to the ground. "Your mother!" he snarls, "I'm glad she's dead! I'm glad she didn't live to see..." the earth tremors begin. Doors rattle, walls totter, ceilings collapse—as if his blasphemy and abuse brought it on. Writer Gladys Hall was on the set during the quake and commented, "I'll just say that... the Almighty never directed one more realistically than William Wellman that afternoon."[622]

Jenny reads a bulletin that lists her young man (actor James Murray before alcohol made him unemployable) among the dead. She attempts to "do the right thing" and joins up with a preacher as a mission worker. When God fails to feed her baby, Jenny turns to gambling and prostitution. The Child Welfare League steps in and Jenny is forced to release her son to be raised by a respectable, well-to-do couple. Jenny gains a reputation as the most notorious woman in San Francisco. Director Wellman pulls no punches when Jenny's syndicate of ladies, whom she jests as being part of San Francisco's "400," gather at her home to tally the monthly revenues. It's been a good month—a convention is in town—time to buy new linens and replace furniture that couldn't "stand the wear and tear."

Years pass. During prohibition, Jenny's connection to slippery lawyer Steve Dutton (Louis Calhern) brings her inevitable downfall. Dutton is in a bootleg scandal and threatens to expose Jenny's past to save his own neck. She shoots to kill and is charged with murder. In a twist on *Madame X*, it is her own son, whom she's secretly been protecting, who does a bang-up job of convicting her. Jenny keeps her true identity from him and heads for the gallows—her sacrifice meeting all the requirements for tears as well as a recalcitrant nod to censorship. Ruth considered *Frisco Jenny* one of her favorite films. Upon release, theaters were registering more than twice the average opening night business.[623] *The Hollywood*

Gambling and prostitution rake in profits for both Jenny and Warner Brothers. (Helen Jerome Eddy at far right) (Warner)

Reporter enthused, "The phenomenal success of *Frisco Jenny* is attributed to the fact that this picture takes Ruth Chatterton out of the salon and puts her into the saloon."[624]

Bay Area's Wood Soanes congratulated Wellman on his "intelligent direction" and Ruth for "putting aside her drawing room manners, and her English accent." "It is the sort of situation in which Miss Chatterton shines and she takes full advantage of its possibilities," said Soanes. "Whether it will re-establish [her] as a potent cinema force remains to be seen."[625] Another critic said that Chatterton gave "the whole lurid-toned picture authenticity. It is a great testimony to her skill to see how she makes *Frisco Jenny* believable."[626] Even in the face of favorable reviews and positive box office, however, Ruth was more determined than ever to quit Hollywood.

⁂

Chatterton lost some fans by staying away from sophisticated, drawing-room types of characters. Her public was becoming divided. "Frisco Jenny" declared in a Warner ad, "I've slept in gutters and I've slept in silk! I've broken all Ten Commandments, and if they ever make another one, I get first crack at it!" When asked about Jenny, Ruth explained, "Nothing dramatic ever happens to a good woman. Even if it did, her reactions would not develop dramatic interest. All good women are good in the same way."[627] Dramatically speaking, if Ruth wanted to jump into mud puddles, she would. Warner Brothers, after all, was known for guts, not class—that territory belonged to Metro. Ruth's next film, *Lilly Turner*, also fit the bill and required her to play a carnival cooch dancer. But was it a mistake for Chatterton to put her natural gentility, cool lucidity, and discerning taste aside to be something other than ladylike? Ruth didn't think so. Author Jim Tully, whose autobiography, *Beggars for Life*, became a bestseller in 1924, saw his friend Ruth Chatterton as "the most misunderstood woman in Hollywood." Tully, also known as the red-headed "hobo author," met Ruth in 1927 during the run of *The Devil's Plum Tree*. He found her to be straightforward, warmhearted, and genuine. She didn't judge people; she didn't judge the characters she played. Tully elaborated:

> Few women are so deeply interested in two subjects—their own work, and the woes of others. Her mind, a blending of the masculine and feminine, is tireless. I have a vagabond friend who called at my house unexpectedly, with a broken pocket comb, no hat, and a hunger that had long endured. I was just backing out of the driveway for Ruth Chatterton's home. "Would you like to go to Ruth Chatterton's house?" I asked. Never did a more tattered individual enter the sanctum of a star. Ruth entered into the mood of the occasion.
>
> I had never seen her superior to the moment. My rapscallion friend was given food and drink. He became loquacious. Ruth listened attentively and with utmost courtesy. When we left, she said to him, "Come again." My friend remained silent for some miles on the way home. "Do you know, Jim, *I think she meant that.*" "Sure she meant it. That's why she said it. She talks our language."

Author Jim Tully at MGM (1930).

Months later I met Ruth in Los Angeles. "How's your friend, Jim? Give him my regards." "He's been ill." She took my arm. "Let's go see him." When we drew up to the small hotel in a limousine larger than a ham actor's estimate of himself, Ruth carried in her arms a large bouquet of roses. My vagabond friend… could not see for the tears. She made the drab room radiant. We remained an hour. When she sought the landlady to obtain a vase… my friend turned to me and said, "She's real people." When I called upon him the next day he told me how his landlady had entered the room after we had gone, "with a little note from Miss Chatterton." It was a fifty-dollar bill. Long after… Ruth again asked about my friend. "You like him." "Yes," she answered. "He's genuine." "Strange… that's what he said about you."[628]

In 1928, William Wellman had directed a tight, moody silent film, *Beggars of Life*, based on Tully's hobo camp experiences with All-American misfits and castaways. Somber themes would also fuel the Wellman-Chatterton effort *Lilly Turner*.

During the filming of *Frisco Jenny*, Mr. and Mrs. Brent attended the first Los Angeles appearance of petite French soprano Lily Pons. It was reported that the audience paid more attention to Ruth Chatterton, who was wearing an old-fashioned orange evening gown with large puff sleeves and a pinch waist line. Sitting in the same box with her and George was good friend Helen Hayes. When the couple preferred a more rugged environment, they headed for the hills. In January 1933, Ruth and George were snow-bound in their isolated San Bernardino mountain cabin for three days. They arrived home, recovering from partial snow blindness and exposure. Brent told the press that they "mushed" out eight miles on snowshoes through heavy drifts to Lake Arrowhead, where they finally obtained an automobile.[629] Filming on *Lilly Turner* was delayed until February 7 and held up again when Ruth arrived at the studio only to have her hand crushed by an automobile door. She was rushed to the hospital with two broken fingers.

Ruth was reunited with husband Brent for *Lilly Turner*, a screen adaptation of a play by Philip Dunning and George Abbott. Hoping to follow the success of *Frisco Jenny*, Warner also re-teamed Ruth with director Wellman. His son, William Wellman, Jr., recalled in 2009, "They got along perfectly. Ruth Chatterton was very independent and very strong. A lot of directors didn't want to work with her. My father liked the independent woman, the strong woman who could hang out with the guys, the Barbara Stanwycks and Carole Lombards and Ruth Chattertons."[630]

Chatterton and Brent, along with Warner's stock characters, Frank McHugh, Guy Kibbee, and Robert Barrat, create an engaging ensemble. While most of the action occurs in seedy surroundings, the characters come across as human. Critics were hard on the film. *The Hollywood Reporter* put the curse on it, saying that it could "only be classed as garbage. The good work of a fine cast ... no way compensates for the utter drabness and unsavory pall which hangs over *Lilly Turner*. Lilly strikes a fair average by repulsing as many men as she sleeps with."[631] As the film had no moral, it was the perfect target for the moralistic.

By the time Lilly's abusive husband abandons her, we understand her dispirited character. She's a carnival prop, a cooch dancer, about to have a baby. When her husband's *real* wife shows up, we learn that he's a bigamist. "Hangin's too good for him!" she informs Lilly. "You mean ...

I'm not married?" Lilly asks. The woman shakes her head. "Tough luck girlie. I know just how you feel." Frank McHugh does a memorable job as Dan, a booze-loving barker who comes to Lilly's rescue. They marry the day before she's going to deliver. McHugh's hangdog persona is in top form as he asks the hospital admission nurse for a light. She ungraciously tosses him a box of matches, asking if Lilly is legally wed. "Sure!" he says. "Yesterday." The nurse haughtily replies, "Um-hmm, and having a baby today, huh?" Dan throws the matches back at her and snarls, "Uh-huh. Ain't nature wunner-ful?"

Lilly loses her baby, but her troubles have just begun. Sexually harassed by her employer, she and Dan leave the carnival and join up with a bogus medicine show run by Doc McGill (Guy Kibbee). Midway into the film, George Brent arrives to give a good account of himself as Bob, an unemployed engineer who fills in for Fritz, a mentally challenged "Strong Man" (Robert Barret), who had been hauled away to a mental institu-

with Frank McHugh and George Brent in *Lilly Turner* (Warner).

tion. The film's happy interlude occurs while Lilly and Bob, who have fallen in love, relax by a stream. "I feel like I've been born all over again," Lilly sighs. Catching herself, she laughs, "Whoa, Lilly! You're talkin' like an Easter card." McHugh's character appears oblivious. His devotion to booze has kept him from consummating their marriage, let alone recognizing that Lilly is in love with another man. Dashes of humor give the film buoyancy. The ending isn't exactly what you would expect. Lilly bids a fond adieu to Bob and remains loyal to drunken, debilitated Dan, who had helped her out when she was in a tight spot. As *Film Daily's* review of *Lilly Turner* emphasized, "it is not family fare."[632]

Amid a slew of negative reviews, the *Los Angeles Examiner* thought *Lilly Turner* "swell entertainment. Ruth Chatterton... handled her dramatic scenes with intensity, her love scenes with tenderness... and her comedy scenes with a nice ironic twinkle. Frank McHugh... turns in a humorous performance that coaxes the picture right into his vest pocket. You may find it hokey, but you won't be bored."[633] Frank McHugh, with his innate comic notions, is on par with Chatterton. His talent keeps the film afloat, while Dan and Lilly steal your heart. Although the story wasn't exactly fresh, the cast offered striking presentations of their individual characters. For Lilly, Chatterton injected a good dose of melancholy and depression without any telltale sign of self-pity. As Jim Tully's vagabond friend had observed, Ruth personified "real people," off screen as well as on.

⚜

Ruth and George were enthusiastically going over house plans, sketches, and blueprints as they wrapped up *Lilly Turner.* They were planning a new home—but before they dug any deeper into the idea, they took off for Europe. After a week in New York, they sailed on the *Europa* on March 23. While on tour, they were joined by Ronald Colman for a motor trip through Spain. As a trio, their senses were sharpened by new surroundings. They attended bullfights and hobnobbed with Ruth's friend, Rex Smith. Smith took the film stars to a bull ranch and urged them to enter the ring. Colman was game. Fortunately, a banderillero waved his cape the very moment a bull was about to charge for the actor. Ruth entered the ring herself only to be chased by a couple of two-year-old bulls. "Juan Belmonte, the great fighter, laughed heartily," she said. "Of course, I was right to run, and the top of my car was a safer place."[634] A conspicuous dent in the side of the vehicle proved her point. Colman also tagged along to Paris, where Ruth, George, and Ronnie sent a risqué "French postcard" to Louella Parsons.[635] While Ruth delighted in her respite from film acting, she said that she never knew Colman to be so "miserable." It was obvious that he had no desire to "get away from it all."[636]

Film Daily said there was talk of Ruth filming a picture in Cannes. British studios had also submitted offers for Chatterton's services.[637] Instead of making a picture, Ruth focused on seeing Paris, England, and George's Ireland. While she was in England, Ruth was asked by Noel Coward to attend the premier of *Cavalcade* with him. "I'm not asking anyone else," he told her. "I want to sit with you all by myself so I can watch your reactions." They sat in the royal box at the theatre. "For the first half hour I was petrified," said Ruth. "I couldn't think. I simply sat there frozen wondering what I could substitute for a good cry."[638] Once she forgot herself and who she was with, the tears flowed naturally and Noel was happy. While in Germany, Ruth was less enthusiastic about what was going on around her—the hypnotic appeal of Hitler, his rhetoric, and its effect on the German people. "I have never belonged to anything, not even a country club," recalled Ruth years later. "I don't like

September 2, 1933–George and Ruth frolic at Kay
Francis' Barn Dance.

mass stuff. I was in Germany in '32 and '33 and I saw that man coming up, and I said, 'Look out, look out, look out...'"[639]

On May 27, Mr. and Mrs. Brent left Southampton on the *S.S. Berengaria*. George was listed as an "Actor," and Ruth a "Cinema Artist." Upon her return to Hollywood, Ruth was confined to bed with a serious case of bronchitis. Dr. William E. Branch reported that Ruth had a relapse. She had been ill on her way home from Europe. Branch went so far as to indicate that it was a "nervous breakdown."[640] For a cure, Ruth and George headed for the hills of San Bernardino. Once there, they followed Dr. Henry (Hal) Bieler's recommended diet: no salt, no sugar, and plenty of green vegetables. They claimed it did them a world of good. Gloria Swanson was a lifelong advocate of Bieler's idea that "food is your best medicine." Once back in Hollywood, George's sister, Kathleen, visiting from New York, joined in the regimen and stayed around to help Mr. and Mrs. Brent celebrate their first wedding anniversary on August 13.

Before Ruth left for Europe, Warner had bought Donald Clarke's torrid 1933 novel, *Female*, with the idea of casting Chatterton, Barbara Stanwyck, or Bette Davis. Upon Ruth's return, the studio had *The House on 56th Street* ready for her instead and gave the role in *Female* to Stanwyck. Chatterton objected. Kay Francis was assigned *The House on 56th Street* (which became one of her biggest hits) and Ruth took on the controversial material in *Female*. (It was reported that Stanwyck rejected *Female*.) Filming began in mid-July. The content of Clarke's novel had to be thoroughly purged to be acceptable for the screen. In New York, The Society for the Suppression of Vice had attacked *Female* and the book was declared "obscene" by the state's Supreme Court. The original story told of a determined daughter's rise from the back alleys to married life on Park Avenue. One review called it *Fanny Hill* 1933-style. Gutting the original censorable story, screenwriters Gene Markey and Kathryn Scola kept only the idea of a woman executive who dallies with the affections of her male employees.

In *Female*, Ruth is Alison Drake—"Catherine the Great" of the automobile industry. She's single, all business, no nonsense, and has one hobby. She invites young, attractive male employees to her home under the ruse of talking about important business matters. Once there, they find themselves imbibing rounds of Russian vodka to fortify their libido—and receiving a complimentary trip to her boudoir. Everyone seems in awe of Alison. Chatterton cracks dialogue like a whip. She's completely in control and delightfully so. When her personal maid complains about her husband's drinking, Alison jests, "You wouldn't have these problems if you were a fallen woman." *The New York Times* said *Female* was "produced with a sense of humor [and] ... infinitely better than

Chatterton lures her victims with feminine
chic in *Female* (Warner).

its title might lead one to expect. Miss Chatterton acts with the necessary
flair for the role. Mr. Brent does quite well..."[641]   Brent's character, Jim
Thorne, a young engineer whom she meets at an amusement park one
evening, chastises her behavior and piques her interest. He tells Alison
he doesn't take home pick-ups and leaves her cold. A couple of street-
walkers call out, "Must be something wrong with your technique, dearie."
Alison fires back, "Ah! Shut up!" She doesn't mince words when explaining herself to an old school chum: "I'm going to travel the same open road
that men have always traveled."

Alison Drake was an unusual character for 1933. She was a woman
with a powerful professional role who indulged in routine sexual relationships. She wasn't seen as unfeminine or romantically deprived. When

Jim Thorne offers marriage, she refuses. "Don't let's spoil everything," she insists. Sex without matrimony suits her fine. Not until her company is in a financial crisis does she promise to head for the altar, telling Jim that he can resolve the crisis and run the firm. She'll be content to stay home and raise no more than nine children. Of course, it's a cop-out that reflects the times. It is expected that she will fall in love, but to give up a profession she loves? As the trailer for the film promised: "It takes a *real* man to tame this kind of female!"

Even with its compromised ending, *Female* was added to censor king Joseph Breen's list of films to be recalled after its release. In one instance, when Alison attempts to seduce a handsome lad (Philip Reed) by the pool, he refuses her vodka and only wants to talk about the arts and reincarnation. "You don't know much about women, do you?" she asks. As author Mark A. Vieira put it, "Her expression betrays the realization that her intended conquest is an invert."[642] *Film Daily* found the film to be "snappy fun." At the Los Angeles preview, columnist Jimmy Starr called *Female* "a smart and sparkling comedy-drama. It is not only surprising, but definitely pleasing

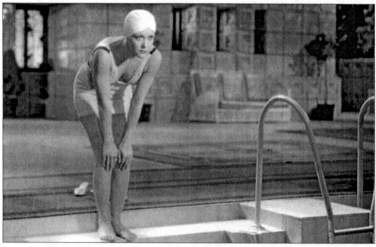

Preparing for a poolside seduction that goes awry in *Female* (Warner).

to the utmost to see one of our dramatic stars turn comedienne."[643] In Mick LaSalle's *Complicated Women* (2000), he complimented Chatterton's performance in *Female*, saying, "Chatterton had not only the sex appeal, but the years, the force, and the brains to pull off such a role."[644] LaSalle felt that Chatterton provided "a vision of total female authority" in her all screen roles. She personified the feminist ideal of women's rights and equality.

Three directors worked on *Female*. When William Dieterle took ill, William Wellman completed the film. Jack Warner was dissatisfied with the performance of one of Ruth's on screen boy toys (George Blackwood) and had him replaced by Johnny Mack Brown. As Wellman had started another picture, Michael Curtiz re-shot the necessary footage and received sole credit. The Chatterton-Brent team manage to exude chemistry in their fourth and final screen outing. However, by the time of Ruth's next Warner release, the couple had gone their separate ways both professionally and privately.

✦✦✦

The public was losing interest in Ruth Chatterton. After Warner released *One Way Passage* in October 1932, box office receipts indicated that Kay Francis was usurping Ruth's place as Queen of the Warner lot. Francis took on one of the mother-weeper roles that Chatterton rejected, *House on 56th Street*, and made it a huge success. Ruth also rejected *Mandalay* and *Dr. Monica*, which had been a moderate success for Nazimova on Broadway. Both roles proved perfect turf for Francis. *Screenland* saw *Dr. Monica* as a minor triumph and said that Francis injected "heartbreaking realism" into the story. Ruth had a difficult time coming up with a final film project to wrap up her contract.

Curiously, George Brent had also turned down *Mandalay*. He was

**Brent and Chatterton in *Female*. "It takes a real man to
tame this kind of female!" teased the ads (Warner).**

overworked; his star did not rise as expected; and suddenly he found
himself on suspension (October 1933). "It was very much like being in
bondage," he later reflected. Granted, his performances were easygoing,
natural, and competent. He simply didn't catch on like Gable or Cagney.
Brent aired his grievances both publicly and bluntly to his columnist,
friend Jack Grant:

> What am I to do? I'm tied with a contract as firmly and
> securely as a prisoner in dungeon chains. I am not be-
> ing given anything worthwhile on the screen. I can't
> quit, for the contract covers stage and radio, too. If I was
> suspended for insubordination, I could be kept idle the
> balance of my natural life. The months of suspension are
> only tacked on to the end of the contract. I'd never be free
> and acting is the only profession in which I'm trained.[645]

When Grant asked what Ruth had suggested, Brent promptly replied, "I've never asked her, and I never will. If I'm not man enough to work out my own salvation, I'd better chuck the whole business." As tension mounted in their home, Ruth began filming *Journal of a Crime*. She felt it wasn't her place to advise George and told Jack Grant, "He is brooding over this contract thing, until he is nearly insane."[646]

G.W. Pabst was scheduled to direct Ruth in *Journal of a Crime*, based on the French play by Jacques Deval. Pabst was one of the best German directors of his era, noted especially for *Diary of a Lost Girl* (1929) with Louise Brooks. Unfortunately, he rejected the script for *Journal of a Crime*, saying it was beneath his talents. William Keighley got the assignment. Undoubtedly, the psychological aspect of the story as well as its French origins appealed to Ruth. The crime in question was committed by Chatterton's character, who shoots her husband's mistress and lets another man be convicted and executed for her misdeed. The husband (Adolphe Menjou) discovers the truth. There is a sadistic interlude in which he waits for her to break under the strain of what she has done. On the verge of a nervous collapse, she decides to confess. On her way to the District Attorney's office, she is run down by an automobile while rescuing a child in harm's way. She comes out of the ordeal suffering from amnesia.

The Hollywood Reporter agreed that Chatterton "carried the picture" in a "difficult, unsympathetic part." "It is not a gay story," cautioned the review. [647] Los Angeles critic Jacques Perier found the film unique and absorbing, stating, "*Journal of a Crime* affords Ruth Chatterton an opportunity to display her superlative qualities as an emotional actress. She has not appeared in a better screen vehicle for many moons."[648] In one of two jaw-dropping, scenes, Ruth's character dives into desperate chatter in order to avoid hearing the truth from her philandering husband. Chatterton makes it clear that this woman's "love" has put her on the brink mentally. In another scene, she asks a legal advisor about conniving women who tempt husbands, imploring, "Aren't there any laws to help me, to protect me?" New York critics offered mixed impressions: "Miss Chatterton makes her agonies very moving" (*New York Daily Mirror*); "Ruth Chatterton gives another of her highly prima donna performances which leave much to be desired" (*New York Herald Tribune*); "Miss Chatterton gives an excellent performance and is ably assisted by Mr. Menjou" (*New York Journal*). Menjou, however, lacked the looks and charisma to pull off a character that devastates women to such extremes. In spite of a good per-

Adoring Adolphe Menjou in *Journal of a Crime* (Warner).

formance, he was a poor choice. In fact, Menjou tried to back out of doing the film. The film begged for a William Powell as well as a continental approach in creating a compelling, thought-provoking finish. One person who liked *Journal of a Crime* was Zelda Fitzgerald. She wrote her author husband F. Scott, saying, "Go see Ruth Chatterton and Adolphe Menjou in [*Journal of a Crime*]. It's a swell, straight, psychological story."[649]

As Chatterton had predicted, upon completing her contract with Warner Brothers, moviegoers were "richly tired" of her. She was richly tired of Hollywood, as well, and all that went with it, except for the money. She was disappointed with her unhappy, uncommunicative husband. In January 1934, she went to Palm Springs for a month's rest. She suffered from a bad cold as well as a bad marriage. In a matter of weeks, it was reported that she and George had separated. In the meantime, Ruth had discovered a new passion: aviation. It proved to be therapeutic and significantly redefined her life.

Endnotes

610   Harrison Carroll, "Chatterton Moves Over to Warners," *Los Angeles Evening Herald*, November 7, 1931.

611   "Notes from the Hollywood Studios," *New York Times*, July 31, 1932 (Decision made after *The Crash* was completed).

612   "Miss Chatterton and MGM," *New York Times*, December 4, 1932.

613   Clive Hirschhorn, *The Warner Brothers Story*, Crown Publishers, c. 1979, pg 112.

614   "Bits About the Talkies," *Manitowoc Herald News*, April 16, 1932.

615   Edwin Schallert, "Is Chatterton Money-Mad?" *Picture Play*, August 1933.

616   Sonia Lee, "Ruth Chatterton Tells What's *Wrong* with the Movies," *Motion Picture*, June 1933.

617   John McCallum, *Scooper*, Wood and Reber, c. 1960, pg 185.

618   John McCallum, *Scooper*, Wood and Reber, c. 1960, pg 185.

619   John McCallum, *Scooper*, Wood and Reber, c. 1960, pg 185.

620   Dan Van Neste, "Ruth Chatterton—Without a Trace of Affectation," *Films of the Golden Age*, Fall 1997.

621   Alan Hynd, *Professors of Perfidy*, Barns, c. 1963, pg 152.

622   Gladys Hall, "Ruth Chatterton's Own Story of her Second Marriage," *Motion Picture*, January 1933.

623   *Film Daily*, January 9, 1933.

624   "Ruth Bigger Hit In Saloon Than Salon," *Hollywood Reporter*, February 18, 1933.

625   Wood Soanes, review of *Frisco Jenny*, *Oakland Tribune*, January 20, 1933.

626   W.E. Oliver, review for *Frisco Jenny*, *Los Angeles Evening Herald Express*, January 6, 1933.

627   May Allison Quirk, "From Lady to Judy O'Grady," *Photoplay*, March 1933.

628   Jim Tully, "Chatterton, the Fighter," *New Movie*, July 1932.

629   "Ruth Chatterton Trapped in Storm," *Pittsburgh Press*, February 4, 1933.

630   Walter Addiego, "A Wealth of Pre-Code Wellman," *San Francisco Chronicle*, April 12, 2009.

631   Review of *Lilly Turner*, *Hollywood Reporter*, April 20, 1933.

632   Review of *Lilly Turner*, *Film Daily*, June 15, 1933.

633   Harriet Parsons, review of *Lilly Turner*, *Los Angeles Examiner*, June 2, 1933.

634   "Ruth Chatterton Revising 'West of Broadway,'" *Boston Herald*, March 13, 1939.

635   Louella Parsons, "Chatterton Brent," *Syracuse Herald*, June 7, 1933.

636   Ben Maddox, "The Lady Talks Back," *Screenland*, January 1936.

637   "Dick Wallace May Direct Ruth Chatterton Abroad," *Film Daily*, April 5, 1933.

638   "Rialto Show Has Chatterton in Lead," *Laredo Times*, January 14, 1934.

639   Louis Sheaffer, "Curtain Time," *Brooklyn Eagle*, May 22, 1951.

640   "Ruth Chatterton Seriously Ill," *Montana Butte Standard*, June 17, 1933.

641   Mordaunt Hall, review of *Female*, *New York Times*, November 4, 1933.

642   Mark A. Vieira, *Sin in Soft Focus—Pre-Code Hollywood*, Harry N. Abrams, c. 1999, pg 144.

643   Jimmy Starr, review of *Female*, *Los Angeles Evening Herald Express*, October 14, 1933.

644   Mick LaSalle, *Complicated Women*, St. Martin's Press, c. 2000, pg 81.

645   Jack Grant, "Why the Chatterton-Brent Love Died," *Movie Mirror*, June 1934.

646   Jack Grant, "Why the Chatterton-Brent Love Died," *Movie Mirror*, June 1934.

647   Review of *Journal of a Crime*, *Hollywood Reporter*, March 5, 1934.

648   Jacques Perier, review of *Journal of a Crime*, *Los Angeles Illustrated Daily News*, April 13, 1934.

649   Jackson Bryer and Cathy W. Barks, "Dearest Scott, Dearest Zelda," St. Martin's, c. 2002, pg 190-191.

By 1936, Ruth had gained respect and admiration in the field of aviation.

11
Aviatrix—Ruth Chatterton
Sportsman Pilots Derby

"Flying is incomparable relaxing," testified Ruth in 1935. "It reduces all sorts of vexations to inconsequential trifles. And it's the best form of wander lusting that I know."[650] She had indulged in her new passion in earnest for well over a year before resuming her profession as an actress. Whatever emotional wounds and career disappointments Ruth had accrued, she found resolution in the sky—and she was determined to obtain her pilot's license. Her interest in aviation began when she went on one of the first commercial air-mail planes (c. 1926). "After that," said Ruth, "I wanted to fly everywhere and did a lot of it abroad. But then, when a friend of mine was badly injured on the R-101, I suddenly became afraid." The R-101 was a British airship completed in October 1929. It crashed on route to Karachi in October 1930, killing 48 of the 54 passengers—more losses than the Hindenburg disaster of 1937. It was a French aviator who took on the task of getting Ruth to fly again in 1932 and letting *her* take the controls and land the plane. "Of course," Ruth explained, "he was sitting right beside me, so there was no danger, but the thrill of that decided me I must learn to fly and pilot my own ship."[651]

Following her separation from George Brent, it took just four months to win her license and it wasn't long before she made three trips across the country and back. There was a push among U.S. women pilots to go after world records held by women elsewhere. An AP report listed 359 licensed American women pilots—"more according to NAA records than licensed women flyers in all other countries."[652] Amelia Earhart was foremost in establishing records in both speed and distance and would become a friend and mentor of Ruth's.

Agent and future producer Leland Hayward sowed the seed in Chatterton's mind for starting an air derby at Cleveland for amateur flyers. It would be the first of its kind. Hayward had shared his passion for flying (and romance) with client Katharine Hepburn while she filmed the Dorothy Arzner-directed *Christopher Strong* (1933). In this film, Hepburn played an aviatrix. Ruth seemed unconcerned about her own film career and was determined to freelance. "I'd rather fly than make pictures," she would say. Clara Studer, editor of *Sportswoman Magazine*, wrote, "Few people besides the man who taught her and her friend Amelia Earhart, know what an able pilot she actually is." Ruth's instructor, Bob Blair, an aviator with more than twenty years' experience, confirmed, "Ruth Chatterton is not only a natural flyer, but she is one of the most intelligent and courageous pilots I have ever taught."[653] Not that the two didn't have their run-ins. Ruth could be too brave, too headstrong. She seemed to live chiefly in her aviation suit, looking calm and poised. As one reporter observed, she gave the "general impression of having solved the riddle of life to her complete satisfaction."[654]

<hr />

During 1934, Ruth dealt with personal issues and put her career on hold. Her swan songs for Warner Brothers failed to establish her as a box office

April 1, 1936, with instructor Bob Blair
(Roosevelt Field, Cleveland).

draw. The *Motion Picture Herald,* in its January 1934 issue, featured the "Ten Biggest Money Making Stars of 1932-33" and reported that among the women on the Warner lot, Kay Francis ranked 42nd, Joan Blondell 44th, Barbara Stanwyck 46th, and Chatteron 55th. Bette Davis wasn't among those listed. Stanwyck had already taken over Ruth's bungalow. "If Barbara felt any triumph, she concealed it," noted columnist Harrison Carroll, who mentioned the lifelong coolness between the two ladies.[655] Ruth wasn't exactly missed by the Warner crew, either, especially assistant directors.

Ruth was known to exercise her temperament when asked to work late or get up early. Photographer Clarence Bull said that Chatterton was the most difficult actress to get into the gallery for new portraits. "She never could understand why studios needed new pictures every few months," he complained.[656] Had temperament worked to her disadvantage? Freelance writer and future scenarist Katharine Hartley (a.k.a. Ketti Frings) didn't think so. She made note that actresses who were spitfires made good copy. While at RKO to do a story on Ginger Rogers, Hartley dropped Ginger the second she heard "a familiar high-pitched, voice squawking, 'You pig! You *are* a pig! Yes, you heard me… p-i-g—pig! Don't you ever come near me again!'" It was none other than Katharine Hepburn, who went on shouting long after "Mr. Pig" retreated from earshot. ("Pig" was one of Hepburn's favorite monikers for those who displeased her.) Hartley found Hepburn inspiring and said, "I would rather endure Hepburn's ire than be soothed by a more pleasant star's smile." Apparently, she felt the same about Ruth. "Chatterton is feared by most," wrote Hartley. "Her tantrums… her wrath have made history in this town. Chatterton, like the temperamental artist that she is, had to rule the roost, and she did: lock, stock and barrel, even husband. Helen Hayes has always been nice to everyone. With the result that Helen Hayes is still just plain Helen Hayes, while we still speak of Ruth as 'La Chatterton.' And in that little 'la' is a world of difference."[657] Ruth's own take on her reputation as being temperamental was to deny it. "I don't know how this idea got started," she said. "All the complaints I have made were in the constructive phase—before actual work was begun—and only when I really thought some cooperation on my part might be of use."[658]

George Brent's quarrel with Warner Brothers aggravated the split between him and Ruth. Brent went seven months without a single film release. Ruth attempted to rally friends to cheer him up, but he was anything but cordial when they appeared at their doorstep. Occasionally, he was downright rude. He wouldn't speak to Ruth for over a week at a time. Finally, they separated. In March 1934, Ruth, accompanied by her mother, boarded a train for New York.[659] During a stopover in Chicago,

June 16, 1935, with Richard Barthelmess and Carole Lombard at
Lombard's Venice Pier Fun House Party. Chatterton offered her
impersonations of famous people at the event.

Ruth issued a statement: "Hollywood gossips seemingly resent married
happiness. There is no strife in the Brent household."[660] In private, Ruth
had promised herself a week to think things over. She wired George back
on March 26, saying that a separation was the only solution.[661] By then,
George's sister, Kathleen, had arrived from Chicago to help him settle
into his apartment at the Town House. When asked, George stated that
he had "learned the lesson that two people in the same line of endeavor
should not be married."[662]

Ironically, Brent also took up aviation during his career lull and purchased a deep cream-colored plane with red leather upholstery. Then he
ran low on funds. "I just had to eat crow and go back to work," he said.
Upon patching things up with Warner, Brent moved from $250 to $1000 a
week, but his roles continued to be unrewarding. He was highly displeased

with his next Warner feature, *Housewife*. [663] This disappointment was best summed up by his co-star Bette Davis, "Dear God! What a horror!"[664] In the aftermath of his ordeals, Brent told columnist Jerry Lane, "I swallowed enough pride back there to float the Mauritania. Maybe it'll agree with me."[665] While Ruth never made comment on Jack Warner, Brent, whose contract with the studio terminated in 1943, revealed, "Jack Warner used to refer to us as 'the peons down on the set.' They were ruthless."[666]

In June 1934, Ruth joined Grace Moore, Virginia Bruce, Bee Stewart (wife of playwright Donald Ogden Stewart), and Frances Goldwyn at a farewell luncheon for Kay Francis. Maurice Chevalier had left for Europe and his love interest, Francis, wasn't far behind. However, by the time she arrived in Paris via Naples, Kay had a "damn attractive" Italian in hot pursuit named Paolo.[667] Ruth, on the other hand, kept her libido at bay for the time being. Instead, she negotiated with RKO producer Pandro Berman for the lead in *By Your Leave*. The story concerned a married couple who decide to take a week's vacation from each other. Claudette Colbert also had her eye on the role. This so-so variation of *The Seven Year Itch* ended up in the hands of Genevieve Tobin and Frank Mor-

1935. Ruth as Josephine Baker and Clifton Webb as Fu Manchu. Dorothy DiFrasso's "Come As The Person You Most Admire" party.

gan. Director Edmund Goulding wanted Ruth for a story titled *Counterpoint* (re-titled *The Flame Within*), in which she would play a psychiatrist.   Goulding had plans to reunite Ruth with Clive Brook as leading man. Ruth told Goulding that it didn't suit her. After Garbo declined the project, the roles went to Ann Harding and Herbert Marshall. It would be over a year before Ruth made another film.

Night out on the town with Philip Reed (her unconsummated conquest in *Female*).

In August, Ruth came out of seclusion to entertain at her Beverly Hills home. A midnight supper in honor of her friend Grace Moore's successful Hollywood Bowl concert included guests: Norma Shearer and Irving Thalberg, the Samuel Goldwyns, the Harry Cohns (Columbia), pianist Jose Iturbi, Maurice Chevalier, Ronald Colman, Edmund Goulding, and a few others. It was now reported that Ruth would sign with Columbia ($100,000 for four pictures).[668] As Grace Moore had a tremendous hit with Columbia's *One Night of Love*, it was predicted that Ruth would try her luck with the studio's abrasive, tight-fisted producer, Harry Cohn. Los Angeles columnist Elizabeth Yeaman minced no words when she described the merger as an attempt to "salvage" Chatterton's sagging career. Highly incensed, Ruth contacted reporter Harrison Carroll, begging him to say that she "wouldn't think of working for $25,000 a picture."[669] While gossips debated her fate, Ruth, along with Miss Moore, spent afternoons sunbathing atop the Chatterton roof.

In the fall, Ruth rented former oil baron William Miller Graham's house at La Quinta. She enjoyed long desert walks; the company of Jackie and Liz, her Sealyham terriers; and taking a daily plunge into the pool.[670] On October 4, Ruth obtained an interlocutory decree in her divorce proceedings, claiming that Brent had been "sulky, unreasonable, and domineering." She took the witness stand wearing a black suit, felt hat to match, double silver fox furs, gray gloves, and gray and black slippers. Her new, svelte figure, she claimed, was due to "great and grievous mental pain and suffering."[671] Her testimony, "I lost twelve pounds the last week we lived together as man and wife," garnered the headline: "Ruth Chatterton, 12 Pounds Lighter, Is Given Divorce."[672] Ruth's secretary, Rita Gray, also took the stand to say, "Miss Chatterton was almost on the verge of a nervous breakdown and it was because of the way that Mr. Brent treated her."[673] One reporter deduced that the "black-haired, hazel-eyed Dublin chap… who was made a movie star by Miss Chatterton, took to domesticity like a bull in a china shop."[674] At least the reporter gave credit where credit was due. Brent's screen career had all but fizzled until Chatterton uttered her famous cry, "Where has *he* been … ?"

Brent did not contest the suit, but let it be known that he was tired of having Ralph Forbes around the house "even at breakfast." Apparently, Forbes had a permanent place reserved in their boudoir as well. Brent claimed that Ruth insisted on keeping a photo of Ralph on her nightstand. "Of course, I love Ralph," Ruth said prior to her split with Brent. "It's different, of course. George is my husband. Ralph is the best kind of a friend."[675] Gossips predicted that Ruth and Ralph would remarry after her divorce, but the rumors were quashed when Ralph married the young English actress Heather Angel. Forbes had previously proposed to Lucille Ball. "He was terribly British," recalled Ball years later, "and so was his whole family; they impressed the hell out of me. But when he proposed, I cooled off in a hurry. I was more than half in love with him, but I managed to turn him down."[676] Ball was convinced she made the right decision. Before she knew it, he had eloped to Yuma with Heather Angel.

Brent relished being on his own again. "I think any man likes his freedom once in a while," he grinned. "He can read his newspaper at the table; he doesn't have to dress for dinner… *He doesn't have to talk when he gets home from the studio dead tired.*"[677] After flying around with young, blonde Warner contract player Jean Muir, Brent found consolation from none other than Greta Garbo. She specifically requested him to play her lover in MGM's *The Painted Veil* (1934). They began to spend time together playing handball and canoeing. She would frequent Brent's small bachelor house at Toluca Lake. With Garbo, Brent could enjoy companionship, just as he did with his pug dog, Whiskey, and not be concerned with matrimony. Brent and Garbo were seen together constantly. In author Barry Paris' *Garbo*, he wrote, "Brent built a wall around his Toluca Lake mansion (sic) so Garbo could lie about, unseen and unmolested, and play tennis and swim with him in privacy… Both were loners. Brent's athleticism and introversion were very much like—and compatible with—the Swede's."[678] Of course, reporters began to refer to Brent as the "Male Garbo." Greta had been threatening to return to Sweden and devote her talent to the legitimate stage and raising potatoes. Then it was disclosed that she would stay in Hollywood, most likely because of Brent. Newshounds had a field day conjuring up headlines, such as, "Ay tank ay stay here now" and "Greta Garbo Wants to Be Alone, With George Brent."[679] Their idyll lasted for over a year. When columnist Franc Dillon asked George if he would marry again, Brent was emphatic: "If I do, I hope someone hits me on the head with a baseball bat."[680]

Following their divorce, Ruth never said a word about George Brent. No one would have dared ask. However, by 1942, a Canadian journalist, Regine Kurlander, braved the subject of Brent when Ruth was guest of honor at a Canadian officers' cocktail party. "You see," Ruth replied wistfully, "I never knew him very well. We were only married three years."[681] Technically, she was correct on both accounts. Ruth never really understood the emotional burden that George Brendan Nolan carried from his childhood—a mother he resented and claimed to be dead. George was genuinely a man who was shy of people/strangers and preferred his own company. "I can't be chummy on short notice," he would explain.[682] As far as their marriage lasting three years—the final decree for divorce was not entered in superior court until October 14, 1935.[683] George remained clueless when it came to Ruth's real age. Earlier that year, when submitting a declaration of intention for U.S. citizenship, he put down Ruth's birth date as, "December 24, 1896 (I think)."[684]

In November, Chatterton made her dramatic radio debut in Lux Theatre's presentation of Donald Ogden Stewart's play, *Rebound*. The hour-long program was the only professional acting she did in 1934. Columbia had brought Dorothy Arzner on board as both associate producer and director in hopes to get a Chatterton project underway, but Ruth couldn't be coaxed into filming anything. She celebrated Christmas Eve at the home of Richard Barthelmess, who had also been ousted from Warner Brothers. Ruth, Kay Francis, and Richard's wife, Jessica, stayed up to talk until the wee hours of the morning. Kay, undoubtedly, had lots to say about filming her new picture, *The Goose and the Gander*. Her two leading men were none other than George Brent and Ralph Forbes. It was reported that the two gents enjoyed lunching together on the set.[685]

Ruth's sabbatical from love came to an end when she began seeing Spanish conductor/pianist Jose Iturbi.   His superb musicianship and inspired fingers seemed to have no limitations when he packed the Los Angeles Philharmonic Auditorium in January 1935.   Kay Francis accompanied Ruth for the opening concert.   Ruth's personal interest and connection to Iturbi made his unerring, rippling, rendition of Chopin's *Impromptu in A flat, Op. 29* and his careless grace in performing Brahms' *Intermezzo* seem all the more… intimate.   Louella Parsons offered a random note: "Ruth Chatterton looking supremely happy these days; so is Jose Iturbi, famous pianist.   All their friends say it's a romance."[686]   Iturbi, a widower, and Chatterton were often seen dining out.   Iturbi, who was also taking flying lessons, was constantly in the air while guest conducting in North and South America.   On one flight, Iturbi's plane crashed and capsized in the waters near Trinidad.   This didn't stop him from getting on the next available plane or performing at his next engagement.   Ruth, who acquired a reputation of ignoring storm warnings for aircraft, had the same attitude.   "As for taking so-called unnecessary risks," she said, "I don't think I take nearly as much risk flying as I do driving an automobile around southern California traffic."[687]

<hr/>

Ruth's reputation as "Cinema's Amelia Earhart" gained momentum in the spring of 1935.   She began flying lessons with Bob Blair, a veteran pilot stationed at the Los Angeles Municipal Airport.   Blair had won the Carnegie Medal for saving an aviator from a burning plane.   He also taught Henry Fonda, Cary Grant, and Wallace Beery how to fly.   Ruth's first plane was a shiny, black, four-seated Stinson with a Lycoming engine and cruising speed of 130 miles per hour.   After 50 hours of student flying instruction, she obtained her license and became the first actress to fly her own plane cross-country. Ruth said that she felt "new born." She wrote an article, "Fly Your Own Ship," for *Sportswoman* magazine in which she expressed her hope that the government would assist young people without the financial means to take flying lessons and "have their chance."[688] Ruth enjoyed taking friends up in her plane, like Fay Bainter and Ruth Gordon. Gordon, who was doing a screen test at MGM, was Chatterton's houseguest for four weeks. Tailing along with Chatterton for morning flying lessons or riding horseback, Gordon was dazzled by Chatterton's life. In her autobiography, she elaborated:

> [Ruth's] career was on the blink, so was mine, her love
> life gone to hell, so had mine, her finances zero, so were
> mine, but gallant Ruth behaved as though it was still the
> grand days. She ordered grand clothes from Howard
> Greer, mornings rode her five-gaited saddle horse in the
> Burbank hills. 'Why don't you ride, Ruthie?' she asked
> me. I'd never ridden, but why not? Home to an exquisite
> lunch in her *small* dining room off the walnut paneled
> grand dining room for dinner parties... around Ruth's
> table... place cards for Ronald Colman, Grace Moore,
> Maurice Chevalier, Kay Francis, Noel Coward, Cary
> Grant, Charles and Pat Boyer, William Powell, Carole
> Lombard! Something to write home about![689]

Eventually, Gordon told MGM "to go to hell," then left for Chicago. Chatterton "dickered" with Warner to play the fiery southern belle in *Jezebel*, but was more tempted by Columbia's offer to star in A.R. Wylie's *A Feather in Her Hat*.[690] After signing a contract in April, she booked passage for Spain. Ruth had appointments to keep: the Moroccan desert; the

Easter bullfights; and the arms of Rex Smith. "I love the bullfights," Ruth cooed to reporters as she boarded the Italian ocean liner *Conte de Savoia* for Seville. Ruth and Rex had delayed a rendezvous from the previous summer as Ruth was preoccupied with her divorce. A disappointed Rex had written a letter that underscored his ardor and devotion.

Dearest Ruth,   June 24, 1934 (Madrid)

Of course, I'll postpone our date—but with a heavy heart… because you will not be with me tonight. Nothing can go wrong with you, more than a little, because you are too fine… We should plan for a May visit next year. That is a good month for the bull fights in Madrid. Naturally, I want you before—anytime you can come.

Why don't you think of a British picture? Bob Milton is crazy for you to do our Russian story—that earthy tale I told you one afternoon in Chicote's Bar—over swell cocktails. We have done nothing about it since and refused the Radio offer—laziness, and the hope we could find you available sometime. If you would be interested I could send you the synopsis. This way, I would take a vacation, work with you, and have you to myself for a long time. I am going along here—loving Spain—missing you—gradually preparing material for later writings when I can retire. Say, when we set forth on that lovely journey you lost on the wager, we shall aim together.

Ruth, Darling—remember always—no matter what happens—there will always be Rex, unchanged and ready to serve you loyally any way you need.[691]

Rex

May 14, 1935. Returning home from her rendezvous in Europe.
Inset photo of Rex Smith—a photo that Ruth held onto
until she died (courtesy of Brenda Holman).

Rex's letter, along with his photograph, was among the very few mementos that Ruth held onto for the rest of her life. Rex also updated Ruth on the condition of the injured toreador Nicanor Villalta—Hemingway's "praying mantis" of the bullring. However, tension in the bullring was nothing compared to the revolt in the streets of Spain during Ruth's 1935 visit. News headlines reported that the atmosphere was tense, the enforcement of martial law inevitable. Ruth returned home on May 14 and Rex was back permanently in the U.S. by the end of June. His assignment in Madrid was terminated prior to the Franco uprising and the Spanish Civil War. Smith began a new career with *Newsweek*, where he launched an editorial formula that was readable and caught the tempo of Americans. It wasn't long before he was the magazine's editor.

⚜

While in Spain, Ruth was awarded a private pilot's license by the Department of Commerce.[692] She returned to New York and took possession of her license as well as a new Stinson plane at Roosevelt Field. After a trial spin, she landed and announced her intention for a cross-country flight. News flashes followed her progress over the next two days. On May 24, Ruth left Roosevelt at 11:32 a.m., accompanied by Bob Blair and Brenda Forbes, Ralph's sister. With Ruth at the controls, they arrived shortly before sundown at St. Louis for an overnight stop. Ruth had decided not to attempt night flying. She left instructions for her plane to be serviced and ready by 8 a.m. the next morning. She overslept. Leaving St. Louis at 10 a.m., she intended to fly to Kansas City, but rerouted to Tulsa for lunch and fuel. When she didn't show up in Kansas City, some feared for her safety. "I'm sorry we caused any worry," Ruth apologized to reporters.[693] She was also overdue for her evening stop in Amarillo—raising concern that her transcontinental hop had run into trouble over the rugged Guadalupe Mountains. While friends and family eagerly stayed tuned to the news, Ruth decided to re-route to El Paso due to stormy weather. She registered incognito at the city's Hotel Hussmann as Mrs. Ralph Forbes and escaped recognition for hours. Ruth was back at the controls at 7 a.m. Her first coast-to-coast flight was safely completed at 4:58 p.m. following a smooth landing at the Los Angeles Municipal Airport. "It was a great trip—I like flying immensely," was her only comment.[694]   While she didn't break any transcontinental elapsed time records, her mission was accomplished.

⚜

Producer Harry Cohn was still determined to put Ruth back in the spotlight. She began rehearsals for Columbia's *Feather in Her Hat* soon after completing her coast-to-coast flight. Filming began in July with veteran director Alfred Santell. Being cast as a self-sacrificing, middle-aged mother of a grown son proved to be too much for Ruth. She walked out after four days of shooting. She thought her character "too old a woman."[695]   Veteran stage actress Pauline Lord flew in from New York to take over the role. Louella Parsons explained, "The problem of making Ruth Chatterton fit the type of a middle aged cockney mother was too great, so both Ruth and Sam Briskin [producer] decided… that it would be wiser to rush preparations for *A Modern Lady*."[696]   Columnist Robbin Coons was more to the point, saying, "The reason Ruth Chatterton quit the comeback… was that the character grows old. She will be a younger woman in the substitute picture."[697]   Ruth's "age anxiety" mirrored the character of Fran Dodsworth, whom she would portray with devastating effect on screen the following year. During her brief stay on the Columbia set, Ruth and Louis Hayward, who arrived from London to play her adoptive son, hit it off. She began giving flying lessons to Hayward and fellow actor Brian Aherne. In the meantime, *A Modern Lady* also bit the dust. Harry Cohn, known for his temper, must have been fuming.

Louis Hayward, with Ruth's encouragement, would return to England to obtain his pilot's license.[698] After encouraging Aherne to take the controls of her Stinson, she cried, "Well done! You have an instinct for flying!" Aherne was impressed by her coolness and efficiency. The two were often seen lunching together. "I easily succumbed to her flattery," he recalled later, "and then and there agreed to take ten hours' lessons from Bob Blair."[699] Ruth reinforced in Aherne the idea that "Flying is good for the mind." Due to Ruth's passion for aviation, Aherne reaped the rewards of self-reliance. He had nothing but praise for her.

> It was Ruth to whom I telephoned from the hangar with the news of my [first] solo. It was she who introduced me to the miracle of flying, whose enthusiasm never faltered when I was tempted to despair, who gloried in my little successes, my first cross-country, the winning of my license, the purchase of my plane—she was my first passenger.[700]

The following year, Aherne and Chatterton teamed for a Lux Radio presentation of James M. Barrie's gentle love story, *Quality Street.* Aherne planned to participate in the second Ruth Chatterton Air Derby. "I wanted so badly to win her trophy," lamented Aherne, "but I'm grounded by Lloyds."[701] He was busy filming Goldwyn's *Beloved Enemy.* Columnist Sheilah Graham insisted that Ruth was "basking in the attentions of Brian Aherne" at the time—while referring to her "ex-heart interest" as director Fritz Lang—who Ruth also persuaded into taking an occasional hop in her… airplane.[702]

Six days after backing out of *A Feather in Her Hat,* Ruth announced her offer of $1,000 prize money for a transcontinental air derby as part of the 1935 National Air Races. It was open to male and female non-professional pilots. She would not compete, but fly her own Stinson as a pacemaker. The Ruth Chatterton Air Derby was scheduled for August 25-30, from Los Angeles to Cleveland Municipal Airport. The derby consisted of a series of noon to night individual laps over a southern route. The national winner at Cleveland would receive $450 and possession of the Ruth Chatterton trophy. The 2nd to 5th place contestants would also receive monetary rewards. The focus was not on speed, but on pilot skill and navigation. Shortly before the event, Ruth tested her acting skills for NBC radio audiences. Al Jolson's *Chateau Hour* provided her a spot to enact a scene from Katharine Hepburn's ill-fated Broadway flop *The Lake.* The selected scene did not include Hepburn's famous: "The calla lilies are in bloom again…" Instead, the radio audience heard a brief episode filled with trembling declarations of love until a car crash mercifully brings them to a screeching halt.

August 27, 1935, (Cleveland) with ex-sister-in-law Brenda Forbes.

National Air Derby officials in Cleveland had little time to persuade amateur flyers to enter the Chatterton event. Even so, they managed to get twenty participants. Then, on August 15, came the sad news of Will Rogers' death in an Arctic plane crash. The loss of America's beloved hu-

morist and aviation advocate came as a terrible shock. One by one, en-
trants in the Chatterton Derby scratched their names until only six were
left (three men and three women). Ruth's reaction? "If Will Rogers' death
had discouraged flying," she said, "I think that would have been the greatest tragedy for him. He believed in it so, and did so much for aviation."[703]
Regardless, the Chatterton Derby turned out to be a huge success.

On August 25, the Los Angeles-to-Yuma leg of the Chatterton derby
was headed by Leland Hayward. His relief pilot was none other than actor
James Stewart. Earl Ricks of Hot Springs, Arkansas, however, scored the
most points. Arriving first didn't mean you had won the lap. Getting off
course; excessive or slow flying; failure to observe safety factors in landing—were penalized. Ruth arrived ahead of the contestants at 1:20 p.m.
in her red Stinson, accompanied by three passengers: her maid, Brenda
Forbes, and Bob Blair. The following day, the derby was greeted by the
mayor in El Paso. Fans looked on as Ruth stepped off her plane wearing
a white silk shirt and gray slacks. "The trip was beautiful, but bumpy," she
said. "We're all having a big time."[704] Hayward, in his blue Waco cabin ship,
won the lap prize. An overnight stop in Abilene included a festive barbeque.
Grace Prescott of San Diego was first across the line in Oklahoma City the
next day and she gained a 27-point lead the following day as she glided into
Indianapolis. Hayward had been handicapped by an overheated engine. At
this point, fliers had logged 2,100 miles. On the 29th, Ruth stepped off her
plane in Toledo. She hurriedly powdered her nose, then cracked her head
on the side of her ship and cried, "Ouch!" After gaining her composure, she
immediately began jotting down plane numbers as her derby contingent
arrived. The Chamber of Commerce provided a luncheon where ace pilots
and guest stars feted the Chatterton Derby. Major Jimmy Doolittle, Captain Eddie Rickenbacker, and Penny Rogers, flying cousin of the late Will
Rogers, offered a few words of encouragement to the participants.[705]

In Cleveland, Grace Prescott, a twenty-three-year-old opera singer, copped the honors. Ruth presented her with the Chatterton Cup—an Egyptian bronze trophy. Prescott was followed by realtor Everett Woodson of Coronado and Leland Hayward in third place. Another contestant, 19-year-old Cecile Hamilton, may have tailed behind, but by the end of the year, with Bob Blair as her instructor, she became licensed as the youngest transport pilot of either sex in America. Ruth Chatterton was the centerpiece for Cleveland's national air races opening August 31. 60,000 aviation enthusiasts welcomed the Chatterton Derby contingent "and roared with approbation as the popular screen star, stepped from her plane."[706] Heads turned up to the sky while forty-seven military planes performed flight formations and a spectacular mass parachute jump. Ruth considered her sponsorship for the derby an honor of which she was "intensely proud."[707]

❧❧❀❧❧

Following the Cleveland event, Ruth flew en route to New York City. Ignoring storm warnings, she got as far as Syracuse. On her way to the hotel, she told reporters, "I've 150 flying hours to my credit and I'm going to have thousands more." Turning to news photographers, she was emphatic: "I'll not pose for a single picture—I'll not stand still."[708] The next morning, Amboy Airport officials warned Chatterton that crosswinds and dense fog over the Mohawk Valley could jeopardize the rest of her trip. Five other veteran pilots refused to risk the weather. Ruth said, "I'll take my chances. I'll fly this plane as far as it will go and then I'll land." Bob Blair admitted that he would rather they took a train—as did Brenda Forbes and Ruth's maid. Ruth stood her ground. "And I," she stated firmly, "I would rather fly. Why shouldn't we fly?" Blair informed her that there was poor visibility over Little Falls and a zero-zero ceiling—the bugaboo of all fliers. "What does that mean?" she asked, wide-eyed. "It means danger," Blair emphasized. "We'll fly," Ruth declared. Blair cautioned further that there were lots of mountains in the region. Ignoring him, Ruth quibbled, "That will be nice scenery."[709]

Surrendering, Blair headed across the field to start the engine. Officials informed Ruth that she would have to walk a hundred feet over a cinder path to reach her plane. "Can't we drive the car to the field?" she asked. A mechanic explained, "It's never been permitted before." "How nice," said Ruth. "This will be the first time," and drove off in a taxi. Two dozen spectators gasped during Ruth's takeoff—as her Stinson narrowly missed striking the tip of the main hangar. "They'll be lucky if they get beyond Utica," said one official, "and they'll be luckier if they land at Utica." The headstrong Miss Chatterton nosed her ship into the pelting rain. She bypassed Utica, but was forced down in Albany, where she, Blair, and party, prepared to proceed to New York City... by train.

Ruth's aeronautic notoriety gave her clout wherever she went. While at CBS for a radio broadcast, her table at the studio commissary was clogged with photographers and reporters when she was greeted by André Kostelanetz. The famous conductor had been working feverishly on a new orchestration during a rehearsal with Lily Pons and Nino Martini. He dropped everything the second he heard "La Chatterton" had requested his presence. CBS executives burned while the two "chatted casually about their common enthusiasm—flying."[710] After a two-week stay in New York, Ruth flew back to Hollywood, accompanied by her houseguest Fay Bainter and Bob Blair. Tilly and a few friends met them at the airport.

Dorothy Arzner was originally set to direct *Maid of Honor*. Zoe Akins adapted the scenario from the Katherine Brush novel. It would be like old times. However, by the time filming began in October, Marion Gering was directing the newly re-titled, *No More Yesterdays*. Columnist Paul Harrison joined Ruth on the set. Together, they watched Marian Marsh, the new ingénue who was playing her daughter. "Notice all her different expressions," Ruth whispered. "And when she smiles she looks like Marlene Dietrich."[711] Marsh, who had also battled Warner, was asked in 1998 what it was like to work with Chatterton. "She was terrific!" said Marsh. "I can tell you a funny story. She wasn't too crazy about [playing a mother]. The first day we had the wedding scene. It was really in the middle of the picture, but they had [the set] already built. The designer made me the most beautiful gown you could imagine. I looked terrific in

With Robert Allen in *Lady of Secrets* (Columbia).

it. Well, Ruth walked off the set! She didn't like what they had made for her to wear. Everyone was aghast! So, we did other things in the meantime. The next morning, they had made another dress for her that she liked."[712] Marsh described what turned out to be a friendly connection between the two actresses:

> I rode a horse every morning… for recreation. I was riding to Griffith Park… and I spied Ruth quite a ways from me on a horse [her chestnut mare "Lady Pat"]. So, I thought, well, maybe I can break the ice. I casually rode by her and acted as if I didn't recognize her. All of a sudden I heard this galloping behind me. And she came up and met me. She said, "I didn't know you rode a horse! I didn't know you liked horses!" And I said, "I can't start the day without getting on a horse." She said, "That's wonderful!" Well, from then on we were friends! When we got back to the set the next day… they were talking about me working on Saturday, and I said, "Oh, but that's the USC football game, and I have tickets!" Right away she interrupted, "Let's do her scenes first, so she won't have to come on Saturday." From then on she took care of me throughout the picture! She was just wonderful and acted just like a mother then!

Production for *Maid of Honor* ended on November 18, but the film was not released for three months. Critics were unanimous in targeting the rechristened *Lady of Secrets* as routine, creaky, mother-love nonsense. The genre had already been bled dry by Ruth. This time round, she played Celia Whittaker, a woman whose troubled past easily surfaces into emotional outbursts. A Fourth of July parade with marching soldiers outside her window sets her off like a firecracker. "Put on your uniforms and beat your drums!" she cries. "Tell the world that war is glorious. Let's have another one!" After calming down, she wistfully calls out, "Michael… Michael… I've got to learn to forget." We assume that the man she speaks of is among the dear departed.

Celia's younger sister, Joan (Marian Marsh), punishes the young man she loves by announcing her engagement to a middle-aged millionaire (Otto Kruger). Celia cordially lets the fiancé know, "I don't feel this marriage should take place. If I find I'm right, I shall declare war on it." He confesses that he isn't exactly convinced he's doing the right thing, either. The simpatico between Chatterton and Kruger is tangible. So far, *Lady of Secrets* holds one's interest. Halfway into the film, the sisters quarrel. Joan accuses Celia of never having had romantic feelings. Celia is left alone to reminisce. We then have the misfortune of experiencing a flashback which hammers more nails than necessary into the cross she bears, as well as the film's coffin. Any subtlety *Lady of Secrets* had quickly vanishes. Instead, we look aghast as Chatterton is asked to portray Celia as a sixteen-year-old. A younger shade of blonde, giddy innocence and clever lighting cannot disguise the fact that Baby Jane Hudson (Chatterton was 43) is attempting a comeback. 17 minutes of drudging things up that we already suspect deflates any delicacy the story possessed. This unfortunate plot twist allowed Ruth the satisfaction of appearing "young" on screen.

When *Lady of Secrets* returns to 1936, Celia is about to tell her "sister" that she is really her mother when the father intervenes (as did the Hays office).[713] Celia is taken into custody by a couple of strong-arm nurses who believe her to be delusional. All is resolved when Celia "escapes" and interrupts Joan's wedding rehearsal. Relieved, Joan admits she loves someone else and the wedding is called off. However, it's too late to save any of the charm, tempo, and poignancy that *Lady of Secrets* possessed. The inflated flashback has become a burdensome anchor, dragging its weight and the film with it.

From a Dallas film critic: "It would be advisable for Miss Chatterton to stick to her flying and derby races."[714] As a comeback picture, the reviewer felt that poor photography and equally bad editing exposed "Miss Chatterton in all her 40 odd years." Bosley Crowther, for *The New York Times*, admitted that Ruth was "forced to lean with increasing heaviness on the person who attends to lighting effects." While Crowther thought her performance "worthy," he found the film to be "formless." "The result," he deduced, "in the curious mathematics of the cinema, is zero."[715] Los Angeles critic Eleanor Barnes sub-titled her review, "Poor Ruthie," saying, "Nothing worse could have been perpetrated on the possessor of broad A's and society attitude than this. No wonder she took up aviation. Katherine Brush's story, creaky and antiquated, turns out to be a hilarious comedy instead of the serious drawing room drama that Ruthie undoubtedly expected."[716] Aside from the unfortunate flashback, Chatterton's neurotic, unhappy Celia held the audience's sympathy. Her easy grace and commendable reserve, abetted by Otto Kruger's performance, were the film's main assets.

⁂

Ignoring the critical tongue-lashings from her big "comeback," Ruth simply hopped aboard her $25,000 Stinson Reliant. Shortly before the film's release, she had made headlines after a forced landing near Fort Bragg. She lost her way on a flight to San Francisco. Taking an inland route to avoid fog, Ruth found herself over Lakeport—90 miles north of the city. Alone, in semi-darkness, her fuel supply diminished, Ruth finally nosed out over the Pacific Ocean, where she managed a forced landing in a sheep

La Chatterton ponders her next move in *Lady of Secrets* (Columbia).

pasture along the coast—125 miles from her original destination. "Her skill at the plane's controls and calmness in the face of an emergency were credited with avoiding a crash," stated one report.[717] Ruth explained, "You see it was 1:15 in the afternoon when I decided to fly to San Francisco for a few hours' visit with friends. I took the valley route to escape fog banks, and had intended to turn northwest when I reached a point south of San Francisco. I became mixed up somehow... before I realized I was badly off my course. But, oh, those mountains and deep gorges and tall trees! I never saw such rough country." She remained overnight in Fort Bragg, refueled the next morning, and then "hopped off" for San Francisco before a large assemblage of spectators.

In 1960, Ruth's publicist, Scoop Conlon, wrote about another flying incident that he said was characteristic of "the real Ruth." A few of Ruth's male buddies were having cocktails at her home in a small lounge that she called the "Glory Hole." She suddenly burst out with, "Who would like to take a flight with me tomorrow afternoon, three o'clock, in my new Stinson cabin plane?" William Powell quickly excused himself, saying he had another appointment. Richard Barthelmess offered the same excuse. Maurice Chevalier was the only honest one in the bunch and admitted, "To be perfectly frank, I'm afraid to fly with you." Ruth smiled at Conlon and said, "I know *one* man who isn't afraid to fly with me. Are you, ducky?" Conlon went on to say,

> The following afternoon I reluctantly showed up... purposely an hour late. If I had any idea that Ruth would give me up for lost—I was mistaken. She was sitting patiently on a truck near her plane, looking very pleased at the sight of me. "Good boy," she said cheerfully. "You didn't let me down." An hour later we were flying back from the Sierras when one of those terrible California fogs suddenly closed in. I said nothing because Ruth had only soloed a few weeks before [Fort Bragg fiasco] and I figured it wouldn't be a good idea to make her nervous. After a few minutes she spoke to me. I looked at her. She was smiling warmly. "Looks bad, doesn't it, ducky? Are you scared?"
>
> "I'm so scared, Ruthie, that I can't even say a prayer." She laughed. "So am I... but we'll make it somehow. Suddenly, we heard the roar of a motor over our heads, going in our direction. Ruth now was all business. She piloted the little plane right on the 'heels' of the big transport, and shortly we spotted a hole in the fog. She wasted no time making a near-perfect landing on the home field. Waiting for us was an angry Bob Blair. He had been hav-

ing terrible visions of his star pupil crashing to her death. He was understandably frightened.[718]

⚜

Christmas Eve 1935-Ruth, surrounded by good friends, celebrated her birthday. Grace Moore sang "Minnie the Moocher" accompanied by Jose Iturbi, followed by Miss Moore's rendition of "Smoke Gets In Your Eyes" with the song's composer, Jerome Kern, at the keyboard. The most important Christmas gift for Ruth came from Samuel Goldwyn. The producer was "very eager," according to Louella Parsons, to have Ruth play the Fay Bainter role in *Dodsworth*.[719] Ruth hesitated to take the role of a heavy, but the role of Fran Dodsworth would turn out to be the saving grace of her cinematic career.

Endnotes

650   "Ruth Chatterton Finds Flying Is Incomparable Recreation," *San Antonio Express*, December 29, 1935.

651   "Ruth Chatterton Finds Flying Is Incomparable Recreation," *San Antonio Express*, December 29, 1935.

652   "U.S. Women Pilots Grit Teeth, Plan to Go After World Records," *San Antonio Express*, May 25, 1935.

653   Clara Studer, "Not For Publicity," *Sportswoman*, November 1936.

654   "Ruth Chatterton Finds Flying Is Incomparable Recreation," *San Antonio Express*, December 29, 1935.

655   Harrison Carroll column, *Los Angeles Evening Herald Express*, January 5, 1934.

656   Charles G. Sampas, "New York – Hollywood," *Lowell Sun*, July 6, 1940.

657   Kay (Katharine) Hartley, "Can a Nice Girl Be a Big Success?" *Modern Screen*, January 1935 (Hartley would write *Hold Back the Dawn* and *Look Homeward, Angel*).

658   Kelly Woolpert, "Ruth Chatterton Denies the Soft Impeachment," *Freeport Journal Standard*, August 7, 1936.

659   "Shivering Fans Get An Icy Turndown From Ruth Chatterton," *Albuquerque Journal*, March 19, 1934.

660   "Ruth Chatterton Denies Separation," *Corsicana Daily* (TX), March 20, 1934.

661   "Ruth Chatterton and George Brent Separate," *Telegraph-Herald and Times Journal*, March 27, 1934.

662   "George Brent Blames Career For Discord," *Nevada State Journal*, March 29, 1934.

663   "Brent Entertains Press; Says 'Uncle,'" *Hollywood Reporter*, March 29, 1934.

664   Clive Hirschorn, *The Warner Bros. Story*, Crown Pub., c. 1979, pg 144.

665   Jerry Lane, "He's Jinx-Proof Now," *Photoplay*, November 1934.

666   Bill Kelly, "George Brent in 'Born Again' Role," *Santa Ana Orange County Register*, May 28, 1978.

667   Kay Francis, diary, July 19, 1934, Kay Francis collection, Wesleyan Cinema Archives, Wesleyan University, Middletown, CT.

668   Harrison Carroll, "Behind the Scenes in Hollywood," *Tyrone Daily Herald*, July 17, 1934.

669   Harrison Carroll, "Behind the Scenes in Hollywood," *San Mateo Times*, July 25, 1934.

670   Mollie Merrick, "Hollywood in Person," *Milwaukee Journal*, November 2, 1934.

671   George Brent Moody, Says Actress in Suit," *Ogden Standard*, September 18, 1930.

672   "Ruth Chatterton Granted Divorce From Geo. Brent," *Lewiston Daily Sun*, October 3, 1934.

673   Walter B. Clausen, "Noted Actress Given Divorce in Los Angeles," *Schenectady Gazette*, October 5, 1934.

674   "Ruth Chatterton Granted Decree, Says Actor Domineering," *The Border Cities Star*, October 4, 1934.

675   "Ruth Chatterton Divorce Catches Gossips Napping," *Pittsburgh Press*, March 15, 1934.

676   Lucille Ball, *Love, Lucy*, Putnam (New York), c. 1996, pg 78.

677   Franc Dillon, "George Brent Is On His Own Now—And Likes It," *Movie Classic*, October 1934.

678   Barry Paris, *Garbo*, Alfred A. Knopf, c. 1995, pgs. 313-320.

679   "Ay Tank Ay Stay Here Now," *Mason City Globe-Gazette*, December 20, 1934, and *Manitowoc Herald Times*, December 27, 1934.

680   Franc Dillon, "George Brent Is On His Own Now—And Likes It," *Movie Classic*, October 1934.

681   Regine Kurlander, "This—and Glamour, Too," *Plain Dealer*, November 12, 1942.

682   James Reid, "Hollywood's Champion Lone Wolf," *Motion Picture*, February 1940.

683   "Ruth Chatterton's Divorce Is Final," *Sandusky Register* (OH), October 15, 1935.

684   George Brent, "Declaration of Intention," County of Los Angeles, #70088, March 18, 1935.

685   Elizabeth Yeaman column, *Hollywood Citizen News*, January 15, 1935.

686   Louella Parsons, "Snapshots of Hollywood," *San Antonio Light*, January 8, 1935.

687   Ruth Chatterton, "Fly Your Own Ship," *Sportswoman*, November 1936.

688   Ruth Chatterton, "Fly Your Own Ship," *Sportswoman*, November 1936.

689   Ruth Gordon, *My Side: The Autobiography of Ruth Gordon*, Harper & Row, c. 1976, pg 318.

690   Woods Soanes, "Curtain Calls," *Oakland Tribune*, March 13, 1935.

691   Rex Smith, letter written to Ruth Chatterton, June 24, 1934, from Madrid (from Brenda Holman collection).

692   "Wings Awaiting For Film Star," *Ogden Standard Examiner*, April 26, 1935.

693   "Ruth Chatterton Resumes Flight," *Arizona Independent Republic*, May 26, 1935.

694   "Ruth Chatterton Completes Flight," *Reading Eagle*, May 27, 1935.

695   Dan Thomas, "Career in Balance," *Lowell Sun*, October 22, 1935.

696   Louella Parsons column, *San Antonio Light*, July 19, 1935.

697   Robbin Coons, "No Old-Age for Ruth," *Lowell Sun*, July 26, 1935.

698   "Louis Hayward Needs No Double," *San Antonio Light*, December 31, 1936.

699   Brian Aherne, *A Proper Job*, Houghton-Mifflin, c. 1969, pg 227, 232.

700   Brian Aherne, *A Proper Job*, Houghton-Mifflin, c. 1969, pg 230.

701   Sheilah Graham, "Hollywood In Person," *The Dallas Morning News*, August 31, 1936.

702   Sheilah Graham, "Hollywood In Person," *The Dallas Morning News*, September 2, 1936.

703   "Ruth Chatterton Finds Flying Is Incomparable Recreation," *San Antonio Express*, December 29, 1935.

704   "Hayward Wins Lap To El Paso," *El Paso Herald*, August 26, 1935.

705   "Ruth's Derby Arrives Here," *Toledo News-Bee*, August 29, 1935.

706   "First in Chatterton Race; Cleveland Show Opens," *Rochester Journal*, August 31, 1935.

707   Ruth Chatterton, "Fly Your Own Ship," *Sportswoman*, November 1936.

708   "Ruth Chatterton's Plane Defies Storm After Star's Brief Surprise Visit in City," *Syracuse Herald*, September 4, 1935.

709   "Ruth Chatterton's Plane Defies Storm After Star's Brief Surprise Visit in City," *Syracuse Herald*, September 4, 1935.

710   Bernes Robert, "The Radio Reporter," *Oakland Tribune*, October 13, 1935.

711   Paul Harrison, "Stars of Broadway Offset Lowly Film Role Seekers," *Port Arthur News*, October 14, 1935.

712   Dan Van Neste, "An Interview: Marian Marsh," *Films of the Golden Age*, Winter 1998.

713   AFI Catalogue of Feature Film Notes (According to the file on the film in the MPAA/PCA Collection at the AMPAS Library, in the original ending, "Celia" tells "Joan" that she is her mother; however, the Hays Office insisted that the film end with "Celia" continuing "to keep this secret to herself as part of her expiation.").

714   J.H., "Miss Chatterton Follows Routine In Movie Return," *Dallas Morning News*, April 15, 1935.

715   Bosley Crowther, review of *Lady of Scandal*, *New York Times*, February 22, 1936.

716   Eleanor Barnes, "Poor Ruthie," *Los Angeles Illustrated Daily News*, February 14, 1936.

717   "Movie Stars Plane Lands In A Pasture," *Ukiah Republican Press*, December 25, 1935.

718   John McCallum, *Scooper*, Wood & Reber, c. 1960, pgs 180-181.

719   Louella Parsons column, *San Antonio Light*, December 3, 1935.

With Walter Huston in *Dodsworth* (Samuel Goldwyn–United Artists).

12
Dodsworth

"You're simply rushing at old age, Sam,
and I'm not ready for that yet!"
- Fran Dodsworth

In 2005, *Time's* Richard Corliss and Richard Schickel placed *Dodsworth* among the "All-Time 100 Greatest Films" made since 1923. When Ruth signed on for the role of Fran Dodsworth on February 4, 1936, she emphasized her delight in portraying a character that was not only brilliant and showy, but unsympathetic. She was tired of playing for audience sympathy and told Benjamin Crisler of *The New York Times* that she wanted the American public to know that "she can dish it out as well as take it."[720] For over a year, Samuel Goldwyn had been persistent in coaxing Chatterton to take the role, saying it would be the high point of her career. Goldwyn was right. *Dodsworth* was nominated for seven Academy Awards, including Best Picture. However, MGM's elephantine *The Great Ziegfeld* won in that category thanks to Louis B. Mayer. In fact, five of the ten films nominated for Best Picture were filmed on Mayer's lot. Studio politics still had clout, influencing the winners as well as the nominees. Ruth was snubbed. Following the Academy Award presentations in 1937, columnist Jimmy Fiddler headlined his column, saying, "The failure to include Ruth Chatterton as a 1936 best performance nominee, was a shame that the Academy of Motion Picture Arts and Sciences will never live down."[721] Fiddler had led a campaign protest on Ruth's behalf causing "several members to write her name on their ballots."[722] Kay Francis put in her two cents' worth to the press when asked about the Academy Awards. "It is unfortunate when such brilliant artists as Ruth Chatterton ... are lost in the shuffle."[723] In the 1987 publication *Oscar Dearest: Six Decades of Scandal, Politics and Greed Behind Hollywood's Academy Awards*, author Peter H. Brown put a sobering slant on the Academy bypassing Ruth. "A maverick (such as Ruth Chatterton) could give the finest performance in years (such as her work in *Dodsworth*) and remain Un-Oscared. If an actor, no matter how fine, refused to play the studio game, then just don't nominate him."[724] Ruth had announced that studio contracts interfered with her independence; she was determined to freelance; and she paid the price.

Chatterton's performance in *Dodsworth* continues to impress. Laura Linney, who has been nominated twice for an Academy Award, lists *Dodsworth* as her favorite film. Her reason is simple and brief. "I love *Dodsworth*," she says. "Ruth Chatterton's deep portrayal of a very superficial person is amazing to watch."[725] In 2009, New York writer David Noh offered a succinct appraisal of Ruth's ability, describing her portrayal of Fran as being "selfish to a fault—an amoral and an annoying cock-tease–often despicable, but through it all, Chatterton makes her deeply human, with a kind of searing empathy which makes us all see a little Fran in ourselves, however unwillingly. In her skilful hands, the usual dilemma of such a premise–why the hell does Sam Dodsworth stay with this bitch?–disappears, such is the actress' fecund allure, mitigating charm and momentarily contrite, convincing fits of remorse."[726] In a 2010 Broadway revival of *Dodsworth*, Noh recalled that the actress playing Fran (Lisa Riegel) said she could barely watch the film version because she hated Ruth so much. "Which is probably the greatest compliment she could have paid her performance," said Noh.[727]

⚜

The New Year 1936 found Ruth frequently flying to Palm Springs, enjoying her daily massage, dining tête-à-tête with Jose Iturbi at Café Lamaze, or the Cocoanut Grove. She did back-to-back programs for radio's popular *Hollywood Hotel*—doing scenes from *Lady of Secrets* as well as Ruth's favorite James Barrie play, *Mary Rose.* One radio reporter noted that Ruth chewed gum "faster than a hat-check girl" during the broad-

**January 31, 1936- Ruth takes a "Cole Porter break"
from Jose Iturbi and Fritz Lang**

casts. She was a frequent visitor to the MGM set of *Fury*, where she observed Fritz Lang directing his unforgiving study of mob violence. Ruth told columnist Robbin Coons that, in her opinion, Lang's *M* (1931) was the greatest film ever made. She had seen it four times.[728] In turn, Lang would make frequent visits to the set of *Dodsworth*, where Ruth faced daily confrontations with director William Wyler. Through his friendship with Ruth, Fritz became a flying enthusiast and it was reported that he was taking lessons from Bob Blair.[729]

In late January, the sea-battered body of test pilot Lt. Arthur Skaer, missing since July 30, 1935, was discovered near Santa Monica. Twenty-four-year-old Skaer disappeared while doing a test flight for the U.S. Army. For over a month, the Coast Guard, private aircraft, and horsemen had scoured Southern California looking for Skaer. Long after the search was abandoned, Ruth used her private plane to pilot members of Skaer's family over the hills and canyons near Alhambra, thirty miles inland. Skaer's young bride, Dorothy, told Ruth that a spiritualist had said that her husband's body "would be found in the hills."[730] Although their search proved futile, it became obvious that Ruth's talent as an aviatrix wasn't limited to pleasure and air derbies. Still, she followed through with her plan for a second annual Chatterton competition.

At the end of March, Ruth flew east with Bob Blair to map out a course for her August 1936 derby.[731] Blair had encouraged Ruth to invest $2,000 for a two-way radio. Lucky thing he did. As they approached the Allegheny Mountains, her new transmitter indicated that the range was impassable. She took a southern route instead. Two hours later, Fred Harvey, pilot and WWI hero, crashed to a horrific death a few miles from where Ruth had changed course. Tilly went along on this adventure. Ruth admitted that having her mother on board reversed the usual emotions of a flier in that she felt safest "whizzing along under a dangerously low ceiling" so the ground below was visible.[732] "My best passenger is my mother," Ruth said. "She thinks I'm a great pilot."[733] A week after arriving in New York, tragedy struck again. On April 8, Leland Hayward and Bob Blair were injured when Hayward's cabin plane crash-landed at Roosevelt Field. Blair's student flier on board was killed. While Ruth would make numerous forced landings, Lady Luck was on her side. Two weeks later, the recovered Hayward accompanied Ruth back to Hollywood.[734]

In late April, Ruth returned to film-making at Twentieth-Century-Fox. She battled influenza while making *Girl's Dormitory*. Disobeying doctor's orders to stay in bed, she brought a nurse to the studio to monitor her fever and to administer shots of adrenalin. "I've been taught to stay on the job," said Ruth, "show or no show."[735] She persevered to give a moving, low-key performance that lent authenticity to her role as Anna, an instructor at an all-girls school in the Swiss Alps. Her leading man, Herbert Marshall, played the headmaster, Dr. Stephen Dominik. Third billed, making her American film debut was French actress Simone Simon playing Marie, a student who develops a crush on Dr. Dominik. Comparisons were being made between the film's theme of budding sexuality and the 1931 German-made, lesbian-themed *Madchen in Uniform*, in which a young girl professes her love for a female teacher at an all-girls boarding school. Upon completion, *Girl's Dormitory* was a well-written, dramatically sound film. Unfortunately, Darryl Zanuck decided to tamper with it. In doing so, he lost both the backbone and fragility of the original work by Hungarian playwright Ladislas Fodor.

In Fodor's play, the unrequited love of Anna for headmaster Dominik is resolved with poignancy and heart. Writer Basil Woon noted, "The

**Simone Simon, Herbert Marshall, Ruth, and director Irving Cummings
on the set of** *Girl's Dormitory* **(20th Century-Fox)**

script [and play] called for Ruth Chatterton... to win [Herbert Marshall] away from his infatuation for the pouting Simone."[736] Zanuck turned the ending on its head purely for publicity purposes—he wanted to make a star of the young, kittenish Simon, who received an unprecedented six-page spread in *Film Daily* prior to the film's release. The film's pressbook was an overblown promotion for her. *Variety* also commented on Simon's "auspicious build-up." On the cutting room floor, regrettably, lay the original, adult Chatterton-Marshall love story. In its place, the headmaster and pubescent Marie share the fadeout kiss. This change made a number of critics cringe. Marshall's headmaster comes across as a pedophile. Looking all of fifteen on screen, Simon, who was actually twenty-one (some sources say twenty-six), next to the forty-five-year-old

Marshall made the proceedings more disturbing than romantic.[737] "The culmination of this definitely absurd romance," said Los Angeles critic Elizabeth Yeaman, "is a jarring note at the conclusion of an otherwise appealing little human interest tale. Marshall... must have squirmed inwardly when he fulfilled the final requirements of his role."[738]

The Hollywood Reporter claimed that Simon's talent "transcends acting," but some critics felt differently. Elizabeth Yeaman found Simon "interesting, but her role... does not require a great deal of her as an actress." Pittsburgh author Florence Fisher Parry elaborated, "I don't know how old the girl is supposed to be, but she doesn't look over fourteen. That is the only weak spot in *Girl's Dormitory*. The girl is too much of a child. Originally the story ended thus: Simone Simon, convinced that Ruth Chatterton and Herbert Marshall are really in love and meant for each other... leaves him. Marshall turns to Ruth, and takes solace in a renewal of their romantic friendship. But after the picture was released, a new ending was manufactured, false and patched and showing concessions in every line."[739]

Variety had high praise for Ruth, saying, "Chatterton gets the best assignment she has had recently and infuses her part as the assistant

With Herbert Marshall in outtake from
Girl's Dormitory (20th Century-Fox).

instructor with a tenderness and understanding she has not always been permitted to reveal of late."[740] When Marie is implicated in a "scandal," it is Chatterton's character, Anna, who allows compassion to override the circumstantial evidence. One scene in particular stood out. New York critic Chester Bahn felt it ought to have been the film's conclusion, saying, "It seems to me that *Girl's Dormitory* would have more approximated adult cinema had director Irving Cummings drawn his curtain with that brilliant scene which finds the understanding Anna waiting for Marie to fall asleep… it was one of the tenderest and loveliest moments in the cinema's year."[741] The scene in question occurs immediately after Marie attempts to take her own life. Anna, fully aware of Marie's romantic interest in the headmaster, is left alone to console her. She tucks Marie into bed, feeds her soup, and quietly listens as Marie shares her hope to dream of Dr. Dominik's declaration of love "all over again." "The way he *looked* at me," she begins, only to be abruptly cut off by Anna. "That's enough Marie!" Marie apologizes, but Anna catches herself. "Oh, darling, forgive me. I shouldn't have spoken to you like that. It's only natural that you should want to talk about it." Anna becomes reflective as Marie explains how *waiting* had been the hardest part. Anna… who had been "waiting" for over a decade to hear Dominik declare the love that he offers instead to a teenager. As Chatterton portrays her, Anna offers the only genuine connection with the girl—and gives the film whatever substance it has.

When Simon and Marshall were called back to the studio to reshoot the ending, a number of extreme close-ups of Simon were inserted throughout the film to exploit her impish appeal. A review from *International Photographer* claimed that the film suffered in the process. It pointed to the "outbursts of mediocre cutting" and "distortion" resulting from "its forced change from a vehicle for Chatterton and Marshall to a builder-upper for Simone."[742] Chatterton's disappointment with *Girls Dormitory* was profound. She placed no blame on director Irving Cummings, who, when asked about her temperament, declared that he had known Ruth for ten years and "haven't yet had an argument with her." [743] Columnist Virginia Vale confirmed, "They do say that Ruth Chatterton is none too happy over the ending of *Girl's Dormitory*. The little Simone, it seems, has a way of getting what she wants, off the screen as well as on. So, a new ending was the result, and a rather unconvincing one it is, too."[744] Uncooperative and quarrelsome, Simon was dismissed by director Frank Lloyd during the filming of *Under Two Flags*—originally slated as Simon's American film debut. She was replaced by Claudette Colbert. A month after *Girl's Dormitory* was released, Chatterton was asked about Simon's being given the lion's share of the publicity as well as getting the leading man at the finish. "I don't mind," Ruth relented. "She's young; let her have her chance."[745]

In the aftermath, Simon became known as "one of Hollywood's most spectacular failures."[746] American audiences weren't interested. She blamed Darryl Zanuck for unsuitable roles and Ernie Westmore for his attempt to "glamorize" her. She appreciated the kindness of Herbert Marshall, however. "I cannot find to say how kind he was to me, that man," she said in her best English. "When I am mixed, he tells me softly the word, so nobody shall hear. When I was so worrying, he would give me a helping look."[747] The girl with the kittenish smile would finally find acclaim in the cult horror classic *Cat People* (1942). The real surprise for Fox was the outpouring of interest in handsome Tyrone Power. On the strength of three small scenes in *Girl's Dormitory*, he was signed to a seven-year contract and given his own massive build-up by the studio. As a side note, Fox remade the film in 1941 as the Jane Withers programmer, *A Very Young Lady*. Withers offered a tomboy version of the Simon role. Nancy Kelly and John Sutton enacted the Chatterton-Marshall roles with the original ending kept intact.

Dodsworth, by Sinclair Lewis, sold 85,000 copies soon after publication in 1929. The following year, Lewis was the first American to be awarded the Nobel Prize in Literature. Lewis was an insightful critic of America's obsession with social status and capitalistic values. Readers enjoyed his story about Sam Dodsworth, a middle-aged, Midwestern automobile magnate who sells his business and retires. While on a European tour, Sam is transformed. He loses some rough edges and gets excited about new ideas for his future... a future without his wife Fran, who indulges in flirtations and affectations and eventually asks for her freedom. In 1932, Henry Miller's son, Gilbert, asked playwright Sidney Howard to adapt it for the stage. The play version, starring Walter Huston and Fay Bainter, was a hit and toured for almost a year following its Broadway run. Samuel Goldwyn purchased the screen rights and Walter Huston, the play's strong point, was included in the contract. The sharp-tongued, master craftsman William Wyler was assigned to direct. This was the second of the Goldwyn-Wyler films and helped establish Wyler's reputation as a major director. Fay Bainter was bypassed in favor of Ruth, who reported to Goldwyn's offices the last week in May 1936. Much has been written about the acrimonious Chatterton-Wyler relationship. Wyler persisted in arguing with Ruth, demanding a more sympathetic take on Fran Dodsworth. Ruth decided to take her cue from the book's author, Sinclair Lewis, instead.

Sinclair Lewis had assisted Sidney Howard in the stage adaptation of *Dodsworth*. During rehearsals, Lewis was emotionally involved with how his characters came across. While watching Fay Bainter as Fran, something didn't ring true. Using his pet name for Bainter, he called out, "Come on, Gracie, you can be much bitchier than that!"[748] Bainter complied, offering an unflinching portrait. "If anyone thinks the part of Fran Dodsworth is easy to play," said Bainter, "he should just try it for himself

Scenes with co-stars Paul Lukas and Maria Ouspenskaya in *Dodsworth* (Samuel Goldwyn–United Artists).

some time. Not that I don't love it. But heaven knows there were easier commodities to deal in than the distilled vinegar of my present role."[749] New York University drama coach Dorothy Mulgrave agreed, "Perhaps no woman in contemporary drama is so constantly and appallingly hateful as Fran Dodsworth."[750] Although Fran was atypical of most American wives, she gave face to the ingrained selfishness of the shallow, age-fearing woman. Ruth had to be coaxed for over a year to be in the film, yet she would reap more accolades for her Fran Dodsworth than any other role. She had actually walked out of the Schubert Theatre during the original play, failing to see the last act because she didn't approve of Fran Dodsworth, finding her to be an "unpleasant person."[751]

The role of Edith Cortright, the woman who Sam Dodsworth turns to for love and understanding, was initially offered to Kay Francis. Kay conferred with Samuel Goldwyn on the project in December 1935, but Warner Brothers refused to release their highest paid star—a huge disappointment for her. Francis was still a big box office attraction. Goldwyn considered silent star Dolores Costello and Geraldine Fitzgerald for the part, but in the end, he preferred Mary Astor. In May 1936, Astor successfully tested for and won the coveted role.

The bittersweet tale of *Dodsworth* centers on Sam Dodsworth's love for his wife. He sells his auto factory so they may pursue her fantasy of traveling to Europe. Aboard ship in new surroundings, Fran's true character emerges. She's 41 going on 35 and accepts the attentions of the much younger Captain Lockert (David Niven). In Paris, she meets the distinguished pseudofinancier Arnold Iselin (Paul Lukas). Fran indulges in flirtations with every count of no account, hobnobs with those she considers to be elite when it is obvious that she lacks the restraint of a well-bred woman herself. She swaggers. She tries too hard. Her clothes may be expensive, her hair the latest style, but she is unable to shake her middle-western roots. "You've got to let me have my fling now!" she tells her husband. "You're simply rushing at old age, Sam, and I'm not ready for that yet." Oblivious to reality and the opportunities that surround her, she encourages Sam to go home without her—he's become a distasteful reminder of her past. Sam later returns to Europe in hopes to bring Fran to her senses, but it isn't long before she is set on a getting a divorce. She's determined to marry a young baron, Kurt von Obersdorf (Gregory Gaye). "I'll be happy with Kurt," she tells Sam defiantly. "I'm fighting for life. You can't drag me back."

Dispirited, Sam sojourns to Italy, where the genteel, understanding widow Edith Cortright provides the nurturing affection of which Fran isn't capable. However, all it takes is one phone call from the desperate Fran, whose engagement has been called off by her young nobleman's formidable mother. The scene in which Fran and Baroness von Obersdorf (Maria Ouspenskaya) lock horns is easily the film's high point. The Baroness, looking as if she could find pleasure in sucking on a large slice of lemon, asks Fran, "Have you thought what little happiness there can be for the… old wife… of a young husband?" As if encountering her worst nightmare, Fran unleashes her fury. The Baroness and her son leave posthaste—mission accomplished.

Sam submits to returning home with Fran, but as their ship prepares to leave port, Fran's repentance once more evaporates into caustic remarks and restless self-centeredness. "You know, as I look back, I can't blame myself," she tells Sam. "You were a good deal at fault yourself." Recognizing that their future together is hopeless, Sam speedily debarks and heads back to Italy for a new life with Edith. His last words to Fran are sound advice: "You'll have to stop getting younger someday." When a ship steward

asks about Sam's sudden departure, Fran cries out, "He's gone ashore!...
He's gone ashore!"—facing the realization that Sam's gone for good.

⚜⚜⚜

Mary Astor said that the animosity between Chatterton and Wyler during the hot summer shoot never wavered.

> One battle waxed and waned all through the picture.
> Ruth Chatterton hated Wyler. She disagreed with his di-
> rection of every scene, and he was stubborn and smiling
> and it drove her to furious outbursts. She didn't like the
> role of the wife of Sam Dodsworth, because the charac-
> ter was that of a woman who is trying to hang onto her
> youth—which was exactly what Ruth herself was doing.
> It touched a nerve. But she gave a beautiful performance
> in spite of herself.[752]

Astor found Wyler to be "picky, sarcastic, and impatient."[753] Before
long, he realized that any sharp criticism directed at Astor would bottle
her up. Nothing would come out. He left her alone. With Ruth, he had
met his match. One day, Wyler, dressed in his usual white linen slacks
and white shirt, was sitting directly under the camera. Everything was
lined up for a big close-up of Ruth and just as Wyler gave the order to roll
the camera, she said, "Willie, darling, that *white* suit of yours! It's very dis-
tracting with you sitting so close; it's all I can *see*!" Wyler asked, "Would
you like me to leave the studio, Miss Chatterton?" Without hesitating,
Ruth answered back, "I would indeed, but unfortunately I'm afraid it can't
be arranged."[754] As far as his numerous takes, Ruth would blurt out, "Mr.
Wyler, we've done it so many times already. I really don't know what you

want."[755] On another occasion, Ruth, staying in character, slapped Wyler's face and then locked herself in her dressing room. "It was like pulling teeth with her," said Wyler. "She only wanted to play [Fran] as a selfish bitch."[756] For whatever reason, Wyler wanted a more sympathetic take. But, as Fay Bainter had pointed out, if Fran Dodsworth allowed herself to languish, "it would throw the whole play out of joint."[757] The Sinclair Lewis story had complete masculine sympathy for Sam Dodsworth—a heroic figure, of sorts. Ruth stuck to her guns and as a result of her decision, the motivations of the other players made perfect sense.

David Niven, who played Fran's "escapade" aboard ship, also claimed to be "bloody miserable." Wyler reduced him to a "gibbering wreck" as an actor. "Willie Wyler is one of the world's all-time great directors," acknowledged Niven, "but in 1936, he was a Jekyll-and-Hyde character. The moment he sat in his director's chair he became a fiend."[758] Wyler didn't have much regard for Niven's talent. "He was sort of a playboy around town," said Wyler. "But he fit the part in *Dodsworth*. He played himself."[759]

Astor said that her scenes with Huston were without incident. She found him to be a "warm, easy-going human being." He didn't have to contend with Wyler harping about his performance. Still, Huston felt free to offer his candid opinions on Wyler's technique. Feature writer Alice Tildesley was amazed by the heat, humidity, and "still hotter lights" during the shoot. "Yet over and over, hour after hour, the same scene was repeated," she noted. Huston complained about the number of "takes" Wyler demanded for one small and not too important scene. "It's mechanical," he told Tildesley. "It's tiresome. It's—Hollywood!"[760] Huston pontificated further. "It is a town too full of actors who are making too much money for their own good and for the good of their work. I have seen splendid actors and actresses decline into mediocrity because they have forgotten the real purpose of their profession and have become little more than money grubbers."[761]

Midway into production, Ruth conceded that Fran was the best film role she ever had. Occasionally, the Chatterton-Wyler battle ceased fire. On July 2, Kay Francis made note in her diary of seeing Ruth at home "with Bill Wyler there."[762] More surprising was the sight of Wyler motorcycling around Beverly Hills one evening with none other than Chatterton straddling the rear seat and hanging on for dear life. According to Ruth, Wyler asked her out for dinner in early July and showed up on his bike. It wasn't unusual for him to cycle after work for relaxation. Ruth was game as long as he agreed to fly in her plane.[763] In the process of making *Dodsworth*, it was reported that Wyler and Huston would fly with Ruth to New York; board the *Queen Mary* (on her maiden voyage) at Quarantine; film their scenes; then return to the film capital. [764] In truth, Wyler sent camera crews to New York and Europe for background shots, but the film itself was shot entirely in the studio.

Wyler felt that while actors may cuss him, the day of reckoning— the preview—comes, "And if the picture is good," he said, "they'll forget the way I've treated 'em."[765] He mentioned Miriam Hopkins, who refused to speak to him after completing *These Three*. Hopkins got over it. Her co-star, Joel McCrea felt otherwise. Wyler informed McCrea that he'd rather be working with Leslie Howard. McCrea said that Wyler "tended to look out for one or two actors in a picture, and he would shit on the rest."[766] Joel paid Ruth a visit on the set of Dodsworth and although he had already worked with Wyler, Ruth cautioned him, "Don't work with [Wyler]. He's a stupid little man."[767] Bette Davis would battle Wyler while playing Regina in *The Little Foxes*. "Our quarrels were endless," she recalled. "I ended up feeling I had given one of the worst performances of my life. It took courage to play her the way I did, in the face of such opposition."[768] Davis was nominated for Best Actress. She mentioned that

Chatterton had faced the same problem. "Her hatred for Willie helped her performance, I'm sure," said Davis. "It kept her on edge."[769] Davis shared her Wyler stories with Myrna Loy. "I hear Wyler's a sadist," Loy told Goldwyn before filming *The Best Years of Our Lives* (1946). Typical of Goldwyn, he replied, "That isn't true, he's just a very mean fellow."[770] Regardless of his reputation with actors, Wyler would garner twelve Academy Award nominations as Best Director, *Dodsworth* being the first.

Dodsworth premiered in September 1936. Los Angeles critic Eleanor Barnes praised, "Ruth Chatterton is the star in this film. She climbs right back to stardom by her vivid and satirical interpretation." Barnes noted that Astor's "Madonna-like face" and restraint made "fine foil for the garishness of the Chatterton characterization."[771] In England, the popular *Punch* review of *Dodsworth* by the prolific writer E.V. Lucas agreed with Barnes that the film was very finely played, "principally by Ruth Chatterton," emphasized Lewis, "and next by Walter Huston, whom I was glad to find no longer masquerading as Cecil Rhodes [referring to Huston's previous film failure]."[772]

The destructive drive and conscious charm that propel Chatterton's performance have had staying power. Critics continue to agree that she never hesitates to live the part. In Michael A. Anderegg's biography of Wyler, the author notes that Chatterton's own "eccentricities" mesh convincingly with the character she plays. "Her performance has a touching vibrance," says Anderegg. "Chatterton suggests from the first scene the futility of Fran's ambitions. The cinematic Fran is in the end more sympathetic and complex than Lewis's original... the image of vain, foolish Fran, energetically if helplessly flitting through the watering places of Europe, remains powerfully locked in the memory."[773] *Films of the Golden*

Age featured an excellent piece on Chatterton in which writer Dan Van Neste recognized the "poignant desperation and restlessness" that Chatterton brought to Fran—"a woman long trapped in conformity, and now longing to be free."[774]   In 2008, British film historian David Thomson wrote, "Contemporary critics still marvel at Ruth in *Dodsworth*. While the wife, Fran, could easily be loathed—she is frivolous, selfish, thoughtless—Ruth Chatterton makes her familiar and understandable."[775]

Surprisingly, Ruth told columnist Sheilah Graham that her "marital encounter" with Sam Dodsworth clinched her resolution to remain celibate. "Imagine any woman being married to [such] a Babbit," she said. "He is crude, ignorant, smug. If he were actually my husband, I'd walk out on him during the first five minutes."[776]   Ruth's "marriage" to Sam, following her divorce from Brent, had indeed soured the idea of matrimony. She continued on this subject and then went on to offer a few choice opinions about producers,

> Marriage is a boring institution. I shall never remarry. I'm happier as a single woman. I didn't want to play the role of Fran Dodsworth. She's such a selfish woman. It took Sam Goldwyn a year to persuade me... Of course, I'm glad now that I succumbed, as, from all reports, the picture is a big success. In the seven years I've been in pictures, I've reached the height of film fame, and I've touched low bottom. I'm now resolved only to accept roles that I consider suitable for my talents. Most of them... directors and producers are such ignorant fools. Apart from Sam Goldwyn, whom I consider the genius of the motion picture industry, and the late Irving Thalberg, Hollywood is barren of producers capable of making good films. If the legitimate stage were as crowded

On the *Dodsworth* set: Paul Lukas, Ruth Chatterton, Mary Astor,
Walter Huston (Samuel Goldwyn–United Artists)

August 1936. Author Marc Goodrich, Ruth, and Mary Astor at trial.

with as many incompetents, the theater would have died many, many years ago.[777]

⚜

While filming *Dodsworth*, Mary Astor's diary offered the public a keyhole into her private life. She was involved in a legal battle with her ex-husband, Dr. Richard Thorpe, to gain custody of their four-year-old daughter, Marylyn. As the steamy courtroom drama unfolded, excerpts from Astor's affair as well as sexual activity with playwright George S. Kaufman (*Dinner at Eight*) made headlines. "I had achieved the reputation of being the greatest nympho-courtesan since Pompadour," recalled Astor, "but, it was never very funny to me, really, because it just wasn't true."[778] Night sessions at court were arranged so Astor could complete her role in *Dodsworth*. Astor claimed she gained strength from playing the cool, confident Edith Cortright. "She was a lot of things I wasn't," said Astor, designating it as her favorite role. As the trial got underway, Astor's "friends" dropped out of sight, not wanting to be associated with scandal. Studio executives insisted that Goldwyn invoke the industry's "morals clause" and replace Astor.[779] He had enough class not to. "I remember the opening session of the trial," wrote Astor in her autobiography.

> As I was leaving the studio, Ruth stopped me. "Do you have anyone with you?" she asked me. "Mother will be there," I said. "No," she said, "that's not what I mean. I mean someone to sit in the front row, someone you know is on your team and can give you a wink of encouragement." I laughed. "No, there's no one like that." And she said, "May I drive you down and be with you?" She did, and she was, to the bitter end.[780]

It was Ruth (sometimes in studio makeup) who sat next to Astor in court, offering moral support at every court session. "I admire Miss Astor very much for her courage," she told reporters, "I am for her all the way."[781] Ruth was joined by Florence Eldridge (wife of Fredric March) to be character witnesses for Astor. Astor felt these two women gave her "some solidity and dignity by their presence."[782] Walter Winchell (surprisingly) complimented the ladies, saying, "Let a harvest of orchids be draped on Ruth Chatterton and Florence Eldridge, who risked public damnation by sitting through the trial with Miss Astor. That's moxie in the movie colony, where the biggies have storm cellars to hide in—when a pal needs consolation, comforting, and help."[783] When asked why she would jeopardize her rating with the public to accompany Miss Astor, Ruth put it bluntly. "She looks half dead. Someone's got to stand by her."[784] Occasionally, Fritz Lang would sit directly behind Ruth during the proceedings. Astor's lawyer, Roland "Rich" Wooley, thought Ruth should have been a lawyer. The two had many heated discussions in his office. "I loved Ruth," recalled Astor, "and we became close friends. The success of the trial was partly due to her efforts and help."[785]

Astor was awarded divided custody of her daughter. The infamous diary was impounded and, by court order, burned in 1952.[786] In her autobiography, Astor was candid. "Sexually I was out of control, I was drinking too much, and I was brought up short when I found myself late in the evening thinking someone was 'terribly attractive'—and wondering the next morning, 'Why, why?'"[787] While *Dodsworth* was in production, Sam Goldwyn and other Hollywood producers met with Astor one evening, encouraging her to drop the lawsuit. She found them "pompous." "Besides," said Astor, "Walter Huston and some champagne were waiting for me in my bungalow."[788]

Following the trial and the release of *Dodsworth*, the public had difficulty matching up the gracious Edith Cortright and the "immoral" woman the tabloids created. Fortunately, Astor's fight for custody garnered sympathy. Before filming began, her name could not be counted on to sell tickets, but after the trial, Astor's notoriety spelled box office. At the *Dodsworth* premier, one critic noted that Astor "received more applause than anyone else in the cast—applause that lasted all through her first scene."[789] On a personal level, Astor admitted, "The only result of the trial was that I sharpened my wits and became more cautious. I stayed close to Ruth, to her home and friends. She maintained a constant 'salon'; people came and went, and good food and drink were always plentiful." Astor was overwhelmed by the brilliance of Ruth's guests. Conversation switched from English to French to Spanish and back again. "[Ruth] always had a swarm of admirers, mostly young men, 'sitting at her feet,'" recalled Astor. [790] On one occasion, amidst much "well-behaved drinking," Astor was introduced to young salon admirer Manuel del Campo—her next husband.

Chatterton and Mary Astor hadn't known each other prior to filming. Former editor/columnist for the *New York World* Gretta Palmer praised their friendship, saying, "Sometimes a crisis is needed to bring two Hollywood women together. Ruth Chatterton stood staunchly by Mary Astor. She admitted the indiscretion Miss Astor had shown in keeping a diary, but said, 'She shouldn't be pilloried for that.' It was with Miss Chatterton's help and encouragement that Mary Astor performed her part so well in *Dodsworth*."[791] A thought worth considering.

The New York Film Critics named Walter Huston Best Actor for *Dodsworth*. A critic for *The New York Times* was incensed that Chatterton only placed second in the Best Actress category and scoffed, "Miss Luise Rainer was practically chased over the line by Miss Ruth Chatterton,

Miss Rainer's moment in *The Great Ziegfeld* proving more compelling to the majority than Miss Chatterton's many moments in *Dodsworth*."[792] Huston and Wyler both received Academy Award nominations. Astor's finest work was overlooked while Maria Ouspenskaya, on screen for five minutes, got a Best Supporting Actress nod from the Academy.

Immediately following the film's release, Sinclair Lewis was so impressed with the film treatment of his story that he sent a telegram of congratulations to Sam Goldwyn. The author was quoted as being "highly pleased" with Chatterton's portrayal of Fran.[793] Perhaps more important to Ruth than another Academy Award nomination was the telegram she received from scenarist Sidney Howard. It was among the very few items that Ruth kept from her long career. Her cousin, Brenda Holman, sent the original to this author; it reads:

RUTH DEAR...   (October 26, 1936)

I HAVE ONLY JUST CAUGHT DODSWORTH HERE IN
PITTSFIELD OR YOU WOULD HAVE ALREADY HEARD
MY RAVES ABOUT WHAT IS CERTAINLY ONE OF THE
FINEST SCREEN PERFORMANCES EVER GIVEN IN ANY
PICTURE. YOU KNOW THAT I FELT WITH YOU THAT
YOUR PLAYING THE PART MIGHT NOT BE WISE FOR
YOU BUT I CANNOT BELIEVE THAT ANYTHING SO
BRILLIANT AS WHAT YOU DID WITH IT CAN BE ANY-
THING BUT VERY WISE INDEED. I THANK YOU. IF
ANYTHING COULD MAKE ME LOVE YOU MORE THAN
EVER YOUR FRAN WOULD. ONLY NOTHING COULD.

SIDNEY

Ironically, Ruth refused to see the picture. In 1951, she confirmed, "I never saw *Dodsworth*, either in the rushes or as the completed picture. In fact, I never saw any of my later films. I'm not my own type. It got so that I didn't like the way I looked, the way I talked—I didn't like anything about myself."[794] The themes in *Dodsworth* did inspire a few proposed remakes, none of which came to fruition. In 1963, Goldwyn came out of retirement intending to make a fresh version starring James Stewart, Lana Turner, and Ingrid Bergman under the direction of George Roy Hill.[795] Studios were unresponsive. For several years, Gregory Peck contemplated a remake of *Dodsworth* and tried to lure Grace Kelly out of retirement to play the expatriate who steals Sam's heart.[796]

✦

Ruth was glad to be back in the air after being grounded during *Dodsworth*. Contestants for the second Ruth Chatterton Sportsman Pilots Derby, competing for $5,000 in prize money, were feted at an informal "good luck" dinner in Cleveland on August 28. The event, aboard the showboat *S.S. Moses*, was given in honor of Ruth and forty other women flyers. Sporting a white tweed coat and slacks, she was squired to the event by Tris Speaker, one of the best center fielders in Major League Baseball. Speaker had trained as a naval aviator in WWI. "I have a cold," said Ruth, greeting the audience, "so I won't say much. But I do want to wish you all the luck in our derby."[797] Again, Ruth would fly as pacesetter. Stops included: Cincinnati, Louisville, Nashville, Memphis, Dallas, El Paso, Tucson, Yuma, and San Diego. After arriving in San Diego, they would hop to Los Angeles to open the National Air Races. Over 100 applicants were narrowed down to 40 in order to accommodate capacity limitations of the various airports. Ruth emphasized:

1936–Ruth stands by her Stinson plane at the Chatterton Sportsman Pilots Derby.

August 28, 1936. Aboard the showboat *S.S. Moses*. Ruth shakes the hand of pilot Katherine Cheung. Looking on is Mrs. F.F. Dugan, President of the Women's Chapter of the National Aeronautical Association.

This race is to be a trial for the prudent sportsman pilot. The
stress is upon accurate cruising at a safe altitude over favorable terrain with safety a primary consideration and speed
of secondary importance. Accuracy and not speed wins.[798]

Among the ten women fliers were: Grace Prescott, the previous year's
winner; Peggie Salaman, noted English pilot; and Katherine Cheung, a
native of Canton who aspired to become the Amelia Earhart of China.
Her new plane was partially financed by actress Anna May Wong. Leland
Hayward was lined up for the second time. Jimmy Stewart, with 35 solo
hours to his credit, and James Dunn were all set to throttle down their
engines when their studios made them withdraw. Even though Ruth had
one more scene to shoot in *Dodsworth*, director William Wyler and Sam
Goldwyn made an exception for her. They may have wished otherwise
when headlines reported that she made a forced landing on the derby's
first lap.[799] Ruth casually explained that she was forced down near Ow-
ensville after noting her fuel gauge was low. "I landed the plane... in one
of the flattest, largest and most beautiful fields I have ever seen. We found
that a farmer living nearby not only had a tank of gasoline, but that it was
airplane gasoline which he used in a stove. I think that proves that God
looks after us fliers."[800] Not true. That same day, entrant W.J. Viau of Los
Angeles crashed his plane near South Vienna, Ohio. He was forced out of
the derby with cuts, bruises, and a fractured ankle.[801]

Fifteen thousand people in Hot Springs, Arkansas, welcomed the re-
maining fleet of 36 contestants as well as the five planes filled with reporters and judges. Adding to the excitement, Katherine Cheung, flying the
slowest plane in the race, nearly collided into another contestant while
taxiing in. Mayor McLaughlin appointed Chatterton as deputy mayor
of "Spa City." More important to Ruth was a visit with Earl Ricks, a local
resident who had participated in the 1935 derby. Earlier in August, Ricks

had been hospitalized with third degree burns. His chances for partici-pating in the competition were considered slim until Ruth gave him the necessary spark. Following her pep talk, Ricks boarded his plane the next morning and joined derby flyers as they took off in one minute intervals. The eastern wing of the competition ended in Dallas, where a banquet at Falstaff Tavern was followed by the gala "Cavalcade of Texas" especially dedicated to "the star."[802] Frank Spreckels, sugar heir and wealthy play-boy from San Francisco, was outperforming the other contestants. His navigator was a young woman who got so angry at him that she threw his maps out the window.[803] He won anyway. Spreckels maintained his lead upon arriving in San Diego. With a total of 1184.18 points, he nosed out Jeannette Lempke of Bay City, Michigan, with 1182.52. Winner of the 1935 derby Grace Prescott placed eleventh. Awards were presented at nearby Casa del Ray Moro café.

The Chatterton Derby arrived in Los Angeles on September 4 to be-gin the 16th Annual National Air Races inaugural ceremony. Kay Fran-cis joined Ruth inside the official stand to greet record crowds. Prior to this event, the Hollywood Chamber of Commerce held a luncheon at the Roosevelt Hotel, which was attended by well-known women avia-tors such as Chatterton, Amelia Earhart, Laura Engalls, and Ruth Elder. While 1936 marked the last Chatterton derby, Ruth had gained a solid reputation as an aviator as well as the respect of the aviation community.

⚜

Between the air races and *Dodsworth's* success, Ruth was back in the spot-light. Goldwyn asked her to star in his remake of the landmark silent film *Stella Dallas*. He thought the role made to order for her, but Ruth was focused on joining Brian Aherne for the stage play *Louise von Coburg*, writ-

September 29, 1936. Ruth chats with Kay Francis and their mutual beau (at different times), director Fritz Lang. Photo taken at a Grace Moore party.

ten by Felix Salten. Auriol Lee would direct. "Stella Dallas was a common woman," complained Ruth.[804] The role was eventually assigned to her "good friend" Barbara Stanwyck, which earned her an Oscar nomination.

There would be no Broadway play. After appearing on several radio programs in the fall of 1936, Ruth simply vanished. As Fritz Lang put it: "She gave up her house, her library, her dogs, and disappeared. I didn't hear from her for six years. For a long time we had seen each other every day. Then poof! No more Ruthie."[805]

Endnotes

720   B.R. Crisler, "Miss Chatterton, Aviatrix, Alights Here," *New York Times,* April 12, 1936.

721   Jimmy Fidler, "Fidler Raps Film Academy—Failed to Nominate Ruth Chatterton," *Omaha World Herald,* May 12, 1936.

722   Richard Lawson, The director Hollywood Forgot to Remember," *Screenbook,* August 1937.

723   Richard Lawson, "The Director Hollywood Forgot to Remember," *Screenbook,* August 1937.

724   Peter H. Brown, Jim Pinkston, *Oscar Dearest: Six Decades of Scandal, Politics and Greed Behind Hollywood's Academy Awards,* Perennial Library, c. 1987, pg 89.

725   Robert Abele, "Laura Linney," *Variety,* December 7, 2007.

726   David Noh, "Rediscovering Ruth," http://nohway.wordpress.com/2009/03/, March 23, 2009.

727   David Noh, email to author, July 10, 2011.

728   Robbin Coons, "Ruth Chatterton Rates Freedom Above Contract," *Gettysburg Times,* July 28, 1936.

729   Harrison Carroll, "Behind the Scenes in Hollywood," *The Tyrone Daily Herald,* April 29, 1936.

730   "Mystery Solved When Sea Yields Body Of Aviator," *Times-Picayune,* January 22, 1936.

731   "Plane Landed in N.Y. By Ruth Chatterton," *Salt Lake Tribune,* April 1, 1936.

732   B.R. Crisler, "Miss Chatterton, Aviatrix, Alights Here," *New York Times,* April 12, 1936.

733   Hubbard Keavy, "Screen Life in Hollywood," *San Antonio Express,* July 5, 1936.

734   "One Killed, Two Injured in Crash," *Times-Recorder,* April 9, 1936.

735   Willa Okerr, "The Hollywood Parade," *San Mateo Times,* June 19, 1936.

736   Basil Woon, "Behold The Tender Savage—Simone Simon," *Screenplay,* November 1936.

737   1940 US Census, Simone Simon was listed as being 25 years old (April 1940) while staying at New York's Ambassador Hotel.

738   Elizabeth Yeaman, review of *Girl's Dormitory, Hollywood Citizen News,* September 17, 1936.

739   Florence Fisher Parry, "Hollywood Presents a New Screen Face," *Pittsburgh Press,* August 18, 1936.

740   Chic, review of *Girl's Dormitory, Variety,* September 2, 1936.

741   Chester B. Bahn, review of *Girl's Dormitory, Syracuse Herald,* September 12, 1936.

742   Robert Tobey, review of *Girl's Dormitory, International Photographer,* November 1936.

743   Kelly Woolpert, "Ruth Chatterton Denies The Soft Impeachment," *Freeport Journal Standard* (ILL), August 7, 1936.

744   Virginia Vale, "Star Dust," *Rake Register,* November 19, 1936.

745   Sheilah Graham, "Marriage Boring, Says 'Wife' of 'Dodsworth,'" *Rochester Chronicle,* September 30, 1936.

746   Richard Lamparski, *Whatever Became of … ?* (Second Series) Crown Publishers (NY), c. 1968, pg 70-71.

747   Ida Zeitlin, "Most Exciting Newcomer!" *Screenland,* November 1936.

748   James M. Hutchisson, *The Rise of Sinclair Lewis, 1920-1930,* Pennsylvania State University Press, c. 1996, pg 262.

749   "It's No Ming Toy Says Fay Bainter," *Brooklyn Daily Eagle,* March 4, 1934.

750   Dorothy I. Mulgrave, review of *Dodsworth, Players,* Volume 10, 1934, page 32.

751   Douglas W. Churchill, "A Role Ruth Chatterton Disliked," *New York Times,* October 4, 1936.

752   Mary Astor, *A Life on Film,* Dell, c. 1967, pg 119.

753   Carol Easton, *The Search for Sam Goldwyn,* William Morrow, c. 1975, pg 137.

754   Mary Astor, *A Life on Film,* Dell, c. 1967, pg 119.

755   Jan Herman, *A Talent for Trouble—The Life of Hollywood's Most Acclaimed Director, William Wyler,* Da Capo Press, c. 1997, pg 154.

756   A. Scott Berg, *Goldwyn—A Biography,* Riverhead, c. 1998, pg 278.

757   "It's No Ming Toy Says Fay Bainter," *Brooklyn Daily Eagle,* March 4, 1934.

758   David Niven, *The Moon's a Balloon,* Putnam, c. 1972, pg 199-200.

759   Jan Herman, *A Talent for Trouble: The Life of Hollywood's Most Acclaimed Director, William Wyler,* Da Capo Press, c. 1997, pgs 154-155.

760   Alice L. Tildesley, "What Is Hollywood?" *Oakland Tribune,* October 25, 1936.

761   Walter Huston, "Plaster Paradise," *Oakland Tribune,* August 16, 1936.

762   Kay Francis, diary, July 2/July 8, 1936, Kay Francis collection, Wesleyan cinema Archives, Wesleyan University, Middletown, CT.

763   Hubbard Keavy, "Screen Life in Hollywood," *San Antonio Express,* July 5, 1936.

764   Ralph Wilk, "A Little from Hollywood Lots," *Film Daily,* May 27, 1936.

765   Paul Harrison, "In Hollywood," *Laredo Times*, August 11, 1937.

766   A. Scott Berg, *Goldwyn: A Biography*, Knopf, c. 1989, pg 270.

767   Gerald Peary, "Strong, Righteous, and Rustic" (from a 1982 interview with Joel McCrea), *Bright Lights Film Journal*, May 2009.

768   Axel Madsen, *William Wyler*, Crowell Co., c. 1973, pg 210.

769   Whitney Stine, *'I'd Love To Kiss You'... Conversations with Bette Davis*, Simon & Schuster, c. 1990, pgs 165-166.

770   James Kotsilibas-Davis, Myrna Loy, *"Myrna Loy-Being and Becoming*, Alfred A. Knopf, c. 1987, pg 197.

771   Eleanor Barnes, review of *Dodsworth*, *Los Angeles Illustrated Daily News*, October 3, 1936.

772   E.V. Lucas, review of *Dodsworth*, *Punch*, October 7, 1936.

773   Michael A. Anderegg, *William Wyler*, Twayne Pub., c. 1979, pgs 60-61.

774   Dan Van Neste, "Ruth Chatterton Without a Trace of Affectation," *Films of the Golden Age*, Fall 1997.

775   David Thomson, *Have You Seen...?* Alfred A. Knopf, c. 2008, pg 230.

776   Sheilah Graham, "Marriage Boring, Says 'Wife' of 'Dodsworth,'" *Rochester Chronicle*, September 30, 1936.

777   Sheilah Graham, "Marriage Boring, Says 'Wife' of 'Dodsworth,'" *Rochester Chronicle*, September 30, 1936.

778   Mary Astor, *A Life on Film*, Dell, c. 1967, pg 126.

779   Lawrence Grobel, *The Hustons*, Charles Scribner's, Sons, c. 1989, pg 178.

780   Mary Astor, *My Story*, Doubleday and Co., c. 1959, pg 191.

781   Paul Harrison, "Movie Stars in Hollywood Fearfully Silent Regarding Mary Astor's Court Battle," *Frederick News-Post*, August 12, 1936.

782   Mary Astor, *My Story*, Doubleday and Col, c. 1959, pg 195.

783   Walter Winchell column, *Rochester Journal*, August 18, 1936.

784   Sheilah Graham, "Astor Trouble Is Good Break For Chatterton," *Dallas Morning News*, August 26, 1936.

785   Mary Astor, *My Story*, Doubleday and Co., c. 1959, pg 191, 197.

786   Mary Astor, *My Story*, Doubleday and Co., c. 1959, pg 196.

787   Mary Astor, *My Story*, Doubleday and Co., c. 1959, pg 197.

788   Mary Astor, *My Story*, Doubleday and Co., c. 1959, pg 193.

789   Robert Tobey, review of *Dodsworth*, *International Photographer*, November 1936.

790   Mary Astor, *A Life on Film*, Dell, c. 1967, pg 119.

791   Gretta Palmer, "A Girl's Best Friend Is Her Opposite," *Photoplay*, January 1938.

792   "The Levee In The Rainbow Room," *New York Times*, January 24, 1937.

793   "Film Versions Can Satisfy Authors," *Brooklyn Eagle*, December 1, 1940.

794   Louis Sheaffer, "Curtain Time," *Brooklyn Eagle*, May 22, 1951.

795   "False Starts Remakes of Dodsworth May Finally Be In The Works," *Chicago Tribune*, October 24, 1991.

796   George Hadley-Garcia, "Gregory Peck – The Silent Sex Symbol," *Hollywood Studio Magazine*, September 1983.

797   "34 Pilots In Lineup For Chatterton Hop," *Portsmouth Times*, 8/29/36.

798   "Pilots Compete In 'Ideal Flight,'" *Twin Falls Idaho Evening Times*, August 29, 1936.

799   "Ruth Chatterton Forced Down on Air Derby Trip," *Pampa Daily News*, August 30, 1936.

800   "Fliers Reach Louisville in Trophy Race," *Syracuse Herald*, August 30, 1936.

801   "Thousands Hail Derby Fliers," *Oakland Tribune*, August 30, 1936.

802   "London Debutant And Chinese Girl Are in Air Derby," *Dallas Morning News*, August 30, 1936.

803   Marj Carpenter, "Many Famous People Stopped At Local Port," *Big Spring Herald* (TX), August 19, 1973.

804   Douglas W. Churchill, "A Role Ruth Chatterton Disliked," *New York Times*, October 4, 1936.

805   Fritz Lang, Barry Keith Grant, *Fritz Lang: Interviews*, University of Mississippi, c. 2003, pg 143.

13
To England & Back...
to Broadway

Traveling incognito as "Mrs. R. Brent" in early January 1937, Ruth slipped out of Hollywood after booking passage on the *Queen Mary*. While abroad, Ruth contemplated her next step, personally and professionally. In mid-February, she returned home. Five days later, she packed up her bags again and flew to New York to sail on the *Berengaria* for London. As the 5' 2 ½" actress approached the gangplank, trying to conceal her identity, a cameraman got wise and began following her. He was surrounded by a mob of boisterous Max Baer fans, chanting, "We want Max!" They assumed *she* was the 6' 2 ½" ex-heavyweight champ. Ruth managed to get to her stateroom in one piece. Baer, already on board, was escaping New York, notoriety, contract obligations, process servers, and... the law.[806] Ruth's own escape was more of a new beginning. Tired of Hollywood and not altogether satisfied with opportunities in New York, she had decided to make her London stage debut. George Bernard Shaw's *Pygmalion* or Somerset Maugham's *The Constant Wife* were being considered. It was soon decided that the latter would open the week before the coronation of King George VI (May 12). There were also film offers in England. Ruth's new adventure would keep her abroad for two years.

∗∘⊛∘∗

While in London, Ruth's *terra firma* was a house where the actress Nell Gwynne had once lived—the secret passageway Nell used to visit Charles II remained intact. A longtime mistress of the King who bore him two sons, Gwynne was considered a folk heroine. Charles himself had legalized acting as a profession for women and licensed the formation of two acting companies. As far as ghosts from the past, Ruth was in good company. In April, her revival of Shaw's 1926 play *The Constant Wife* had tryouts in Edinburgh, Manchester, and Brighton. Ruth Gordon was also visiting England at the time and ran into Somerset Maugham at a party. He invited her to attend the play. He wanted her opinion. "Your friend Miss Ruth Chatterton is starring in it," he explained. "Will you meet me in Brighton tomorrow night and see if you can do something about her performance?" He felt Chatterton was ruining his play. Gordon wasn't particularly fond of Maugham, but felt she had no choice. She went. She saw. After the curtain, Mr. Maugham said, "Well?" "Well," said Gordon, "I think Ruth Chatterton is fine. But I think your play has gotten old-fashioned and you should do something about *it*."[807] Gordon admitted that her remark didn't bring them closer together. *The Constant Wife* lasted 36 performances at London's Globe Theatre and did a modest business. London audiences hadn't been any keener on the play when it premiered in 1926. Ruth most likely had selected the play based on her happy experience with the film version, *Charming Sinners*.

Reviews for *The Constant Wife* were mixed. Ruth was received warmly by the press and the British themselves had always been appreciative of her talent. The drama critic for *The Daily Telegraph* called her a "lovely actress who brings out all the delicious little subtleties of this leading part. Her sly humor matches Maugham's highly sophisticated wit, and she is mistress of all the delicate situations."[808] *The London Mercury* also referred to her performance as "delicious." "Indeed, all the acting is first-rate," stated the review, "and in its mirror Mr. Somerset Maugham's craft shows up masterly."[809] Some felt that Ruth wasn't quite in the same key as the rest of the cast. As playwright/novelist Charles Morgan put it,

> Miss Chatterton acts too broadly with her face; she understands the part, enjoys playing it, has vitality and spirit; but her whole performance is loose, she lacks precision and discipline, she gives in the strangest way an impression of being still in rehearsal for she fails again and again in the simplest timing of a comedy line.[810]

Ruth hadn't scrimped when it came to creating a dazzling wardrobe for her English debut. She made a special trip to Paris to be personally fitted in a selection of gowns by Molyneux. Included was a black and white print garden dress with draped short sleeves, lemon-yellow sash, and large yellow picture hat. Molyneux, known for his idle quip "never too rich or too

1937. With Noel Coward at London's annual theatrical garden party in Regent's Park.

thin," was also a friend of Noel Coward. After the play closed, Ruth accompanied Coward to the annual theatrical garden party at Regent's Park in London. It was a benefit for the Actors' orphanage. Coward had accompanied Ann Harding to the event the previous year. Harding had also escaped Hollywood in an attempt to jump-start her waning career. She completed one British film as well as a revival of Shaw's *Candida* at the Globe Theatre. Just as Ruth was settling into her new London environs, Harding was returning to the United States with a new husband, conductor Werner Janssen.

⁂

Newspapers began reporting that Ruth's relationship with Marques Antonio De Portago, an international playboy cum polo player, was leaning towards matrimony. That is, after he divorced his second wife, Olga. Apparently, Ruth and the Marques had been an item for a number of months. Ruth assured Louella Parsons that the romance "was cold" before she had left the United States.[811] Ruth wasn't interested in being the third wife of any man. In 1935, Portago had sunk money (from the $50,000 annual allowance his wife gave him) into the British film *Sanders of the River* with Paul Robeson. Portago, the actor, was given a small role. He was designated as "technical director" for Alexander Korda's *The Private Life of Don Juan*. The film's title underscored the Marques' real expertise. He did come from one of the oldest families in Spain. When Hollywood beckoned in 1936, Portago brought his wife and two children to the U.S. He gained a reputation for giving elaborate parties—one of which placed him face-to-face with Ruth Chatterton.[812] Portago was completely smitten with her. He asked his wife for a divorce. She refused. The couple returned to Spain in time for the Spanish Civil War. Ruth, of course, journeyed to England.

In 1942, Portago would die just as he had lived: recklessly playing polo after his physician had warned him against strenuous activity.

Legally, Ruth still went by Ruth Chatterton Brent, while ex-husband George once again dabbled in matrimony. In May 1937, ten days after his marriage to young Australian actress Constance Worth, Brent asked for an annulment, saying he was "tired of it" and that he had been "pressured."[813] He confessed that it was "a real mess," especially after a government official in Australia asked that George Brent films be banned.[814] Australians felt that Brent had besmirched the good name of Miss Worth. For the time being, Ruth maintained a safe distance from romantic entanglement and enjoyed the company of her gay companions, like Noel Coward and Ivor Novello. Coward was Ruth's constant escort to numerous theatrical productions during her stay in Great Britain.

In mid-summer 1937, Ruth began filming *The Rat,* based on the Ivor Novello play about the French underground. Novello had filmed it as a silent, but due to stage commitments, was unable to co-star with Ruth in the remake. Anton Walbrook, fresh from his success opposite Anna Neagle in *Victoria the Great,* was selected to play "The Rat"—a thief and opportunist. Both roles helped establish Walbrook as one of Britain's most popular stars. Following some location filming in Paris, Ruth was in good spirits during the shoot at London's Denham Studios.

> I have adored the experience of making a film over here and I hope this won't be my last. Everyone has... accepted me as one of themselves from the first day. There is less strain and stress about making pictures in England... and a great friendliness that appeals to me very

much. Also, I get on excellently with my director, Jack
Raymond. He has a grand sense of humor, and that in a
director is a priceless asset.[815]

The Rat's gritty opening scene provides a fascinating contrast between Zelia (Chatterton), a wealthy socialite out slumming, and the brute
strength of Boucheron, a.k.a. "The Rat" (Walbrook), who is obviously up
to no good. During a table-smashing fight in a Montemartre cabaret and
pick-up bar, Zelia makes her grand entrance accompanied by a wealthy
admirer, Luis Stets. "The Rat" is about to stab a man, but Zelia's appearance causes a bigger stir. The fighting stops. Boucheron's intense male
sensuality is accentuated by his sinewy physique. Zelia picks up on it immediately. "Who is the man who is winning?" she inquires. Her escort
begs they leave the unsavory characters and surroundings. "I've known
so many pleasant characters in my life," she says, "all of them bores." She
approaches Boucheron. He ignores her. She persists, asking why he tried
to kill a man. He tells her the man annoyed him. "You always kill people
when they annoy you?" Zelia asks. He accuses her of getting a secondhand kick at his expense. "You must be terribly hard up for emotions of
your own," he snaps. "Perhaps I am," she admits thoughtfully. When
Zelia calls Boucheron "a fool" and says that he is simply throwing away
his power—he listens. He has recently taken on the responsibility of a
young girl, Odile, after her prisoner father went to the guillotine. Zelia
considers Odile's youthful innocence. Although she may be out looking
for thrills, Zelia's underlying assertiveness, sophistication, and compassion offer unusual dimension to the situation.

In the days that follow, Zelia and Boucheron spend a great deal of
time together. She invites him to dinner at her *maison*. When he is received curtly by the butler, he suggests that Zelia get rid of him. "What

would you do... kill him?" she laughs. Meanwhile, the lecherous million-aire Stets, after being dumped by Zelia, zeroes in on the youthful Odile. He claims he wants to be her benefactor, but takes advantage of her. There is much struggle... until a gun goes off. In the aftermath, the girl confesses to murder, but Boucheron takes the rap. At his trial, Zelia takes the stand to confess that Boucheron was in her boudoir on the evening in question. She finds the courage to jeopardize her own reputation in order to save Boucheron as well as his blossoming relationship with Odile. Due to extenuating circumstances, Odile is sentenced to only a year in prison. Through all the turmoil, Zelia realizes that she cares more about people than herself. It is through her effort that Boucheron turns his life around. *The Rat* is absorbing escapist fare. One never loses interest as the story unfolds. Also impressive was Freddie Young's cinematography. He would achieve Oscars for three David Lean successes: *Lawrence of Arabia, Dr. Zhivago,* and *Ryan's Daughter.*

The Rat provides a mature and interesting role for Chatterton. The

With Anton Walbrook in *The Rat* (London Films).

Motion Picture Herald found Ruth's Zelia "polished." Walbrook's impulsive, edgy portrayal was smooth and impressive. *Film Daily* complimented the "sound craftsmanship" of both Walbrook and Chatterton, also noting the film was "lavished" with fine photography.[816] Another critic stated, "Walbrook surpasses himself in this film… and practically steals the picture from Ruth Chatterton, who still maintains her undeniable charm."[817] Mac Tinee of *The Chicago Tribune* found the film "brisk, suspenseful and well acted"—the dialogue "arresting" and the direction "excellent." Tinee was of the opinion that Chatterton had "acquired a necessary finish and sincerity during her long absence from the screen."[818] Frank S. Nugent for *The New York Times* opted for sarcasm, indicating that U.S. Customs inspectors must have looked the other way when *The Rat* came ashore. "*The Rat* is a pitifully made romantic melodrama," Nugent wrote. "Ruth Chatterton is downright Spring Byingtonish."[819] In 1956, *The Rat* was released on American TV. Apparently, Ruth agreed with Nugent's assessment and told columnist Milton Bass that she finally saw *The Rat* "and found it so bad that she enjoyed every second of it."[820]

***

Ruth missed her Stinson plane, which was in Los Angeles. When the subject of flying came up, she paused to pay tribute to Amelia Earhart, who had disappeared over the Central Pacific while circumnavigating the globe in July 1937. "She was a very great friend of mine," said Ruth. "And I can't believe that she is dead. She was an experienced pilot and no daredevil, and her plane was made so that it could have floated on the sea for many hours. It seems incredible that she should have sent out the SOS that she only had petrol for half an hour, and then have disappeared so completely. I still hope that she may have been picked up by some little

Japanese trawler, where the sailors didn't understand what she wanted, and that she will turn up again one day."[821] Ruth and Earhart championed the idea of government subsidizing young fliers. "Miss Earhart believed—and it is my conviction also," added Ruth, "that we should thus be able to build up a generation of new fliers competently trained. I want to carry on, mostly for her sake."[822] Ruth also expressed interest in using her aviation skill for films. One prospect was to have her involved as a female "Scarlet Pimpernel" flying refugees out of Spain.[823]

After completing *The Rat*, Ruth was joined by Tilly, who sailed to Europe at the end of October. The two enjoyed the sights around London for a couple of months. In mid-December, the world press went askew regarding a proposed marriage between Ruth and Carlos Freitas Martins, son of a Portuguese aristocrat and wine merchant. Reportedly, Ruth announced her intentions en route from Lisbon to the island community of Madeira, where the distinguished family resided.[824] From her London home, Ruth expressed complete bewilderment. "I have been in London since November 7," she said. "I never have been in Portugal or Madeira in my life."[825] The more Ruth thought about it, the angrier she got. She declared her intention of filing a suit against the woman who was impersonating her. "I think I have been the victim of a practical joke," said Ruth. "I am placing the matter in the hands of my solicitors and may prosecute."[826] Ruth suspected that it was the same woman who had urgently cabled her in London and Paris asking to meet her in Cannes. When she learned that the mystery woman had a dog named Mitzi, Ruth was able to joke about it. "I have dogs named Matthew, Mark, Luke and John, and even one named Sophocles," she mused, "but I never on any account would call a dog Mitzi." The marriage rumor was finally put to rest when the woman in question, Elsie Alice Snyder, a 35-year-old English woman, angrily told a United Press correspondent, "Leave me alone! I won't talk

with anyone! You can say I am *not* Ruth Chatterton… now go."[827] After
Tilly left for home in January, Ruth retreated to a Paris apartment to re-
group before starting her second British film.

⚜

Ruth's desire to play the ill-fated Empress Josephine was finally realized
when producer Herbert Wilcox, who had produced *The Rat*, agreed to a
screen version of *A Royal Divorce* to be filmed at Denham Studios. Ruth
contributed to the scenario and stated that much of it was based on her
own ideas. She had previously consulted with filmmaker G.W. Pabst
about the project.[828] A *London News* correspondent visited the set and
found Ruth "radiant in an exact replica of Josephine's coronation dress."
They were shooting a scene in which Josephine, feeling that Napoleon
looked undignified waving his arms about, coaches him on hand place-
ment—right hand into the waistcoat, left behind his back. "That incident
is typical of the film," explained Ruth. "The first two thirds of it are light
and satirical." Ruth hoped the end result would be in the same league
as Charles Laughton's *The Private Life of Henry VIII* (1933). "We have
not been afraid to poke fun at history a little," she added. "But all the
same our story is founded on fact. I spent three months in France visiting all the places connected with Napoleon and collecting all the material
that I could."[829] Ruth felt the underlying tragedy of the story would prove
compelling screen fare. In deference to Josephine's past, Ruth would sing
two old Creole songs which a composer friend had acquired from an old
woman on the isle of Martinique. Some predicted that *A Royal Divorce*
would be nothing more than a variation of the old melodrama bearing the
same title and that Ruth's talent was better suited to the modern idiom.
Whatever the case, she had been forewarned.

With Pierre Blanchar in *The Royal Divorce*
(courtesy of Photofest).

As Napoleon, the brilliant French actor Pierre Blanchar felt a little odd portraying the same character Charles Boyer had recently played with success in Garbo's *Conquest* (1937). "It seems we have always been rivals," said Blanchar, "though very friendly ones. We both joined the Paris Conservatory in 1919."[830] Also on board was Auriol Lee as the Emperor's mother. While Blanchar may not have been completely at ease with the English language, critics felt that he outshone the efforts of Chatterton. An Australian review commented on the grace and charm of *A Royal Divorce*—that is, the first half of it. "This light touch still suits Ruth Chatterton nicely—as do the empire gowns. But when the drama comes on the scene... Ruth Chatterton as the soulful, tragic woman is— well, just another actress. On the other hand, Pierre Blanchar... sustains the role and the temperament of his character throughout."[831] Some felt Jack Raymond's direction lacked originality.

On screen, *A Royal Divorce* told of the Little Emperor's campaign for the love and respect of his wife Josephine, who married him for the sole purpose of providing security for her fatherless children. His rise to power and their eventual divorce, which (the picture claimed) Napoleon didn't want, delineated the film's scenario. The ending revealed the last meeting between the two when the defeated Napoleon brings his small son to meet Josephine for her blessing. "It is a touching scene," wrote Harold W. Cohen of the *Pittsburgh Gazette*, "ringed with the darkness of impending doom."[832] Cohen admired the "thorough cunning" in which Blanchar illuminated his down-to-earth Napoleon as well as the "shafts of bright humor" in the photoplay's early sections. "*A Royal Divorce* achieves distinction of a sort despite its academic lethargy and Miss Ruth Chatterton," cautioned Cohen. "Certainly she is hardly the average fellow's idea of a femme fatale these days and her Josephine has all of the deadly charm and fascination of a smoggy, rain-swept fall afternoon in downtown Pittsburgh."[833] *The Chicago Tribune* was unmerciful to Chatterton. "She queers everything," the review stated. "The gracious, ingratiating… woman she is supposed to impersonate, becomes under her crude handling a simpering bar maidish dame of ogling archnesses and an ungainly kittenishness that is truly awful."[834] For all her effort and three years of research, it is a pity that the film fell flat and that Chatterton's performance, by most accounts, was a complete bust. *A Royal Divorce* is considered to be a "lost film," so there is no way to offer a fresh assessment seventy-five years after the fact.

⚜

As German aggression and tension surmounted in Europe, Ruth intuited that heading back to America would be a wise decision. She left Le Havre on the *Il de France* on January 11, 1939, and sailed for New York. Uncle Sam greeted her with a tax lien for $5,338 on her 1935 income. She wasn't alone. He was asking ZaSu Pitts for $20,371 on her 1932-33 return.[835] Ruth responded by condemning the high salaries of film stars in the first place. "The huge salaries they pay stars are really detrimental," she said. "They are applied to the budget of the picture. If you get a big salary you get a low-priced director and a cheap story. Moreover... you pay a major share of it to the government. I stuck with motion pictures because I was lazy. I could finish a picture and then travel, have a good time."[836]

After her "good time" abroad, Ruth wasted no time in getting back to work. Some reports stated that she had gone through her money, which was easy for her to do. Adela Rogers St. Johns observed that for Ruth, money was to spend and give away. "She's a good business woman in driving a bargain," said St. Johns, "but money melts in her presence; it is nothing of itself."[837] Within a month, Ruth was rehearsing *Farewell Appearance*, a play by Marguerite Roberts, as her stage comeback. Auriol Lee directed. The play opened March 6 at Boston's Wilbur Theatre with a new title, *West of Broadway*. The cast included Walter Abel, Will Geer, Josephine Hull, and a young pig named Edna. Ruth Chatterton in person was a definite draw. "Miss Ruth Chatterton, very easy on the eyes," said the *Boston Herald*, "goes into the farcical sequences in excellent spirits. She handles her comedy lines with a neat touch. Walter Abel doesn't fare quite so well... being more than a little stiff."[838] *West of Broadway* concerned two stage co-stars who retreat to a rural farm in Iowa for a change of pace. It isn't long before too much applejack inspires a belated marriage and a new play titled *Dry Rot*. Ruth admitted that Edna the pig stole the show. "I can hear shrieks of laughter even in my dressing room," she said. "They tell me she drowns out the lines entirely."[839] Following a two-week run, Ruth and Auriol Lee decided on revisions and another tryout before playing Broadway's Martin Beck Theatre. "The final act is undergoing principal alterations," said Ruth. Both admitted that *West of*

Broadway was 45 minutes more play than necessary. By April, Ruth and Auriol decided that the play wasn't necessary at all. They chalked it up as a misadventure.

Along came the eminent drama critic George Jean Nathan to the rescue. In 1925, Nathan had accused Ruth of acting with her "powdered tootsies" in *The Little Minister.* Now he was persuading her to tackle all seven lead female characters in a revival of Arthur Schnitzler's one-act comedy, *The Affairs of Anatol*—obviously something that would take more balls than feet. It necessitated that Ruth finally join Actor's Equity. Technically, she had no choice if she intended to play the summer stock circuit. Schnitzler was noted for his interest in sexual psychology, specifically amongst Vienna's upper class. Seven vignettes allowed Ruth to dazzle her audience as a vulgar music hall entertainer, a circus lady, and five other seductresses who tempt Anatol along the path to matrimony. *The Affairs of Anatol* proved to be nothing more than a novel stunt. It closed after one week in Maplewood, New Jersey. If anything, it paired Ruth with actor Barry Thomson, who more than succeeded in filling the shoes of Anatol. He became her next husband. Thomson had worked on the London stage and made his American debut in the Lunts' production of *The Taming of the Shrew.* Ruth and Barry soon became an item for Broadway gossip. "Ruth Chatterton and Barry Thomson, her leading man in summer stock, are yum yum," tooted Dorothy Kilgallen.[840] Walter Winchell described the lovebirds being "thicker than Stalin and Adolf."[841]

Before Ruth (and Barry) attempted another play, she signed up for the WABC drama serial *Big Sister.* In July 1939, Ruth was a three-week replacement for the regular star, Alice Frost. "Radio's trigger-timing and pinpoint precision are really breathtaking," Ruth declared during rehearsal. She played herself and the locale was switched from New Hampshire to Hollywood. Chatterton was introduced as the longtime friend of cast regular Martin Gabel, who played Dr. John Wayne. Agnes Moorehead also played various roles on the program. "The idea of playing yourself is just the least bit obvious," said Ruth, "and it is more or less a matter of reading lines. It also makes one a little bit self-conscious."[842] Bing Crosby had already introduced Ruth to the potential informality of radio when she appeared on his program. "Bing is one of the most disarming people in Hollywood," said Ruth. "I asked him if there was any studio audience and he said 'Oh, no, just a few people who may slip in.' So, I dressed in a pair of old slacks and tied a handkerchief around my head. The place was packed. I was terribly embarrassed, but not after Bing took off his coat and opened his collar at the neck, exposing his gaudy shirt and suspenders. All those people seemed to love it."[843] As far as American films were concerned, Ruth had lost interest. She now leaned towards the French cinema with its innate sophistication and attitudes about the "birds and bees." "In consequence," stated Ruth, "French films are made on a basis of artistic understanding that does not hamper the story."[844]

⚜

Before long, Chatterton-Thomson teamed for the new comedy *Tonight We Dance.* After a tryout in Rhode Island, it played two weeks near Baltimore on the straw-hat circuit. Author Gladys Unger, scenarist for Katharine Hepburn's decidedly off-beat *Sylvia Scarlet* (1935), and co-writer Marcella Burke, both divorcees, thought it amusing that the play was very *anti-*divorce. Much of the plot mirrored Burke's marital experience. While it leaned towards farce, the effect of divorce upon children was emphasized. Chatterton played a volatile, capricious wife and Thomson a mercurial, gambler husband who has depleted their finances. Their three precocious children reflect the weaknesses of the parents. As the marriage crumbles, an amorous musician pursues the wife and a three times divorcee (silent star Lila Lee) lures the husband into being her number four. Though the production was enthusiastically received, Unger and Burke took time out to work on revisions. Ruth and Barry took the opportunity to join the annual Woodstock Country Club Revue on September 11. Their enactment of the Christmas scene from *The Affairs of Anatol* was considered the highlight of the sold out event.

The revised *Tonight We Dance* premiered before a cosmopolitan audience on September 25 at Cleveland's Hanna Theater. Chicago's Harris Theatre scheduled an extended stay for the play and made an ample profit. Among Ruth's admirers applauding in the audience was her old friend Ramon Novarro. *Chicago Tribune* critic Cecil Smith said the play "had neither a good beginning nor a very conclusive end, tho it had a modicum of wit in between." "It served to remind us," added Smith, "that Miss Chatterton is one of the most capable and one of the most economical of all our actresses, and it brought Barry Thomson forward as a first-rate leading man."[845] A memorable moment during the Chicago run occurred when Ruth confronted a man in the audience who yelled out an answer to her character's question. The audience laughed at first. Ruth ignored the intrusion and carried on. When he answered her next cue, and the next, she stopped dead cold and glared at him until two ushers nabbed the culprit by his arms and carried him out of the theater.

Following the Chicago run came St. Louis, Indianapolis, and Pittsburgh, where *Tonight We Dance* lost steam, receiving a new low gross for the season. "Nothing funny was said or done in that first act," complained the *Pittsburgh Press*.[846] English playwright John van Druten, known for his

sharp wit, was brought in to rewrite Act I. He had penned Ruth's unre-
markable *Unfaithful* in 1931. Instead of a December opening on Broadway, Ruth and company attempted another tryout in Boston. A critic for
The Boston Herald found it "reasonably pleasant... and an opportunity for
Ruth Chatterton to hover over an audience with a silky voice and a most
engaging manner."[847] In the meantime, however, van Druten had talked
Ruth into dropping the play completely and "hover over an audience" in
something more serious.

❧❀❧

After his rewrite for *Tonight We Dance*, van Druten had arm surgery. During recovery at New York's posh Gotham Hotel, he was chatting away
one day with fellow writer Christopher Isherwood when Chatterton
showed up. Van Druten began telling her about his new play (*Leave
Her to Heaven*), in which she was to star. "I have never seen anyone put
on such an act," recalled Isherwood. '*Johnny—!*' she tearfully, joyfully
gasped, 'Oh—Johnny, *darling!* Oh—I'm so *glad!*'" Isherwood went on
to say, "John handled her perfectly—he was cool and pleasant, submitting to her kisses without a sign of disgust. I admired him as one admires
an excellent animal trainer."[848] Coming from Isherwood, this was an odd
assessment considering Chatterton's assortment of devoted gay friends.
Besides, there was a decidedly theatrical element in Chatterton and van
Druten's world. It was van Druten who would adapt Isherwood's *Goodbye to Berlin* from *The Berlin Stories* for the stage success *I Am a Camera*,
which in turn inspired the musical *Cabaret* (1966).

Chatterton's tears of joy quickly evaporated when she saw van Druten's final script. She had reasonable doubts regarding the play's potential.
Leave Her to Heaven (in no way related to the 1945 film) focused on trag-

February 27, 1940. Holding telegrams on opening night for *Leave Her to Heaven*.

edy. Van Druten's intention was to illustrate how cataclysmic events could descend on the most ordinary lives. The title, from Shakespeare's *Hamlet*, refers to Queen Gertrude: "Leave her to heaven, and to those thorns that in her bosom lodge to prick and sting her." Van Druten's play was based on a real-life incident in London involving a Mrs. Alma Rattenbury and her eighteen-year-old lover—the family chauffeur, George Stoner. On the night of March 24, 1935, Stoner (ironically on narcotics) took a mallet to Mr. Rattenbury, Alma's rich, aging husband. When the police arrived, Alma said it was she who fractured her husband's skull. Stoner finally confessed and was scheduled for execution. Ostracized by public opinion, Mrs. Rattenbury plunged a dagger into her heart, committing suicide.[849] "The only reason I hesitate to do [the play]," Ruth stated at the time, "is that there is so much tragedy in the world today and people really need to laugh more."[850]   Critics echoed Ruth's concerns—the timing was all wrong for a play. Set in England, Chatterton's sex-inflamed character, Madge Monckton, is married to a much older man (Reynolds Denniston) and has taken up with Robert, the family's young chauffeur (Edmond O'Brien). She has no intention of leaving the security of her husband's fireside and finances. On the other hand, Madge was Robert's first important romance. A fury of jealousy gets the better of him. He bludgeons the husband to death. Upset and inebriated, Madge confesses to the murder. So does Robert, who is sentenced to hang. Madge, in turn, kills herself. It duplicated pretty much what had been front-page news in 1935. There would be no tryout. Auriol Lee would direct. *Leave Her to Heaven* opened cold on February 27, 1940, at Broadway's Longacre Theatre.

Time magazine declared that van Druten "did his best to make his play as dull as it was depressing"—the melodrama was without excitement, the "violence of love" had no poignancy.[851] *Leave Her to Heaven* came across as slow and painful—some suggested it move at a faster clip. Burns Mantel found Chatterton's role to be "anything but appealing," but added, "Miss Chatterton has improved greatly as an actress since she left Broadway. Her individual performance in *Leave Her to Heaven* is quite impressive technically. She has grace and charm and a persuasive approach. She is distressingly convincing as a woman who drinks too much... And, she is pathetically true to character when, in the end, she decides to put an end to her wasted life."[852] "Chatterton had a field day running the emotional gamut," said critic Gerald Bordman, "but the play was too weak to sustain her."[853] Another review noted that newcomer Edmond O'Brien, fresh from playing the fiery Prince Hall to Maurice Evans's Falstaff, brought "so much stridence" to his role as the chauffeur, that Madge's love for him appeared "incomprehensible."[854] Ruth's portrayal of Madge Monckton lasted fifteen performances, closing March 9.

With playwright John Van Druten (c. 1940).

If only she had waited until December and returned to Broadway in van Druten's next real success, *Old Acquaintance,* which Auriol Lee also directed. Lee and van Druten had had a close working relationship for over ten years and were trusted influences in Ruth's decision-making about her own career.

After war was declared in Europe, Ruth was decidedly an isolationist—not an uncommon stance prior to Pearl Harbor. Fellow aviator Charles Lindbergh was perhaps the most famous among those who opposed U.S. involvement. Ruth stated her views thusly,

> This war is illogical. People have been so busy with their isms that they have failed to see what has been creeping up. We ought to… keep our minds on our own affairs. I

have been in Europe for three years and I have seen the thing coming. I just can't make it out. And somehow I still feel that it's not going to go on. I'd be amazed if any large number of planes could get to this country, and if they did we could shoot them down. England, of course, was so completely unprepared. The whole world took a shot at Mr. Chamberlain, who was simply the mouthpiece for people who were not prepared.

There is propaganda everywhere. I'm beginning to come around to the idea that the arms embargo should be done away with. For the last year my mind has been so completely tied up with human beings and the hideous nightmare that has come over a large part of the world. I don't hate the German people or the Russian people. It's just such a frightful pity. [855]

Despite her feelings, Ruth felt that the United States, even though geographically isolated, would eventually get involved. The arms embargo was repealed in November 1939, which allowed munitions to be sold to England and France and prevented American ships from sailing into war zones. In the spring of 1940 came the news of Germany's successful invasion of France. It seemed impossible—Ruth's upcoming tour in Shaw's *Pygmalion* would coincide with Hitler's victory tour of Paris. In such a world, Ruth stated that home to her was wherever she hung her hat. Her remark somehow made perfect sense as countless human beings found themselves plunged into what she called a "hideous nightmare."

Endnotes

806   "Baer Evades Law to Sail for England," *Omaha World Herald*, March 4, 1937.

807   Ruth Gordon, *Myself Among Others*, Atheneum, c. 1971, pgs 181-182.

808   George W. Bishop review of *The Constant Wife*, (excerpt from *The New York Times*) May 20, 1937.

809   Review of *The Constant Wife*, *The London Mercury*, September, 1937.

810   Charles Morgan, review of *the Constant Wife*, *The New York Times*, June 6, 1937 (originally in *The London Times*).

811   Louella Parsons, "Ruth Chatterton's Play 'The Constant Wife' Goes Over Big in London Town," *Syracuse American*, June 20, 1937.

812   John U. Sturdevant, "Slow Fate Ended Olga's Royal Up-and-Down Romance," *Oregonian*, June 14, 1942.

813   "Weddings Okeh Across Border," *Ogden Standard Examiner*, September 14, 1937.

814   James Robert Parish, *The Debonairs*, Arlington House, c. 1975, pg 38.

815   Joan Littlefield, "Ruth Chatterton's Rich Role," *Springfield Republican*, September 23, 1937.

816   Review of *The Rat*, *Film Daily*, January 31, 1938.

817   Review of *The Rat*, *Australian Women's Weekly*, February 18, 1939.

818   Mac Tinee, review of *The Rat*, *Chicago Daily Tribune*, April 16, 1938.

819   Frank S. Nugent, review of *The Rat*, *New York Times*, February 28, 1938.

820   Milton R. Bass, "The Lively Arts," *Berkshire Eagle*, August 30, 1956.

821   Joan Littlefield, "Ruth Chatterton's Rich Role," *Springfield Republican*, September 23, 1937.

822   Russell Landstrom, "Women Asked to Help Aviation," *Appleton Post-Crescent*, November 3, 1939.

823   Joan Littlefield, "Britain on the Screen," December 5, 1937.

824   "Portuguese Will Be Ruth Chatterton's Husband, She Says," *Nevada State Journal*, December 15, 1937.

825   "Ruth Chatterton Denies Lisbon Report of Romance," *Daily Capitol* (MO), December 17, 1937.

826   "Ruth Chatterton Has a Double," *The Gleaner* (Jamaica), December 20, 1937.

827   "Girl Angrily Admits Hoax," *Billings Gazette*, December 17, 1937.

828   "Ruth Chatterton Tired of Hollywood and New York Stage," *The Queenslander* (Brisbane), March 11, 1937.

829   Joan Littlefield, "Ruth Chatterton as Josephine In British Film on Napoleon," *Dallas Morning News*, July 24, 1938.

830   Joan Littlefield, "Ruth Chatterton as Josephine In British Film on Napoleon," *Dallas Morning News*, July 24, 1938.

831   Review of *The Royal Divorce*, *Australian Woman's Weekly*, August 26, 1939.

832   Harold W. Cohen, "Chatterton and Blanchar in 'Royal Divorce,'" *Pittsburgh Post-Gazette*, October 7, 1939.

833   Harold W. Cohen, "Chatterton and Blanchar in 'Royal Divorce,'" *Pittsburgh Post-Gazette*, October 7, 1939.

834   Mac Tinee, "Scores Triumph As Napoleon in *Royal Divorce*, *Chicago Daily Tribune*, October 2, 1939.

835   "U.S. Sues ZaSu Pitts for $20,371 in Taxes," *Omaha World Herald*, January 17, 1939.

836   "Ruth Chatterton Speaks on Film Standards," *Boston Herald*, March 5, 1939.

837   Adela Rogers St. Johns, "The Men in Ruth Chatterton's Life," *Liberty*, January 20, 1934.

838   Elinor Hughes, review of *West of Broadway*, *Boston Herald*, March 7, 1939.

839   Elinor Hughes, "Ruth Chatterton Revising *West of Broadway*, *Boston Herald*, March 13, 1939.

840   Dorothy Kilgallen, "The Voice of Broadway," *Trenton Evening Times*, July 26, 1939.

841   Walter Winchell, "On Broadway," *Logansport Pharos Tribune*, September 5, 1939.

842   Richard B. O'Brien, "Taking A 'Flier' On The Air," *New York Times*, August 6, 1939.

843   Richard B. O'Brien, "Taking A 'Flier' On The Air," *New York Times*, August 6, 1939.

844   "Ruth Chatterton Speaks on Film Standards," *Boston Herald*, March 5, 1939.

845   Cecil Smith, "Looking Back Over 1939-40 Theater Fare," *Chicago Tribune*, June 9, 1940.

846   Kaspar Monahan, "*Tonight We Dance* Stars Chatterton," *Pittsburgh Press*, November 28, 1939.

847   R.F.E., Jr., review of *Tonight We Dance*, *Boston Herald*, December 26, 1939.

848   Christopher Isherwood, *Diaries, 1939-1960*, Methuen, c. 1996, pg 14.

849   "Woman Freed of Killing Mate Stabs Herself, Jumps Into River," *Richmond Times Dispatch*, June 6, 1935.

850   Richard B. O'Brien, "Taking A 'Flier' On The Air," *New York Times*, August 6, 1939.

851   Review of *Leave Her to Heaven*, *Time*, March 11, 1940.

852   Burns Mantle, "Ruth Chatterton's Only Mistake Is Poor Play," *Springfield Republican*, March 14, 1940.

853   Gerald Martin Bordman, *American Theatre: A Chronicle of Comedy and Drama, 1930-1969, Vol. 3,* Oxford University Press, c. 1997, Page 189.

854   Blanches Shoemaker Wagstaff, review of *Leave Her to Heaven, Wilton Bulletin,* March 14, 1940.

855   Roelif Loveland, "War Stage Roils Ruth Chatterton," *Plain Dealer,* September 25, 1939.

c.1940 Publicity shot.

14
Caprice

Following the tepid response to *Leave Her to Heaven*, Chatterton's highly anticipated Broadway "comeback," her career decisions favored intuition—whatever took her fancy. As she approached 50, Ruth played in numerous tryouts and revivals while enjoying the camaraderie of fellow players—all part of her new life on the east coast. The 1940s found her performing in as many as six plays a year—short runs, summer stock, another stab at Broadway, and a number of aborted projects. Ruth's considerable success afforded her a posh apartment at The Pierre facing Central Park in Manhattan. The luxury hotel, with top floors modeled after the Royal Chapel at Versailles, was a recognizable landmark in the New York skyline. Ruth felt right at home. In the fall of 1940, dressed in white taffeta, Ruth enjoyed a reunion at the hotel's Café Pierre with soprano Grace Moore, who was in her preferred pale blue velvet. Moore stated in her autobiography that Ruth was "companionable and utterly fascinating." "Under her rather meek, quiet, subtle charm," wrote Moore, "there lurked a potent lure which was irresistible."[856] Undoubtedly, the two talked about Moore's recent trip to Havana where she opened a new opera house, as well as Ruth's upcoming tour in Shaw's *Pygmalion*.

Pygmalion

While Ruth was in England, George Bernard Shaw (who was very particular) had suggested that she play Eliza Doolittle in *Pygmalion*. The metamorphosis of an English curbstone flower girl into a grand lady was Shaw's most popular play. Auriol Lee, an old friend of Shaw's, arranged his meeting with Ruth and promised to stage the production when things fell into place.[857]   Finally, in May 1940, Ruth and Barry Thomson (as Henry Higgins) opened in *Pygmalion* at the annual Ann Arbor Drama Festival. It was such an overwhelming success that Ruth and Auriol planned a transcontinental tour. "I adore the part because of its gay, light-hearted quality," said Ruth, "and its ability to amuse audiences and take their minds off the dark problems of the world today. It also has the wit and sparkling dialogue of the one and only George Bernard Shaw."[858] Indeed, Shaw's sly suggestion that environment and opportunity are more important than heredity had substance and spirit. By Act V, Eliza comes to the realization: "The difference between a lady and a flower girl is not how she behaves, but how she's treated." Eliza Doolittle proved to be one of Ruth's most acclaimed roles during her post-film career. Curiously, she admitted that she had never seen *Pygmalion* performed. "So you see my Eliza is my own," she said. "It may be a poor thing, but my own."[859]

Chatterton and Thomson opened the summer season at Long Island's Red Barn Theatre, where *Pygmalion* scored once again. Before continuing with Shaw, the duo made their first appearance at the Cape Playhouse in Philip Barry's *Tomorrow and Tomorrow*. This was the production in which John Kerr made his stage debut playing Chatterton's nine-year-old son. He had three lines and made ten dollars for the week. Ruth had a soft spot for her role (which she had filmed in 1931). She would perform it the following year in Stockbridge, where a critic applauded her "quick and malleable portraiture," saying, "Chatterton's understanding of

Eve Redmond... is extraordinarily moving and complete."[860]   There was renewed interest in Philip Barry, especially after *The Philadelphia Story* rejuvenated Katharine Hepburn's career. The Chatterton-Thomson team also opened the Amherst Drama Festival in Noel Coward's *Private Lives*. It was their fifth play as co-stars. Again, full houses greeted the former screen star (52 standees one evening) and reviews were enthusiastic. "Last night Miss Chatterton and Barry Thomson had a field day," said one critic, who found the chatter between acts a revelation. "Everyone was in a happy mood, speaking appreciatively of the merry, hilarious, and, to a certain small degree, naughty fun."[861]

Pygmalion was then offered as a benefit performance for British War Relief at the seaside Bass Rocks Theatre in Gloucester, Massachusetts. After the play, Ruth and Thomson held a reception, greeting audience members in the filled-to-capacity theater. Proceeds from the event afforded a new ambulance, fully equipped, that would be shipped to Gloucester, England. From October 1940–March 1941, Chatterton's tour of *Pygmalion* was credited for its Shavian bite. One review praised Thomson's "zest" and Chatterton's ability to give "the cruder side of Eliza Doolittle its full sound and fury."[862]   Three young producers were backing Chatterton's venture: Harold J. Kennedy and a gay couple—Justus Addis and Hayden Rorke. Rorke, fresh from the tour of Katharine Hepburn's *The Philadelphia Story*, also agreed to play the role of Freddie. "Co-producer Rorke makes the simpering Freddie a standout minor role," observed one critic.[863]   Rorke, Addis, and Kennedy would also co-produce Ruth's next theatrical venture. (In the 1960's, Rorke was a cast regular on TV's popular *I Dream of Jeannie*, starring Barbara Eden. In her autobiography, Eden mentioned the "unashamedly gay" Rorke and Addis living happily for many years in Studio City with their menagerie of dogs.)[864]

In November 1940, Ruth glided into Chicago at the controls of her plane with leading man Thomson. The play was such a hit that it was extended from two weeks to seven. Chicago's Ashton Stevens, considered the dean of American drama critics (and uncle of director George Stevens), appraised Chatterton's performance in *Pygmalion* as "a thrill that has followed me home. Miss Chatterton was incandescently good. She was high comedy with a beautiful flourish."[865] Ruth was an honored guest at the Chicago Art Institute and her numerous personal and radio appearances ensured box office returns. The popular radio quiz show *Speak Up America,* sponsored by the Better Speech Institute, gave Ruth the opportunity to investigate "murders" of the King's English. Dramatic skits were presented with errors in grammar and diction. Ruth competed with two news columnists and Sidney James, the editor of *Time.* She won money for her favorite charity and returned the following week for an encore. Before leaving Chicago, Ruth, along with Lillian Gish, hosted a hotel reception honoring Ruth Gordon's 25th anniversary on stage. Gordon was in town starring in a revival of George Oppenheimer's comedy, *Here Today.*

After Chicago, Ruth took a brief respite from Eliza Doolittle to join Ian Keith in a benefit for the British Red Cross. They paired for Noel Coward's *Tonight at Eight-Thirty* at Evanston, Illinois' Guild Theatre. Ruth and Barry took time out to visit the legendary Alfred Lunt and Lynn Fontanne at their country retreat in Genesee Depot—Ten Chimneys (now a historical landmark). The Lunts were especially fond of Thomson, who had co-starred with them in several plays.

When *Pygmalion* arrived in Santa Fe, Ruth had a reunion with Henry Miller's daughter, Agnes Miller McCoy, who was visiting the area. Agnes' 1920 marriage to Col. Tim McCoy had ended in divorce. She complained that her movie cowboy husband had "gone Hollywood." *Pygmalion* reached the film capital in February 1941. Ruth's Eliza Doolittle received eight curtain calls opening night at the Biltmore. "Chatterton Triumphs In Play," headlined the *Los Angeles Times*. Critic Edwin Schallert felt that Chatterton "achieved results lustrously and movingly" and praised her "understanding and skill" with the role.[866] Louella Parsons raved, "Ruth, for my money, is better than Wendy Hiller in the movie version."[867] On opening night, Ruth, Barry, Auriol, and Tilly reveled with old friends at the Richard Barthelmesses' until the wee hours of the morning. Joining in the merriment were Mary Astor and Manuel del Campo, John van Druten, Mary Pickford and Buddy Rogers, and writer Dorothy Parker. Parker, known for her wit and wisecracks, was writing additional dialogue for the Warner Brothers production of *The Little Foxes*. It had been rumored earlier that Chatterton was offered the lead role of Regina Giddens.[868] Hollywood kept Chatterton in the loop, but Bette Davis, as Queen of the lot, chalked up another Oscar nomination with the role. *The Little Foxes*, however, would later prove to be a much lauded stage role for Ruth. Shortly before *Pygmalion* arrived in Los Angeles, Bette Davis, still a great admirer of Chatterton, suggested to Jack Warner that Ruth play in *Mr. Skeffington*. Davis didn't feel capable of doing justice to the part.[869] George Brent also went to his bosses and argued on his ex-wife's behalf for the role. Unfortunately for Ruth, Warner held out until Davis finally relented to act the spoiled, once too-beautiful Fanny Skeffington, whose looks are ravaged by illness and age.

There was a question as to whether Chatterton, at age 48, was a tad ripe for the role of Eliza Doolittle. A critic for the *San Diego Union* countered with, "Miss Chatterton flabbergasted those who remember seeing her in their own childhood, and were skeptical of her fitness for the part of the young flower girl. She was equal to all demands."[870] Salt Lake City's Paramount Theatre hosted the final performance of the twenty-seven week tour. "Actress Wins Big Applause," raved a local paper. "Ruth Chatterton

As Eliza Doolittle in the tour of *Pygmalion* (1940-41).

proved to a fairly large but rather skeptical audience last night… that she can still play the ingénue roles… and effectively, too."[871] The review mentioned that Chatterton was thinking of taking the play to South America. In truth, she had already begun rehearsing a new comedy, *Treat Her Gently*. The play was sent to her by a complete unknown, a busboy who worked at a New York automat. Once again, producers Kennedy, Addis, and Rorke were a hundred percent behind Ruth's hunch about the play.

"When I did Liza in *Pygmalion*," said Ruth long after the tour, "I was still playing it freshly after thirty-six weeks. I was still creating it because Shaw is such a devil, and I found in my last week a line that I finally understood and which subtly changed the entire performance for me."[872] Before she put Eliza Doolittle to rest, Ruth offered a delicious little scene from *Pygmalion* for radio's *Hollywood Open House* in 1944. Higgins accompanies Eliza to his mother's home to test her conversational skill, cautioning her not to stray from the topics of health and weather. Upon her leave, she is politely asked if she will walk home through the park. "Walk!" she snaps. "Not bloody likely! I'm going 'ome in a taxi!"

George Batson, a twenty-five-year-old busboy, had been writing one act plays right out of high school. During the Depression, government stimulus via a W.P.A. enabled him to take a course in play writing. In early 1941, Batson sent his manuscript of *Treat Her Gently* to Ruth, who, upon recognizing "genius," cut short her tour of *Pygmalion*. Nothing could have been more inspiring—busboy cooks up play for Ruth Chatterton! Ruth and company had yet to meet Batson when they arrived for an opening tryout at Amarillo's Paramount Theatre. On stage, Baston's comedy told of an aggressive, spirited book reviewer named Julia (Chatterton) who has been too busy to bother with love. Her debonair publisher (Thomson) and a young "enlightened socialist" (Rorke) whose book she had panned are about to change all that. An enthusiastic audience stood up for seven curtain calls. Some found the play too risqué, walked out, and demanded their money back. A review from the *Dallas Morning News* assessed that *Treat Her Gently* was rough in spots and slow to start, but "closed with the audience holding their sides."[873] "There's swearing aplenty," commented

Bill Wilson for the *Amarillo News-Globe*, "spicy lines galore. Most of them unprintable."[874] For a new play, un-gauged, Wilson was impressed with Chatterton's ability to time the laughs and pick up her lines. One of the best scenes had her "educating" the young, radical, penniless author. "Listen, young man," she advises, "only the rich buy books. If you want to change the world you must reach the man on the street, the man who buys the five-cent newspaper. If you want to change the world, you should be a columnist—not a Communist." Author Batson missed his play's premier. Wearing his only suit, he was still hitchhiking from New York. A busboy's salary of $15.89 a week didn't afford the luxury of wheels of any kind. Although *Treat Her Gently* never made it to Broadway, Batson would have several moderate hits through the years, his most successful being *Ramshackle Inn*, which was a huge hit for ZaSu Pitts.

By the time Chatterton and company decided to drop *Treat Her Gently*, Rorke and Addis had been paged by Uncle Sam. But Ruth hadn't given up on George Batson. She was determined to try out yet another of his comedies in which she would direct, stage, and star. Once again, Thomson tagged along in a supporting role. The oddly-titled comedy, *Sorrow for Angels*, premiered in August as part of the Cambridge Summer Theater. Amid much talk of sex and a good deal of drinking, Ruth played the mother of a newlywed daughter—a daughter who is unduly anxious to philander with a handsome novelist. "Miss Chatterton literally carries the show and she has the best lines," noted the *Boston Herald*. The review admitted that Batson's *Sorrow for Angels* had some genuinely witty lines, but cautioned, "He also has some cheap ones which don't ring true to his characters. He is lacking in technical ease."[875] Batson was unable to make the audience care about his characters.

Sadder than the sorrows of her new play was Ruth's loss of Auriol Lee, friend, mentor, and director. Sixty-two-year-old Lee, who had recently completed her first American film, Alfred Hitchcock's *Suspicion,* was killed on July 2, 1941, while motoring east from John van Druten's ranch in California. She was preparing to direct Gertrude Lawrence in a revival of van Druten's *Behold We Live.* The playwright arrived in Hutchinson, Kansas, to preside at her funeral. Lee had expressed to him that she be buried wherever she died.[876] Lee was survived by her niece, actress Virginia Field, who Chatterton had brought to the attention of Hollywood in 1935. Ruth and Barry had just opened the season at Stockbridge in *Tomorrow and Tomorrow* and weren't able to attend the graveside service. "Auriol Lee was one of the ten most interesting women I've ever known," wrote Dorothy Kilgallen a few days later. "She was quick, salty, and full of wit." Kilgallen stated that she relished having lunch with Auriol, who loved to tell amusing stories about Chatterton, Merle Oberon, and Madeleine Carroll—women she had directed. "She was full of lore about them," said Kilgallen.[877]

By the fall of 1941, Chatterton was putting her heart and good will into a Canadian tour for British War Relief. Offering free and voluntary aid, she was heard on various radio programs such as *The Ontario Show, Sky Over Britain,* and *War Letters from Britain.*[878] She also starred in a special adaptation of Noel Coward's *Cavalcade* for Canada's coast-to-coast network. The following year, Ruth would be guest of honor at a cocktail party and dance sponsored by Canadian officers. Dressed in a long-sleeve black dinner dress scrolled in scarlet sequins, she reported to the official Officer's Quarters at Stanley Barracks. Ruth was ranked Captain in the "Queens Own" (the only woman so designated) as well as flight lieutenant in the Royal Canadian Air Force. They became two of Ruth's proudest achieve-

Pilot Ruth Chatterton at Soldiers Center in Montgomery, Alabama (1942).

ments.[879] She frequently wore a sport jacket bearing the Royal Canadian Air Corps wings alongside her insignia of the U.S. Air Corps.

While in Canada, Chatterton-Thomson teamed for a slick revival of the Lunt-Fontanne 1929 hit *Caprice*. The charmingly risqué comedy afforded Ruth the opportunity to play a sophisticated woman with an unquenchable thirst for attractive men. Her character goes so far as to seduce her lover's teenaged son, whose infatuation is complete. Ruth was *The Graduate's* "Mrs. Robinson," 1941-style. Newcomer William Eythe played the juvenile. *Caprice* also toured New England where the *Boston Globe* praised, "Miss Chatterton, indeed, treats her role with a deft hand. She takes a line, toys with it a bit, and then flings it out to good effect. Mr.

Thomson and Mr. Eythe are excellent... a remarkable show."[880] It was reported that Eythe, who would later form a lifelong relationship with actor Lon McAllister, preferred to run around with "the older group of ladies" when in New York: Chatterton, Garbo, and Tallulah Bankhead.[881] That is, when he wasn't sunbathing on the balcony of his Greenwich Village apartment.

Eythe enjoyed telling about the time he was on his way up to Ruth's apartment for a party. He got in the elevator, whose only occupant other than the operator was a woman hiding behind a newspaper. He thought it rude and commented, 'Looks like everybody thinks she's Garbo nowadays.' With that, the woman put the paper down. It was Garbo, also on her way to Chatterton's party.[882] Ruth reveled in playing *Caprice* and would pull it out of her hat several times during the 1940s. Of actor Eythe, Ruth commented on his "natural ability" and praised, "He knows instinctively the right thing to do."[883] Bob Francis, for *Billboard*, caught the opening of a 1943 Manhattan performance and felt although the play was no longer the "mild shocker" it had been fifteen years before, Chatterton's "top-drawer playing" made it "tick." "[Miss Chatterton's] entrance sparks the motor and the show begins to move," wrote Francis. "When she's in there pitching, the whole business takes on sparkle. She's a honey."[884]

A few weeks after Pearl Harbor and the U.S. entry into World War II, Ruth announced that she would bring in the New Year with a new comedy, *Bow to the Wittiest*, written by a Chicago columnist. The project was shelved shortly before its Cleveland opening. Katharine Hepburn had also considered doing the play. Luckily, Philip Barry came to Hepburn's rescue by offering her the comedy *Without Love*. In late February 1942, Barry Thomson joined Hepburn's New England tour in a supporting role. Thomson's exit as Ruth's co-star and partner was put permanently on hold by Uncle Sam. In early May, Thomson entered the army. When the cast of *Without Love* threw him a going-away party, Hepburn handed Thomson a sealed brown envelope containing exactly $21—army pay. "A month's salary in advance," she explained.[885] Upon receiving their monthly brown envelope, enlistees were known to complain, "The eagle has landed and took a crap." Surely Thomson resisted in making such a remark to his benefactor, Hepburn.

Uncle Sam was also paging Ruth—for tax returns to the tune of $13,000. Three hundred and forty-six pieces of furniture from her Los Angeles home were being held captive in a warehouse by state and federal authorities until sold.[886] Perhaps it was her reward for raising thousands of dollars in War Bonds. On one occasion, she arrived for a previously announced appearance at the popular department store Forbes & Wallace (Massachusetts). A large crowd broke out in applause as she stayed behind the counter, handing out war bond certificates and making her own change.

Before enlisting, Barry's final theatrical venture was to stage *Private Lives* for the Star Theatre Circuit, starring Ruth and Eddie Nugent. The revival was promptly slammed by *Billboard*, which found it to be "badly acted" with a set design that had all the charm of a "cowbarn."[887] Another critic commented that Ruth was "the star and practically lone actor" on stage. "Only infrequently," the review stated, "did Eddie Nugent gain any momentum or catch the lively give and take."[888] Nugent abruptly left the cast and was replaced by Ralph Forbes. The Chatterton-Forbes combo generated enough steam to keep *Private Lives* public for over a year.

When the play reopened, *The Boston Herald* raved, "Excellent horseplay. Miss Chatterton and Mr. Forbes spared neither themselves nor the properties, and the audience enjoyed it thoroughly."[889] The added fillip of real life ex-mates playing reunited ex-mates on stage certainly helped. Ruth and Ralph's critical and box office success seldom wavered on tour—frequently breaking house records well into 1943. By June of that year, according to Pittsburgh critic Harold Cohen, the brew of Chatterton, Forbes, and Noel Coward had turned from "a bubbling champagne cocktail" to a "glass of heavy stout." "There is such a premeditated deliberateness about their performance," he complained.[890] Chatterton's financial weekly reward on tour was in the range of $500 a week in cash.[891] In 1983, famous ex-mates Elizabeth Taylor and Richard Burton would also maintain their cash flow by reuniting for Coward's fifty-three-year-old chestnut. Some, including the critic for *The New York Times,* saw it as nothing more than "a calculated business venture." The *Times* review felt that Burton and Taylor had "all the vitality of a Madame Tussaud's exhibit."[892]

Gregory Peck had entered the charmed circle of Chatterton co-stars during the summer of '42. In July, she and Forbes took a week off from Noel Coward to do Donald Ogden Stewart's comedy *Rebound* at the Cape Playhouse. Ironically, Peck had recently played opposite Jane Cowl in busboy Batson's revamped *Treat Her Gently,* which had been rechristened *Punch and Julia.* It did a big belly flop. *Rebound,* however, was considered a success for twenty-six-year-old Peck, who played Chatterton's suitor. "There is a young actor named Gregory Peck playing with Miss Chatterton who strikes us as the complete actor," raved the *Boston Record.* "Inside and out he gives an electrifying performance."[893] In late August, Ruth was announced to play Victoria Woodhull, the women's rights advocate who had run for U.S. President in 1872. Unfortunately, *The Incredible Woodhull,* penned by Frederick Schlick, was never produced. Schlick's play was also considered by Frances Farmer and Katharine Hepburn.

⁂

With Barry Thomson in the army, Ruth surrounded herself in safe male territory. Aside from ex-husband Ralph, there were her gay pals, such as Monty Woolley, Cole Porter, Leonard Hanna, a wealthy patron of the arts, and actor Phil Coolidge. Woolley, Porter, and Hanna had been friends since 1909. Coolidge had played the alcoholic church organist in the original production of Thornton Wilder's *Our Town*—a role speculated to represent a closeted gay man who, as one Wilder character put it, "ain't made for small-town life." Ruth would enjoy evenings out with the aforementioned quartet—all creatures of the night—at the intimate, luxurious 1-2-3- Club on East 54th Street, which was said to appeal to those who "loathed the privacy of their own home."[894] Host Roger Stearns, a favorite pianist of Porter, entertained, along with people like astrologer Myra Kingsley. While she was on vacation, Dorothy Kilgallen once asked Stearns to be her guest columnist. Under the heading "Food Foibles of the Famous," Stearns gave the low-down on the appetites of his numerous friends who frequented the club: Woolley, Porter, Hanna, John Geilgud, Alfred Lunt, and John van Druten. Naturally, he included Ruth in the mix, saying, "Ruth Chatterton, a dainty eater, picks up one pea at a time—on her fork, of course."[895]

Barry Thomson's army assignment was primarily as a soldier actor. By June 1943, he was directing a troupe from headquarters at 52 Broadway. He was billed Gordon B. Thomson, Sgt. 1204 SCSU, for a one-night fundraiser called *The Army Play by Play*. The production resulted from a playwriting contest open exclusively to enlisted men. The event raised $100,000 for the soldiers and sailors club. It reopened a month later and closed September 4 after forty-one performances. Thomson also served in the Air Transport Command. His enlistment record (May 1942) indicates that the 5' 11", 163 lbs. Sgt. Thomson was born in 1908 in New York. He had four years of high school and he was divorced.[896] In 1940, Dorothy Kilgallen had predicted that Ruth and Barry would be married by Labor Day. When that didn't happen, it was rumored they eloped to Mexico in April 1941 during the run of *Treat Her Gently*. They did, in fact, have a "honeymoon" in Mexico, but Ruth wasn't referring to Barry as her husband upon their return. Army records put to rest the rumor of Chatterton-Thomson nuptials. Ruth was questioned in November 1942 about the possibility of a rekindled romance with Ralph Forbes. She explained, "You see [Ralph] is very much in love with someone else… and so am I."[897] Ruth kept her private life private and her relationship to Thomson a mystery.

Ruth's exes weren't as fortunate. Their romances were still making headlines. In May 1940, George Brent and Warner's reigning sex goddess, Ann Sheridan, were seen out double-dating with Ralph Forbes and his wife Heather Angel at the Hollywood Tropics. Apparently, the two men got along better. They had recently returned from a month-long voyage to Honolulu together without Ann or Heather.[898] A year later, Heather filed for a divorce, charging that she "became virtually a widow at night."[899] She was rapidly losing weight worrying until the wee hours of the morning. Forbes provided no explanation as to his whereabouts. "Slaps Wife–Finds Himself Divorced" were typical headlines that described the Forbes-Angel breakup. At the time of their split, Ralph received consolation from Ruth while dining tête-à-tête at the Algonquin.[900] Brent and the down-to-earth Sheridan dated steadily. They had offered fans a 56-second screen kiss in Warner's *Honeymoon For Three*. It caused a furor in Kansas, where a women's league fought to limit on-screen osculation.[901] The duo eventually eloped to Palm Beach. Sheridan, touted as the star with "Oomph," failed to quash Brent's reputation for being noncommittal. After nine months, he walked out, telling Ann to "go get a divorce."[902] For an anniversary present in 1943, a Mexico divorce was granted. When asked about the marriage, Sheridan put it brusquely, "We didn't part friends."[903] She kept a donkey that Brent had given her as a memento—to remind her of what she thought of him.

Sheridan's experience had been a repeat of Chatterton's. "George suffers from a shyness that is out of this world," Sheridan revealed. "I used to think he was pretending when he said he didn't like people, but after I married him I discovered that it was really a phobia. Someone at the studio would invite us to dinner, and George would accept with the utmost charm. But by the time we'd gotten home and ready to dress for dinner, George would've talked himself into a state of abject misery. We'd end up staying home."[904] Like Chatterton, Sheridan wasn't being critical. She acknowledged a simple fact: Brent was too steeped in his gloom to do much about it. In 1947, Ruth and Ann finally had an opportunity to chat. Ruth walked into the Stork Club, spotted Sheridan, and feeling that she and Ann were practically related, asked to meet her. Before long Ann and Ruth were sharing their experiences at Warner. Sheridan, who had recently gone through a long, drawn-out battle with the studio, was accompanied by her current beau, publicist Steve Hannagan. Ann offered Chatterton her heartfelt thanks. "In arranging Miss Sheridan's contract with Warner Bros.," joked Hannagan, "I made sure to insert the 'Ruth Chatterton' clause—the clause which protects her against what the studio did to you."[905]

Chatterton's name also popped up in the peculiar marital woes of Juliette Compton, a former Ziegfeld beauty who had supported Ruth in *Anybody's Woman* and *Unfaithful*. Compton married a wealthy Australian businessman, James Bartram, in 1931. During their 1942 divorce trial, Compton mentioned the time she and her husband were dining at Ruth's home. Bartram objected to sitting next to Ruth. "If it is punishment to Mr. Bartram to sit by me," offered Ruth, "I can change the seating." After this embarrassment, Compton attempted to smooth things over by extending a dinner invitation to Ruth and Ralph. Ruth accepted and wore a diamond necklace for the occasion. Bartram took one look at her and grumbled, "Must you wear the entire crystal chandelier around your neck?" Compton's major complaint was Bartram's hobby of dressing himself up as a woman. "He used my wigs and artificial eyelashes," Compton testified. "He made himself up, with false busts, and photographed himself night after night."[906] Bartram admitted that he had dressed as a bar maid in order to seduce "an old school chum."[907] He wanted to "teach him a lesson." Such escapades, Compton insisted, amounted to nothing more than "mental cruelty." Compton ended up teaching her *husband* a lesson. She got her decree.

Ruth's stage appearances were interspersed with commitments to the Women's Division of the National War Fund Drive. In March 1943, she was escorted by Indiana State police from Chicago to Whiting, Illinois, to appear as the "climax" for a women's bond drive. She raised $25,000 in two hours, bringing the region's total to $446,325. Ruth cautioned the women behind the drive: "A success such as this must not mean the cessation of effort. The boys 'over there' know nothing about quitting— we must keep on and on, making each success merely a stepping stone to the next."[908] Ruth also participated in the drama *Untitled* by Norman Corwin—an all-star fundraiser held at the Astor Gallery of the Waldorf-Astoria. The play was a dramatic case history of an average American soldier who dies in battle. Joining her on stage were Myrna Loy, Gertrude Lawrence, Helen Hayes, and Mary Martin.

In June, *Private Lives* wrapped up its successful year-long tour. Ralph Forbes, after a four-year screen absence, was paged by Paramount for the flamboyant costume drama *Frenchman's Creek*. He was assigned the role of Joan Fontaine's husband, a baron who pimps her off to a bewigged Ba-

With Ralph Forbes in *Private Lives* tour (1942-43).

sil Rathbone. During his stay in Los Angeles, Ralph stayed with Tilly Chatterton. By the time the film wrapped in October, Ruth had found another new play for her and Ralph. She poured her pocketbook into *The Lady Comes Home*, a spy comedy. Draped in gowns by Mainbocher (haute couture next door to Tiffany's), she played the glamorous Daisy de Beaudreau, who returns to the United States after twelve years' absence. Her ex-husband, a Washington official, looks askance while she attempts to shake her past and reunite with their son. It was no secret that her connections with officers in the German High Command crowned her as "Queen of Nazified Paris." *The Lady Comes Home* came and went after two weeks. As one wag put it, "It would have been better for actors and audience if this lady hadn't come home."[909] Ruth wasn't really feeling up to par and had to postpone both opening nights in Pittsburgh and

Philadelphia. The box office promptly took a nose dive. Theater managers had to refund $2,000 in advance sales. Forbes quickly signed on with producer George Abbott for *A Highland Fling*, which made it to Broadway for a month's stay.

In early 1944, Ruth took time-out from acting to host radio's *Bondwagon* and attend the season at the Metropolitan Opera. Her friend Grace Moore delivered what critic Olin Downes called a lusty interpretation of *Tosca*. After the performance, Ruth attended Moore's party at the Stork Club's "Blessed Event Room" along with fifty other "intimate" friends. The real excitement for Ruth during her sabbatical from the stage was taking navigation lessons from the second-best navigator in the Air Transport Command (ATC). The ATC was a semi-military organization. It focused on transporting military personnel and cargo overseas. Although Ruth wasn't recruited for military activity, she never turned down an opportunity to hone her skills as an aviator. She missed flying her own plane, which she sold during the war.

Aside from a one week run of *Private Lives* (without Ralph) that fall, the rest of Ruth's acting assignments in 1944 were on radio. Ronald Colman invited her to appear on his program in the charming comedy *Holy Matrimony*. It was her first acting assignment in Hollywood in six years. She also did the Katharine Cornell hit *No Time for Comedy* for radio's *Theatre of Romance*. There were rumors of numerous film roles Chatterton was considering. She was given various scripts to read while visiting her mother in Los Angeles. When asked about a potential film deal, Ruth hesitated. "I am superstitious, and won't want to say a word until its signed, sealed and delivered."[910] Louella Parsons reported that Chatterton was up for an important role in a Warner film titled *Happiness*, which was to star Ida Lupino. A week later, Hedda Hopper announced that Ruth would play Diana Lynn's mother in Paramount's *The Trouble with Women*. A few months later, Sheilah Graham mentioned Ruth was going to play the sister who is killed in Universal's *Strange Affair of Uncle Harry*. RKO joined in the chorus to offer Chatterton a role in *Prodigal Women*. None of these film projects really tempted Ruth. By the spring of 1945, she toyed with the idea of doing a play by Aben Kandel. Kandel, known for cinematic gems like *I Was a Teenage Werewolf* (1957), would provide Joan Crawford her last gasps on screen: *Berserk* (1967) and the forgettable *Trog* (1970). Kandel was determined to have Ruth star in *You Only Twinkle Once*—about a film star beyond her prime. Instead of being a film star, or playing one, Ruth invested her time and energy in helping her friend Kay Francis make her stage comeback after a 15-year absence.

⚜

In the summer of 1945, Ruth asked Kay Francis to take the lead in *Windy Hill*, written by their mutual friend, former silent star Patsy Ruth Miller. Ruth would produce and direct. She had considered the lead role for herself at first. In the fall of 1944, there was talk of having Ruth co-star in *Windy Hill* with the handsome Pacific war hero Captain Bob Hartzell, the former "Flying Tiger" who rescued Major Jimmy Doolittle out of Japanese-held territory in China.[911] Kay was familiar with the play as she had visited Ruth and Patsy several times in New York while they were working on it. Kay's Hollywood career was winding down. She had been co-producing her own films at Monogram Studio and intermittently entertaining the troops in Europe. She was anxious to leave films and return to the east coast. *Windy Hill* was her opportunity.

Miller's story told of a veteran newspaper woman (Francis) who falls into the arms of a returned war correspondent (Roger Pryor). Together they experiment in "free love"—no ties, no promises. Chatterton wanted actor Lee Tracy, famous for his portrayals of newsmen, for the male lead, but he was unavailable. She cast newcomer Judy Holliday to play Kay's dumb-bunny actress friend. When it premiered in Montclair, reviews agreed that the cast and Chatterton's direction were excellent, but *Windy Hill* the play was a "disappointment" that made for a "dull evening." The theater overflowed with patrons, as was the case for subsequent tryouts in New Haven, Philadelphia, Pittsburgh... people came in droves to see Kay Francis, the "movie star." When Holliday left the show early on, she was replaced by Jetti Preminger Ames, who shared with this author numerous stories about the tour.

> The play was rewritten every night, literally. Ruth and Patsy would rewrite until two or three in the morning and hand it to us at ten! Kay and I would wonder, 'Now which version are we playing tonight?' It was never ready to come to New York. Everybody out on the road loved Kay and... every house was sold out. They were on their feet cheering her. They didn't really care how good the play was."[912]

A discouraged Patsy Ruth Miller disappeared, leaving Ruth and Kay to their own devices. The rewrites took a toll on them emotionally. Even Chatterton began missing performances. When John van Druten popped in after a show to offer his advice, Kay blew up. She released her pent-up frustration and broke four bottles of Ballantine Scotch. "Shit on this production!" Kay screamed for all to hear when a prop door failed to open at Pittsburgh's Nixon Theater. Roger Pryor was forced to come out of what had firmly been established as a clothes closet.[913] The audience howled with delight. After three weeks of ironing out kinks, the play reached Baltimore. "Out of touch with reality," said the review from the *Baltimore*

Sun. "Another Horror Opening," jotted Francis into her diary.[914] One sage review advised, "There's one place *Windy Hill* should positively stay away from—Broadway. If Misses Miller, Chatterton and Francis just content themselves with the road, maybe they'll all make a lousy fortune."[915] Kay's diary continued to be peppered with angst. "Leaving for Washington, D.C. Chatterton rehearsing on train and rewriting. Christ!"[916] After D.C., Kay fumed, "Blew up and threw new script away!"[917] In Toledo, "Discussion on new version—will cut my own throat!"[918] In May 1946, the play closed in Chicago, where it played for three months. Kay was all smiles afterward. "What a show," she said. "I swear I had ninety-seven sides... as big as the lead in *Strange Interlude.* We kept revising... but it was fun, good trouping. I really enjoyed it."[919]

When Patsy Ruth Miller got around to writing her autobiography, she didn't mince words about her "friendship" with Ruth while they worked on *Windy Hill.*

> When I was living with Ruth Chatterton, who was directing *Windy Hill...* I nearly lost my mind. Ruth was a brilliant actress, but she was one of those people who knew everything, and would brook no contradiction. It was during the War; hotels were so crowded... so I stayed with Ruth and went slowly mad. To give you an example, she made a pronouncement about our 94 senators being hopelessly archaic. At that time, there were 48 states, therefore 96 senators. When I pointed this out to her, she replied firmly, "No, dear, there are 94 senators. I happen to know."[920]

Miller complained about Ruth to Gloria Swanson, who lived on 5th Avenue. Swanson, who was busy with her own stage career, invited

Miller to stay with her. It wasn't long, Miller claimed, before she was listening to Gloria purr into the phone during chats with Joseph Kennedy. Despite their contretemps, Miller emphasized that Chatterton turned out to be "a damned good director."[921] Those of the opinion that Ruth thought she knew everything included producers Harold J. Kennedy and Homer Curran. As Curran put it: "She knows so much, she really does, that it's a great pity she thinks she knows just a little bit more than she does know."[922] Curiously, in the fall of 1944, when Ruth and Patsy were roomies, the U.S. Senate was, in fact, briefly whittled down from 96 to 94 (November 17-20). If we can allow that the discussion took place then—Ruth can rest her case

After the war, Barry Thomson was back in the picture, both as a husband (so they said) and co-star on Broadway. And Ruth felt younger than ever. When she landed at LaGuardia Airport from Toronto in July of '45, she listed her birth date as December 24, 1905. Chatterton and Barry were reunited on stage at Carnegie Hall for *The Chosen Uninvited*, a Jewish-themed presentation that was sponsored by The American League for a Free Palestine. It set into motion Ruth's work on behalf of the organization and its goals. It also triggered her desire to become a writer.

Endnotes

856   Grace Moore, *You're Only Human Once*, Doubleday, c. 1944, pg 176.
857   "Chatterton Shaw Star," *Los Angeles Times*, February 8, 1941.
858   Alice Pardoe West, "Ruth Chatterton to Appear in Shaw Play 'Pygmalion,'" *Ogden Standard Examiner*, Marcy 16, 1941.
859   "Ruth Chatterton Eyes Life on Eastern Farm," *Milwaukee Sentinel*, January 13, 1941.
860   Louise Mace, "Berkshire Playhouse Opens, Starring Ruth Chatterton," *Springfield Republican*, July 1, 1941.
861   Review of *Private Lives*, *Springfield Republican*, August 13, 1940.
862   Keith Wilson, "Chatterton's Show Pleases," *Omaha World Herald*, January 25, 1941.
863   Keith Wilson, "Chatterton's Show Pleases," *Omaha World Herald*, January 25, 1941.
864   Barbara Eden, *Out of the Bottle*, Random House, c. 2011, pgs 154.
865   Ashton Stevens review of *Pygmalion*, *Herald-American* (c. December 1941).

866   Edwin Schallert, "Chatterton Triumphs In Play," *Los Angeles Times*, February 11, 1941.

867   Louella Parsons column, *San Antonio Light*, February 13, 1941.

868   Alice Pardoe West column, *Ogden Standard Examiner*, June 23, 1940.

869   Arthur T. Shea, "See Tallulah in Warner's 'Skeffington'—Bette Davis Suggests Chatterton," *Omaha World Herald*, January 20, 1941.

870   R.T., "Ruth Chatterton Scores Hit Here," *San Diego Union*, February 18, 1941.

871   Alice Pardoe West, "Actress Wins Big Applause," *Ogden Standard Examiner*, March 26, 1941.

872   Harvey Breit, "Talk With Miss Chatterton," *New York Times*, August 27, 1950.

873   Bill Wilson, "Chatterton's New Vehicle in Premier," *Dallas Morning News*, March 31, 1941.

874   Bill Wilson, review of *Treat Her Gently*, *Amarillo News-Globe*, March 30, 1941.

875   Alexander Williams, review of *Sorrow for Angels*, *Boston Herald*, August 27, 1941.

876   "Famous Actress' Rites Are Today," *Plain Dealer*, July 4, 1941.

877   Dorothy Kilgallen column, *Trenton Evening Times*, July 10, 1941.

878   "Air Waves," *The Calgary Herald*, October 22, 1941.

879   Regine Kurlander, "This—and Glamour, Too," *Plain Dealer*, November 12, 1942 (one source gives the date July 18, 1941, for Chatterton being designated as the first female in the Royal Canadian Air Force).

880   Review of *Caprice*, *Daily Boston Globe*, July 29, 1941.

881   Sheilah Graham, "Studio Gossip," *Plain Dealer*, August 19, 1945.

882   Louella Parsons column, *Lowell Sun*, April 27, 1945.

883   James Robert Parish, *Hollywood Players: The Forties*, Arlington House, c. 1976, pg 212.

884   Bob Francis, review of *Caprice*, *Billboard*, September 4, 1943.

885   Leonard Lyons, "The Lyons Den," *New York Post*, May 15, 1942.

886   "Ruth Chatterton has Tax Troubles," *San Antonio Light*, March 24, 1943.

887   "Springfield Stock Try Flops; Show Weak," *Billboard*, April 25, 1942.

888   Louise Mace, "Ruth Chatterton Gives Performance at Temple," *Springfield Republican*, April 11, 1942.

889   E.L.H., review of *Private Lives*, *Boston Herald*, June 9, 1942.

890   Harold V. Cohen, "Chatterton In Comedy By Coward," *Pittsburgh Post-Gazette*, June 1, 1943.

891   Dorothy Kilgallen, "Ohio Summer Theater Operator Appears to Have Right Approach," *Leader-Herald*, July 23, 1964 (Interview with John Kenley of Kenley Players).

892   Frank Rich, "Theatre: 'Private Lives,' Burton and Miss Taylor," *New York Times*, May 9, 1983.

893   Elliot Norton, review of *Rebound*, *Boston Record*, c. July 1942.

894   William McBrien, *Cole Porter*, Random House, c. 2000, pg 251.

895   Roger Stearns, "Voice of Broadway," *Schenectady Gazette*, May 7, 1947.

896   Gordon B. Thomson, U.S. World War II Army Enlistment Records, 1938-1946.

897   Regine Kurlander, "This—and Glamour, Too," *Plain Dealer*, November 12, 1942.

898   Harry Lang, "The Talkie Town Tattler," *Motion Picture*, June 1940 (Brent and Forbes were passengers on the S.S. *Lurline* voyage #156, departing Los Angeles for Honolulu February 16, 1940; they arrived back in Los Angeles March 15, 1940 on S.S. *Lurline* voyage #157).

899   "Divorce Suit Filed by Heather Angel," *Omaha World Herald*, July 3, 1941.

900   Dorothy Kilgallen, "The Voice of Broadway," *Trenton Evening Times*, May 8, 1941.

901   Charles Sampas, "New York – Hollywood," *Lowell Sun*, September 7, 1940.

902   Rosalind Leigh, 'Oomph' Can't Hold Husbands," *Sunday Times* (Perth), June 6, 1943.

903   Ann Sheridan, "We Didn't Part Friends," *Hollywood*, February 1943.

904   Liza, "Why the Sheridan-Brent Marriage Failed," *Screenland*, January 1943.

905   Leonard Lyons, "The Lyons Den," *Advocate*, November 18, 1947.

906   "Former Stage Beauty names Secretary as 'Other Woman,'" *Racine Journal-Times*, March 5, 1942.

907   Fred Dickenson, "Won the Fun Crown—Lost a Wife," *Omaha World-Herald Magazine*, May 3, 1942.

908   "Women Praised for $446,325 War Bond Total," *Hammond Times*, March 6, 1943.

909   Andrew Davis, *America's Longest Run: A History of the Walnut Street Theatre*, Penn State Press, c. 2010, pg 240.

910   Louella Parsons column, *Lowell Sun*, May 20, 1944.

911   Harrison Carroll column, *Evening Independent*, November 30, 1944.

912   Conversations with Jetti Preminger Ames, February 18, 2003, & December 23, 2003.

913   George Eells, *Ginger, Loretta and Irene Who?* Simon & Schuster, c. 1976, pg 234.

914   Kay Francis Diary, October 8, 1945, Wesleyan Cinema Archives.

915   Harold V. Cohen, "Kay Francis At Nixon In *Windy Hill*," *Pittsburgh Post-Gazette*, October 16, 1945.

916   Kay Francis Diary, January 27, 1946, Wesleyan Cinema Archives.

917   Kay Francis Diary, February 7, 1946, Wesleyan Cinema Archives.

918   Kay Francis Diary, November 23, 1945, Wesleyan Cinema Archives.

919   "Kay Francis Returns to Broadway," *New York World Telegram*, August 28, 1946.

920   Patsy Ruth Miller, *My Hollywood, When Both of Us Were Young,* O'Raghailligh Ltd., c. 1988, pg 116.

921   Patsy Ruth Miller, *My Hollywood, When Both of Us Were Young,* O'Raghailligh Ltd., c. 1988, pg 116.

922   Harold J. Kennedy, *No Pickle, No Performance,* Doubleday & Co., c. 1977, pg 56.

As Anne Hathaway in *Second Best Bed* (1946).
Barry Thomson as William Shakespeare.

15
I Can't Help It ...

"I'm a born crusader who wants to fight social injustices." [923]
- Ruth Chatterton

Ruth's home in Beverly Hills, filled with furniture, was tied up by a writ of attachment in 1945. Shreve & Co., a New York jeweler, had filed suit for nonpayment of diamond- ruby clips and a ring to the tune of $2,243.00. [924] Profits from *Windy Hill* resolved the problem and also afforded Ruth another try at Broadway. Finances would continue to plague her, but Chatterton had a miraculous charm that kept her afloat. It seemed to be the central theme of her final years. By 1948, she refocused and redefined her *raison d'etre...* she was compelled to write. Chatterton immersed herself in her "calling" and come hell or high water, she would be heard. In the aftermath of World War II, millions of people were in transition. New beginnings and visions of what was possible captured the imagination. Ruth participated wholeheartedly and wanted to be part of the change that could make a difference in the real world. She allowed the moment to carry her into new territory. One of her top priorities was the creation of the Free State of Israel.

Theatre continued to provide Ruth the steady income which allowed her to devote time and energy for the Palestine movement. Before *Windy Hill* closed in Chicago, she co-produced a return to Broadway in playwright N. Richard Nash's *Second Best Bed*. Barry Thomson and Ralph Forbes co-starred. After tryouts in Schenectady, Detroit, Toronto, and Boston, the play premiered at the Ethel Barrymore Theatre on June 3, 1946. Critics weren't impressed with Nash's one track mind. The tale of William Shakespeare (Thomson) returning from London to find wife Anne Hathaway (Chatterton) smitten with the local bailiff (Forbes) who, in turn, falls for the town trollop "missed the boat," according to *Billboard*. "What might have developed into a lusty Elizabethan farce," said the review, "turns up as three acts of... queasy smut."[925] When out on the road with the play, Ruth had countered, "It's not in the least suggestive, but out-and-out direct to the point."[926] It was mentioned that while Ruth looked "fetching" on stage, she and Thomson were inclined "to be cute." Columnist Jack O'Brian thought *Second Best Bed* "one of the dreariest comedies of any season [with] some of the decade's most sleep-inducing dialogue."[927] *The New York Times* found it "a silly and tedious affair."[928] Drama editor Robert Garland placed the play among the "worst" of 1946 and pegged Thomson as rendering one of the "worst performances."[929] The production may nod to the historical fact that Shakespeare willed Anne Hathaway his second-best bed, but the critical consensus declared *Second Best Bed* second-rate theatre.

Ruth spent the rest of the summer touring in *Caprice*. She also pulled out the old Clyde Fitch social satire *The Truth*. A prolific as well as controversial author, Fitch's passionate 1889 affair with Oscar Wilde is well-documented in love letters. "Make me what you will," he had begged Wilde, "but keep me yours forever."[930] Oscar kept his distance. For a time, Fitch rejoiced in being the wounded lover. By 1906, he had read Ibsen. He no longer held a romantic worldview. In *The Truth*, he delved into the polished facades of social propriety. Chatterton's revival of Fitch's character Becky Warder, a consummate liar who only tells the truth by accident, played for two weeks at the Cape Playhouse. Becky believes that lying protects her from unpleasantness. As public figures, this was territory with which both Fitch and Chatterton were familiar, especially in regard to their personal relationships. *The Truth* had set Spencer Tracy free in 1921. He dropped plans to become a plastic surgeon after playing in Fitch's play at college. What would *The Truth* do for Ruth? In the summer of 1946, publicity for *Second Best Bed* emphasized that Ruth and Barry were husband and wife in real life.[931] Was it a fact or merely a convenient truth that Ruth and Barry decided to adhere to?

Gordon John Barry Thomson

"There was some conjecture about Barry and Ruth even being married," said Ruth's cousin, Brenda Holman, in 2012. "We knew he was younger than she, but my mother felt they were a devoted couple."[932] Brenda's mother, Olive Wehbring, speculated that no marriage ever took place. In a 1958 interview, Ruth mentioned that she and Barry had celebrated their 17th wedding anniversary.[933] If true, their wedding would have taken

Barry Thomson (c. 1942).

place in June of 1941. The fact remains that Thomson's enlistment records the following year designate him as a divorced man with no dependents. Whatever the case, Ruth and Barry's commitment to each other was rooted in a devotion to the theatrical arts and, more importantly, to each other.

Gordon John Barry Thomson was born September 30, 1908, in New York. Like Ruth, he was an only child raised in a well-to-do household. His father was a prominent surgeon in Melbourne, Australia, where young Barry, who went by "Jack," spent his childhood. In his late teens, Barry spent two years in Europe. He studied voice and music in Milan, Italy, as well as the Royal Academy of Music in London. Along with fellow student Charles Laughton, Barry pursued acting at the Royal Academy of Dramatic Art and he toured England playing juvenile roles. At eighteen, Barry sailed on the *S.S. Lancastria* from England to New York and after joining Actors Equity, remained there for six months. In 1928, he returned to Melbourne, assumed the stage name John Barry, and toured in a company run by actress Muriel Starr.[934] In 1929, Barry co-starred in the Australian silent film *Tiger Island*. His film debut was doomed to early oblivion. "If it was five times better acted and five times better photographed," said one critic, "it would still be entirely negligible."[935]

Barry sailed to San Francisco in June 1930. Here, he played in the Pulitzer Prize-winning play *They Knew What They Wanted* with veteran trouper Leo Carrillo. While on the West Coast, Barry essayed dramatic roles with Helen Gahagan and Anna Q. Nilsson. Heading to Canada in 1934, Barry played thirty weeks in stock. In New York, the tall, black-haired, brown-eyed, mustachioed thespian made an impression during his audition for the Theater Guild, which was the leading purveyor of non-commercial theater in the country. Through the Guild and its connection to the legendary team of Alfred Lunt and Lynn Fontanne, Barry firmly established his acting career. He performed in their 1935 revival, *The Taming of the Shrew* (Hortensio). The following year, Thomson joined the Lunts for Robert Sherwood's anti-war comedy, *Idiot's Delight*. After the San Francisco premier of *Amphitryon 38*, in which Thomson played the title role, *Variety* stated that he handled "the title assignment in an acceptable, if not distinguished manner."[936] Five months later, when the Lunts reached Broadway, the drama critic for *The Socialist Call* found Thomson "incomparable" and *Amphitryon 38* a welcome relief from the "sound and fury of class struggle."[937] Sydney Greenstreet was also featured in these Lunt-Fontanne productions—all substantial hits. *Idiot's Delight* ran for 300 performances.

During a summer break from *Idiot's Delight* in 1936, Barry costarred with Blanche Yurka in Aristophanes' *Lysistrata*, the classic war tale of women who withhold sex until their men negotiate peace. Offstage, a petite young actress named Marion Shockley gave in to co-star Thomson's "negotiations." They tied the marital knot. Shockley, along with Ginger Rogers and Gloria Stuart, had been selected as filmland's WAMPAS Baby stars in 1932. Shockley appeared in a number of shorts as well as a Tim McCoy serial before concentrating on the stage and radio. The Thomson-Shockley marriage was short-lived. By December 1937, Walter Winchell was predicting the couple would "tell it to a judge."[938] They did. In 1939, Marion married CBS executive George Zachary. A third marriage followed with radio-TV's Bud Collyer.

In 1938, when Thomson traveled with the Lunts to London, he had an opportunity to meet Ruth. She saw him in *Amphitryon 38* and persuaded him to co-star with her after they returned to the United States.[939] "I stole him from the Lunts," Ruth would jest.[940] When they reconnected the following year, Barry was fresh from touring with the great Laurette Taylor in Shaw's *Candida*. "You have an opportunity to discover how liquid human speech can be," mused critic Brooks Atkinson—referring to Taylor's propensity to imbibe before each performance.[941] Atkinson thought Thomson "good enough," but lacking the pompousness required for the clergyman husband.

Ruth and Barry obviously felt a strong connection, but were skeptical about matrimony. By 1946, after eight years and numerous plays together, at least one critic declared the Chatterton-Thomson combination "a delightful stage team."[942] The duo moved in together at the luxurious Ritz Tower, which housed neighbors like Greta Garbo. In January 1946, Ruth and Barry hosted a wedding ceremony in their Ritz apartment, 14E, not for themselves, but for Ralph Forbes and his new bride, actress Dora Sayers. It wasn't long before Ruth began writing postscripts on Barry's letters to his mother in Australia. She made no mention, however, that she had become her daughter-in-law.[943] But by 1948, their "marriage" was old news and Ruth was referring to Barry's mother as "Mummy Melbourne" during their long-distant phone chats.[944]

After "Mr. and Mrs. Thomson" co-starred in *Second Best Bed*, it would be a few years before they worked together on stage again. Thomson focused on radio and since 1945 had taken the lead role of the hugely popular series *Dick Tracy*. In the fall of 1946, Ruth involved herself more deeply with those committed to creating the state of Israel.

⚜

A Flag Is Born was Broadway's plea for a Hebrew Homeland. At the end of WWII, there were hundreds of thousands of displaced Jewish Holocaust survivors. The producers of the play were straightforward about their intent. "*A Flag is Born* is not ordinary theatre," said the publicity. "It was not written to amuse or beguile. *A Flag is Born* was written to make

Ruth visits director Irving Pichel on the set of Paramount's *A Medal for Benny*
(1945). A press release stated that she had "returned to Hollywood with the
intention of resuming her screen career" (courtesy of James Stettler).

money—to make money to provide ships to get Hebrews to Palestine."[945]
The political drama was written by Academy Award-winning scenarist
Ben Hecht. In the 1920s, Hecht wrote human interest stories for the *Chicago Daily News*. He gathered material from wandering through ethnic
and class-divided neighborhoods. Hecht looked for real life under the
edge of everyday headlines. *A Flag is Born* involved concentration camp
survivors who were attempting to travel to Israel. Luther Adler directed a
revolving cast which included Paul Muni, Marlon Brando, Sidney Lumet,
Rita Gam, and author/radio commentator Quentin Reynolds. When
the play moved from Broadway's Alvin Theatre, Reynolds bowed out.
Chatterton took over his role as "The Speaker" when it began its run at

The Music Box, October 22, 1946. Most critics praised *A Flag is Born* as powerful propaganda. It had bite and the ability to stir emotion, especially when twenty-two-year-old Brando addressed the audience directly, shouting, "You let six million people die!" He brought down the house every night. The British press, however, had a different view. *The London Evening Standard* called it "the most anti-British play ever staged in the United States."[946]

Profits from *A Flag is Born* came close to $1,000,000 for the American League for a Free Palestine (ALFP).[947] A portion of that money helped to purchase a ship, renamed the *S.S. Ben Hecht.* In early 1947, the vessel carried 600 Holocaust survivors to Palestine. This was done in defiance of British immigration restrictions. The voyage was intercepted by the British shortly before landing. Refugees were sent to detention camps on Cyprus. This crisis made international headlines. The end result of *A Flag Is Born* was its ability to create awareness in the American public and prove instrumental in bringing about London's decision to withdraw from the Holy Land.

Ruth's commitment to resolve the plight of the Jewish people actually began before the close of WWII. In December 1944, she was paged by the Emergency Committee to Save the Jewish People of Europe. She represented the theatrical community at a dinner held at the Hotel Commodore.[948] This was followed by a benefit performance of the play *The Chosen Uninvited,* in which Barry Thomson also was cast. In early 1946, Ruth joined a radio panel discussion, "Palestine or Mass Suicide," in which she and former Iowa Senator Guy Gillette detailed the grave political situation in Palestine. Gillette charged that Great Britain had violated the "letter and spirit" of her mandate power.[949] In June 1947, Ruth, along with Ben Hecht and Will Rogers, Jr., hosted a dinner at Boston's Hotel Somerset in honor of Senator Gillette, who was President of the ALFP.

Ruth also traveled to Boston on behalf of the ALFP to give a speech titled "Americans for Freedom." The event, held at Boston's Jordan Hall, included a stirring presentation by Yale University's Fowler Harper titled, "It's '1776' in Palestine." Harper was a significant sounding board for Chatterton while she wrote her second novel, *The Betrayers.*

The Palestine issue was getting even "hotter" in the fall of 1947. Chatterton, Ben Hecht, author Louis Bromfield, Will Rogers, Jr., and William Ziff, who had written *The Rape of Palestine* criticizing British policy, were now designated as executive board members of the ALFP. The league made the controversial charge that the British were supporting the brigands of Arabs who were invading the Holy Land. Many felt that Britain had usurped authority granted to them by the League of Nations and denying fundamental rights to the Hebrew People. Prior to these events, Ben Hecht had penned a second pageant for ALFP titled *The Terrorist.* It was anti-British propaganda and played for two nights at Carnegie Hall. *The Terrorist* encouraged support for the Irgun Zvai Leumi, one of three rival Jewish underground militias. Chatterton was a featured artist in this controversial tribute based on the last hours of the Hebrew patriot Dov Gruner.

❧❧❧

Chatterton was a public figure—recognizable and willing to lend her name to causes she believed in. She appreciated the recognition that Hollywood had given her and recognized that it afforded her opportunities she may not have had otherwise. As a pilot, she had talked about forced landings in remote places; people would run up to her plane and say, "That's Ruth Chatterton!" "*That's* the movies," Ruth would chuckle to herself. Aside from her involvement with the ALFP, she recognized her need to create new challenges on stage. Ruth admitted that, as an actress, she didn't thrive on audience adoration. She was on stage to make characters and ideas "come alive." "The only fun for me is creating a part," said Ruth. "I'm a pretty quick study and after a month or two I've gone as far as I can go. I know my limitations. I want to dine late, take things easy, and it becomes a chore going on night after night in the same play. I'm not an exhibitionist and I don't enjoy just getting up in front of an audience and showing off."[950] In 1947, Ruth tackled the reputable Lillian Hellman play *The Little Foxes* and made it her own. Critics and co-stars marveled at the indelible mark Ruth cast upon Regina Giddens, a manipulative woman whose lust for money and power achieves her great wealth and unfathomable loneliness.

The Little Foxes

When Ruth's tour of *The Little Foxes* premiered at the Ogunquit Playhouse, it broke all attendance records in the theater's fourteen-year history.[951] She left a lasting impression on her co-stars. Thirty years later, Marian Selder, who played the daughter role, thought Ruth's Regina Giddens "one of the finest performances I had seen."[952] This melodrama of bitterness and greed, which opened on Broadway in 1939, has long been considered Lillian Hellman at her best. The play had starred Tallulah Bankhead, who keyed her powerful and unique personality to create a performance which won the New York Drama Critics Circle Award. Bankhead played the role as if she were fighting for survival. In 1941, director William Wyler asked Bette Davis, cast as Regina for the Warner film, to see Bankhead in the play. Afterward, Davis felt compelled to put her own spin on Regina as a cold, conniving, and vicious woman, even though she felt Bankhead "had played it the only way it could be played." "Miss Hellman's Regina was written with such definition that it could only be played one way," Davis wrote in her 1962 autobiography.[953] Ruth disagreed, saying, "There are so many ways to play Regina Giddens, none necessarily better than another, but different. I play her not as a virago but as an astute, greedy woman who would move Heaven and earth to get what she wanted."[954]

The character of Regina Giddens had its Southern roots in Lillian Hellman's own family—specifically, her maternal grandmother. As the story unravels, Regina's independently wealthy brothers, heirs to the family fortune, approach her sickly husband, Horace, for funds to invest in a new cotton mill. His refusal propels the avaricious siblings to indulge in theft and blackmail in order to achieve their ends. Regina goes so far as to refuse husband Horace his medicine during a fatal heart attack. In the process of getting what she wants, Regina loses the love and respect of her seventeen-year-old daughter. Chatterton felt that Regina had some remnant of appeal and connection to her own flesh and blood. "Regina must have been a woman who could be charming when she wanted," Ruth pointed out. "After all, her husband, even after 20 years of difficulties, is still in love with her. I play the scenes between Regina and her daughter rather softly except in the second act when things have crashed all about her and Regina goes completely to pieces."[955] During a Detroit run of *The Little Foxes* in 1948, future First Lady Nancy Davis Reagan played the daughter. *Variety* thought the twenty-seven-year-old Davis a bit mature for the role, but said she came close to "top honors" as an actress.[956] When biographer Bob Colacello questioned Nancy Reagan (c. 2000) about her two-week run playing Chatterton's daughter, Reagan didn't recall being in the play at all. "But her scrapbook contains seven clippings about it," wrote Colacello, "as well as a sheaf of telegrams."[957] *The Little Foxes* marked the end of Nancy's stage career.

The Little Foxes provided one of three roles that Chatterton thoroughly enjoyed. *Mary Rose* and *Pygmalion* were the others. From 1947-1958, she would revive Regina Giddens on an almost annual basis. Audiences were drawn by Chatterton's personal magnetism as much as they recoiled from the Regina she created. "Ruth Chatterton is giving a distinctive, skilled and blood-chilling performance of rapacious Regina Giddens," raved critic Cyrus Durgin following a Boston Summer Theatre performance. "She has conceived Regina logically as a woman whose passion has been channeled into greed for pleasure, comfort and money. She is no monster, but her nature encompasses malevolence as well as affection for her daughter—so long as the child's path does not cross hers. That scene when her despised husband, Horace, dies for lack of the medicine that Regina refuses to fetch, comes off with blood-curdling precision."[958] Ruth never saw Tallulah Bankhead in the play and decided it was a good thing. "You pick up mannerisms from the person you are watching," she said. "But I love the part of Regina. She's a tough one."[959]

Bankhead, apparently, had displeased Ruth upon their first meeting in 1931. Cameras were grinding away at Paramount's Long Island studio when Chatterton showed up during one of Bankhead's scenes for *Tarnished Lady*. "Stop!" Tallulah shrieked in her familiar drawn-out drawl. Cameras came to a halt. After a few obligatory pleasantries between the two stars, Bankhead asked, in her "sweetest voice," "Would you mind leaving the set while I do this scene?" With a quick smile, Ruth replied, "Not at all. I'll be going." Bankhead called out after her, "We're living in the same hotel." Ruth hollered back, "See you in the lobby sometime."[960]

In the summer of 1952, Christopher Plummer co-starred with Ruth and Barry in *The Little Foxes* on the island of Bermuda. Plummer was part of the Bermuda Repertory Theatre that season and was cast as Regina's older brother, Ben. In 2009, Plummer recalled that Chatterton, "brought things out of us we didn't know we had." "There was an aura of seductive world-weariness about her," said Plummer, "that made her Regina... so deadly frightening and so very much her own. Lillian Hellman told me years later that of all the Reginas, Ruth's was by far the best. Of course, it was universally known that its creator, Tallulah Bankhead, and Lillian were mortal enemies. Nevertheless, Ruth was superb."[961] Plummer described in detail Chatterton's take on one particular scene.

> There is a moment just before Regina decides to kill Horace when she is alone on stage. I shall never forget the frightful effect Ruth produced to make that moment stay in the mind forever. Like a panther she prowled about the stage. Arriving at her decision, she came to a dead stop. Her absolute stillness and repose when she knew the dreadful moment had come were terrifying and beautiful both at once. This vampire became, before our eyes, silkily feminine, soft, almost innocent. Then with two sharp little clicks of her fingers that rang through the theater like gunshots, she softly whistled a little tune between her teeth, silently turned on her heels, and slithered up the stairs toward her kill.[962]

Barry Thomson played husband Horace and Plummer was quick to point out Barry's "kind, soft nature." The domination of Regina over Horace, Plummer felt, was "precariously close" to the real-life Chatterton-Thomson relationship. They both lavished Plummer with "unbelievable kindness and attention." Plummer felt *The Little Foxes'* week run at the Bermudiana Theatre surpassed anything the repertory group had done. "It was all due to Ruth," he praised, lump in throat. "She had turned us into a proper company of players."[963]

While Ruth and Barry played the New England summer circuit, they were drawn to make the area their home. "You know, I've fallen in love with Cohasset," Ruth told a Boston reporter. "I think it's one of the prettiest towns anywhere in New England. For that matter, I think New England is about the most beautiful country I know, and I've lived nearly everywhere in the world. My husband and I drive around and he just simply stares in silent pleasure at the countryside."[964] During a Boston run of *The Little Foxes*, the duo commuted from Cohasset. They stayed in the same tower room with seven windows where Thornton Wilder finished writing his bestseller, *The Ides of March*. "I hope I can finish my own novel there," said Ruth, "because I think occupying that same room is a good omen." *Homeward Borne* would confirm her hunch. Ruth and Barry's dream of relocating gained momentum after they were booted out of their Ritz Tower apartment.

In March 1949, the Ritz Tower sought an injunction to stop Ruth from cooking in her 14th-floor kitchenette. They charged in a State Supreme Court that "decidedly unpleasant" odors were permeating the luxury hotel and that she was making the Ritz Tower "smell like a hamburger stand."[965] Hotel management, after deodorizing the halls, stated that kitchenettes were meant only for making ice and serving hors d'oevres. Ruth was accused of the heinous crime of cooking with garlic, onions, heady cheese, and octopi. Her attorney, Hyman L. Goldstein, insisted, "She never cooked an octopus."[966] In fact, it was nothing more than *escargot bourgoinnaise*. Columnist Bob Considine mused, "If La Chatterton loses this one many thousands of New Yorkers in search of a quiet meal at home will have to take it intravenously."[967] On March 20, Ruth promised she would stay out of her kitchenette and take her "cooking smells" elsewhere. Before she and Barry began a search for new living quarters in the East Seventies, Ruth toured in *Lovers and Friends* by English playwright Dodie Smith of *101 Dalmatians* fame.

Katharine Cornell, taking a break from Chekov and Shaw, had introduced the lightweight *Lovers and Friends* on Broadway in 1943. The crux of Smith's play involves a husband who drops the bombshell that he's having an affair. It invariably provided Cornell the opportunity to "shine faultlessly," according to *Billboard's* review.[968] After Eleanor Roosevelt saw the play, she mentioned in her syndicated news column that she liked it because it "was full of subtle meaning" and "real people." "The play shows that it is not the people who happen to attract each other temporarily who really matter," she observed.[969] The husband invariably finds out that the "other woman" who has fed his ego is a pathological liar. Ruth stated that she had handpicked the cast and was determined to encourage more interest in live theater. Her determination and cheek made a lasting impression on the cast at Chapel Playhouse in Guilford, Connecticut. In her book *Broadway in a Barn*, producer Charlotte Harmon shared vivid recollections of Ruth's visit.

> Miss Chatterton didn't arrive until... the day before the opening. Apparently she wasn't happy with what the director had done with the play and when he refused to take her directions she told him to sit quietly in the back; she would do the directing from then on. The director, so meek and mild up to this point, now blew his stack. Miss Chatterton then ordered him to leave the building. By this time the whole company had the jitters. Miss Chatterton continued to raise hell... although we realized she knew what she was talking about.[970]

It was quietly suggested to Ruth that, as director, she should have been there to rehearse all week. Ruth haughtily informed them that she had been by the sea visiting her dear friend Kit Cornell. Things simmered down temporarily. Charlotte and her husband, Lewis, who had been Ruth's press agent for the *Pygmalion* tour, were then interrupted by a phone call during dinner. The stage manager was frantic. "Come right away," he begged hysterically. "Miss Chatterton says she won't play tonight unless the set is repainted and the lights changed. Also, she's kind of sore because of what Tony said." "What did Tony say?" asked Charlotte. "He told her she was an old bitch," came the reply. Tony was the electrician. Charlotte and Lewis found him, arms akimbo, stomping around growling he'd make no changes. "Because she's an old bag, she wants all pinks," he fumed, "but believe me no color lights will make *her* look any younger."[971] Lewis had a special fondness for Ruth and tried to mediate. He told her that the electrician and designer had "a lot of right on their side." "With an '*et tu, Brute*' look on her face," said Charlotte, "Ruth announced, 'If that's the way you feel, I won't play tonight.'"[972] After her ultimatum, Lewis appealed once more to the crew and got them to yield a little. "Chatterton was sweet and charming to everyone backstage for the remainder of the engagement," recalled Charlotte. "Even the electrician admitted she was terrific and said the next time she could have any lights she wanted."[973]

Poor Ruth also had to contend with management of the Sheldon House, a conservative, upscale family hotel. They refused to allow her into their formal dining room to partake of their famous French cuisine. She was dressed in slacks. Ruth was indignant. She told them that except for stage clothes, she owned no dresses. They would not yield. Like a naughty child, Ruth was served meals in her room. Charlotte Harmon admitted that the real headaches among the stars were: John Barrymore, Jr., Shelley Winters, Constance Bennett and Ilka Chase (tying for third), and the husband of Jean Parker, a partially blind insurance broker who insisted that his actress wife's costumes allow her bosoms to "stand up straight and firm like two soldiers."[974]   In August 1952, Charlotte and Lewis drove to Hartford to see Ruth, who was playing in *Old Acquaintance*. Afterward, Ruth dropped by Chapel Playhouse to observe rehearsals for the first play Charlotte had written, *That Foolish Age*. Charlotte recalled: "Ruth said that my theme, a woman's fear of growing older and less attractive to men, was *so* United States, because it was only here that the worship of the very young female prevailed. On the continent, she said, women were considered more attractive as they grew older and more experienced."[975]   The fine line between Ruth and Fran Dodsworth had remained intact.

During her summer tour in *Lovers and Friends*, Chatterton was top choice for the lead in a film adaptation of Tennessee Williams' *The Glass Menagerie*. Warner Brothers was "dickering" with her for the role that had revived Laurette Taylor's stage career.[976]   "The dark horse and the actress who is a mile out in front for the coveted role of the mother... is Ruth Chatterton," claimed Louella Parsons, who added that producer Charles Feldman had gone to New York to talk to Ruth. "He has already made a screen test," added Parsons, "which I am told is the best yet."[977]   In the fall, Dorothy Manners said that Ruth never made a test. "But another famous star," noted Manners, "leave her unnamed out of sheer kindness, was dreadful."[978]   Years later, the film's director, Irving Rapper, confirmed, "I did a test with Miriam Hopkins, who was terrible."[979]   In late September 1949, it was announced that the role would go to Gertrude Lawrence. "She beat out Tallulah Bankhead and Ruth Chatterton," reported Erskine Johnson in his "Hollywood Roundup." Rapper considered Lawrence a compromise. Bankhead actually had the role in her pocket. After making an impressive screen test, she showed up drunk the next day to feed lines, off-camera, to a supporting player. According to reports, she "reeled onto the set cursing and swaggering."[980]   As a result, Jack Warner refused to hire her.[981]

The Glass Menagerie was the last time that Chatterton was a viable contender for an important film role. Although she may have toyed with the idea, Ruth had no desire to return to the grind of film-making, especially in a mother role. "It's dreadful, uninspiring, hard work," she stated in 1951. "Life's too short. You have to get up so early and go to the studio to have your hair washed every morning so it will match the way it looked the day before. You work and they say, 'Cut' and put in into a can."[982] Ruth's attitude was well-known in Hollywood. "They don't quite approve of me out there, you know," she told columnist Phyllis Battelle, who noted Ruth's "couldn't-care-less grin."[983]

⁂

On May 14, 1948, the British Mandate for Palestine was terminated. The State of Israel was established the following day. In July, Ruth joined conductor Leonard Bernstein, who was headlining a pro-Irgun concert at the Waldorf Astoria. This was after Henry Fonda and baritone Robert Merrill had buckled under pressure and backed out of the controversial fundraiser. Unruffled by picketers, Ruth and Luther Adler gave speeches. Mainstream Jewish organizations considered the Irgun to be terrorists by definition and action. One promoter for the Irgun stated in 1960 that Bernstein "acted from the heart, not the head," a remark that no doubt mirrored Chatterton's own involvement.[984] The ideal of a peaceful Jewish homeland would remain controversial and violence continued to fuel the hope for something better.

In the summer of '48, Ruth also let it be known she was adding "author" to her résumé. "I have felt awfully deeply about the Jewish situation," she remarked. "The fate of children going from one place to another—I can't think of anything more tragic or terrible."[985] Ruth did more than talk and write a militant and humanitarian line. "Through Marshall Field," she said, "who's chairman of an organization for placing displaced children, I learned of a reception center in the Bronx for refugee youngsters up to the age of 18." Following the release of *Homeward Borne*, Ruth scheduled regular visits to the center to take children on a day's outing, lunch, the movies, sometimes to Central Park. "I never was a great moviegoer," laughed Ruth, "but I've seen more movies in the past year than practically the rest of my life combined." "Always Westerns," she groaned humorously—"the children love Westerns."[986]

Ruth kept busy with book signings, touring in plays, and speaking engagements for groups like the National Council of Jewish Women, who put progressive ideals into action. In 1951, Chatterton, along with author Fannie Hurst and economist/journalist Sylvia Porter, received a Women of Achievement Citation from the Federation of Jewish Women's Organizations.[987] American literary critic and historian Harry Hansen wrote a tribute to author Ruth Chatterton, comparing her to other famous authors: Henry James, William Faulkner, and Eugene O'Neill. Hansen elaborated:

> Miss Chatterton's distinction as an actress is an asset of our generation. [She] reads everything of any value, has clean cut views on the issues of the day, and, when writing, takes up an individual or social problem and follows it thru to a solution. Her thinking is in a straight line... in which each character says something. This comes from her training in the theater, where every speech must advance the play.[988]

Ruth adored Henry James and had a complete set of first editions. She continued to read incessantly. Topical books she praised included John Hersey's *The Wall*, which detailed the origin and devastation of the Warsaw Ghetto. "I'd say it belongs with the greatest 100 novels of the world," she said. "I almost resented it because *Cry, the Beloved Country* had been my favorite novel."[989] Ruth was a perfect candidate for reviewing books for the *New York Times*, which she did for several years. And she hadn't given up on Broadway. When Maurice Evans suggested she revive the Robert E. Sherwood hit *Idiot's Delight*, Ruth was hesitant at first. "Then I read the script," she said, "and it was magnificent. Back in '35 Sherwood sensed what was going to happen. In the play he spoke out against all the dangers threatening us. The play is still very timely. We're so swept by the fear of Communism, and I realize what a great danger it is, that we forget about the others, the munitions kings, greed, Fascism, which is another form of totalitarianism, just as Russia is."[990] Ruth felt that the playwright showed remarkable prescience in *Idiot's Delight*. She relished the dialogue and the opportunity to play Irene, the consort of a wealthy munitions maker. Fortunately, a revival of the Sherwood classic provided Ruth both a critically acclaimed comeback and swansong for Broadway.

Endnotes

923   Glenn C. Pullen, "Ruth Chatterton Can't Quit Stage," *Plain Dealer*, July 27, 1958.
924   "Ruth Chatterton's Home is Attached," *Seattle Times*, August 10, 1945.
925   Review of *Second Best Bed*, *Billboard*, June 15, 1946.
926   "Theatre," *Winnipeg Free Press*, May 13, 1946.
927   Jack O'Brian, "Broadway Letter," *Dallas Morning News*, June 9, 1946.
928   Lewis Nichols, "Annie Shouldn't Live Here," *New York Times*, June 4, 1946.
929   Robert Garland, column, *Marietta Journal*, January 5, 1947.
930   Neil McKenna, *The Secret Life of Oscar Wilde*, Basic Books, c. 2006, pg 110-112.
931   "*Second Best Bed* Opens at Erie Tonight," *Schenectady Gazette*, May 3, 1946.
932   Brenda Holman, email sent August 28, 2012.
933   Glenn C. Pullen, "Ruth Chatterton Can't Quit Stage," *Plain Dealer*, July 27, 1958.
934   News article from *Western Mail* (Perth, Australia), March 29, 1928.
935   Review for *Tiger Island*, *The Bulletin* (Australia), March 26, 1930.
936   Review of *Amphitryon 38'*, *Variety*, July 6, 1937.
937   Michael C. Arcone, "Class Angle," *Socialist Call*, November 27, 1937.
938   Walter Winchell, "On Broadway," December 30, 1937.
939   "John B. Thomson," *Bridgeport Post*, August 29, 1960.
940   Ann V. Masters, "Ruth Chatterton Steps Again Before the Footlights," *Bridgeport Post*, August 21, 1955.
941   Brooks Atkinson, review of *Candida*, *New York Times*, August 31, 1938.
942   "*Second Best Bed* Marked By Good Acting," *Schenectady Gazette*, May 4, 1946.
943   "Postscripts," *The Argus* (Melbourne), February 6, 1945.
944   "The Life in Melbourne," *The Argus* (Melbourne), January 10, 1948.

945 Dr. Rafael Medoff, "Ben Hecht's *A Flag is Born*: A Play That Changed History," The David S. Wyman Institute for Holocaust Studies (wymaninstitute.org), April 2004.
946 Dr. Rafael Medoff, "Ben Hecht's *A Flag is Born*: A Play That Changed History," The David S. Wyman Institute for Holocaust Studies (wymaninstitute.org), April 2004.
947 Matthew Silver, *Our Exodus: Leon Uris and the Americanization of Israel's Founding Story*, Wayne State University Press, c. 2010, pg 21.
948 "Theater Notes," *Variety*, December 19, 1944.
949 "U.S. Asked To Lead In Palestine Aid," *New York Times*, February 24, 1946.
950 Louis Sheaffer, "Curtain Time," *Brooklyn Eagle*, May 22, 1951.
951 "Ruth Chatterton Stars in *Caprice* At Ogunquit Playhouse This Week," *Portland Press Herald*, August 17, 1947.
952 Marian Selder, *The Bright Lights*, Houghton Mifflin, Boston, c. 1978, pg 147.
953 Bette Davis, *The Lonely Life*, Putnam, c. 1962, pg 207.
954 Cyrus Durgin, "Actress Ruth Chatterton May Soon Be Known as an Author," *Boston Globe*, August 1, 1948.
955 Cyrus Durgin, "Actress Ruth Chatterton May Soon Be Known as an Author," *Boston Globe*, August 1, 1948.
956 Review of *The Little Foxes*, *Variety*, July 17, 1948.
957 Bob Colacello, *Ronnie and Nancy: Their Path to the White House—1911-1980*, Warner Books, c. 2004, pg 191.
958 Cyrus Durgin, "Summer Stage," *Boston Globe*, August 3, 1948.
959 "Notes and Footnotes," *Berkshire Eagle*, August 28, 1956.
960 Cal York (pseudonym for various *Photoplay* columnists) "Hollywood Goings-On," *Photoplay*, May 1931.
961 Christopher Plummer, *In Spite of Myself: A Memoir*, Random House, c. 2009, pgs 99-100.
962 Christopher Plummer, *In Spite of Myself: A Memoir*, Random House, c. 2009, pg 100.
963 Christopher Plummer, *In Spite of Myself: A Memoir*, Random House, c. 2009, pg 100.
964 Cyrus Durgin, "Actress Ruth Chatterton May Soon Be Known as an Author," *Boston Globe*, August 1, 1948.
965 "Ritz Wins War With Actress," *Oakland Tribune*, March 20, 1949.
966 "Actress' Attorney Denies She Ever Cooked Octopus," *Long Beach Press Telegram*, March 18, 1949.
967 Bob Considine, "Where Do We Eat?" *Deseret News*, March 23, 1949.
968 Bob Francis, review of *Lovers and Friends*, *Billboard*, December 11, 1943.
969 Eleanor Roosevelt, David Emblidge (ed.) *My Day: The Best Of Eleanor Roosevelt's Acclaimed Newspaper Columns, 1936-1962*, Da Capo Pr., c. 2001, pg 88-89.
970 Charlotte Harmon, Rosemary Taylor, *Broadway in a Barn*, Crowell, c. 1957, pg 105.
971 Charlotte Harmon, Rosemary Taylor, *Broadway in a Barn*, Crowell, c. 1957, pg 106.
972 Charlotte Harmon, Rosemary Taylor, *Broadway in a Barn*, Crowell, c. 1957, pg 106.
973 Charlotte Harmon, Rosemary Taylor, *Broadway in a Barn*, Crowell, c. 1957, pg 106.
974 Charlotte Harmon, Rosemary Taylor, *Broadway in a Barn*, Crowell, c. 1957, pg 55.
975 Charlotte Harmon, Rosemary Taylor, *Broadway in a Barn*, Crowell, c. 1957, pg 162.
976 "Chatterton May Do Menagerie for WB," *Variety*, May 4, 1949.
977 Louella Parsons, "Ruth Chatterton Sure to Get Role in *Glass Menagerie*," *San Diego Union*, April 11, 1949.
978 Dorothy Manners, "Hollywood," September 6, 1949.
979 Michael Buckley, Irving Rapper, *Films in Review*, August/September 1986, pg 396.
980 Jeffrey L. Carrier, *Tallulah Bankhead: a bio-bibliography*, Greenwood Pr., c. 1991, pg 33.
981 Henry Jenkins III, Tara McPherson, Jane Shattuc, *Hop on Pop: The Politics and Pleasures of Popular Culture*, Duke University Pr., c. 2003, pg 326.
982 "Typical Film Star in Looks," *Pittsburgh Post-Gazette*, August 4, 1951.
983 Phyllis Battelle, "Veteran Actress Ruth Chatterton Is Preparing To Try Hand At Television," *Avalanche Journal*, April 12, 1953.
984 Rafael Medoff, "When Leonard Bernstein 'Dug' the Irgun," *The Jewish Daily Forward*, September 12, 2008.
985 Harvey Breit, "Talk With Miss Chatterton," *New York Times*, August 27, 1950.
986 Louis Sheaffer, "Curtain Time," *Brooklyn Eagle*, May 22, 1951.
987 "Home-Front Unity of Women Urged," *New York Times*, January 18, 1951.
988 Harry Hansen, "The Personalities of Authors, and the Dynamic Ruth Chatterton," *Chicago Daily Tribune*, August 22, 1954.
989 Harvey Breit, "Talk With Miss Chatterton," *New York Times*, August 27, 1950.
990 Louis Sheaffer, "Curtain Time," *Brooklyn Eagle*, May 22, 1951.

With Lee Tracy in the 1951 Broadway revival
of *Idiot's Delight* (courtesy of James Stettler).

16
Reluctant Actress

After the release of *Homeward Borne,* writing was first and foremost in the mind of Ruth Chatterton. It had become her passion and would remain so. She discovered that creating new characters for the written page had become more satisfying. When she did return to the stage, it was by request, as a favor, or to get money. Whatever the case, acting for Chatterton was now on the back burner. Her 1957 summer tour in the British comedy *Reluctant Debutante* would be strictly for cash and director Walt Witcover was dumbfounded by the minimal effort Ruth put into her role. "Not only did I have to listen to her read me another chapter of her new novel [*The Southern Wild*]," he complained, "she spent all too little time learning her lines."[991] According to Witcover, Ruth never read the play before rehearsal and was completely unprepared for her characters' lengthy telephone speeches. "Finally, we had to hook up a line on stage to the stage manager off stage," he said, "who would read her lines to her before she could utter them. As Ruth was a pro, the audience never got wind of this arrangement."[992] Even so, the play would often run 15 minutes overtime. Fortunately, as a reluctant actress, Chatterton still managed to pull in good reviews. Her earnings and royalties, however, continued to slip through her fingers. Kay Francis, according to biographer George Eels, had come to Ruth's rescue on at least one occasion. While Kay could be a real tightwad and "raise hell over an excessive tip… she spontaneously sent $5,000 to the high-living Ruth Chatterton, who had run through her earnings."[993] Toward the end of her life, Ruth relied on the financial generosity of several friends and acquaintances.

⚜

January 1950. Garson Kanin, playwright/director husband of Ruth Gordon, had been cajoling Chatterton to do his new play, *The Sky Is Falling*. She kept resisting his offer while working on her second novel. When she did take a break, it was to enjoy a reunion with Noel Coward. One evening, the two dined at the New York apartment of Guthrie McClintic and Kit Cornell along with Alec Guinness and Bob Hope. "We sat up until three talking pure theater and it was lovely," Coward noted in his diary.[994] By June, Ruth relented to Kanin's wish, but only if she could do another

May 3, 1950. Ruth shares Amelia Earhart
biography with Sam Ross and Bob J. Casey
at an author luncheon.

one of his plays, *The Smile of the World*. She liked the idea of playing a phi-landering wife of a narrow-minded Supreme Court Justice—a conserva-tive reactionary who had compromised the liberal politics of his youth. The play had been a five performance flop on Broadway. Unsurprisingly, the sky also fell on Chatterton's revival—in spite of her many curtain calls on opening night.[995] It bombed—pulling in the poorest business for Bucks County Playhouse since the theater opened eleven years prior. The good news that *Homeward Borne* had made *The New York Times* Best-Seller List found Chatterton riding the crest of a different kind of wave. For the remainder of the year, she was engaged with promotional tours and interviews. She then faced the loss of someone who had been one of the important anchors in her life.

On March 31, 1951, Ralph Forbes died following an operation at Montefiore Hospital, The Bronx. He had been ill for several weeks.[996] His wife, Dora, a lovely woman with a grand sense of humor, had become good friends with Ruth. They were both at Ralph's hospital bedside when he passed away.[997] The ex-mates hadn't worked together since *Second Best Bed*. According to his sister Brenda, Ruth was always drawn to Ralph's matter-of-factness and "jolly boyishness." Part of this attraction was Ralph's ability to make Ruth laugh at herself. She enjoyed repeating his remark, "Don't tangle with Ruth on any subject. She's got the fastest mind of anyone you've ever known." He would add with a grin, "Shallow, of course."[998]

In the summer of 1951, Chatterton's successful two-week revival of Rob-ert Sherwood's 1935 treatise on the idiocy of war, *Idiot's Delight*, was a tonic for her. She glided on stage playing the role of Irene, a pseudo-Rus-sian adventuress traveling through the Swiss Alps with her companion, a cynical and self-satisfied munitions mogul. When Irene is confronted about her vaudeville past by Harry Van, an American entertainer/con artist, she maintains her charade. The abrasive, fast-talking Lee Tracy was perfect for the role of Harry. Tracy's reputation for wild spontaneity served him well in *Idiot's Delight.* It had also gotten him into a lot of trouble. In 1933, the intoxicated actor relieved himself from a fourth-story window at Mexico City's St. Regis Hotel just as a military parade was passing by. During his stream of consciousness, he yelled, "Go to hell!" to the crowd below.[999] He was arrested. A local paper stated that Tracy, unclothed at the time, had insulted the Mexican flag.[1000] Tracy, who was on location filming MGM's *Viva Villa!,* boasted, "I'd been to a cabaret on a gay party and, like any drunk I was noisy; but I didn't thumb my nose at anybody."[1001] Louis B. Mayer, after apologizing to the President of Mexico, invoked the morals clause, fired Tracy, and tore up the actor's five-year contract.[1002] Tracy fled to El Paso, where he fumed to reporters, "Tell Hollywood to go to hell!"[1003] Somebody listened. He was relegated to a string of mostly "B" pictures.

Before *Idiot's Delight* opened at New York's City Center Theatre, Chatterton explained, "I'm doing this, because Maurice Evans asked me months ago. It only takes me two minutes to say yes, and the rest of my life to regret it. When he first asked me I figured it was safely off in the future, but now…"[1004] She needn't have worried. Veteran reporter Mark Barron (co-writer of the play *Gentlemen of the Press*) felt that the Pulitzer Prize-winning play was timelier than ever. The world was now dealing with the threat of atomic bombs. "The point that Mr. Sherwood made in his play… is much more applicable to the present state of world affairs," said Barron. "Miss Chatterton and Lee Tracy give it all the verve it needs for an up-to-the-minute production."[1005] Critics agreed that bad boy Tracy's brash personality was made-to-order for the American hoofer who brings Chatterton's airy character back down to earth. Brooks Atkinson, for *The New York Times*, praised the exuberance of the "excellently directed" play. He thought Lee Tracy "irresistible" and that Chatterton, "witty and sparkling," appeared to float through all the hokum and dry humor. As the United States was currently at war in Korea, the City Center management cautiously inserted a program note to remind patrons that the anti-war play was written four years before Hitler marched into Poland. Atkinson disagreed with Mark Barron and decided for his readers that munitions-makers were not "evil geniuses of carnage" after all. "That was the sophistry of the Thirties," Atkinson sniffed,"—the easy way out for intellectuals in search of a villain."[1006]

Following one evening performance of *Idiot's Delight*, Ruth's cousin, Olive Wehbring, and her sixteen-year-old daughter Brenda came backstage. "I remember seeing Ruth in *Idiot's Delight*," recalled Brenda. "It was amazing. She just breezed through it. While the adults had champagne backstage, Barry went next door to a restaurant and brought me ginger ale."[1007]

After the two-week run of *Idiot's Delight*, Ruth and Barry toured in another Lunt-Fontanne revival. Terence Rattigan's *O Mistress Mine* was all about a man who lived happily with his mistress, a Mrs. Brown, while his wife lived happily alone. A divorce would only ruin his career. When Mrs. Brown's son learns of his mother's adultery, he begs her to return the husband to the wife—who doesn't want him. The play ends with the son reconciled to the fact that the parties concerned were much better off living in sin. It brought back echoes of *Monsieur Brotonneau*—which Ruth had translated for the stage in 1930. A Pittsburgh review commented,

Miss Chatterton plays Mrs. Brown with sympathy and

sincerity. An experienced master of her craft, she is always the Mistress Mine. Quite sure in her own mind of
the sanctity of her arrangement... she is just as convincing as she drops out of the agreement at the blandish-
ments of her talkative son. It is altogether an engaging
portrayal and one in which Miss Chatterton can take
much pride.[1008]

Bette Davis gave Ruth some stiff competition one evening when *O
Mistress Mine* reached Ogunquit, Maine. Davis, who had remained a loyal
fan of Ruth Chatterton, attempted to make an inconspicuous entrance to
see the play. Instead, "the crowd stood up and applauded insistently," but
Davis refused to pay them any attention.[1009] The "ohs" and "ahs" continued
to buzz throughout the performance. Davis and husband Gary Merrill
had driven from their new home in nearby Prout's Neck for the occasion.

TV & Hamlet

Chatterton had done six teleplays before filming Maurice Evans' *Hamlet* in 1953. Her television dramatic debut was on December 19, 1948,
in *Suspect*, based on the Broadway play. In the intensely emotional role,
Ruth played a woman who had once been accused of a brutal murder.
One critic felt that Chatterton anchored the production and then went
on to say that while her emotional values were "convincing enough," they
were more appropriate for the stage than the intimacy of the small screen.
"Miss Chatterton was too obvious," he said and suggested she use a more
"natural" approach for television.[1010] It was a problem that faced many
actors during TV's infancy.

In October 1950, Ruth revived Fran Dodsworth for *Prudential Family Playhouse*. Walter Abel adequately handled the role of Sam and Eva
Marie Saint as the daughter, Emily, played with natural ease. "I don't
think I had worked with quite a star as Miss Chatterton," Saint told this

author in a 2011 telephone interview. "I had such respect for her work. She was lovely on the set. She knew I was young and starting out. She was very giving and very dear. That's about all I can say… I have no bad memories. It was very exciting. She and Walter Abel were just charming. The more you are with giants like that; you learn how they handle themselves. They were such pros. They were nurturing. I loved being on that set."[1011] Despite technical limitations, the televised *Dodsworth* was a worthwhile effort and maintained some semblance of the original film's dramatic intensity. It was a definite stretch for Chatterton, though still attractive, to pull off lines such as, "They think I'm young!" Fourteen years had passed since the original film's release. A bit of rasp in Ruth's emotionally-charged voice also added pathos to her character's futile attempt to pass as Sam Dodsworth's child wife. Claire Trevor and Fredric March would also team for a 1956 "live" colorcast TV remake. "I never dreamed I'd be doing *Dodsworth* myself," exclaimed Trevor, who, years earlier, had purchased the ermine wrap worn by Chatterton in the film.[1012]

In 1951, Chatterton teamed with Edna Best for John van Druten's *Old Acquaintance*. As an author who writes seldom, but brilliantly, the role was obviously a shoo-in for Ruth. In his book *Theatre: from Stage to Screen to Television*, William T. Leonard found the teleplay to be "expertly directed by Fred Coe, with telling, professionally polished performances by Edna Best and Ruth Chatterton."[1013] *Variety* agreed: "The Chatterton-Best tandem for van Druten's sharp-shafted treatise on unattached forty-ish femmes… was inspired casting."[1014] The following year, Ruth took *Old Acquaintance* out on the road with good results. *The Hartford Courant* praised, "Miss Chatterton manages to get a world of wisdom and tolerance into the role… with a gracefulness and understanding that would be difficult for any but a seasoned actress to make convincing."[1015]

Along with Otto Kruger and Ilka Chase, Ruth teamed for two episodes of the popular TV series *Pulitzer Prize Playhouse*. Included was Susan Glaspell's *Alison's House*, inspired by the life of poet Emily Dickinson. Ruth, as the niece of a deceased spinster poet, discovers they both have similar skeletons in the family closet... affairs with married men. Columnist Charles Sampas noted that Chatterton and Kruger were "wearing their years gracefully."[1016] When English actor Maurice Evans asked Ruth to play Queen Gertrude for the first televised *Hamlet,* she didn't hesitate. "He called to offer me the part while I was at the hairdressers," she said. "I said yes immediately. This will be a nice change."[1017] Chatterton's only Shakespearean role had been in 1910 stock as the plump, middle-aged Maria in *Twelfth Night.* Even so, her confidence on the subject of Shakespeare had guaranteed her a spot on a 1947 special radio broadcast which discussed his longest play, *The Tragedy of Hamlet, Prince of Denmark.*

The televised *Hamlet* was a two-hour *Hallmark Hall of Fame* special. It was considered TV's most prestigious production to date, costing $180,000. After three weeks of rehearsal, director George Schaefer, who had collaborated with Evans doing Shakespearean plays for troops overseas, felt the cast was ready for "live television." This was no easy task as the new medium had a reputation for disastrous mishaps—and, in this case, there would be a potential 16,000,000 witnesses glued to their television screens. As one critic barbed, "TV or Not TV—Hamlet Gets His Answer."[1018] The *Chicago Tribune* called the production a "spectacular success" and Maurice Evans, making his television debut, "the finest Hamlet of our time." The review then added, "One-time movie star Ruth Chatterton, as Queen Gertrude, skidded in her opening lines, but recovered quickly."[1019] Evans, of course, had no problems. He had played the role close to 800 times. Only one line in Act I had actually stuck in Chatterton's throat. While cautioning son Hamlet about his grief, she stumbled, "Do not forever with-with thy veiled lids look-look for thy father in the dust." Mayhap the dead king's prophecy for Queen Gertrude in Scene V had already taken effect: "Leave her to heaven and to those thorns that in her bosom lodge, to prick and sting her."

The use of dissolves allowed for "dramatic continuity" and another "startling effect" was the use of superimposition for the ghost of King Hamlet. No less than five cameras, shooting from various directions, allowed for spaciousness, intimacy, and, at times, a feeling of commotion. Threatening booms, cameras, assorted technicians invited the inevitable. When Christopher Plummer recalled watching Evans and Chatterton on TV, he pointed to the famous soliloquy scene: "Now I am alone..." "He wasn't," said Plummer. "Only a few feet behind him in full view of the camera was a beefy, unshaven stagehand peering around a pillar chawing at an oversized deli sandwich."[1020]

While columnist/critic Ed Brooks thought Joseph Schildkraut as Claudius lacked characterization, he felt Chatterton "an excellent choice" for Queen Gertrude.[1021] Jack Gould for *The New York Times* argued that Chatterton "seemed lacking in assurance."[1022] As a play, *Hamlet* is clouded with uncertainty. The fine line between "lacking in assurance" as a performer and the uncertainties of the character she was playing indeed compromised Chatterton's performance following her opening scene.

Not everyone shined to Evans' *Hamlet*. Reigning television critic John Crosby bluntly announced that he found the production "fairly appalling" and Evans' performance "terribly monotonous." "Evans' voice is one of the great organs of our stage," wrote Crosby, "but it seems to have got stuck in one key. I found it unpardonable." "Mr. Schildkraut and Miss Chatterton are fine as actor and actress," added Crosby, "but this—to put it charitably—was not their day."[1023] Where Crosby missed the mark was after Hamlet murders Polonius. Crosby mused that Chatterton "seemed merely cross with her boy." For all the tears and emotional anguish she displayed, it was an unfair assessment. But then, Crosby's caustic remarks were designed to entertain readers. *Boston Globe's* Ted Ashby's review of *Hamlet* was gruff and included an unpardonable gaff. "Ruth Chatterton as Queen Claudia," he blundered, "was fine… [after] she kicked around a line or two. The stage was strewn with dead and dying near the play's end. Viewers with a yen for the bloodthirsty… must have felt they had hit the jackpot."[1024] To accent the timelessness of the play, the traditional Tudor setting was updated to the 19th century; the costumes, however, weren't in sync. Joseph Schildkraut, according to John Crosby, looked as if he had wandered in from the operetta *The Student Prince*. Chatterton's plunging neckline was also an unwanted distraction for Crosby. Crosby

Daggers enter the ears of Queen Gertrude.
With Maurice Evans in TV's *Hamlet* (1953).

had a valid point in these trifling matters. After seeing Sarah Churchill's overdressed Ophelia, I kept waiting for Hamlet to tell her, "Get thee to a cocktail party!"

While the voice of Maurice Evans resonated, admirers mostly overlooked its frequent quaver, something that was more appropriate for the pulpit. However, the main thing that works against his Hamlet was his age. He was almost fifty-two and looked older than Uncle Claudius. "Youthful" revenge may have escaped the televised production, but the mix of madness, suicide, murder, and corruption easily fulfill Hamlet's "What a piece of work is a man."

In hindsight, fifty years later, Kenneth Sprague Rothwell's A History of Shakespeare on Screen compliments director Schaefer and goes on to say that TV's Hamlet was "most memorable for the really stunning Gertrude played by Ruth Chatterton."[1025] Chatterton comes into her own in Act III, Scene IV, during Gertrude's confrontation with Hamlet. This takes place in her boudoir, where she is witness to her son's murder of the eavesdropper, Polonius. "O, what a rash and bloody deed this is!" she cries. Suspecting he has gone mad, Gertrude listens as "the coinage of his brain" confronts her regarding her own duplicity and marriage to Claudius, her brother-in-law. "You cannot call it love," he tells her. "For at your age the hey-day in the blood is tame." It must have struck a chord. Chatterton's queen is convincingly distraught by this bit of news as she pleads with him, "O, speak to me no more; these words, like daggers, enter in mine ears."

In Act V, when Chatterton grasps the poison cup that Queen Gertrude knows is intended for Hamlet, she shows newfound purpose and strength. Claudius demands she not drink, but she has finally seen through him and condescendingly replies, "I will, my lord; I pray you pardon me." While watching the final duel between Hamlet and Laertes, the viewer anticipates the poisoned Queen's doom. In a grip of convulsion, Chatterton almost steals the show. "The drink, the drink!" she cries. "O, my dear Hamlet. I am… poisoned." Chatterton turns her final word in a sing-song fashion with uncanny effect.

※⊙◎⊙※

While Ruth never wrote her own memoirs, she generated interest in the genre as a critic for *The New York Times.* Her review of actress Eva Le Gallienne's *With a Quiet Heart* in the spring of 1953 found the effort "detailed and rather pedestrian"—lacking in "humor and incident." Not that Le Gallienne would open the closet door to reveal her lesbianism, but the painful reversals in her personal and public life were also missing from her story—the price of discretion. Chatterton felt that although Le Gallienne had given much to theatre, her "single-mindedness" was out of touch with "the swift pace and violent changes of the past two decades."[1026] In 1951, Chatterton had placed herself at the feet of Ethel Waters when reviewing *His Eye Is On The Sparrow.* "When I had finished reading," wrote Chatterton, "I felt as if I had curled up in front of a fire listening as Ethel Waters bared her soul and told me the intimate fascinating and, at times, terrible story of her life." As the illegitimate daughter of a twelve-year-old, Waters left nothing out. Chatterton found that the "bawdy, lusty and profane" language allowed for a "brutal frankness and… touching compassion." Waters was guileless in her conceit as she was candid about her frailties. When she expressed her outrage and "fear of not being able to count on anything in this white man's world"—Chatterton wept. The overall verdict: "eloquence… which comes from [an] unbreakable heart."[1027]

Before completing the manuscript for her third book, *The Pride of the Peacock,* Ruth took a break to star in Rachel Crothers' *Susan and God.* The production played for two weeks in Evanston, Illinois. As a middle-aged socialite smitten by a pseudo-evangelistic movement, Ruth rose to the occasion to satirize the lives of the idle rich while spouting Crothers' witty dialogue. *Susan and God* was an insightful commentary on social issues; in this case, the need to scare away emptiness with "pipe dreams." The *Chicago Daily Tribune* acknowledged Chatterton's "excellent portrayal of Susan," but remarked that the fumbling of lines by the supporting cast marred the overall production.[1028] Praises were also given to Barry as the alcoholic husband. Next up, Ruth returned to the small screen for a guest appearance in one of TV's more stimulating discussion sessions, *Author Meets the Critics.* She listened while lawyers Leo Cherne of the Research Institute of America and Arthur Garfield Hayes of the American Civil Liberties Union battled it out over Ruth's book, *The Betrayers.* Hays, who had taken part in the famous Scopes trial; the Sacco and Vanzetti case; and the Scottsboro trial, argued in favor of Chatterton's work. Cherne argued that the book attacked all subversive groups, which Chatterton readily denied. He called her "politically unsophisticated." According to one viewer, Ruth "didn't take to that description too kindly."[1029] Hays focused on the damage done to liberty by such committees as the HUAC. The damage, countered Hays, outweighed any facts they had dug up.

Chatterton remained politically active and stuck to her convictions regarding Israel. In 1956, when Israel's Premier Ben-Gurion pressed the United States for weapons to match those delivered to Egypt by the Communist bloc, Ruth gave him her full support. Along with author Louis Bromfield, she helped form the Committee to Save the Middle East from Communism. The group's name was more of a ploy to gain bi-partisan support for Ben-Gurion's request. The organization's first rally at Town Hall included speeches by Chatterton and the prominent lawyer Paul O'Dwyer.[1030] While it was true that Soviet arms sales to Egypt threatened peace, the real problem pointed to Arab hostility along the Gaza Strip. The Gaza Strip would remain a volatile hotbed of fighting long after the "threat" of Soviet Communism bit the dust.

Ruth's novels were now being published in England, Italy, and Norway. As she pounded away seven or eight hours a day on her typewriter, she said she didn't miss the theater. "There is more satisfaction as an author," she explained. "A novel is more elastic and you can go where you like. I'm my own mistress and I make my own mistakes."[1031] *Pride of the Peacock* told of a self-centered, attractive woman, Alexandra "Zan" Payton, who throws her family into a bewildering state of discord. She deserts her husband and teenage daughter for an Italian pianist who "could play Bach like an angel." Three years later, Zan's "angel" leaves her when she runs out of money. She returns home to face the consequences: a daughter who has withdrawn into a shell of confusion; is wary of marriage; and sees her mother as competition. Zan had done a good job of making her daughter feel inferior. Zan's husband, Jock, is a down-to-earth guy—an investor who, when asked about Wall Street, deftly replies, "The Korean mess seems to have goosed it a bit."[1032] He's not as clever when it comes to Zan. Knowing full well her penchant for male admirers, Jock welcomes her back. But their reunion is short-lived. Jock finally sees through his fantasy and falls for a nurturing, middle-aged woman named Christine, who Zan calls a "frump." Zan is stuck—devoted only to vanity and sexual passion whenever "her uneasy body [becomes] restless and hungry for warmth and relaxation."[1033]

Although the topic was less controversial than her first two novels, Ruth challenged readers. The plot wasn't new, but the telling of it was unique, especially her way of advancing the narrative. The reader is intimately immersed in the thought processes of Zan, her husband Jock, and their daughter, Jenny as they alternate telling the story. *Kirkus Reviews* praised, "This is probably the most sparkling and best written of the novels by the actress-turned-author."[1034] Edmund Fuller for the *Chicago Daily Tribune* argued that Chatterton's book was "mature and subtle... executed with skill and precision."[1035] Charlotte Capers for *The New York Times* felt otherwise, saying Chatterton was nothing less than "a cliché expert... whose characters deliver hackneyed lines in predictable situations."[1036] On the contrary, *The Pride of the Peacock* is a page-turner which easily pulls the reader into the mindset of three individuals with fresh, interesting results. As they let go of self-doubt, the trio begin to understand themselves and each other. A well-realized scene occurs between the two women when Christine shrewdly tells Zan, "It didn't occur to you that a woman whom [Jock] loved would have to have less than you have—not more!" Zan also finds a better choice for a husband—one with all her bad attributes. "Could this be it?" she asks herself. "He likes music— *and* he was driving a Cadillac!"[1037] Chatterton is adept in showing how individuals punish themselves by the thoughts they entertain. Her book echoes the sentiment expressed by author Carlos Castaneda: "The trick is what one emphasizes. We either make ourselves miserable or we make ourselves stronger. The amount of work is the same."[1038]

As an author, Ruth knew Zan Payton intimately. All she had to do was look in the mirror and mull over her own past: Henry Miller; the odd trio of Ralph, Ruth, and George; European escapades with journalist Rex Smith. Zan's coterie of male admirers was something that Chatterton herself relished. Exactly what kind of mother Ruth would have been becomes quite clear. Fortunately for her, Ruth knew that she was not mother material. If Zan lacked anything, it was Chatterton's ability

Ruth, Barry, and their "black monsters"–New York–
Summer 1954 (Courtesy of the Everett Collection).

to match her ambition with intelligence. Harry Hansen for the *Chicago Daily Tribune* also felt that Ruth's own personality projected into her narrative. "Ruth Chatterton's well organized personality," he wrote, "is responsible for the clear dynamic story telling in her third novel, *The Pride of the Peacock.*"[1039]

Shortly after the release of *The Pride of the Peacock* on October 29, 1954, Lilian Chatterton passed away at the age of eighty-seven in her Beverly Hills home. Ruth had visited Tilly whenever she could and always made a point to be with her mother when she was ill. Chatterton's ties to Los Angeles were now completely severed. Soon after Lilian's death, Ruth and Barry managed to realize their dream of living in New England.

In March 1955, Ruth and Barry leased, with an option to buy, what locals referred to as the Ault House on Putnam Park Road in Redding, Connecticut. It was the original homestead of John Read, the founder of Redding, that is, after he "acquired" 500 acres from the Potatuck Native Americans—a farming and fishing culture. The Thomsons and their three black poodles settled into Connecticut permanently. Ruth hadn't been to Europe since 1939 and had lost interest in traveling. "I don't quite care to go back," she explained. "I have too many memories of what it was before the war. I lived in France, which I dearly love... Spain is a country that gets in your blood, and once it's in, you love it forever."[1040] The seclusion of Redding provided just what Ruth wanted out of life. Even though she would read until four in the morning, she said she "had to get out of bed in time to see that big blazing ball ascend the heavens."[1041] Aside from writing, Ruth enjoyed cooking (especially curry dishes) and working in her vegetable garden. If good friends like Noel Coward or Maurice

Chevalier hit New York, Ruth could be persuaded to zip into town for an evening of conversation. "When I'm in the country," Ruth would say, "nothing gets me out." However, as bills piled up, Chatterton's lectures and stage performances were essentials. Barry's revenues came mostly from his radio TV role as Dr. Bart Thompson on the popular soap opera *The Guiding Light*. After he was written out, he toured with Sylvia Sidney in *Anniversary Waltz*.

Once settled into her handsome, pre-Revolutionary, colonial residence, Ruth offered a two-performance tryout of Ettore Rella's play, *Sign of Winter*. Rella championed the use of blank verse in theater and Ruth shared his enthusiasm. During rehearsals, Ann V. Masters, a reporter from nearby Bridgeport, interviewed Ruth against the backdrop of the new home's spacious lawns. Ruth, "tanned and comfortably dressed in halter and shorts," held court while ensconced on her chaise lounge. "Her rich timbred voice," noted Masters, "splendid in its sureness rose and fell as the group led by the young director, Sherwood Arthur, ran through a scene."[1042] Chatterton played the role of a boozy mistress of a Manhattan rooming house that had once been her childhood home.

Sign of Winter, which Chatterton felt appealed to intellectuals, had intrigued her for several years. Financial backing was a problem. Blank verse wasn't considered box office. When Lucille Lortel offered a two-day stint for the production at her White Barn Theater, noted for serving experimental plays, Chatterton grasped the opportunity. "So here we are," smiled Ruth. "The lines come curiously alive when they're played. I'm madly in love with it." Not everyone was. Eva Le Gallienne stormed out of the theatre the evening of the second performance after noticing the carefully plumped up bodice of Ruth's co-player, Anne Meacham. "Why do actresses have to wear falsies," Le Gallienne huffed.[1043] Or perhaps the veteran actress had suddenly recalled Chatterton's scathing review of Le Gallienne's autobiography in *The New York Times*. On opening night, there had been even more excitement. The audience was less intrigued by the play than the presence of a blonde movie star in their midst: Marilyn Monroe. Monroe arrived at the White Barn wearing a simple white blouse and black skirt, accompanied by her future biographer Norman Rosten. During intermission, all eyes were on Marilyn, who chatted away with Lortel's housekeeper.

Lucille Lortel considered *Sign of Winter*, despite its esoteric qualities, one of the more important entries for her summer theater. The play paired Anne Meacham, who played Chatterton's daughter, with an African-American lover. Meacham later remarked that she "found the depth and complication of this relationship way ahead of its time."[1044] Two weeks' rehearsal, however, wasn't enough to grasp hold of Rella's sprawling, pretentious work. One review praised, "It was apparent [Chatterton] believed deeply in the play and the writing, for she brought to it all her acting skill."[1045] Theater journalist Ira Bilowit praised, "Chatterton ably maintains and projects the appearance and determination of a drunken, disappointed widow, who is first and finally a mother who cares."[1046]

⚜

In 1956, Ruth signed on for a lecture circuit as well as two new stage roles: S.N. Behrman's *Jane* and *The Chalk Garden* by Enid Bagnold. In *Jane*, Behrman's sparkling wit managed to keep afloat the story of a middle-aged widow who has a charming knack for telling truths no one wants to hear. During a fall tour of *The Chalk Garden*, "artistic differences" between Gladys Cooper and Judith Anderson had allowed Ruth to take over for Cooper in St. Louis. In the role of Mrs. St. Maugham, Chatterton played an aging socialite struggling to raise her emotionally damaged pubescent granddaughter and a flower garden that subsists on a subsoil of chalk. A

Milwaukee critic favored Chatterton's performance over co-star Anderson, who played the newly hired governess with a secret past. "Miss Chatterton is excellent as Mrs. St. Maugham," noted the review, "a soul as shallow as her garden topsoil, but full of amusing twists and turns of conversation. Miss Anderson seems to overpower the role of Miss Madrigal."[1047] After four weeks, Ruth withdrew from the cast. Confined to her hotel room, she was diagnosed with a virus infection.[1048] She flew home to Connecticut. The dark comedy was scheduled to tour for another nineteen weeks. The road company's producers filed suit, saying that "Miss Chatterton had not been cooperative."[1049] Ruth denied the charge. Ruth's claims were upheld in a 2-1 arbitration decision against the management. She was rewarded $15,000. The virus, combined with pleurisy, was something she had been battling since wrapping up her lectures at the end of October.

The Lyceum-Tulane (a.k.a. "Knife and Fork") lecture series consisted of six well-known talents, including Arthur C. Clarke, who would go on to write *2001: A Space Odyssey*, and Ninette de Valois, formerly of the Ballet Russe. In Chatterton's lecture, she stressed the importance of supporting local theatrical productions. "The theater is important in our lives today," cautioned Ruth, "but she is a very sick girl."[1050] Chatterton felt that Americans were "more concerned with dishwashing machines than art."[1051] She emphasized that legitimate theater had fallen into the hands of those who were "out to make a quick buck." Theater at its best, according to Ruth, was a powerful implement to bring about the correction of social problems and "an indispensable tool to the maintenance of democracy."[1052] The *Pittsburgh Press* reported that "Without help of scenery, cast or costume, Ruth Chatterton held members of the Twentieth Century club spellbound. The actress... had the collective imagination of her audience building scenes, designing costumes and conjuring her fellow characters. She gave an actors-eye-view of the difference between stage and screen performances to the capacity crowd."[1053] Ruth made use of a self-interrupting "Cut" while doing scenes from *Dodsworth*. She would then enact the make-up man adjusting one of her eyelashes before filming resumed. In contrast, she demonstrated the fluidity of stage acting with scenes from Shaw's *Pygmalion*.

On September 20, while lecturing in Spokane, Chatterton met some real competition—the Vice President of the United States. Richard Nixon was hot on the '56 campaign trail. During her ill-timed presentation at the Davenport Hotel, the management made arrangements to have loudspeakers in the same room as Ruth so those in attendance could hear Nixon's scheduled speech in the spacious hotel lobby.[1054] An hour into her presentation, she was upstaged by the Vice President, who took a break from railing against Communist infiltration. Instead, he addressed charges made against him for using smear tactics, catering to special interest groups, and the accusation that the Eisenhower administration was "concerned only with the welfare of the rich and well born."[1055] It was reported that a crowd of 2,500 roared with approval. Undoubtedly, Ruth had a difficult time holding back her reputable and articulate tongue in response to Mr. Nixon's diatribe.

❧❀❧

When Ruth finally recovered from the virus which forced her out of *The Chalk Garden*, she was ready for another battle. "Actress Assails New Road Plan," headlined *The Bridgeport Post* on May 17, 1957. Ruth fought the State Highway Commission over a proposed road in front of her residence on Putnam Road. She went so far as to drive to the state capitol to confer with the governor. She threatened that she would move to New York if the project were completed. A reporter outside Governor Ribicoff's office got an earful. "I came to this state," asserted Ruth, "because it's a beautiful state, and a wonderful place to live. But if they're going to take all the beauty away, then what's the use. I might as well move out. Why do they need a new road where we are? We've got one already."[1056] The newsman made a point of Chatterton's "sharply-clipped theatrical voice." After her meeting with the Governor, Ruth felt she had made some headway. When she learned otherwise, she followed through with her ultimatum and moved. She and Barry relocated to another vintage home three miles away on a secluded 17-acre lot.

In the summer of 1957, 5' 2" Ruth co-starred on tour as the wife of 6' 4" English actor Arthur Treacher. The British comedy hit, *Reluctant Debutante*, had the duo as parents of a debutante, played by a young actress named Sandy Dennis. It was Dennis' first commercial leading role. Her quirky "method" style of acting was quite different from that of consummate pros like Chatterton and Treacher, who became concerned about Dennis' ability. The play's director, Walt Witcover, assured Ruth that the young actress, whom he found "delightfully vague and often absent-minded," would pull through. "She held her own on stage with these veterans," recalled Witcover. In fact, one review felt that Dennis "dominated the performance with charm and skill."[1057] Witcover found Treacher "impeccable, amiable and thoroughly professional." "But Miss Chatterton!" he moaned. "It turned out she was doing this tour only to make enough money to pay the mortgage on her Connecticut home." Witcover felt that Ruth didn't want to put any effort into the role of a neurotic wife who was trying to find her daughter a suitable husband. Evidently, it wasn't necessary. A critic for *The Bridgeport Post* observed that "Miss Chatterton gets a lot of fun out of the rather stuffy role of the mother." [1058] Chatterton's performance was also nominated for Chicago's prestigious Sarah Siddons Society Award for Best Actress. Among the other twenty-two contenders were: Geraldine Page, Celeste Holm, Jessica Tandy, Gertrude Berg, Agnes

Moorehead, and Fay Bainter. The winner was English actress Anne Rogers, who played Eliza Doolittle in the first national tour of *My Fair Lady*.

Reluctant Debutante toured from New England to South Carolina. When it played in Connecticut, Ruth arranged a rehearsal at her home *without* director Witcover. She told the cast that Witcover was too much of a "perfectionist." During this impromptu rehearsal, Witcover consoled himself by having a "brief romantic encounter with a very attractive young actor" whose wife, it so happened, was the star on the current bill at Westport Country Playhouse.[1059] In Illinois, the *Chicago Daily Tribune* reported that Chatterton, true to form, was "busier with the typewriter than with rehearsals."[1060] Ruth had an October deadline for her fourth novel and stated that she found it difficult to make the changeover from the characters in her book to those in *The Reluctant Debutante*. She obvi-

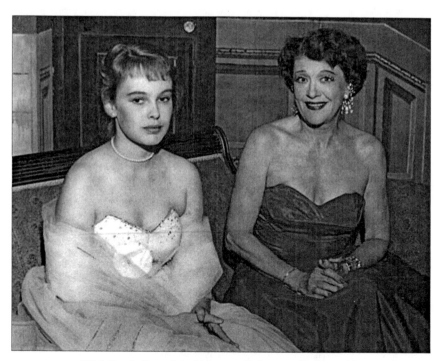

With Sandy Dennis in *Reluctant Debutante* (July 1957).

ously thought more of her own novel and told director Witcover that her stage character was a silly woman, unworthy of serious attention. When the play reached the Paper Mill Playhouse in Milburn, New Jersey, Witcover's aunt and uncle hosted a reception for the cast. A chill factor set in, however, when his aunt walked into the kitchen to discover Ruth trying to talk their devoted maid, Hannah, into coming to work for *her*.

When *Reluctant Debutante* finally closed in Myrtle Beach, Witcover, who had a reputation as a soft-spoken, polite young director, had reached his wits' end thanks to Ruth Chatterton. He found himself screaming at the crew, "Let's do the fucking thing! Let's do it!"[1061] Witcover declared the tour of *Reluctant Debutante* "minimally satisfying." Ruth considered it merely an intrusion. With a sigh of relief, she was able to meet her publisher's October deadline.

Endnotes

991   Walt Witcover, *My Road, Less Traveled: Becoming an Actor, Director, a Teacher*, Xlibris, c. 2011, pg 237.

992   Walt Witcover, *My Road, Less Traveled: Becoming an Actor, Director, a Teacher*, Xlibris, c. 2011, pgs 237-238.

993   George Eels, *Ginger, Loretta and Irene Who?*, Simon & Schuster, c. 1976, pg 193-194.

994   Noel Coward, ed. Graham Payn and Sheridan Morley, *The Noel Coward Diaries*, Little, Brown & Co., c. 1982, pg 143 (entry February 12, 1950).

995   Review of *The Smile of the World*, *Variety*, June 7, 1950.

996   "Ralph Forbes, 45, Pioneer Stage, Film Actor, Dies," *Long Beach Telegram*, April 2, 1951.

997   John McCallum, *Scooper*, Wood & Reber, c. 1960, pgs 190-191.

998   Ann V. Masters, "Ruth Chatterton Steps Again Before the Footlights," *Bridgeport Post*, August 21, 1955.

999   Jessie Henderson, "Tracy's Side of the Incident in Mexico," *Omaha World Herald*, December 5, 1933 (In many news reports, Tracy claimed he was wearing "a blanket." Eyewitness, including a lawyer and his 12-year-old-daughter, felt otherwise. Following his arrest, Tracy spent time in a Mexican jail before fleeing the country while still under investigation on morals charges.).

1000   Dorothy Donnell, "Did Lee Tracy 'Insult' Mexico, Or Did That Report Insult Him?" *Motion Picture*, February 1934.

1001   Dorothy Donnell, "Did Lee Tracy 'Insult' Mexico, Or Did That Report Insult Him?" *Motion Picture*, February 1934.

1002   Imogen Sara Smith, "Lee Tracy-A Manic, Scalding Passion for Success," *Bright Lights Film Journal*, May 2009.

1003   Dorothy Donnell, "Did Lee Tracy 'Insult' Mexico, Or Did That Report Insult Him?" *Motion Picture*, February 1934.

1004   Louis Sheaffer, "Curtain Time, *Brooklyn Eagle*, May 22, 1951.

1005   Mark Barron, review of *Idiot's Delight*, *Dallas Morning News*, May 24, 1951.

1006   Brooks Atkinson, review of *Idiot's Delight*, *New York Times*, May 24, 1951.

1007   Conversation with and email from Brenda Holman, January 16, 2012 and August 28, 2012.

1008   Donald Steinfirst, 'O Mistress Mine' Stars Ruth Chatterton at Arena," *Pittsburgh Post-Gazette*, August 7, 1951.

1009   The Scribbler, "The Open Door," *Portsmouth Herald*, July 20, 1951.

1010   Robert S. Stephan, "*Television Playhouse* Show Needs Less of Stagy Touch," *Cleveland Plain Dealer*, December 21, 1948.

1011   Conversation with Eva Marie Saint, September 1, 2011.

1012   "Claire Trevor Gets Star TV Role in *Dodsworth*," *Logansport Pharos-Tribune*, April 25, 1956.

1013   William T. Leonard, *Theatre: from Stage to Screen to Television*, Scarecrow, c. 1981, pg 1129.

1014   Review of *Old Acquaintance*, *Variety*, November 21, 1951.

1015   E.N.D., "Ruth Chatterton, Clinton Star In Van Druten Play," *Hartford Courant*, August 13, 1952.

1016   Charles G. Sampas, "Scampascoopies," *Lowell Sun*, January 16, 1952.

1017   Phyllis Battelle, "Veteran Actress Ruth Chatterton Preparing To Try Hand At Television," *Avalanche Journal*, April 26, 1953.

1018   Martin Lee, "TV or Not TV? Hamlet Gets His Answer on NBC Sunday," *Herald*, April 26, 1953.

1019   Anton Remenih, "Television News And Views," *Chicago Daily Tribune*, April 28, 1953.

1020   Christopher Plummer, *In Spite of Myself: A Memoir*, Random House, c. 2009, pg 126-127.

1021   Jack Gould, "Television In Review," *New York Times*, April 27, 1953.

1022   Ed Brooks, "*Hamlet* Hit New High in Quality Drama on Video," *Times-Picayune*, April 28, 1953.

1023   John Crosby, "Radio and Television," *Portsmouth Times*, May 25, 1953.

1024   Ted Ashby, "Coarse Death," *Boston Globe*, April 27, 1953.

1025   Kenneth Sprague Rothwell, *A History of Shakespeare on Screen*, Cambridge University Pr., c. 2004, pg 98.

1026   Ruth Chatterton, "A Deep Love of Theatre," *New York Times*, April 26, 1953.

1027   Ruth Chatterton, "With Songs And a Tear," *New York Times*, March 4, 1951.

1028   Ray Simmons, "Line Fumbling Mars New Play At Showcase," *Chicago Tribune*, December 31, 1953.

1029   Review of *Author Meets The Critics*, *Variety*, January 20, 1954.

1030   "Ben-Gurion Spurs Demand Upon U.S.," *New York Times*, March 1, 1956.

1031   Ann V. Masters, "Ruth Chatterton Steps Again Before the Footlights," *Bridgeport Post*, August 21, 1955.

1032   Ruth Chatterton, *The Pride of the Peacock*, Doubleday and Co., c. 1954, pg 53.

1033   Ruth Chatterton, *The Pride of the Peacock*, Doubleday and Co., c. 1954, pg 122.

1034   George Freedley, review of *The Pride of the Peacock*, *Kirkus Reviews*, June 15, 1954.

1035   Edmund Fuller, "Mature and Subtle," *Chicago Daily Tribune*, August 22, 1954.

1036   Charlotte Capers, "Grandma Takes Over," *New York Times*, August 22, 1954.

1037   Ruth Chatterton, *The Pride of the Peacock*, Doubleday and Co., c. 1954, pg 314.

1038   Carlos Castaneda, *Journey to Ixtlan*, Simon & Schuster, c. 1972, pg 184.

1039   Harry Hansen, "The Personalities of Authors, and the Dynamic Ruth Chatterton," *Chicago Daily Tribune*, August 22, 1954.

1040   Cyrus Durgin, "Actress Ruth Chatterton May Soon Be Known as an Author," *Boston Globe*, August 1, 1948.

1041   Milton R. Bass, "The Lively Arts," *Berkshire Eagle*, August 30, 1956.

1042   Ann V. Masters, "Ruth Chatterton Steps Again Before the Footlights," *Bridgeport Post*, August 21, 1955.

1043   Robert A. Schanke, *Shattered Applause: the Lives of Eva Le Gallienne*, SIU Press, c. 2010, pg 195

1044   Alexis Greene, *Lucille Lortel: The Queen of Off Broadway*, Hal Leonard Corp., c. 2004, pg 127.

1045   Rita Hassan, review of *Sign of Winter*, *Show Business* (c. 1955).

1046   Ira Bilowit, review of *Sign of Winter*, *Show Business* (c. 1955).

1047   Edward P. Halline, "*The Chalk Garden* Intriguing at Pabst," *Milwaukee Sentinel*, November 27, 1956.

1048   "Ruth Chatterton Ill; Withdraws From Play Cast," *Janesville Daily Gazette*, November 30, 1956.

1049   Sam Zolotow, "Ruling for Ruth Chatterton," *New York Times*, October 16, 1957.

1050   "Actress Opens Club Season," *Billings Gazette*, September 29, 1956.

1051   Don Whittinghill, "Star Stresses Theater's Role," *Times Picayune*, October 9, 1956.

1052   "Knife & Fork Season to Open," *Idaho State Journal*, September 11, 1956.

1053   Grace Proven, "Living Theater Still Full of Life," *Pittsburg Press*, January 24, 1956.

1054   "Knife, Fork Club Will Hear Star," *Spokane Daily Chronicle*, September 20, 1956.

1055   "Nixon Sees Low Tactics," *Oregonian*, September 21, 1956.

1056   Actress Assails New Road Plan," *Bridgeport Post*, May 17, 1957.

1057   Fred Russell, review of *The Reluctant Debutante*, *The Bridgeport Post*, July 9, 1957.

1058   Fred Russell, review of *The Reluctant Debutante*, *The Bridgeport Post*, July 9, 1957.

1059   Walt Witcover, *My Road, Less Traveled: Becoming an Actor, Director, a Teacher*, Xlibris, c. 2011, pg 238.

1060   Kathryn Loring, "Her Novel's the Star Nowadays in Life of Ruth Chatterton," *Chicago Daily Tribune*, August 11, 1957.

1061   Walt Witcover, *My Road, Less Traveled: Becoming an Actor, Director, a Teacher*, Xlibris, c. 2011, pg 240.

1961. Ruth holding court in her Redding home. Here with Albert Hubbell and his wife Miriam (Ruth's private collection–courtesy of Brenda Holman).

17

La Bonne Chance...
et L'Adieu

I n the 1950s, Chatterton had pitched in without reserve to try and elect presidential candidate Adlai Stevenson. Although he lost to Eisenhower, Ruth found solace in her belief that the written page was a persuasive tool in making cultural change. She enjoyed releasing political feelings in her novels. In the fall of 1960, John F. Kennedy, whom Chatterton had known since he was fifteen, was elected to the Oval Office. By that time, Ruth's friends thought her less driven by causes. Literally speaking, she had made her point. Upon completing her fourth novel, *The Southern Wild*, Ruth began a fifth, emphasizing that it would be strictly a novel with no agenda. She continued to accept a stage role or two each year, but focused on writing and her pet poodles. Her financial extravagance and surmounting debt, often resulting from her own generosity, remained Ruth's modus operandi. After all, she had her relationship with Barry, her friendships, her talent, and... her luck.

The Southern Wild was released in June 1958 by Doubleday. It concerned the Merediths, a decidedly arrogant family steeped in the traditions of the Old South. They were being confronted by a young generation of whites and blacks who had come to the realization that times had changed. The story begins with the funeral of Jason Meredith, who had helped torture and drown a black student enrolled in an all-white college. When police finally make the effort to investigate, Jason is convinced they wouldn't shoot a white boy. He was wrong—dead wrong. The chasm between the two races—the immensity of it—was shifting. Chatterton takes head-on the multiple layers of tradition, heritage, religious myth, and political stagnation—blacks who are allowed to pray, but not vote. And, despite introducing eighty-eight characters in the course of thirty-nine chapters, she keeps the momentum of her story alive and readable. One of Chatterton's younger characters, a black politician from the north, makes the observation: "All Americans are in a hurry, and it's easier for them to accept the status quo than to do something about it."[1062] Chatterton, as the exception in this equation, attempts to create a ripple in the collective consciousness. As an author, she focused on action that was appropriate for the whole, not a select few.

A critic for *The Bridgeport Post* found the book "unforgettable… a passionate story of a tradition-bound world that slowly, but surely, is getting in step with the rest of the universe."[1063] The realization that people are people regardless of skin color or religious heritage was being put "into practice, thanks in part… to Miss Chatterton." Marjorie B. Snyder for the *Chicago Daily News* called Chatterton a "skilled novelist" and found *The Southern Wild* a "strong story of love and hate and violence… that advances by explosions." "With extraordinary vividness," said Snyder, "Miss Chatterton has created some remarkable characters. It's an awe-full lot of book that ends with hope for the future."[1064]

At the time of the book's release, the shocking events of Little Rock, Arkansas, loomed in every state below the Mason Dixon line. Shortly before Ruth submitted her final manuscript, President Eisenhower called the U.S. Army to protect nine African-American students who had en-rolled in the racially segregated Little Rock Central High. This was after the Governor of the state, Orval Faubus, sided with the segregationists. The KKK eventually put out a $10,000 reward for anyone who would injure the black students, who were already being subjected to physical and verbal abuse. One girl, Melba Pattillo, was locked in a bathroom stall while white students tried to set her on fire.[1065] The newspapers down South were, needless to say, less than enthusiastic about Chatterton's latest novel. *The Greensboro Record* (North Carolina) called the book "unrealistic... sprinkled with wild misconceptions." "Miss Chatterton does not know the South," said reviewer Claire Russell Cheney. "Anyone who has lived in the south for any length of time knows that in many cases a real affection exists between the two races."[1066] *The Miami News'* review claimed that *The Southern Wild* was "certainly enough to drive any Southerner wild." "Miss Chatterton," it cautioned, "specializes in writ-ing books with a message, but the message in this book... is laid on with such a heavy hand it is apt to sicken the average reader. It certainly isn't dull [and] will probably sell like hotcakes."[1067] *The Galveston Daily News* railed that Chatterton's book was "heavily slanted" in favor of integration and "unduly harsh" on the attitudes and traditions of the Old South. The review also criticized Chatterton's portrayal of southern "peace officers," saying it was "grossly unfair and unrealistic." In truth, the book was about as "unrealistic" as the steady stream of "live" TV newscasts showing the brutal attacks on blacks by white southern "peace officers."

During her book promotion for *The Southern Wild*, Ruth often con-cluded her "talks" by singing a spiritual that she felt reflected the book's theme as well as the African-American experience of struggle, forbear-ance, and hope. Juliette Benton, a reputed lecturer on literature and drama, arranged for one of Ruth's appearances and aptly summed up

Chatterton as "a vital woman with deep humanitarian interests which transcended all faiths and nationalities."[1068]

⚜

In an August 1958 interview with Associated Press correspondent Cynthia Lowry, Ruth waxed enthusiastic about writing. "It is hard work but satisfying," she said. "After all, it seems to me that the training of an actor is ideal for a writer. Acting stimulates the imagination, sharpens the ear to catch accents and ways of speech—and we are disciplined to emphasize dramatic moments."[1069] Ruth proved her point once again during her seventh revival of *The Little Foxes*. The Valley Playhouse in Chagrin Falls, Ohio, hosted a two-week stay for the Hellman play. Ruth stated that she was "growing mellow" after being considered a "devastatingly candid hot-head most of her life."[1070] "I'm no longer stage-struck although I can't seem to escape from the theater," she declared. Even so, Ruth found it difficult to be pulled away from her home, Barry, and her three "lovable black monsters"—which is how she referred to her poodles. The lure of playing the power-hungry Regina Giddens still tempted her. She considered it one of the "most powerful, glamorous parts in the contemporary theater." She found many of Broadway's current plays "too vaguely symbolic, verbose and bloodless." "My literary agent," Ruth added proudly, "commented that all my books are too controversial for Hollywood filming."

Playing opposite the sixty-five-year-old actress was a twenty-two-year-old newcomer named Alan Alda. A critic for the *Plain Dealer* commented: "Gray hair, a limp and a wheelchair… fail to conceal the ruddy youthfulness of Alan Alda, who carries it off fairly plausibly."[1071] The review emphasized the "melodramatic wallop" of Chatterton's "sadistic glee" during the scene where Regina watches her husband die. "When

Miss Chatterton sweeps out in an elegant long velvet gown ... the revived drama takes on fresh fire. She assumes full command in a colorful, compelling portrayal."

⚜

As Ruth Chatterton graduated into the "Whatever Happened To..." category, gossip queen Hedda Hopper was as out of touch as her spies. "She hasn't acted for years," Hopper reported in an October 1958 column, which made brief mention of Chatterton's novels.[1072] Ruth's stage roles in 1959 included her second revival of *Jane* at Arizona's Sombrero Theatre in Phoenix. Chatterton also visited Towson State Teachers' College in New Jersey, where she lectured on drama and literature as well as starred in the Glen Players production of Giraudoux' *The Madwoman of Chaillot.* She was the second resident artist to visit the school under the auspices of the American National Theater Academy program—the first being Aline MacMahon, who was at Warner during Ruth's brief reign at the studio. After quietly moving into a guest room in the girls' dormitory, Ruth chatted, dined, and mingled with students before rehearsals began. Sporting a simple gray suit, white blouse, gold charm bracelet, and sunglasses, Ruth took a break one afternoon while hobbling around campus in her high-heeled brown alligator shoes. "I burst a blood vessel in my foot and it's exactly like walking on an egg," she explained to Muriel Dobbin, a freelance reporter—soon to become a White House correspondent. "I'm trying to rest it, and these shoes—I don't like clothes, never have. I would much rather wear comfortable flat heels and slacks." After a pause, Dobbin asked the star a few questions. Why was she on campus? "I enjoy doing this because I love being around young people," Ruth explained. "I like the atmosphere of college and especially I like ambitious youngsters."[1073] Ruth was enthused that her second novel, *The Betrayers*, was being adapted for television. She was still on the defensive, however, and stated sharply, "I did a lot of research for that book. I went to libraries, and I read the entire Constitution getting material for the trial scene." Ruth mused that she was always asked what she was going to write about when she ran out of causes. "My next book," she smiled, "is going to be strictly a novel—no cause."

Ruth explained to reporter Dobbin that when she did get upset, cooking was her new method of working out frustrations. "I go in the kitchen and concoct something exotic," Ruth laughed. When Dobbin asked who had remained friends from her Hollywood days, Ruth listed the late Ronald Colman, Bette Davis, Noel Coward, and William Powell. "People are so sad in Hollywood," Ruth added, "so dedicated to keeping their faces young and keeping them on the screen. When they go out for the evening they discuss the psychology of their last role and their next. The $10,000 a week set never mixes with the $5,000 a week set." Ruth stated that she hadn't done any television acting roles since *Hamlet*—that she disliked doing it. "It makes me nervous," she admitted. Ruth said she found life in Connecticut agreeable. She read a lot, watched dramatic shows on television, and sometimes entertained. She loved conversation. "I like people I *like* around me," she told Dobbin, "and I am a snob about intelligence." Which brought her to the subject of bees. "I read a book about bees," said Ruth, "and, you know they are as intelligent as dogs. I became so fascinated that I ended up keeping bees myself. They knew me and they let me put my hand in to get honey, but no one else. Of course there are always half a dozen bees with ugly dispositions… but that isn't bad, out of 5,000."[1074] Following ten days of rehearsing her role as Countess Aurelia, the eccentric *Madwoman of Chaillot*, Chatterton and her cast were ready for three nights of performances. While Chatterton no longer fought causes with her pen, her new stage persona took on corporate executives who schemed to dig up the streets of Paris strictly for profit… and oil.

⚜⚜⚜

In January 1960, Ruth aligned herself with author William Faulkner and national figures such as Dr. Martin Luther King and Eleanor Roosevelt in a group called "Friends of P.D. East"—a courageous white publisher/author who resided in the heart of Mississippi. A zealous and outspoken liberal, East ran a country newsletter, *The Petal Paper*, which was threatened with closure after he began lampooning the KKK and The White Citizen's Council.[1075] Through the efforts of people like Chatterton, he was able to continue writing and publish his autobiography, *The Magnolia Jungle*. In May, Ruth signed up for what was legally termed "Old-Age Insurance Benefits" under the Social Security Act of 1935: $106.70 a month.[1076] Undoubtedly, this "award" was but a mere pittance for a woman who lived well beyond her means.

Chatterton's final stage appearance was also in 1960. She signed on with Bucks County Playhouse in Pennsylvania for a two-week engagement of a new play titled *Happy Ending*. The story, by Nellise Child, was an amiable study of life at a boarding home for elders. Ruth's co-star was another vintage screen star, Conrad Nagel. Also on hand were Pert Kelton and, in a small role, organist Ethel Smith. During rehearsal on August 12, Ruth received word that Barry had suffered a heart attack. At midnight, she left to be with him at Danbury Hospital in Connecticut.[1077] While she missed the play's opening on August 15, she reported that Barry was doing much better. On August 17, Ruth said she was returning to the playhouse that day to resume her role.[1078] Her plans changed. Barry took a turn for the worse. Two days later, Thomson passed away following a second heart attack.[1079] He was fifty-two. Pennsylvania's *Daily Intelligencer* confirmed that actress Ruth Gregory would fill in for Chatterton for the remainder of the play's performances. On August 20, a private memorial service was conducted on Thomson's behalf at the Hull Funeral Home in Danbury.[1080] His parents were both deceased. Thomson was cremated and his burial at Beechwoods Cemetery in New Rochelle was postponed until the spring of 1961.

The day after Barry's funeral, Buck's County Playhouse director Michael Ellis telephoned Chatterton, asking if she would like to come back and finish the final week for *Happy Ending*. "I think that's a marvelous idea!" came her quick reply.[1081] Ruth piled her three large French poodles (Henry, Lisa, and Lili) into her Buick station wagon and drove to Pennsylvania. On Tuesday, August 23, she rehearsed all afternoon with the cast prior to the evening's performance. Ruth held her own during the performances, but there came a point where stage tears turned into real ones. Her role as Miss Manchester included a scene which paralleled Ruth's own unhappy experience losing Barry. She had difficulty controlling her emotions during her many curtain calls. During the Wednesday evening performance, she broke down completely.[1082] Ruth's final performance on Saturday evening, August 27, would be the last stage appearance of her career.

<hr />

Some acquaintances said that Barry's death hadn't discouraged Chatterton's drive. Theatre critic Ward Morehouse reported in October 1960 that the actress/novelist was working steadily on her fifth novel, looked "perfectly beautiful," and had "the energy of four devils."[1083] That same month, Chatterton received an award for her outstanding contribution and humanitarian effort on behalf of Israel. It was presented to her by Governor David Lawrence of Pennsylvania. The gala event was held October 31, 1960, in the ballroom of the Bellevue Stratford Hotel in Philadelphia. Wearing a simple gunmetal gray surge dress with a corsage modestly attached to her belt, Ruth appeared to be enjoying herself. One of the highlights in the early afternoon was the "surprise" appearance of Senator John F. Kennedy. Ruth gave rapt attention to his winning manner and "excellent campaigning" for the U.S. Presidency. Following a luncheon, Ruth was called upon to speak. She calmly took to the stand and graciously acknowledged her "Star of David" plaque award. "I don't deserve it," Ruth said, "but I will hold on to it, tightly. You have been my friends. You have helped me, and *I shall never fail you.*"[1084]

The winter of 1960-61 kept Chatterton mostly indoors and briefly snowbound. Her longtime friend, screenwriter Frances Marion, visited Redding and for several days the two huddled indoors while Ruth's French poodle gave birth to two pups.[1085] The papers that Ruth's cousin Brenda forwarded to this author contained the first chapter of a book, most likely Chatterton's fifth novel, titled *Entente Cordiale*. It begins in New York and the first scene takes place at café society's popular Colony restaurant on East 61st Street. Chatterton's experience as a beekeeper provided the proper simile for the opening line: "As usual, every table in the Colony was occupied that particular Friday, and the steady hum of female voices sounded like a beehive on the eve before a swarm." Chatterton's bee colony included a young heiress whose love life and bank account were being controlled from the grave by her dear departed grandfather. The chapter establishes that the beautiful granddaughter is caught between two men: a married English nobleman and an attractive red-headed detective who has been trailing her. The narrative flows with wit and personality. An element of intrigue and uncertainty compel the

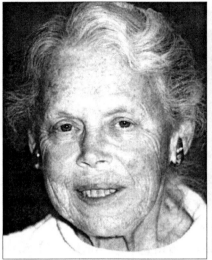

Ruth's favorite cousin–Olive Minuse Wehbring (1998).
Ruth's "firecracker" cousin Melba Moore holding Olive Minuse (c. 1906)
(Courtesy of Brenda Holman).

reader to immediately dive into the next chapter, which sadly, after sixty-two years, appears to have disappeared along with the rest of the book. For some reason, this first chapter was returned to Ruth for corrections by her literary agent, Margot Johnson. The postmark from New York was dated August 13, 1961. Johnson was quoted as saying that Ruth was still "in a fog" after the "terrible jolt" of losing Barry. She sensed that Ruth was unable to "snap out of it."[1086] Not an unusual plight after twenty years of living together.

Olive Wehbring-Ruth's favorite cousin

Olive Wehbring was a "chip off the old block" when it came to having the fortitude and ambition of her older cousin, Ruth Chatterton. Shortly after Olive passed away at the age of ninety-five, she was, in fact, honored by California Congresswoman Susan Davis in Washington, D.C. In January 2001, the Speaker of the House gave Davis five minutes to pay tribute to Olive's involvement as a political activist. In the 1950s, Olive, a reference librarian and mother of three children, served as President of the United Nations Association of Westchester County. After relocating to San Diego in 1970 with her husband Leon, a retired social worker, Olive served as President of the League of Women Voters. As an author, she wrote a guide to the city's structure and operation. In 2012, Olive's oldest son John mentioned his mother's admiration for her cousin Ruth and visiting her in Connecticut. "I knew that Ruth was well-known and in the movies," John told me. "When you're a kid you don't think much about it. If she had been a baseball player—*that* would have been different!"[1087] While John was unable to elaborate on his celebrity cousin, who wasn't Babe Ruth, his sister, Brenda Wehbring Holman, had plenty to say.

> I spent time with Ruth. She was my mother's cousin, but there were [twelve] years between them. When Ruth lived in Connecticut, we lived in White Plains. They began to see each other regularly. Ruth was very exotic to me—not really gorgeous, but magnetic. First of all, the voice that comes over in *Dodsworth* was very high, but in fact her voice was... much lower in pitch, very clear and very sharp. One time we were at dinner, and we began to talk about Mary Astor. I had read something... I was in my early twenties. Then Ruth said, "Well, you know... John Barrymore really took advantage of her sexually. He did—he raped her!" I remember thinking "Okay, I see."

For Brenda, cousin Ruth had upped the ante in the art of dinner conversation. When I asked Astor's daughter, Marylyn Roh, if her mother had ever mentioned her feelings for "Jack" Barrymore, she answered, "Oh, my yes! She and Jack were a duo. He coached her in speech (and other things!). He wanted her to marry him. I wonder what things would have been like—would they have both been helpless alcoholics? He was pathetic at the end."[1088] In her memoirs, Astor admitted that Barrymore kept trying to get the seventeen-year-old actress alone and away from her parents—to tutor her. He succeeded. She found the forty-one-year-old Barrymore to be a gentle lover.[1089] In 1941, Astor had stated, "One of my best and closest friends next to Bette [Davis] is Ruth Chatterton."[1090] Astor, who would become the author of five novels herself, also paid homage to Ruth in her sensational 1959 bestseller, *My Story: An Autobiography.*

Brenda Holman's recollections underscored her cousin Ruth's generosity.

> Ruth was interested in people with brains—and, very much in the moment. My mother just loved Ruth to death—and, bright they were. Ruth was very generous. One summer we stayed with her at Lake Sunapee. Ruth had rented the Vanderbilt place, horses, boats and all. I remember she was a very good cook. And, hostess. We would visit her home and have lobster salad made from scratch. She'd go out and buy fifteen lobsters and make stuff. She had beautiful silverware. The table setting was always perfect. The car was older, but the table setting was perfect. We always ate with linens—my mother, Ruth and I, and my little children running around. I wish my mother were alive. I wish I could channel her. I'm sure you didn't get much from my brother, John. It's a shame that people don't talk about these things. My mother was sure full of stories.[1091]

Olive and her daughter Brenda (c. 1990) (courtesy of Brenda Holman).

By 1961, Ruth had no illusions about returning to the stage. If the "show must go on" for Ruth Chatterton, it remained on home turf. Friends just assumed that Ruth wouldn't leave her writing or her poodles. That fall, Ruth was pleasantly surprised when asked to join the cast of *A Passage to India*, but politely refused. The play, based on the E.M. Forster novel, would debut on Broadway that winter.[1092] Gladys Cooper took the role intended for Chatterton. While completing her fifth novel, Ruth took a break to contribute an excellent short story for the Alfred Hitchcock anthology *Alfred Hitchcock Presents: Stories For Late At Night*, which was released in August.

Hitchcock introduced the Random House publication by asking, "What is more delightful than a domestic crime, when it is executed with subtlety and imagination?" Chatterton's contribution, *Lady's Man*, detailed an experience at Noel Coward's English country home, Goldenhurst. During her guest stay, she was given the only ground floor bedroom. Late one evening, a voice called out, "Ruth!" The door swung open... she only saw blackness and heard the sound of footsteps... a definite male presence. In sheer terror, she closed her eyes. She awoke the next morning, deciding to dismiss what had occurred. However, during a conversation with Coward and another female guest, she learns the real truth. "What's most striking about the story," said publisher/editor Levi Stahl in 2009, "is that, rather than a piece of fiction crafted to thrill the readers of Hitchcock… *Lady's Man* appears to be a straight-up ghost story."[1093]

In 1961, Ruth also hosted an episode of *Memoirs of the Movies*—an oral history project sponsored by Columbia University. Her guests included: Adolph Zukor (former President of Paramount Pictures), Broncho Billy Anderson, Paul Newman, Joanne Woodward, producer Jerry Wald, Sessue Hayakawa, Janet Gaynor, Roddy McDowell, Zachary Scott, Jack Lemmon, and Ruth's old friend, scenarist Ben Hecht. Chatterton's narration ties together numerous interviews recorded in 1959. The films covered were noted for rising above trite formula and cliché. Roddy McDowell talked about John Ford's *How Green Was My Valley*; Joanne Woodward commented about *The Three Faces of Eve*, a film shot in straight continuity; in *The Left Handed Gun*, Paul Newman's thoughtful approach in playing Billy the Kid was explored—how the actor allowed the young outlaw to accept his own doom and thereby "recognize things he had never really seen before—the sunsets, the colors and wheat fields"; Jack Lemmon offered his breathless enthusiasm for Billy Wilder's *Some Like It Hot*; Sessue Hayakawa told of his hesitancy in accepting Sam Spiegle's offer to play in *Bridge of the River Kwai*; and Ben Hecht revealed the chaos surrounding his assignment for writing scenes for *Gone With the Wind*. The clarity of Chatterton's familiar voice, registering a notch lower, was the perfect component to tie together her guests' remarks. "To me," Chatterton concluded, "memories of the movies are part of my life, and will always have a mixture of frustration and fascination."[1094]

Chatterton's final book review for *The New York Times* was *The Art of Ruth Draper* by Morton Zabel. She found this 1960 publication about the recently deceased actress a "miserable failure." "Miss Draper's family tree has been carefully authenticated," scoffed Chatterton. "[Zabel] reiterates ad infinitum... his admiration and awe of her. When I closed the book, I knew no more about the woman who was Ruth Draper than I did when I opened it."[1095] In 1930, Chatterton admitted that she had saved no clippings from her own career. She had made it clear that she "wanted to be spared" from being the kind of actress "who continually lives in the 'past.'"[1096] Ruth wasn't the type to dwell on old stories that obscured her presence. The moment at hand is what counted. She felt that writing a novel was "more elastic" than biography. "I don't think actresses and actors are interesting," she admitted in 1955. "They only know one thing."[1097]

A longtime fan did write a biography on Chatterton, but it was never published. Ruth Moesel, who passed away in 1982, was a Pennsylvania preschool teacher who had amassed a collection of 32 Chatterton scrapbooks. Moesel met Chatterton several times. She had seen every play Ruth appeared in from 1939-1960. In 1962, Moesel wrote a letter to the editor of the *New York Times Book Review* in pursuit of information on Chatterton's personal life. She wrote Chatterton's friends and acquaintances. While most responded, there was a hint of reservation in many of their remarks. Guthrie McClintic offered Moesel an abrupt, "I would say I knew her very well, but I do not think she lends herself to 'anecdotes.'" Helen Hayes, "I have no anecdotes to pass on to you." Brenda Forbes, "I'm afraid there is nothing more that I can tell you... that you do not know already." A letter from Ruth's physician, Dr. Eugene Beck, was plainspoken. "I was very surprised to hear from you. I don't see how I could add anything more than we have discussed on a number of phone conversations. I have no reason to belabor this any longer, since we both lost a friend."[1098] Some of the respondents Moesel heard from simply expressed their deep affection for the actress. Katharine Cornell called Ruth "a very gallant woman [who] didn't know the meaning of 'defeat' or 'self-pity.'" Pollster pioneer and close neighbor Elmo Roper was "impressed" that Chatterton "wanted to be very much more than an actress. She wanted to be a fully participating citizen in what to her was the greatest of all dramas—life, as it is lived daily, in a democracy." Veteran stage actress Peggy Wood's comment raises lots of questions. "I felt [Ruth] was given a very unfair deal in the matter of her rights of ownership in the Henry Miller Theatre."[1099]

Moesel's draft of Chatterton's story finally made the rounds in the late 1960s and early 70s. Author Mary Cantwell recalled that she read Moesel's manuscript no less than three times for three different New York publishers. "There could not have been a publisher's reader in the city who had not seen it once," said Cantwell.[1100] In 1973, it was mentioned that Moesel, a former "personal acquaintance" of Chatterton, was still revising her manuscript.[1101] Cantwell gave no specifics as to why Moesel's effort ran up against numerous rejections. If anything, Moesel was persistent. She even made the 1974-75 edition of Who's Who of American Women for her Chatterton collection. Brenda Holman recalled something that might provide a further clue to the Moesel story. "My mother had nothing but scorn for a woman whom she called 'the fan,'" said Brenda. "She lurked in the background of Ruth's life at the end and bought Ruth's fur coat at the auction of her belongings."[1102] During Moesel's visit, she went so far as to go into Chatterton's bedroom and take a snapshot of the deceased star's canopy bed.[1103]

To all appearances, Ruth was cheerful to the end and busy. She also enjoyed relaxing with friends and playing countless games of bridge with her local "gang." She had not been to a doctor, nor had she needed one in the last twelve years. Brenda Holman said that Ruth's mind remained sharp. In the fall of 1961, Ruth had a series of small strokes. For a while, she was under a nurse's care, but then seemed to be on the road to recovery. On Friday, November 17, 1961, Chatterton was putting finishing touches on her fifth novel when she suffered a cerebral hemorrhage. She was home alone when it occurred. On Tuesday, her neighbor, Mrs. Thew Wright, became concerned when Ruth didn't answer the phone and went over to her house. She found Ruth lying on the floor of the TV room where she did her writing. She was unconscious. The lights were still on, likewise the TV. Untouched snacks were about and the telephone receiver askew.[1104] Mrs. Wright called Ruth's physician, who had Ruth rushed to Norwalk Hospital. Chatterton passed away that Friday, November 24, without regaining consciousness."[1105] One of Ruth's cousins saw her in the oxygen tent that last day and remarked afterward, "She looked about 25 years old."[1106] Most likely, this would have been Olive Wehbring or her younger sister, Elva Minuse. Ruth's remains were taken to a funeral parlor in Danbury, where she was cremated.

Ironically, on the day Ruth died, her friend Amelia Earhart also made headlines. Many newspapers featured front page stories about the two women. Chatterton was praised for her reputable stage and film career, her successful turn as an author and interest in aviation. The mystery surrounding Earhart's disappearance was renewed when bone fragments were found on the island of Saipan. Natives had told of a white woman and man that were held captive by the Japanese in July 1937. Both had died in captivity. After an official investigation, however, the remains proved valueless. The Earhart mystery remained intact.[1107]

. Brian Aherne made mention that he and his wife visited Ruth shortly before she died. He had never forgotten her. "She had brought aviation into my life," he said, "and this was to prove a great blessing to me."[1108] Ruth's bar was surrounded with photos of friends she had lavishly entertained in Beverly Hills. The actor asked Ruth if she ever heard from any of them. She replied, "No," and went on to say that none of them had sent a word backstage when she played in Los Angeles some years before. Aherne, with a dash of creative license, went on to say that Chatterton "was alone with her four dogs when she died, and her body lay for three days on the floor, watched by her dogs and surrounded by the mute faces of her former friends."

Ruth's old nemesis, Dorothy Kilgallen, in her year-end roundup of newsworthy events, cattily remarked, "Ruth Chatterton, once a great name in the movies, died a lonely death in obscurity."[1109] Kilgallen ignored the tributes paid to Ruth by more than 70 friends and family members who gathered in her memory shortly after her death. Ethel Beckwith for the *Bridgeport Sunday Herald* did an impressive job of capturing the spirit of the occasion, which was held at Ruth's home on Sunday, November 26, 1961.

> The curtain went down most quietly for Ruth Chatterton, but the script was hers. The actress, who… lived in Redding, often said, "Funerals are barbarous. When I die I don't want an audience." And—there was none. From the moment she died at Norwalk Hospital, her body remained unseen. Two days later an audience came to the house on Sanfordtown Road. The star was absent but about 75 other notables were there including Katharine Cornell, Frances Starr, and Lois Wilson. Noel Coward cabled his regrets from London. They were received by

women cousins of Miss Chatterton. Carefully the relatives explained that this was not to be a service. Then the guests sat down to hear a tribute delivered by Professor Fowler Harper who teaches international relations at Yale. The professor's talk was all. But as audiences do, this one departed discussing the theme. They wondered "how Ruth made out, really."[1110]

Harper mentioned the "vigorous contributions" that Chatterton had given the world, referring to her as "a rebel in this society which values diplomacy highly."[1111] At the time, he was fighting vigorously for the fundamental "right of privacy"—Connecticut was prohibiting the use of contraceptives. In a landmark Supreme Court ruling, the law was overturned, thanks to Harper. Beckwith mentioned no other speakers, but Brenda Holman recalled, "Katharine Cornell, *I know*, spoke about Ruth. And, a man and his wife, it may have been Ruth's vet, spoke lovingly and emotionally about her. The couple was very young, and knew nothing of her background."[1112] To the vet and his wife, Ruth was simply the wonderful lady with the black poodles.

The "women cousins" who hosted the event were Olive, her sister Elva, and Melba Lugar Moore. Moore, a former Corporal in the Women's Army Corps (WAC), lived in Germany. Brenda Holman thought Melba to be a "real corker." "Melba was really overbearing, garish," recalled Brenda. "I could never understand when my mother called her the 'life of the party.' I guess she and Ruth kicked up their heels. Melba hung around with a lot of gay men. She left $50,000 to her cats."[1113] Ruth's cousin, Elva Minuse, was devoted to scientific research. As Associate Professor of Epidemiology, Elva taught at University of Michigan's School of Public Health. Her research and experience with the influenza viruses was legendary. In 1945, she had teamed with Jonas Salk, who was famous for developing the first polio vaccine in 1955. "We always joked that Elva taught Jonas Salk everything he knew," recalled Brenda.[1114]

Others in attendance at the gathering, aside from neighbors, were Ruth's physician, Dr. O'Neill, her godchild, Reggie Venable (son of Fay Bainter), playwright Nancy Hamilton (previously the lover of Ralph Forbes' sister Brenda, now companion to Katharine Cornell), George Batson (who had penned Ruth's *Treat Her Gently*), Elmo Roper, Beatrice Ames Stewart, Mr. and Mrs. Albert Hubbell, and Jane Gray, who had been Ruth's secretary in Hollywood. Beckwith went on to say that some neighbors felt that Ruth's "cheerful outlook was good acting"— that she "was up against it." And she was financially. When I talked with Brenda Holman, she readily admitted, "Ruth did not own her home. The man who owned that house let her live there rent free. She had all those French Poodles—everyone just loved them—and, she owed the vet a lot of money. The vet just adored her. When he came to the funeral he told us, 'Never mind'—but not everybody did that." At the time of her death, Ruth was considering a move to a smaller, more economical place. Her current lease, in theory, was set at $175 per month.[1115]

<hr />

Brenda stayed at Ruth's colonial home after the gathering. She detailed an amusing story about Ruth's close friend, Albert Hubbell, who was a cover illustrator for *The New Yorker*. Ruth had dedicated her book, *The Southern Wild*, to Albert and his wife Marion.

> I stayed in the house after Ruth died ... because there was silver, and some jewelry and my mother didn't want the house empty. Hubbell came over one day and there were some porcelain figures on the mantle. He said, "See those

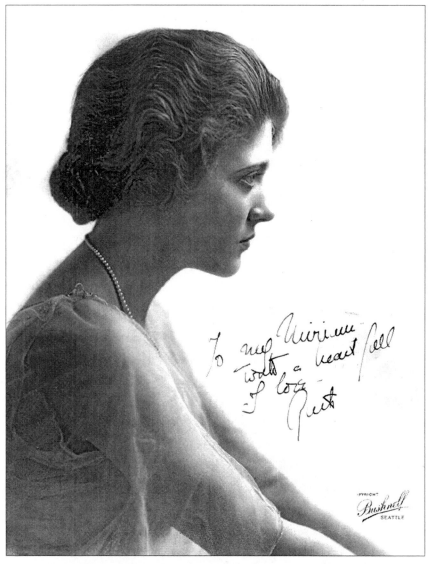

1917 photo that Ruth sent to her Aunt Miriam, Olive's mother. "To My Miriam-with a heart full of love-Ruth" (courtesy of Brenda Holman).

two figurines? Ruth always promised them to me." Well, he was like sixty-five and I was in my twenties. What did I know? I knew that they were friends. Well, he wasn't a robber or anything. So, he took them. Several months later when we had to auction off her things, my mother said "Where are those figurines?" I said "Albert Hubbell took them." She said, "Oh my God! They were worth thousands." And he had them. I did not do my job well. They were trying to pay off her debts.[1116]

Ruth's ashes were laid to rest in the Lugar Mausoleum at Beechwoods Cemetery in New Rochelle on January 5, 1962. Her furnishings were auctioned off at her home on May 26. The day prior, there was an exhibit and auction of her collection of more than 1,600 books. O. Rundle Gilbert, who specialized in Americana of the 19th and early 20th centuries, was auctioneer.[1117] Aside from antique and modern Italian furniture, there was an ebony Steinway grand piano and a mahogany J. Broadwood spinet. As Brenda mentioned, there was also silver and china—a 14 karat gold dresser set, portraits, and paintings as well as Ruth's 1959 Buick sedan. "My mother took the colonial-style 4-poster bed which she used

R.P. Lugar Mausoleum at Beechwoods Cemetary (New Rochelle). Though her ashes remain in the family crypt, it is Ruth's essence that continues to propel hearts and minds though her writing and screen roles.

until the day she died in 2000," said Brenda. It wasn't until 1963 that the Redding Probate Court appointed three commissioners to decide upon claims against the estate of Ruth Chatterton Thomson. It was reputed as being "hopelessly insolvent."[1118] Chatterton must have been chuckling in her grave and quoting Oscar Wilde: "Anyone who lives within their means suffers from a lack of imagination."[1119]

In a 1955 interview, Ruth reflected back to 1912. It was opening night for *The Rainbow* when that electric moment came, her first entrance. She stepped onto the empty stage. She stood there silently, before an audience that had never seen her—when suddenly, an ovation rocked the theater. Their reaction had always given her pause. "I've never understood it," pondered Ruth. "I hadn't done a thing. Some magnetic quality apparently reached the audience. I was lucky."[1120]

Endnotes

1062   Ruth Chatterton, *The Southern Wild*, Doubleday, c. 1958, pg 29.

1063   Taylor F. Glenn, "Books and Authors," *Bridgeport Post*, June 22, 1958.

1064   Marjorie B. Snyder, "Witch's Brew of Excitement in the South," *Chicago Daily Tribune*, June 22, 1958.

1065   Melba Pattillo Beals, *Warriors Don't Cry*, Simon & Schuster, c. 2007, pg 120 (After Governor Faubus closed Little Rock's high school the following year, Melba, with the help of the NAACP, transferred to Montgomery High School in Santa Rosa, California, where she completed her senior year).

1066   Claire Russell Cheney, "The Literary Lantern," *Greensboro Record*, June 21, 1958.

1067   Jack Roberts, "Message Is Heavy In Novel of South," *Miami News*, June 22, 1958.

1068   Comment taken from the Ruth Moesel manuscript held at the New York Public Library at Lincoln Center (Benton was in attendance for Chatterton's book talk at the Larchmont Women's Club (New York)).

1069   Cynthia Lowry, "Ruth Chatterton, Once A Bright Star, In Second Career As Serious Writer," *The Register-News* (IL), August 27, 1958.

1070   Glenn C. Pullen, "Ruth Chatterton Can't Quit Stage," *Plain Dealer*, July 27, 1958.

1071   Glenn C. Pullen, "Play is Hit for Ruth Chatterton," *Plain Dealer*, July 23, 1958.

1072   Hedda Hopper, "Where Did Stars Go?" *Times Picayune*, October 16, 1958.

1073   Muriel Dobbin, "A Star Shines On Towson," *The Sun*, October 25, 1959.

1074   Muriel Dobbin, "A Star Shines On Towson," *The Sun*, October 25, 1959.

1075   "National Figures Appeal for Funds for P.D. East," *Los Angeles Tribune*, January 21, 1960.

1076   "Certificate of Social Insurance Award" Claim Number 143-12-4067A (Among the papers that Ruth's cousin Brenda Holman forwarded the author).

1077   "Ruth Chatterton Goes to Stricken Husband," *Trenton Evening Times*, August 16, 1960.

1078   "Redding-Georgetown," *Wilton Bulletin*, August 17, 1960.

1079   "Barry Thomson, Stage, TV Actor," *Springfield Union*, August 20, 1960.

1080 "Barry Thomson Dies in Danbury," *Wilton Bulletin*, August 24, 1960.

1081 Ruth Moesel manuscript held at the New York Public Library at Lincoln Center (page 326).

1082 Ruth Moesel manuscript held at the New York Public Library at Lincoln Center (page 327).

1083 Ward Morehouse, "Broadway After Dark," *Long Island Star Journal*, October 10, 1960.

1084 Ruth Moesel manuscript held at the New York Public Library at Lincoln Center (page 328).

1085 Hedda Hopper, "Looking Over Hollywood," *Springfield Union*, February 9, 1961.

1086 Ruth Moesel manuscript held at the New York Public Library at Lincoln Center (page 329).

1087 John Lugar Wehbring, phone conversation, January 9, 2012.

1088 Marylyn Roh, email dated April 21, 2012.

1089 Mary Astor, *Mary Astor My Story*, Doubleday, c. 1959, pg 75.

1090 Dorothy Manners column, *Los Angeles Examiner*, April 13, 1941.

1091 Brenda Wehbring Holman, phone conversation, January 16, 2012.

1092 Ethel Beckwith, "Famed Ruth Chatterton Gets Her Last Wish: 'No Barbarous Funeral Rites,'" *Sunday Herald*, December 3, 1961.

1093 Levi Stahl, Ivebeenreadinglately (Blog), February 27, 2009.

1094 Ruth Chatterton, *Memoirs of the Movies*, WNYC Radio, c. 1961 (available from Archival Television Audio, Inc. (New York).

1095 Ruth Chatterton, "A Woman Of Parts," *New York Times*, May 29, 1960.

1096 Radie Harris, "Star Gazing," *Chester Times*, October 23, 1930.

1097 Ann V. Masters, "Ruth Chatterton Steps Again Before the Footlights," *Bridgeport Post*, August 21, 1955.

1098 Eugene C. Beck, letter to Ruth Moesel, February 24, 1962 (Ruth Moesel collection held at the New York Public Library at Lincoln Center).

1099 All excerpts from these letters were taken from the Ruth Moesel manuscript held at the New York Public Library at Lincoln Center.

1100 Mary Cantwell, *Manhattan, When I Was Young*, Houghton, Mifflin, Harcourt, c. 1995, pg 125.

1101 "Members in the News," *Broadside*, Summer 1973.

1102 Brenda Wehbring Holman, email, November 8, 2012.

1103 Photo captioned, "Bedroom of actress Ruth Chatterton–W. Redding, Conn. (Sun.) Dec. 3, 1961. Photo by: (Miss) Ruth L. Moesel, 961 Wheeler Ave., Scranton 10, Pa. (among papers forwarded to author by Brenda Wehbring Holman)

1104 Ruth Moesel manuscript held at the New York Public Library at Lincoln Center (page 332).

1105 "Ruth Chatterton's Friends Gather In Her Memory," *Wilton Bulletin*, November 29, 1961.

1106 Ethel Beckwith, "Famed Ruth Chatterton Gets Her Last Wish: 'No Barbarous Funeral Rites,'" *Sunday Herald*, December 3, 1961.

1107 "Amelia Earhart Mystery Is Revived By Bone Fragments," *The Daily News* (PA) November 25, 1961 ("Ruth Chatterton, Actress Of Yesteryear, Dies," was also on the front page).

1108 Brian Aherne, *A Proper Job*, Houghton-Mifflin, c. 1969, pg 232.

1109 Dorothy Kilgallen, "1961, Year of Broken Hearts, Bomb Shelters," *Hamilton Daily News Journal*, January 2, 1962.

1110 Ethel Beckwith, "Famed Ruth Chatterton Gets Her Last Wish: 'No Barbarous Funeral Rites,'" *Sunday Herald*, December 3, 1961.

1111 "Friends Pay Tribute to Ruth Chatterton," *Bridgeport Post*, November 27, 1961.

1112 Brenda Wehbring Holman, phone conversation, October 22, 2012.

1113 Brenda Wehbring Holman, phone conversation, February 28, 2012.

1114 Brenda Wehbring Holman, phone conversation, October 22, 2012.

1115 Lease between Bradley Murray (Lessor) and Ruth Chatterton, signed August 1, 1961, specified $175 "per month on the 1st day of each and every month commencing July 1, 1961" (Document sent to author by Brenda Holman).

1116 Brenda Wehbring Holman, phone conversation, January 16, 2012.

1117 "Sale Offers Items of Late Actress," *Bridgeport Post*, May 19, 1962.

1118 "Ruth Chatterton's Estate Insolvent," *Wilton Bulletin*, January 9, 1963.

1119 Michael Powell, *The Mammoth Book of Great British Humor*, Running Press, c. 2010, pg 347.

1120 Ann V. Masters, "Ruth Chatterton Steps Again Before the Footlights," *Bridgeport Post*, August 21, 1955.

AFTERTHOUGHT –
from Garson Kanin

As far as Garson Kanin was concerned, Ruth had the innate ability to convince her listener about anything. In his frequently hilarious novel about backstage show biz, *Smash* (1980), one of Kanin's characters, Larry, an assistant stage manager, noticed during a rehearsal that Ruth pronounced the word "scenario" as "shenario." Kanin wrote:

> It was so positive, so confident, so convincingly correct, that no one questioned it. The rest of the company began saying it that way. So did I, until about a year later, a brilliant girl I had—a poet—said to me, "Why are you saying that word in such an outré fashion?" And we looked it up in twelve different dictionaries, and of course, there *is* no such pronunciation. That Ruth Chatterton![1121]

Endnotes
1121 Garson Kanin, *Smash*, Viking, c. 1980, pg 490.

ACKNOWLEDGEMENTS

"Silent gratitude isn't very much use to anyone," said Gertrude Stein.[1122] Ruth Chatterton was quick to point out those who nurtured her multiple careers: Julia Dean, Henry Miller, Myron Selznick, Emil Jannings, pilot/instructor Bob Blair, literary agent Margot Johnson, Yale professor Fowler Harper, among others. This biography, like Ruth's career, was nurtured along by a number of people—a collective effort. Most importantly, I would like to express my gratitude to Brenda Holman. Brenda is the daughter of Ruth's favorite cousin, Olive Minuse Wehbring. Brenda stayed in Ruth's home after she passed away, looking after things and pondering the life and career of her famous first cousin once removed. Fifty years later, Brenda enthusiastically shared her memories with me. This was after I tracked her down using, as a start, the details provided in a 1903 *New York Times* article. Ruth was mentioned as being maid of honor at the wedding of her aunt Miriam (Olive's mother). Fortunately, Olive's own accomplishments made it possible for me to locate her children, including Brenda. If anyone has a lasting connection to Ruth Chatterton, it is Brenda. Ruth's ashes reside in the Lugar Mausoleum in New Rochelle, New York. "I have the only key," says Brenda. "My son, Christopher Chatterton Holman has been to visit it with me."[1123]

Suzanne Brent, daughter of George Brent, Ruth's second husband, offered a brief glimpse into what she referred to as her father's "mysterious life." She and her brother Barry are currently working on a project about their famous father. Locating co-stars of Ruth Chatterton proved challenging. I was hoping that the late John Kerr would have something to share. Both Kerr's father Geoffrey and grandfather Frederick had worked with Ruth in films. John himself had played her son on stage in a 1940 revival of *Tomorrow and Tomorrow*. In April 2012, Kerr wrote back to me, "I've been ill for a long time and no longer reply…"[1124] Recalling something from seventy-two years ago can prove challenging. During the 1950s, John often pointed out that it was Ruth who suggested him to Guthrie McClintic for *Bernadine*, the play that set his career in motion. I had also sent a letter to Christopher Plummer, who had an uncanny knack of resurrecting Ruth Chatterton in the pages of his memoirs. Plummer praised Chatterton for being the real catalyst behind his career. Although I didn't hear back from him, Plummer's delightful comments concerning Ruth are peppered throughout a couple of chapters in this biography.

Also typical was the response of Linc Sparks, who had posed for a news photo with Chatterton when she guest starred in *The Madwoman of Chaillot*—a student production at Towson State Teachers College in 1959. "I am sorry to disappoint you," Sparks wrote to me, "I really have no specific recollection of working with Miss Chatterton."[1125] Fifty-three years had passed, and *Madwoman…* was one of the last stage appearances in which Chatterton appeared. Director Arthur Hiller, who directed the 1956 teleplay of Chatterton's novel *Homeward Borne*, informed me that he never got to meet Ruth during the production and apologized for not being able to help.[1126] Others who didn't respond to my queries were: Patricia Barry (who worked with Ruth in *Old Acquaintance* in 1952), Herbert Marshall's daughter Sarah (who was in the cast of Chatterton's 1951 revival of *Idiot's Delight*), and William Smithers (who played Laertes in the 1953 televised production of *Hamlet*). Understandably, Chatterton's "youthful" co-stars are now in their eighties and nineties. The youngest of all is Alan Alda, who was only twenty-two when he played Ruth's husband in a 1958 production of Lillian Hellman's *The Little Foxes*. Alda wished me luck, but was sorry that he, too, was "not able to help."[1127]

Fortunately, I did have favorable response from Eva Marie Saint, who played Ruth's daughter in TV's *Prudential Family Playhouse* presentation of *Dodsworth*. Saint telephoned me upon receiving my letter and graciously offered a lengthy conversation with details about the production and working with Ruth and Walter Abel. We also got a bit off track talking about our mutual favorite film of hers, *All Fall Down...* and her bittersweet memories of Brandon de Wilde.

Among the fellow writers and researchers who generously offered input is Graceann Macleod. Graceann proofed and edited my previous work, *Ann Harding – Cinema's Gallant Lady*. Her grammatical competence, talent as a writer, and input bolstered the narrative and helped it flow. Check out her splendid webpage: silentsgirl.wordpress.com. Author James Robert Parish has been an anchor for all my writing endeavors and his enthusiasm for my Chatterton project has never wavered. His 1975 publication, *The Debonairs*, was the perfect reference for detailing the career of Chatterton's second husband and leading man, George Brent. G.D. Hamann's publication *Ruth Chatterton In the 30's* provided Los Angeles news coverage concerning Chatterton during the decade she was making films. Hamann was also kind enough to send additional PDF files as I pursued my research. April Lane offered a thorough perusal of Ruth Moesel's manuscript on Chatterton held at the New York Public Library for the

Performing Arts (Lincoln Center). Check out April's detailed website on cinema's master director John Ford: http://directedbyjohnford.com/.

Archivist Mike Rinella has done extensive research on stage performances by Hollywood actors. He generously offered to scrutinize my list of Chatterton's stage credits (1939-1960) and provide some reviews of her performances. Canadian film researcher/writer Joseph Worrell shared his in-depth knowledge on vintage film actresses and has been an excellent sounding board. Author William M. Drew (author of *Speaking of Silents: First Ladies of the Screen* and *At the Center of the Frame: Leading Ladies of the Twenties and Thirties*, both of which contain interviews with women who worked with Ruth Chatterton) supplied numerous rare news articles. Special thanks, also, to James Stettler, who supplied amazing photos as well as insights into Chatterton's career. My good friends Jenny Paxson and Larry Smith of Culpepper's Library of Congress Film Archive were helpful in locating DVDs as well as reviews and notes regarding the teleplay adaptation of Chatterton's novel *Homeward Borne*.

Gratitude also goes out to: Alycia Hesse, who is currently writing a biography of the California poet and friend of Chatterton, George Sterling; Santa Fe author/poet Alex Gildzen; documentary filmmaker Eric Monder; Kenton Bymaster of Warner Brothers Archival Mastering; Natalie Olsen for sharing her experience and knowledge of women and aviation; Author Axel Nissen, of Oslo, Norway; writer David Noh of New York's *Gay City News*; Minae Hatakeyama (creator of the John Kerr Website); Eve Golden (watch for her upcoming biography *John Gilbert: The Last of the Silent Film Stars*); Marylyn Roh (daughter of Mary Astor); Fernando Silva for his translation of "Los Mercaderes de Estrellas"; my longtime friend and mentor Craig Smith; and writer/editor Moira Finney, creator of the excellent *Silver Screen Oasis* (website) and *Skeins of Thought* (blog). Irish filmmaker Brian Reddin was a real catalyst for me to dig deeper into the life of Chatterton's second husband, George Brent. This was in preparation for being interviewed for Reddin's documentary, *Hollywood Rebel* (2013). The film deals with Brent's involvement with the Irish Revolution as well as his nonconformist attitude during his Hollywood heyday.

Once again, my partner Joel Bellagio shared the journey into the life of an undeservedly forgotten film icon. He helped create and now maintains my website: scottobrienauthor.com. Joel keeps insisting I write about Maria Ouspenskaya and I keep countering, "How do you solve a problem like... Ouspenskaya?" But who could ever forget the scene from *Dodsworth* where Ouspenskaya leans toward Chatterton and asks the chilling question, "Have you thought what little happiness there can be for the... old wife... of a young husband?"

Dan and Darlene Swanson of Van-garde Imagery have done another remarkable job with an elegant book cover design—just as they did for my biographies on Virginia Bruce and Ann Harding. In closing, I want to thank publisher Ben Ohmart. BearManor Media has created a legacy for preserving, in print, stories of important artists in the entertainment field whose contributions and talents have been unjustly neglected. Check out www.bearmanormedia.com/ and download an amazing catalog encompassing film, radio, TV, music, and theater. You will be surprised by what you discover.

Endnotes

1122 J. Michael Mahoney, *Topsy Turvy: A Book of Quotations*, AuthorHouse, c. 2008, pg. 238 (the quote is also credited to English writer G.B. Stern).

1123 Letter from Brenda Holman, dated February 13, 2012.

1124 Letter from John Kerr, April 30, 2012.

1125 Linc Sparks, email dated: October 18, 2012.

1126 Arthur Hiller (via his assistant Brenda White) email dated: February 1, 2012.

1127 Email from Jean Cheney, assistant to Alan Alda, dated: November 20, 2012.

Credits

Ruth Chatterton on Stage

1909:

(Washington, D.C.-Columbia Stock Co. Columbia Theatre)

Merely Mary Ann (May) (by Israel Zangwill) Starring: Julia Dean, Ruth Chatterton (Polly), Miss Wright, Mr. Calvert, Tom Chatterton

The Prince Chap (June) (by Edward Peple) Starring: Julia Dean, Ruth Chatterton (Claudia), Helen Brown (Hayes)

Are You A Mason? (June) (adapted from *Die Logenbruder* by Carl Laufs and Curt Kraatz) Starring: Orme Caldara, Tom Chatterton, Julia Dean, Ruth Chatterton

My Wife (June) (by Michael Morton – adapted from a French play, *Mademoiselle Josette, Ma Femme*, by Paul Gavault and Robert Charvay) Starring: Julia Dean, Ruth Chatterton (Mary)

The Man on the Box (June) (adapted from the novel by Harold McGrath) Starring: Orme Calderra, Julia Dean, Ruth Chatterton (Cora)

The Bishop's Carriage (June) (by Channing Pollock – adapted from the novel by Miriam Michelson) Starring: Julia Dean, Ruth Chatterton (Mrs. Wallace)

Cousin Kate (August) (by Hubert Henry Davies) Starring Julia Dean, Orme Caldara, Laura Oakman, Alexander F. Frank, Everett Butterfield, Ruth Chatterton (Jane)

Charlie's Aunt (August) (by Brandon Thomas) Frederick A. Thomson (d) – Starring: Everett Butterfield, Edith Luckett, Ruth Chatterton (Amy Spettigue), Louise Reed

The Girl From the Circus (August) (by Sidney Grundy) Starring: Everett Butterfield, James A. Bliss, Robert Cain, James W. Shaw, Louise Reed, Ruth D. Blake, James W. Shaw, Ruth Chatterton (Barbara), Daisy Maitland, Edith Luckett

1909–1910:

(Milwaukee/Worcester Theatre Stock Companies – incomplete list of plays and dates. Ruth played light leads/juveniles.)

Milwaukee:
Held by the Enemy (by William Gillette)

David Copperfield (play from the novel by Charles Dickens) Starring: Lowell Sherman (David), Ruth Chatterton (Dora)

Twelfth Night (by William Shakespeare) Starring: Ruth Chatterton (Maria)

Worcester:
The College Widow (by George Ade) Starring: Ruth Chatterton (Flora Wiggins)

The Little Minister (by James M. Barrie) Starring: Ruth Chatterton (Micah Dow)

1910:
Miss Patsy (October) Belasco Theatre, Washington, D.C. (by Sewell Collins) Henry W. Savage (p) Starring: Gertrude Quinlan, Hardee Kirkland, Ruth Chatterton (Clara Gilroy), Wallace Worsley, Dorothy Tennant, Nellie Malcomb, Ione Bright, Jennie La Mont, Maud Earle (note: Chatterton joined the cast in Washington, D.C., after *Miss Patsy* played on Broadway. The play closed while on tour in Philadelphia on October 22)

1911:
The Great Name (December 26, 1910–October 1911) on tour and Broadway's Lyric Theatre and 39th Street Theatre for 21 performances (by James Clarence Harvey) Henry W. Savage (p) Starring: Henry Kolker, Russ Whytal, Sam Edwards, Hardee Kirkland, Ruth Chatterton (Isolde Brand) (Chatterton's Broadway debut)

Standing Pat (November–December 1911) on tour (by Bayard Veiller – originally titled: *Gordon's Wife*) Fred. G. Latham (d) Starring: Zelda Sears, William McVey, Eric Blind, Thomas Tobin, Jr., Ruth Chatterton (Helen Thomas), Milton Sills

1912:

The Rainbow (March 1912–January 1914) on tour and Broadway's Liberty Theatre for 104 performances (by A. E. Thomas). Henry Miller (producer/director) Starring: Henry Miller, Charles Hammond, Effingham Pinto, Edith Barker, Laura Hope Crews, Ruth Chatterton (Cynthia), Hope Latham, Louise Closser Hale, etc. (Opened on Broadway March 11, 1912; Closed 3rd week in June 1912 before going out on the road)

Susan's Gentleman (August 1912) Proctor's Fifth Avenue Theatre (one-act vaudeville sketch by Kate Jordan) Starring: Ruth Chatterton (Susan), House Peters, Daniel Pennell. On same bill: Fanny Brice, George White

1913:

My Wife (July) Columbia Theatre, Washington, D.C. (by Michael Morton – adapted from the French play *Mademoiselle Josette, Ma Femme* by Paul Gavault and Robert Charvay) Harry Andrews (d) Starring: A.H. Van Buren, Helen Holmes, Everett Butterfield, Craig Weston, George Barbier. According to the *Washington Herald*, Ruth Chatterton returned one week to the Columbia to play a small role.

1914–1916:

Daddy Long-Legs (February 1914–April 1916) on tour and Broadway's Gaiety Theatre for 264 performances (by Jean Webster) Henry Miller (producer/director) Starring: Ruth Chatterton (Judy), Charles Waldron, Charles Trowbridge, Cora Witherspoon

1916:

Frederic LeMaitre (December 1, 1916) one performance at New Amsterdam Theatre (one act play by Clyde Fitch) Starring: Ruth Chatterton (Madeleine), Henry Miller Testimonial benefit on behalf of F.F. Mackay of the Actors Fund of America.

1916–1918:

Come Out Of The Kitchen (August 1916–June 1918) on tour and at Broadway's Cohan Theatre for 224 performances (by A.E. "Al" Thomas, adapted from a magazine serial story by Alice Duer Miller) Henry Miller (producer/director) Starring: Ruth Chatterton (Olivia Dangerfield/Jane Ellen), Walter Connolly, Bruce McRae, Cecile Kelly, Alice Baxter, Raymond Walburn, Minna Gombell, Charles Trowbridge, Frances Stirling Clarke, Robert Ames

1917:

The New York Idea (June) Columbia Theatre – San Francisco (by Langdon Mitchell) Starring: Ruth Chatterton, Henry Miller, Lucille Watson, O.P. Heggie, Bruce McRea, Robert Ames, Raymond Walburn, Frances Goodrich

A Bit O' Love (July) Columbia Theatre – San Francisco (by John Galsworthy) Starring: Henry Miller, Ruth Chatterton, O.P. Heggie

Anthony in Wonderland (July) Columbia Theatre – San Francisco (by Monckton Hoffe) Starring: Henry Miller, Ruth Chatterton (All Aloney), Lucille Watson, Frances Goodrich, Walter Connolly, Raymond Walburn, Robert Ames, O.P. Heggie, Bruce McRae

1918:

Perkins (October–November) Henry Miller's Theatre for 23 performances (by Douglas Murray) Starring: Ruth Chatterton (Mrs. Calthorpe), Henry Miller, Frank Kemble Cooper, Tempe Pigott, Florence Wollerson

Daddy Long-Legs (November) two-week revival at Henry Miller's Theatre (by Jean Webster) Henry Miller (producer/director) Starring: Ruth Chatterton (Judy), Henry Miller, Bessie Lea, Lucia Moore

A Marriage of Convenience (August 1918–January 1919) on tour (by Sydney Grundy from *Un Mariage de Louis XV* by Alexandre Dumas) Starring: Ruth Chatterton (Comtesse de Condale), Henry Miller, Lucille Watson, Charles Trowbridge, David Glassford, Willard Barton

1919:

Chloe in Love (rehearsed in January 1919 and then aborted) (by William J. Hurlbut)

Merrie Month of May (previously titled: *Moonlight and Honeysuckle*) (March

1919–March 1920) on tour and Henry Miller's Theatre for 97 performances (by George Scarborough) Henry Miller (Producer/director) Starring: Ruth Chatterton (Judith Baldwin), Katherine Emmet, James Rennie, Sydney Booth, Charles Trowbridge, Flora Sheffield, Lucille Watson, Auriol Lee

Frederic LeMaitre (July 1919) benefit performance Columbia Theatre – San Francisco (by Clyde Fitch) Starring: Ruth Chatterton (Madeleine), Henry Miller, Laura Hope Crews

1920:

Pygmalion and Galatea (c. April 1920) one performance – all-star charity event (by W.S. Gilbert) Starring: Ruth Chatterton, Blanche Bates, Zelda Sears, Ina Claire, Fay Bainter, William Collier, George M. Cohan

The Maker of Dreams (April 27 and May 1, 1920) Knickerbocker Theatre – benefit for the Actor's Fidelity League (by Oliphant Down) Starring: Ruth Chatterton (Pierrette), Jose Rubens

1920-1922:

Mary Rose (December 1920–January 1922) on tour and Broadway's Empire Theatre for 127 performances (by James M. Barrie) Iden Payne (d) Starring: Ruth Chatterton (Mary Rose), Tom Nesbitt, Winifred Fraser, Ada King, Leo G. Carroll, Patricia Collinge

1921:

Into the Sunlight (September 27–30) Columbia Theatre – San Francisco (by Salisbury Field and Felton Elkins) Starring: Ruth Chatterton (Marion Boyden), Henry Miller, Blanche Bates, Tom Nesbitt, Boyd Irwin, Betty Hall, Mignon O'Doherty

1922:

He Stoops to Conquer (May) Columbia Theatre – San Francisco (by Thompson Buchanan and Henry Miller) Ruth Chatterton, Henry Miller, Blanch Bates, Bruce McRae

The Awful Truth (May) Columbia Theatre – San Francisco (by Arthur Richman) Henry Miller (d) Starring: Ruth Chatterton (Lucy Warriner), Bruce McRae, Geoffrey Kerr, Paul Harvey, Cora Witherspoon

Her Friend the King (Summer 1922) Columbia Theatre – San Francisco (by A.E. Thomas and Harrison Rhodes) Starring: Ruth Chatterton, Henry Miller, Blanche Bates, Bruce McRae, Paul Harvey

La Tendresse (1922) (May 1922–January 1923) on tour and Broadway's Empire Theatre for 64 performances (by Henri Bataille – translated from the French by Ruth Chatterton) Henry Miller (d) Starring: Ruth Chatterton (Marthe Dellieres), Henry Miller, Blanche Bates, Bruce McRae, Ronald Colman (Warren William took over the Colman role when he left the cast)

1923:
The Changelings (1923–1924) on tour and Broadway's Henry Miller's Theatre for 128 performances (by Lee Wilson Dodd) Starring: Ruth Chatterton (Kay Faber), Henry Miller, Laura Hope Crews, Blanche Bates, Emma Dunn, Geoffrey Kerr

1924:
The Man in Evening Clothes (December) Henry Miller's Theatre – closed after eleven performances (by Andre Picard and Yves Mirande – *L'Homme En Habit* translated from the French by Ruth Chatterton) Starring: Henry Miller, Marjorie Gateson

Magnolia Lady (November–December) on tour and Broadway's Shubert Theatre for 47 performances (musical version of *Come Out of the Kitchen* by A.E. Thomas and Alice Duer Miller) Henry Miller (p) Hassard Short (d) Starring: Ruth Chatterton (Lily Lou Ravenel), Ralph Forbes, Skeets Gallagher

1925:
The Little Minister (March–April) on tour and Broadway's Globe Theater for 16 performances (by James M. Barrie) Charles Dillingham (p) Basil Dean (d) Starring: Ruth Chatterton (Lady Babbie), Ralph Forbes, J.M. Kerrigan, Hubert Druce

Women and Ladies (May) one week Washington, D.C. – Belasco Theatre (by Louis Verneuil adapted from the French by Cosmo Hamilton) Starring: Ruth Chatterton, Ralph Forbes, Auriol Lee, Robert Rendel, Frederick Perry, Ernest Stallard, William Leith

The Siren's Daughter (May) played in Philadelphia – Adelphi Theatre (by Mrs. Wallace Irwin) Starring: Ruth Chatterton, Ralph Forbes, Auriol Lee

The Man With A Load Of Mischief (October–November) on tour and Broadway's Ritz Theatre for 16 performances (by Ashley Dukes) Lee Shubert (p) Ruth Chatterton (d) Starring: Ruth Chatterton (A Lady), Ralph Forbes, McKay Morris, Bertha Mann, A.G. Andrews, Robert Loraine, Bertha Mann, Jessie Ralph

1926:

The Conflict (January–April) vaudeville on tour and at New York's Palace and Albee Theatre (by Vincent Lawrence) Starring: Ruth Chatterton, Minor Watson

The Green Hat (August–January 1927) west coast tour (by Michael Arlen) Edward E. Smith (p) Starring: Ruth Chatterton (Iris March), Ralph Forbes, William H. Turner, Gareth Hughes, Montague Shaw, Charles A. Stevenson, Mira Adoree (sister of Renee), Catherine Bennett (sister of Enid)

1927:

The Devil's Plum Tree (September–December) west coast tour (adapted by John Colton from the Hungarian play by Miliam Begovic) Lou Wissel (p) Irving Pichel (d) Starring: Ruth Chatterton (Mara), Kenneth Thompson, Ivis Goulding (sister of director Edmund), Montague Shaw, Mary Forbes (Ralph's mother), Edward Leiter (future husband of Madame Sylvia of Hollywood)

1930:

Monsieur Brotonneau London (Ruth Chatterton translation of the French play by Robert de Flers and Gaston de Caillavet) Starring: Ivor Barnard, Louise Gervais

1932:

Let Us Divorce (April–May) west coast tour (from the play *Counsel's Opinion* by Gilbert Wakefield) Ruth Chatterton (producer/director) Starring: Ralph Forbes, Rose Hobart, Lowden Adams, Hugh Huntley, Mary Gordon (Filmed as *The Divorce of Lady X* in 1938 starring Laurence Olivier and Merle Oberon)

1937:

The Constant Wife (April–June 1937) on tour and at London's Globe Theatre (by Somerset Maugham) Starring: Ruth Chatterton (Constance Middleton), Cecil Parker (closed at the Globe after 36 performances)

1939:

West of Broadway (March) two weeks in Boston – Wilbur Theatre (by Marguerite
Roberts – previously titled *Farewell Appearance*) Albert Lewis (p) Auriol Lee (d)
Starring: Ruth Chatterton (Theodora Varner), Walter Abel, James Bell, Jeanne
Dante, Josephine Hull, Will Geer

Affairs of Anatol (May) one week Maplewood, NJ (by Arthur Schnitzler) Starring:
Ruth Chatterton (Annie/Cora/Bianca/Elsa/Emilie/Ilona/Gabriele), Barry
Thomson, Wilton Graff

Tonight We Dance (July 1939–January 1940) on tour (by Gladys Unger and Marcella
Burke – originally titled *You Can't Eat Goldfish*) Thom Conroy (d1), Auriol Lee
(d2) Starring: Ruth Chatterton (Romona Flack), Barry Thomson, Lila Lee, Robert
Wallston, Roy Johnson, Marcel Journet, Tina Thayer, Shirley Poirier, Thomas Hume

1940:

Leave Her to Heaven (February–March) Broadway's Longacre Theatre – 15 per-
formances (by John Van Druten) Dwight Deere Wimon (p), Auriol Lee (d)
Starring: Ruth Chatterton (Madge Monckton), Edmond O'Brien, Reynolds
Denniston, Frances Compton, A.G. Andrews, Esther Mitchell, Hilda Plowright,
Edmond Stevens, Guy Spaull, Neil Fitzgerald, Bettina Cerf, Eldon Gorst, J. Mal-
colm Dunn, William Packer

Pygmalion (May 1940–March 1941) various tour dates (by George Bernard Shaw)
Harold J. Kennedy, Justus Addis, Hayden Rorke (producers), Auriol Lee (d) Star-
ring: Ruth Chatterton (Eliza Doolittle), Barry Thomson, Richard Temple, Alice
John, Hayden Rorke, Dennis Hoey, Eleanor Wilson, Mytle Tannahill, Mortimre
H. Weldon, Arthur Gilmore, Margaret Moffat, Vilma Royton, Richard Bowler

Tomorrow and Tomorrow (August) one week Cape Playhouse – Dennis, MA (by
Philip Barry) Arthur Sircom (d) Starring: Ruth Chatterton (Eve Redmond),
Barry Thomson, John Kerr

Private Lives (June–October) various tour dates (by Noel Coward) Frederic Lyn-
wood (d) Starring: Ruth Chatterton (Amanda Prynne), Barry Thomson, Louise
Kirtland, Robert Perry, Harry E. Lowell, Emmett Rogers

1941:

Tonight at 8:30 (January 12, 1941) benefit performance for British Red Cross – Evanston, IL – Guild Theatre (by Noel Coward) Starring: Ruth Chatterton (Leonora Vail), Ian Keith

Treat Her Gently (March–April) various tour dates (by George D. Batson) Harold J. Kennedy, Justus Addis, Hayden Rorke (producers), Ruth Chatterton (d) Starring: Ruth Chatterton (Julia), Barry Thomson, Hayden Rorke, Alice John, Elaine Ellis

Tomorrow and Tomorrow (June–July) on tour (by Philip Barry) Starring: Ruth Chatterton (Eve Redmond), Barry Thomson, Ann Dere, Lewis Martin, Ellen Hall, Whit Bissell, Robert Allen

The Constant Wife (July–August) on tour (by Somerset Maugham) Harold J. Kennedy (p) Starring: Ruth Chatterton (Constance Middleton), Barry Thomson, Clay Clement, Dorothy Sands, Fraye Gilbert, Bijou Fernandez, A.J. Herbert, Diane de Bret, Douglas Gilmore

Caprice (July–August) on tour (by Sil-Vara) Starring: Ruth Chatterton (Ilse), Barry Thomson, William Eythe, Muriel Kirkland

Sorrow for Angels (August) one week – Cambridge, MA – Brattle Hall (by George D. Batson) Ruth Chatterton (d) Starring: Ruth Chatterton, Barry Thomson, Katherine Wyman, Wilson Lehr, Nina Wentworth, Robert Wilcox, William Mendrek

1942:

Private Lives (April) on tour (by Noel Coward) Barry Thomson (d) Starring: Ruth Chatterton (Amanda Prynne), Eddie Nugent, Leila Ernst

Private Lives (June–November) on tour (by Noel Coward) Robert Perry (d) Starring: Ruth Chatterton (Amanda Prynne), Ralph Forbes, Louise Kanasireff, John Grogan, Michael Castille

Rebound (July) on tour (by Donald Ogden Stewart) Arthur Sircom (d) Starring: Ruth Chatterton (Sara Jaffrey), Ralph Forbes, Gregory Peck, Otto Hulett, Harry Ellerbe, Muriel Williams, Cora Witherspoon

1943:

Private Lives (February–September) on tour (by Noel Coward) Starring: Ruth Chatterton (Amanda Prynne), Ralph Forbes

Caprice (August–September) on tour (by Sil-Vara) Starring: Ruth Chatterton (Ilse), Donald Buka, Alexander Clark, Dora Sayres

Untitled (November 9, 1943) all-star fund raiser at the Astor Gallery for the Women's Division of the National War Fund Committee (by Norman Corwin) Starring: Ruth Chatterton (The Voice), Myrna Loy, Gertrude Lawrence, Helen Hayes, Mary Martin

The Lady Comes Home (December) on tour (by Ethel Borden and Jacques Thery) K. Elmo Lowe (d) Starring: Ruth Chatterton (Daisy le Beaudreau), Ralph Forbes, Frank Conroy, Margaret Bannerman, Charles McClelland, John Crogan, Henry Barnard

1944:
Private Lives (October) one week – Long Island – Queensboro Theatre (by Noel Coward) Starring: Ruth Chatterton (Amanda Prynne)

1945:
The Chosen Uninvited (April 19) benefit performance (by Paul Eldridge) Dorothy Tierney Keith (d) Starring: Ruth Chatterton, Barry Thomson, Horace Braham, Moishe Oysher

Windy Hill (August 1945–May 1946) on tour (by Patsy Ruth Miller) Ruth Chatterton (d) Starring: Kay Francis (Antonia Connors), Roger Pryor, Judy Holliday, Jetti Preminger, Eileen Heckert, Donald McClelland, Ruth Conley, Eulabelle Moore, James Hagen, Edward Colebrook, Grant Gordon, Earle Mayo, Lawrence Fletcher

1946:
Second Best Bed (May–June) on tour – Broadway's Ethel Barrymore Theatre – closed after 8 performances (by N. Richard Nash) Ruth Chatterton and John Huntington (p) Ruth Chatterton and N. Richard Nash (d) Starring: Ruth Chatterton (Anne Hathaway), Ralph Forbes, Barry Thomson, John McKee, John Gay, Elizabeth Eustis, Peter Boyne, Ralph Cullinan, Max Stamm, Richard Dyer-Bennet

Caprice (July–September) on tour (by Sil-Vara) Starring: Ruth Chatterton (Ilse), Shirling Oliver, Richard Camp, Esther Mitchel

The Truth (August) (by Clyde Fitch) Arthur Sircom (d) Starring: Ruth Chatterton, William Post, Josephine Brown, Morton L. Stevens

A Flag Is Born (October–November) New York – Music Box Theatre (by Ben Hecht) Luther Adler (d) Starring: Ruth Chatterton (Speaker), Luther Adler, Celia Adler, Sidney Lumet, Marlon Brando, Richard Monti (play had numerous cast replacements; Ruth was replaced by Alexander Scourby when the play moved to the Alvin Theatre)

1947:

The Terrorist (September 20-21) Carnegie Hall (by Ben Hecht) Moe Hack (d) Starring: Ruth Chatterton (presented by The American League for a Free Palestine)

Caprice (August and December) Ogunquit, ME and Reading, PA (Kenley Players) (by Sil-Vara) Starring: Ruth Chatterton (Ilse), Jean Muir, Shirling Oliver

The Little Foxes (June–August) on tour (by Lillian Hellman) Alex Segal and others (d) Starring: Ruth Chatterton (Regina Giddens), Blaine Gardner, Katherine Squire

1948:

The Little Foxes (July–November) on tour (by Lillian Hellman) Alexander Kirkland (d) Starring: Ruth Chatterton (Regina Giddens), Clark Chesney, Robert Emhardt, Howard Wendell, Nancy Davis, Paul Marlin, Dorothy Blackburn, Archie Smith, Eugenia Rawls

1949:

Lovers and Friends (April–August) on tour (by English playwright Dodie Smith) Harry Ellerbe (d) Starring: Ruth Chatterton (Stella), Stiano Braggiotti, Margaret Bannerman, Edward Ashley

1950:

The Smile Of The World (June) New Hope, PA – Bucks County Playhouse (by Garson Kanin) Henry Jones (d) Starring: Ruth Chatterton (Sara Boulting), Donald Buka, Harry Mehaffey, Ruth Amos, James Doolan, Elizabeth Dewing

The Little Foxes (June) Chicago – Chevy Chase Summer Theatre (by Lillian Hellman) Starring: Ruth Chatterton (Regina Giddens), Barry Thomson, John Albert, Maurice Copeland, Wiley Hancock

O Mistress Mine (July–August) on tour (by Terence Ratigan – original title *Love in Idleness*) Starring: Ruth Chatterton (Olivia Brown), Barry Thomson

1951:

Idiot's Delight (May–June) limited engagement on Broadway – City Center Theater – closed after 16 performances (by Robert E. Sherwood) George Schaefer (d) Maurice Evans (artistic supervisor) Starring: Ruth Chatterton (Irene), Lee Tracy, Stiano Braggiotti, Sarah Marshall, Stefan Schnabel, Louis Borell

O Mistress Mine (July–August) on tour (by Terence Ratigan – original title *Love in Idleness*) Starring: Ruth Chatterton (Olivia Brown), Barry Thomson, Ethel Barrymore Colt

The Little Foxes (September) Mountainhome, PA – Pocono Playhouse (by Lillian Hellman) Starring: Ruth Chatterton (Regina Giddens)

1952:

The Little Foxes (March–July) on tour (by Lillian Hellman) Starring: Ruth Chatterton (Regina Giddens), Barry Thomson, Christopher Plummer

The Constant Wife (May) Hamilton, Bermuda – Bermudiana Theatre (by Somerset Maugham) Starring: Ruth Chatterton (Constance), Christopher Plummer

O Mistress Mine (April–May) on tour (originally titled *Love in Idleness* by Terence Ratigan) Starring: Ruth Chatterton (Olivia Brown), Barry Thomson

Old Acquaintance (July–August) on tour (by John Van Druten) Starring: Ruth Chatterton (Katherine Markham), Margaret Bannerman, June Dayton, John Haragrey, Patricia Barry, Carol Goodner

1953:

Highlights of the Empire (May 24) Commemorating the passing of the 60-year-old Empire Theatre. Starring: Ruth Chatterton, Judith Anderson, Shirley Booth, Basil Rathbone, Cornelia Otis Skinner

Susan and God (December–January 1954) Evanston, IL – Showcase Theatre (by Rachel Crothers) Hope Summers (p) Starring: Ruth Chatterton (Susan Trexel), Barry Thomson, Marian Brown

1954:

Old Acquaintance (September) (by John Van Druten) Starring: Ruth Chatterton (Katherine Markham)

1955:

Old Acquaintance (July) Myrtle Beach, SC (by John Van Druten) Starring: Ruth Chatterton (Katherine Markham)

The Sign of Winter (August 27-28) Westport, CT – White Barn Theatre (by Ettore Rella, previously titled *Stars for the Dark Cave*) Sherwood Arthur (d) Starring: Ruth Chatterton, Anne Meacham, Ian Martin, Rai Saunders

1956:

Knife and Fork Lecture Circuit (January, September–October) on tour

The Little Foxes (February, August–September) (by Lillian Hellman) William Miles (d) Starring: Ruth Chatterton (Regina Giddens), Eleanor Wilson, Maurice Wells, Bert Thorn, John Marriott, Patricia Lamson

Jane (July) White River, IN – Avondale Playhouse (by S.N. Behrman) Starring: Ruth Chatterton (Jane Fowler), Barry Thomson

The Chalk Garden (November) on tour (by Enid Bagnold) Starring: Ruth Chatterton (Mrs. St. Maugham), Judith Anderson (Chatterton withdrew in Milwaukee and was replaced by Audrey Ridgewell)

1957:

O Mistress Mine (March) Palm Beach Playhouse (original title *Love in Idleness* by Terence Ratigan) Starring: Ruth Chatterton (Olivia Brown), Barry Thomson

The Reluctant Debutante (June–September) on tour (by William Douglas-Home) Walt Whitcover (d) Starring: Ruth Chatterton (Sheila Broadbent), Arthur Treacher, Sandy Dennis, Ralph Purdum, Peter Craig, Harriet MacGibbon, Ruth Estler

1958:

The Little Foxes (July) Chagrin Falls, OH – Chagrin Valley Playhouse (by Lillian Hellman) Robert Belfance/Howard da Silva (d) Starring: Ruth Chatterton (Regina Giddens), Alan Alda, Lawrence Kuhl, Gerri Cenza, Mark Fleischman, Keith Mackey, Alfredina Brown, Charles Grimes

1959:

Jane (January–February) Phoenix, AZ – Sombrero Theatre (by S.N. Behrman) Starring: Ruth Chatterton (Jane Fowler), Wilton Graff

Madwoman of Chaillot (October 28-30) Towson State Teachers College – Maryland (translated from *La Folle de Chaillot* by Jean Giraudoux) William C. Kramer (d) Starring: Ruth Chatterton (Countess Aurelia), Sharie Lacey, Linc Sparks

1960:

Happy Ending (August 23-27) New Hope, PA – Bucks County Playhouse (by Nellise Child) Michael Ellis (p) Jack Ragotzy (d) Starring: Ruth Chatterton (Miss Manchester), Conrad Nagel, Pert Kelton, Ethel Smith, Nell Harrison, David Hurst, Nat Burns

1932 Warner publicity shot

Ruth Chatterton – Films

1) *Sins of the Fathers* (1928) Paramount (silent with one musical sound sequence) – 87m (from the story by Norman Burnstine) Ludwig Berger (d) Cast: Emil Jannings, Ruth Chatterton (Greta Blanke), Barry Norton, ZaSu Pitts, Jean Arthur, Frank Reicher, Jack Luden, Matthew Betz, Anne Shirley (billed as Dawn O'Day)

2) *The Doctor's Secret* (1929) Paramount – 61m (from the James M. Barrie play *Half an Hour*) William de Mille (d) Cast: Ruth Chatterton (Lillian Garson), H.B. Warner, John Loder, Robert Edeson, Wilfred Noy, Ethel Wales, Nancy Price

3) *The Dummy* (1929) Paramount – 60m (from the play by Harriet Ford and Harvey J. O'Higgins) Robert Milton (d) Cast: Ruth Chatterton (Agnes Meredith), Fredric March, John Cromwell, Fred Kohler, Mickey Bennett, Vondell Darr, Jack Oakie, ZaSu Pitts, Richard Tucker, Eugene Pallette

4) *Madame X* (1929) MGM – 95m (from the play by Alexandre Bisson) Lionel Barrymore (d) Cast: Lewis Stone, Ruth Chatterton (Jacqueline), Raymond Hackett, Holmes Herbert, Eugenie Besserer, John P. Edington, Mitchell Lewis, Ullrich Haupt, Sidney Toler, Richard Carle, Carroll Nye, Claude King, Chappell Dossett, Dickie Moore

   Nominated 1930 - Best Actress: Ruth Chatterton

   Nominated 1930 - Best Director: Lionel Barrymore

   (DVD: WB Archive Collection)

5) *Charming Sinners* (1929) Paramount – 66m (from the play *The Constant Wife* by W. Somerset Maugham) Robert Milton (d) Cast: Ruth Chatterton (Kathryn Miles), Clive Brook, Mary Nolan, William Powell, Laura Hope Crews, Florence Eldridge, Montagu Love, Juliette Crosby, Lorraine MacLean, Claud Allister (DVD: lovingtheclassics.com & eMoviez)

6) *The Laughing Lady* (1929) Paramount – 80m (from the play by Alfred Sutro) Victor Schertzinger (d) Cast: Ruth Chatterton (Marjorie Lee), Clive Brook, Dan Healy, Nat Pendleton, Raymond Walburn, Dorothy Hall, Nedda Harrigan

7) *Sarah and Son* (1930) Paramount – 86m (from the novel by Timothy Shea) Dorothy Arzner (d) Cast: Ruth Chatterton (Sarah Storm), Fredric March, Fuller Mellish, Jr., Gilbert Emery, Doris Lloyd, William Stack, Phillipe de Lacy, Edgar Norton

Nominated 1931 - Best Actress: Ruth Chatterton

(DVD: lovingtheclassics.com & eMoviez)

8)   *Paramount on Parade* (1930) Paramount – 102m (original print) Victor Schertz-inger (director for *Montmartre Girl*) Cast: Ruth Chatterton (Floozie), Fredric March, Stuart Erwin, Skeets Gallagher, Stanley Smith, Jack Pennick (DVD: lovingtheclassics.com)

9)   *The Lady of Scandal* (1930) MGM – 76m (from the play *The High Road* by Fred-erick Lonsdale) Cast: Ruth Chatterton (Elsie), Basil Rathbone, Ralph Forbes, Nance O'Neil, Frederick Kerr, Herbert Bunston, Cyril Chadwick, Effie Ellsler, Robert Bolder, Moon Carroll, Mackenzie Ward, Edgar Norton

10) *Anybody's Woman* (1930) Paramount – 80m (from the story by Gouveneur Morris) Dorothy Arzner (d) Cast: Ruth Chatterton (Pansy Gray), Clive Brook, Paul Lukas, Huntley Gordon, Virginia Hammond, Tom Patricola, Juliette Compton, Cecil Cunningham, Charles K. Gerrard, Harvey Clark, Sidney Bracey, Mary Gordon

(DVD: lovingtheclassics.com)

11) *The Right to Love* (1930) Paramount – 79m (from the story *Brook Evans* by Susan Glaspell) Dorothy Arzner (d) Cast: Ruth Chatterton (Brook Evans/Naomi Kellogg), Paul Lukas, David Manners, Irving Pichel, Louise Mackintosh, Oscar Apfel, Veda Buckland, Robert Parish, Lillian West

Nominated 1931 - Best Cinematography: Charles Lang

12) *Unfaithful* (1931) Paramount – 85m (story by John Van Druten) John Cromwell (d) Cast: Ruth Chatterton (Lady Fay Kilkerry), Paul Lukas, Paul Cavanagh, Juliette Compton, Donald Cook, Emily Fitzroy, Leslie Palmer (DVD: lovingth-eclassics.com)

13) *The House That Shadows Built* (1931) Paramount – 47m (Documentary celebrat-ing Paramount's 20th anniversary) Scenes include the aborted *Stepdaughters of War* written by Helen Zenna Smith. (3 minutes) Dorothy Arzner (d) Cast: Ruth Chatterton (Smith)

14) *The Magnificent Lie* (1931) Paramount – 81m (from the Leonard Merrick story *Laurels and the Lady*) Berthold Viertel (d) Cast: Ruth Chatterton (Poll), Ralph Bellamy, Stuart Erwin, Francoise Rosay, Sam Hardy, Charles Boyer, Tyler Brooke, Tyrell Davis, Jean De Val, Bess Flowers, Bill Elliott (DVD: eMoviez)

15) *Once a Lady* (1931) Paramount – 80m (from the play *Das Zweite Leben* by Bernauer Osterreicher) Guthrie McClintic (d) Cast: Ruth Chatterton (Anna Keremazoff), Ivor Novello, Jill Esmond, Geoffrey Kerr, Doris Lloyd, Herbert Bunston, Gwendolyn Logan, Stella Moore, Edith Kingdon, Bramwell Fletcher, Theodore von Eltz (DVD: lovingtheclassics.com & eMoviez)

16) *Tomorrow and Tomorrow* (1931) Paramount – 80m (from the play by Philip Barry) Richard Wallace (d) Cast: Ruth Chatterton (Eve Redman), Robert Ames, Paul Lukas, Harold Minjir, Tad Alexander, Walter Walker

17) *The Rich Are Always With Us* (1932) Warner – 71m (from the novel by Ethel Pettit) Alfred E. Green (d) Cast: Ruth Chatterton (Caroline Grannard), George Brent, Bette Davis, John Miljan, Adrienne Dore, John Wray, Robert Warwick, Walter Walker, Virginia Hammond, Berton Churchill, Edith Allen, Cecil Cunningham (DVD: WB Archive Collection)

18) *The Crash* (1932) Warner – 58m (from the Larry Barretto novel *Children of Pleasure*) William Dieterle (d) Cast: Ruth Chatterton (Linda Gault), George Brent, Paul Cavanagh, Barbara Leonard, Henry Kolker, Lois Wilson, Hardie Albright, Virginia Hammond, Helen Vinson (DVD: WB Archive Collection)

19) *Frisco Jenny* (1933) Warner – 73m (from the short story *Common Ground* by Gerald Beaumont) William A. Wellman (d) Cast: Ruth Chatterton (Jenny Sandoval), Louis Calhern, Donald Cook, James Murray, Helen Jerome Eddy, Hallam Cooley (DVD: TCM Archives *Forbidden Hollywood Collection* Volume 3)

20) *Lilly Turner* (1933) Warner – 65m (from the play by George Abbott and Philip Dunning) William A. Wellman (d) Cast: Ruth Chatterton (Lilly Turner), George Brent, Frank McHugh, Guy Kibbee, Robert Barrat, Ruth Donnelly, Marjorie Gateson, Gordon Westcott, Arthur Vinton, Grant Mitchell, Margaret Seddon, Mae Busch

21) *Female* (1933) Warner – 60m (from the novel by Donald Henderson Clarke) Michael Curtiz (d) (William Dieterle, William A. Wellman un-credited directors) Cast: Ruth Chatterton (Alison Drake), George Brent, Philip Reed, Ferdinand Gottschalk, Ruth Donnelly, Johnny Mack Brown, Lois Wilson, Gavin Gordon, Kenneth Thompson (DVD: TCM Archives *Forbidden Hollywood Collection* Volume 2)

22) *Journal of a Crime* (1934) Warner – 65m (from the play *Une Vie Perdue* by Jacques Deval) William Keighley (d) Cast: Ruth Chatterton (Francoise Mollet), Adolphe Menjou, Claire Dodd, George Barbier, Douglass Dumbrille, Noel

Madison, Henry O'Neill, Phillip Reed, Henry Kolker, Frank Reicher, Edward McWade, Walter Pidgeon, Jane Darwell

23) *David O. Selznick: 'Your New Producer'* (1935) 25m – Highlights from the career of producer David O. Selznick. Host Robert Benchley introduces various clips, including a scene from *Sarah and Son* (1930) with Ruth Chatterton and Fredric March.

24) *Lady of Secrets* (1936) Columbia – 73m (from the story *Maid of Honor* by Katharine Brush) Marion Gering (d) Cast: Ruth Chatterton (Celia Whittaker), Otto Kruger, Lionel Atwill, Marian Marsh, Lloyd Nolan, Robert Allen, Dorothy Appleby, Nana Bryant, Esther Dale (DVD: lovingtheclassics.com & eMoviez))

25) *Girls Dormitory* (1936) 20th Century Fox – 66m (from the play *Matura* by Ladislas Fodor) Irving Cummings (d) Cast: Ruth Chatterton (Anna Mathe), Herbert Marshall, Simon Simone, Constance Collier, J. Edward Bromberg, Dixie Dunbar, John Qualen, Shirley Deane, Tyrone Power, Frank Reicher, Christian Rub, Baby Peggy, Lynn Bari (DVD: *Tyrone Power Matinee Idol Collection*)

26) *Dodsworth* (1936) Samuel Goldwyn – United Artists – 101m (from the play by Sidney Howard, adapted from the novel by Sinclair Lewis) William Wyler (d) Cast: Walter Huston, Ruth Chatterton (Fran Dodsworth), Mary Astor, Paul Lukas, David Niven, Maria Ouspenskaya, Gregory Gaye, Spring Byington, Kathryn Marlowe, John Payne, Odette Myrtil, Bess Flowers

   Nominated 1936 – Best Picture

   Best Director – William Wyler

   Best Actor – Walter Huston

   Best Supporting Actress – Maria Ouspenskaya

   Best Writing – Sidney Howard

   Best Sound – Oscar Lagerstrom

   Best Art Direction – Richard Day (won)

   (DVD: MGM DVD)

27) *The Rat* (1938) London Films – RKO – 72m (from the play by Ivor Novello and Constance Collier) Jack Raymond (d) Cast: Ruth Chatterton (Zelia de Chaumont), Anton Walbrook, Rene Ray, Beatrix Lehmann, Mary Clare, Leo Genn, Felix Aylmer

28) *The Royal Divorce* (1938) Imperator-Paramount – 85m (from the novel *Josephine*
by Jacques Thery) Jack Raymond (d) Cast: Ruth Chatterton (Josephine de Beau-
harnais), Pierre Blanchar, Frank Cellier, Carol Goodner, Auriol Lee, Jack Hawkins

*The *Washington Times* (Washington, D.C.) for November 19, 1914, listed the
following Famous Players-Lasky (4 reels) title:

Wildflower – released October 15, 1914. The story of the love of two brothers for
the same girl. Allan Dwan (d) Starring: Marguerite Clark, Harold Lockwood,
James Cooley, Jack Pickford, E.L. Davenport, Jane Fernley, Ruth Chatterton,
James Neill, Wal Clarendon

Wildflower was filmed in New York during March–April, 1914. The *Washington
Times* appears to be the only publication which lists Chatterton as one of the players.

Ruth Chatterton on Radio

1924:
December 22: Interview (**WHN New York**) RC (guest)

1929:
September 24: **The Paramount Hour** (**CBS**) (program's inaugural broadcast) RC
(guest), Clive Brook, Buddy Rogers, Fredric March, Jack Oakie, Nancy Carroll

1930:
April 26: **The Paramount Hour** (**CBS**) (dialogue and stories by Frederic Longsdale)
Nancy Carroll/Clara Bow (hosts) RC (guest), Buddy Rogers, Skeets Gallagher,
Gary Cooper

1931:
April 8: **Sunkist Musical Cocktail** (**ABC**) Louella Parsons (host) interviews RC

1933:
September 30: **NRA** (**National Recovery Administration**) **Program** RC (guest),
Marion Davies, J. Farrell MacDonald

Publicity shot of Ruth for the CBS series "Big Sister"
(July 1939) (courtesy of James Stettler).

1934:

March 10: **45 Minutes in Hollywood** (CBS) RC (guest)

November 18: **Lux Theatre** (NBC) *Rebound* (by Donald Ogden Stewart) Starring:
RC (Sarah), Earle Larimore

1935:

March 22: **Hollywood Hotel** (CBS) *Sarah and Son* (from Timothy Shea novel) Starring: RC (Sarah), Louis Hayward. Also Dick Powell, Harry Warren, Al Dubin

May 19: **Lux Theatre** (NBC) *The Lion and the Mouse* (play by Charles Klein) Starring:
RC (Shirley Ross), Robert T. Haines. Drama about the attempted impeachment
of a Federal Judge and a woman's battle with a business tycoon.

July 27: **Shell Chateau Hour (NBC)** *The Lake* (play by Dorothy Massingham and Murray MacDonald) Starring: RC (Stella Surrege). Al Jolson (host)

August 30: **Air Race Broadcast (NBC)** RC interview

September 9: **Lux Theatre (NBC)** *Petticoat Influence* (play by Neil Grant) Starring: RC (Peggy Chalfont)

1936:

January 10: **Hollywood Hotel (CBS)** scene from *No More Yesterdays* (from Katharine Brush story – re-titled *Lady of Secrets* for the screen) Starring: RC (Celia). Dick Powell (host)

January 17: **Hollywood Hotel (CBS)** scenes from *Mary Rose* (by James M. Barrie) Starring: RC (Mary Rose). Dick Powell (host). With Anne Jamison, Igor Gorin

April 16: **Fleischmann Variety Hour (NBC)** Rudy Vallee (host). RC stars in the monodrama *The Beloved Boy*. Comic Eddie Green

August 21: **Hollywood Hotel (CBS)** scenes from *Dodsworth* with RC and Walter Huston. With Frances Langford, Igor Gorin

September 14: **Lux Theatre (NBC)** *Quality Street* (by James M. Barrie) Starring: RC (Phoebe Throssel), Brian Aherne

October 15: **Kraft Music Hall (NBC)** Bing Crosby (master of ceremonies) RC (guest), Bob Burns, Ethel Rethberg, Jimmy Dorsey Orchestra

October 24: **Irvin S. Cobb's Paducah Plantation (NBC)** RC (guest), Clarence Muse (actor/baritone), Mills Brothers

December 22: **The Radio Camel Caravan (CBS)** *A Marriage Has Been Arranged* (by Alfred Sutro) with RC (Lady Aline de Vaux) and Otto Kruger. Wini Shaw (soloist)

1937:

February 25: **Maxwell House Showboat Program (NBC)** scene from *Mary Rose* (by James M. Barrie) Starring: RC (Mary Rose). With Lanny Ross

1939:

May 28: **The Magic Key (NBC)** dramatic sketch *The Anniversary* Starring: RC. With George Gaul, Joan Edwards (songstress)

July 3-21: **Big Sister (CBS)** RC guest star on morning dramatic series (Monday–Friday) with Martin Gabel

1940:

January 31: **Texaco Star Theatre (CBS)** Ken Murray (host) *The Last of Mrs. Cheney* (by Frederick Lonsdale) Starring: RC, Barry Thomson. Burns Mantel (commentator)

June 14: **Fifth Row Center (WGN)** *Beautiful Lady* starring: RC, Francis X. Bushman, Marvin Mueller, Ed Prentiss, and Cleveland Towne

August 13: **Playhouse Personalities (WMAS)** RC guest star

November 14: **In Chicago Tonight (Mutual)** *Page Five, Column Two* (by Ashmead Scott and William A. Bacher) Starring: RC (Evelyn Vane) Chatterton played both mother and daughter roles as the duo fight to escape notoriety after the mother is acquitted of murder. With Billy Gilbert (comedy sketch)

November 30: **Celebrity Circle (WBBM)** Tommy Bartlett (host), RC (guest)

December 8: **Speak Up America! (NBC)** Quiz show. RC (guest), Roy Atwell

December 15: **Speak Up America! (NBC)** RC (guest), columnists June Provines and Robert M. Yoder, editor Arnold Gingrich

December 17: **Club Matinee (Blue Network)** RC (guest)

December 22: **Speak Up America! (NBC)** RC (guest). With Avery Brundage, Sidney James (editor of *Time*)

1941:

May 16: **CBS Playhouse** *Alien Corn* (play by Sidney Howard) Starring: RC (Elsa Brandt)

June 1: **The Ontario Show (WMAS)** Variety show. Lemuell Q. Stopnagel (host) RC (guest)

July 3: **Berkshire Broadway (WOKO)** RC (guest)

September 19: **War Letters from Britain (WMCA)** (drama) Starring: RC

October 22: **War Savings Program (CBC)** *Cavalcade* (by Noel Coward) Starring: RC (Jane Marryot)

November 17: **Sky Over Britain (Mutual)** *Remember the Living* Starring: RC

1942:

February 7: **Lincoln Highway (NBC)** (drama) Starring: RC, Vincent Price

May 22: **Navy Show** RC (guest)

June 9: **Ruth Chatterton (WEEI)** 15-minute program with RC (guest)

1943:

August 7: **Saturday Night Bond Wagon (WOR)** *Miss Anstruther's Letters* (based on a short story by Rose Macaulay) Starring: RC. Jose Ferrer (guest director)

October 23: **Saturday Night Bond Wagon (Mutual)** *Paris Underground* (based on the book by Etta Shiber) Starring: RC (Kitty de Mornay)

1944:

February 5: **Saturday Night Bond Wagon (WOR)** RC (Mistress of ceremonies), Opera star Helen Jepson

May 2: **Everything for the Boys (NBC)** *Holy Matrimony* (based on Arnold Bennett's comedy *Buried Alive*) Starring: RC (Alice Challice) and Ronald Colman.

July 8: **Hollywood Theatre of Stars (NBC)** *Silver Gown* (by Roger Q. Denny) Starring: RC

August 19: **Stars Over Hollywood (ABC)** *Mrs. Miniver Jones* Starring: RC

September 22: **Stage Door Canteen (ABC)** RC (guest), Dana Andrews, Bert Lahr

October 28: **Chattam Shopper (WMAQ)** Lois Long (hostess), RC (guest)

November 19: **Hollywood Open House (NBC)** Jim Ameche (host), RC in a scene from Shaw's *Pygmalion*. With Patricia Gilmore

November 30: **Hollywood Open House (NBC)** Jim Ameche (host), RC (guest)

December 12: **Theatre of Romance (ABC)** *No Time for Comedy* (based on S.N. Behrman's play) Starring: RC (Linda). Marc Loeb producer/director

December 16: **"Women's Fight for Victory" (WOR)** RC (guest), Eleanor Roosevelt, Mrs. Jimmy Doolittle, Jane Powell, Mrs. Pat O'Brien, Mrs. Edna Standing

1945:

January 4: **Hollywood Open House (NBC)** Jim Ameche (host), RC (guest)

November 11: **Hollywood Open House (NBC)** Jim Ameche (host), RC (guest)

1946:

February, 23: **Palestine or Mass Suicide (WBCA)** Discussion on ALFP. RC (guest), former Senator Guy M. Gillette, Senator Warren G. Magnuson, Louis Bromfield

September 30: **Dinner for Paul Muni (WMCA)** RC (guest), Quentin Reynolds

October 5: **Interview with a Star (WMCA)** Host Jack Shafer interviews RC, Barry Thomson

November 18: **Broadway Talks Back (WOR)** RC (guest). The play *A Flag is Born* is discussed. Luther Adler, Kay Norton

November 23: **American Melodies (ABC)** *Revolt of the Alphabet* Starring: RC (narrator), Vladimir Selinsky (conductor)

November–December 1946 (no exact date – *Billboard*): **Martha Deane Show (WOR)** RC (guest)

1947:

August 15: **Special Broadcast** (Bangor, Maine) RC discusses the play *Hamlet.* With Earle Rankin, Leon Shalek

1948:

January 8: **Hollywood Open House (Mutual)** RC (guest)

April 26: **American Cancer Society Broadcast (ABC)** *Between You and Me* Starring: RC and Eddie Dowling (dramatic sketch which drove home the importance of treating cancer in its early stages). With Frank Sinatra, Jo Stafford, Jack Benny, Harry Morgan

1949:

April 1949: **Curtain Calls at Kaysey's (WAVZ)** RC is interviewed by George Thomas and Jack Abels (exact date unknown)

1950:

March 10: **Hollywood Theatre (WOR)** *Silver Gown* Starring: RC and Howard Duff

May 1: **Barbara Welles Show (NBC)** RC (guest)

1951:

October 24: **Hollywood Open House (NBC)** RC (guest)

1953:

September 28: *The Harvest Years* **(ABC)** United Jewish Appeal drama starring RC and Everett Sloane as a refugee couple finding rejuvenation of spirit and renewed hope for the future in Israel.

October 18: **Book Page of the Air (WHDH)** Alice Dixon Bond (host), RC (guest). Discussion of *The Betrayers*

1954:

January 24: **Author Meets the Critics (WOR)** *The Betrayers* is discussed. RC (guest). With Leo Cherne, Arthur Garfield Hays, Virginia Peterson (moderator)

August 22: **Sunday with Dave Garroway (NBC)** Guests: RC (discussing *Pride of the Peacock*), Mae West, Hermione Gingold, Errol Garner, Art Buchwald

August 26: **Author Meets the Critics (WOR)** *The Pride of the Peacock* is discussed. RC (guest), Isabel Leighton, Howard Whitman (Originally an August 22 TV broadcast)

September 12: **Book Page of the Air (WHDH)** Discussion of *The Pride of the Peacock*. Alice Dixon Bond (host), RC (guest)

September 16: **Mike and Buff Show (WBBM Chicago)** RC (guest), Mike Wallace (host)

1958:

June 24: **The Last Word (CBS-Radio)** RC (guest), McGeorge Bundy, Dr. Bergen Evans, John Mason Brown

July 22: **The Last Word (CBS-Radio)** RC (guest), McGeorge Bundy

1959:

November 29: **Sunday at Stonehenge (WLAD)** RC interview with Victor Gilbert in Ridgefield, CT.

1960:

January 31: **Sunday at Stonehenge (WLAD)** RC second interview with Victor Gilbert.

1961:

Fall of 1961: **Memoirs of the Movies (WBC)** RC hosts an episode of a spoken memoir of the movies as part of the Oral History Research Project of Columbia University. Guests: Myrna Loy (introduction), Adolf Zukor, Broncho Billy Anderson, Paul Newman, Joanne Woodward, Jerry Wald, Sessue Hayakawa, Arthur Mayer, Janet Gaynor, Roddy McDowell, Zachary Scott, Jack Lemmon, film distributor Arthur Mayer, and scenarist Ben Hecht. (27 minutes) (Series of 16 half-hour broadcasts which aired in 1961 and 1964. Most interviews were originally recorded in 1959 by producers Joan and Robert Franklin.)

Ruth Chatterton on TV

1948:

December 19: **Philco-Goodyear Television Playhouse (NBC)** *Suspect* (based on the 1940 Broadway play by Edward Percy and Reginald Denham) Bert Lytell (host) Starring: RC (Mrs. Smith), Bramwell Fletcher, Michael Duane, Mary Orr, Perc Mayo

1950:

September 24: **This is Show Business (CBS)** RC (guest panelist) with George Kaufman, Abe Burrows

October 2: **This Is Show Business (CBS)** RC (guest panelist), Clifton Fadman (host) with Vivian Blaine, Sam Levenson, Bill Callihan

October 24: **Prudential Family Playhouse (CBS)** *Dodsworth* (based on the play by Sidney Howard; adapted from the novel by Sinclair Lewis) Donald Davis (director) Starring: RC (Fran), Walter Abel (Sam), Eva Marie Saint (Emily), John Baragrey (Kurt), Barbara Robbins (Edith), Cliff Hall (Tubby), Edith King

(Matey), Archie Smith (Harry), Leslie Barrie (Lockert), Riza Royce (Mme. Penable), Lili Valenty (Baroness)

1951:

November 14: **Celanese Theatre (ABC)** *Old Acquaintance* (based on the play by John Van Druten) Fred Coe (director) Starring: RC (Kit Marlowe), Edna Best, Scott McKay, Pat Breslin, Robert Wallsten

1952:

January 2: **Pulitzer Prize Playhouse (ABC)** *Fatal Weakness* (based on the 1946 play by George Kelly) Starring: RC (Mrs. Espenshade), Otto Kruger, Ilka Chase

January 13: **Pulitzer Prize Playhouse (ABC)** *Alison's House* (based on the 1930 play by Susan Glaspell) Starring: RC (Elsa), Otto Kruger, Ilka Chase

(Note: IMDB lists the December 31, 1952 telecast "The Paper Moon" as a Chatterton credit. No newspaper listing at that time confirms her appearance.)

1953:

April 26: **Hallmark Hall of Fame (NBC)** *Hamlet* (by William Shakespeare) Albert McCleery (director) Starring: Maurice Evans (Hamlet), RC (Queen Gertrude), Joseph Schildkraut (Claudius), Sarah Churchill (Ophelia), Barry Jones (Polonius), Wesley Addy (Horatio), William Smithers (Laertes), Malcolm Keen, Neva Patterson, Noel Leslie, Frances Bethencourt, Alan Shayne, Winston Ross, Chester Stratton

December 26: **DeLux Events of the Week (WBBM-Chicago)** Jim Conway (host), RC (guest). Chatterton was playing in *Susan and God* at Evanston Showcase Theatre.

1954:

January 17: **Author Meets the Critics (DuMont)** Virginia Peterson (moderator), RC (guest). *The Betrayers* is discussed by Leo Cherne and Arthur Garfield Hayes (also broadcast on radio).

August 22: **Author Meets the Critics (DuMont)** RC (guest) *Pride of the Peacock* is discussed by Howard Whitman and Isabelle Leighton (also broadcast on radio)

September 3: **Home (NBC)** Arlene Francis (host), a visit at home with Ruth Chatterton

1958:

June 22: **The Last Word (CBS)** Dr. Bergen Evans (moderator), RC (guest), McGeorge Bundy, John Mason Brown – Discussion of the correct usage of modern English.

July 17: **Dorothy Fuldheim (ABC)** RC (guest) Cleveland evening news program

July 28: **The One O'Clock Club (ABC) (WEWS Cleveland)** Dorothy Fuldheim (host), RC (guest)

Ruth Chatterton author

Homeward Borne (1950) New York, Simon & Schuster – 312 pages (on *The New York Times* Best-Seller List for twenty-three weeks)

The Betrayers (1953) Boston, Houghton Mifflin Co. – 310 pages

A Present From the Past (c. January 13, 1953) Barry Thomson (co-author) Original TV Script

The Pride of the Peacock (1954) New York, Doubleday – 315 pages

The Southern Wild (1958) New York, Doubleday – 487 pages

Lady's Man from *Alfred Hitchcock presents: Stories For Late At Night* Random House (1961) New York, Random House – 469 pages (*Lady's Man* pgs. 45–59)

Entente Cordiale (1961) – unpublished

Ruth Chatterton - Recordings

Ruth Chatterton tells about *The Revolt of the Alphabet* (1947) 78 Rpm (Tiffany - Merry-Go-Sound children's records)

The Revolt of the Alphabet, which Ruth narrated, was written by John Byrne. The story detailed the rebellion of four letters that band against the letter "X" and its celebrity status. After all, "X" marks the spot. The letters in question drop out of the alphabet. "X" convinces the rebels that envy is something to be dodged. Maestro Vladimir Selinsky provided the orchestral accompaniment.

Ruth told columnist Jack O'Brian that it was "a platter of chattering fun." *Billboard* (6/14/47) found it to be "an engaging and fascinating kiddie set ... original and novel in content. And Miss Chatterton, in spite of her heavy dramatic overtones, has an easy time of it in arresting the attention." Barry Thomson would follow suit and make his own children's recording—a musical version of *The Shoemaker and the Elves* (1949).

PHOTO CREDITS

Every effort has been made to trace the copyright holders of the photographs included in this book; if any have been inadvertently overlooked, the author and publisher will be pleased to make the necessary changes.

All Warner Bros./ First National photos c. Warner Bros. Entertainment Inc. Co. All Rights Reserved.

All MGM and United Artists photos c. Metro-Goldwyn-Mayer Studio Inc. All Rights Reserved.

All 20th Century-Fox photos c. 20th Century-Fox Film Corp. All Rights Reserved

All Paramount photos c. Paramount Pictures. All Rights Reserved.

All Columbia photos Columbia Pictures-Sony Entertainment. All Rights Reserved

All photos, unless otherwise noted, are from the author's collection. The author would like to express his thanks to the following individuals for the lending of photos: Brenda Holman, Howard Mandelbaum (of Photofest), Wisconsin Center for Film and Theater Research, Jenny Paxson and Larry Smith, James Stettler, Brian Reddin, and Joseph Worrell.

Front cover photos: (from top) 1) publicity for *Lady of Secrets* (Columbia) 2) c. 1922 3) c.1936 4) August 29, 1936 Cleveland, Air Derby (Acme Photo) 5) publicity for *Pygmalion* (author's collection).

Back cover photos: (from top) 1) August 1912 issue of *The Theatre* 2) Ad for *Female* (Warners) 3) *Screen Book* October 1929 4) with Walter Huston in *Dodsworth* (Samuel Goldwyn-United Artists) (author's collection).

About the Author

Scott O'Brien has written three previous film biographies: *Kay Francis – I Can't Wait to be Forgotten* (2006), *Virginia Bruce – Under My Skin* (2008), and *Ann Harding – Cinema's Gallant Lady* (2010). He has penned articles for the publications *Films of the Golden Age, Classic Images,* and *Filmfax.* As a guest author, O'Brien has introduced films at the Library of Congress Film Archive in Culpeper, Virginia, and been interviewed on such film websites as TCM's *Movie Morlocks* and *Silver Screen Oasis.* O'Brien is featured in the film documentary *Queer Icon – the Cult of Bette Davis* (2009) as well as the upcoming Irish film documentary *George Brent – Hollywood Rebel* (2013). O'Brien appeared on Bay Area Emmy-winning producer Jan Wahl's "Inside Entertainment," for KRON-TV. Radio's *Silver Screen Audio* and KRCB's *A Novel Idea* have also invited the author to talk about his research and writing. Scott lives in Northern California's Sonoma County with his partner Joel Bellagio. Website: www.scottobrienauthor.com

INDEX

CPSIA information can be obtained at www.ICGtesting.com
Printed in the USA
LVOW08s2124140713

342845LV00011B/221/P